Anne Hardy

Where to Eat in Canada

THIRTY-SIXTH YEAR

06-07

First published July 1971. Reprinted September 1971, November 1971, January 1972. Second edition published June 1972. Reprinted July 1972. Third edition published June 1973. Reprinted July 1973. Fourth edition published June 1974. Fifth edition published June 1975. Book-of-the-Month Club edition published July 1975. Sixth edition published June 1976. Seventh edition published June 1977. Eighth edition published June 1978. Ninth edition published June 1979. Tenth edition published June 1980. Eleventh edition published June 1981. Twelfth edition published June 1982. Thirteenth edition published June 1983. Fourteenth edition published June 1984. Fifteenth edition published June 1985. Sixteenth edition published June 1986. Seventeenth edition published June 1987. Eighteenth edition published June 1988. Nineteenth edition published June 1989. Twentieth edition published June 1990. Twenty-first edition published June 1991. Twenty-second edition published June 1992. Twenty-third edition published June 1993. Twenty-fourth edition published June 1994. Twenty-fifth edition published June 1995. Twenty-sixth edition published June 1996. Twenty-seventh edition published June 1997. Twenty-eighth edition published June 1998. Twenty-ninth edition published June 1999. Thirtieth edition published June 2000. Thirty-first edition published June 2001. Thirty-second edition published June 2002. Thirty-third edition published June 2003. Thirty-fourth edition published June 2004. Thirty-fifth edition published June 2005. Thirty-sixth edition published June 2006.

ISBN 0 7780 1284 0

Photo by R. Ian Lloyd/Masterfile.

Printed in Northern Ireland by W. & G. Baird Limited

PUBLISHED IN CANADA BY OBERON PRESS

HOW TO USE THIS GUIDE

The restaurants recommended in this guide have been arranged alphabetically by location, from Abbotsford in British Columbia to Yellowknife in the Northwest Territories. Each entry begins with the name of the city, town or village in which the restaurant is located, followed by the name and address of the restaurant and its telephone number. Next comes the entry itself, printed in roman type, followed by two or three lines, in italic type, indicating the hours during which the restaurant is open for business. The entry ends with a quantity of other useful information: does the restaurant have a full liquor licence or is it licensed for beer and wine only? What credit cards does it take? Is there an area for non-smokers or is it a smoking-only restaurant? Is smoking permitted anywhere on the premises? If the restaurant is in an urban centre, does it have free off-street parking? Do you need to book a table? Is there wheelchair access to the washrooms?

If you already know what restaurant you want to go to, look up the restaurant in the guide, selecting first the name of the centre and then the name of the restaurant. You will find a heading like this:

SYDNEY MINES, N.S.	**MAP 216**
THE GOWRIE HOUSE	☆☆
840 Shore Road	**$115 ($300)**
(902) 544-1050	

At left, you will find the name, address and telephone number of the restaurant, all arranged under Sydney Mines. The first line on the right means that Sydney is represented by Map Number 216. Look for Number 216 on the map of Eastern Quebec & the Maritimes. Once you've found it, consult your road-map for the most convenient route to Sydney Mines. Often a quick check of the entry in the guide will help you to find your way.

The second line indicates how many stars the restaurant has earned. The maximum is three, and there are only twenty-nine restaurants in the guide that have earned this rating. Fifty-three have earned two stars and 126 have earned one. We consider a further 70 restaurants to be good buys, which doesn't necessarily mean that they are unusually cheap, though it usually does. They are indicated by a pointing finger.

The third line indicates the price. The first (and often the only) figure indicates the average cost of dinner for two with a modest wine, applicable taxes and a tip of 15%. Dinner for two is taken to mean two appetizers, two main courses, one sweet, two coffees and three glasses of an open wine. Where a restaurant has earned two stars, the cost of half a bottle of wine is included. Where a restaurant has earned three stars, the cost of a full bottle is part of the estimated price. The wines chosen are not the cheapest the establishment has to offer, nor are they the most expensive. Where, as in the case of the Gowrie House, a second figure in parentheses follows the first, this second figure indicates the average cost of dinner, bed and breakfast. The presence of this figure means that we recommend not only dinner but also, if convenient, an overnight stay.

If you don't know where you want to go, turn to the maps. Find yourself on the map that shows the province you are in. Select the nearest number and then look it up in the Index. Under the number you'll find all the centres represented by that number. Let's suppose that the nearest number is 223, which stands for the city of Toronto. Look up Toronto in the Index to Southern Ontario and you'll find that there are six other centres with the same number, each enclosed in parentheses. This means that these centres are all in the immediate vicinity of Toronto, too close to be given a number of their own. They are: Ajax, Creemore, Kleinburg, Nobleton, Oakville and Whitby. Now look up Toronto in the main body of the guide, where you will find all 33 restaurants that we recommend in the city. If you then look up each of the other six centres, you will find six more restaurants in the area that are recommended.

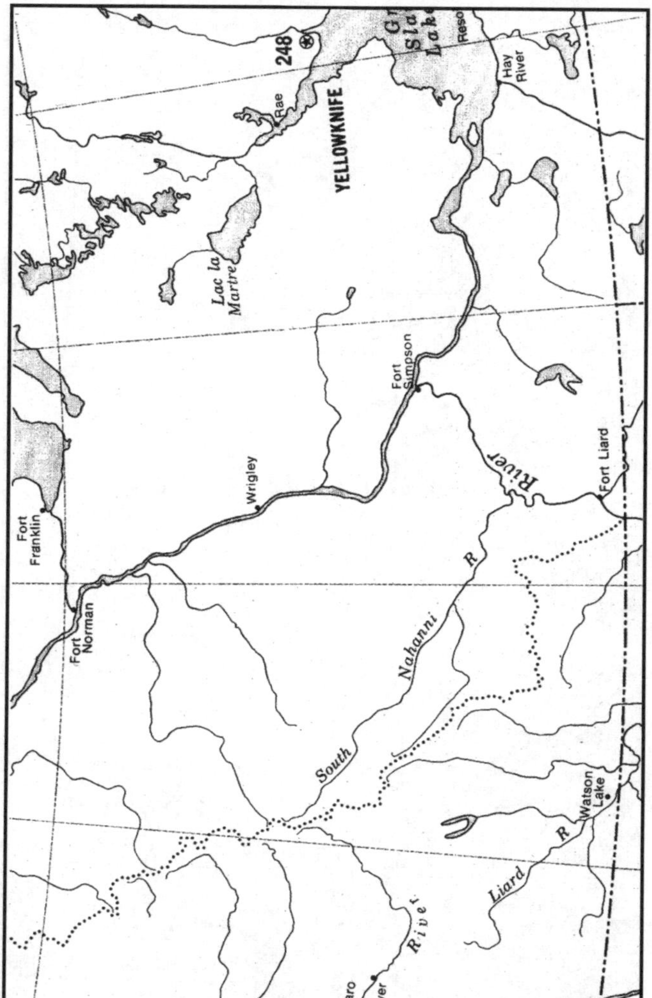

YUKON & NORTHWEST TERRITORIES

BRITISH COLUMBIA

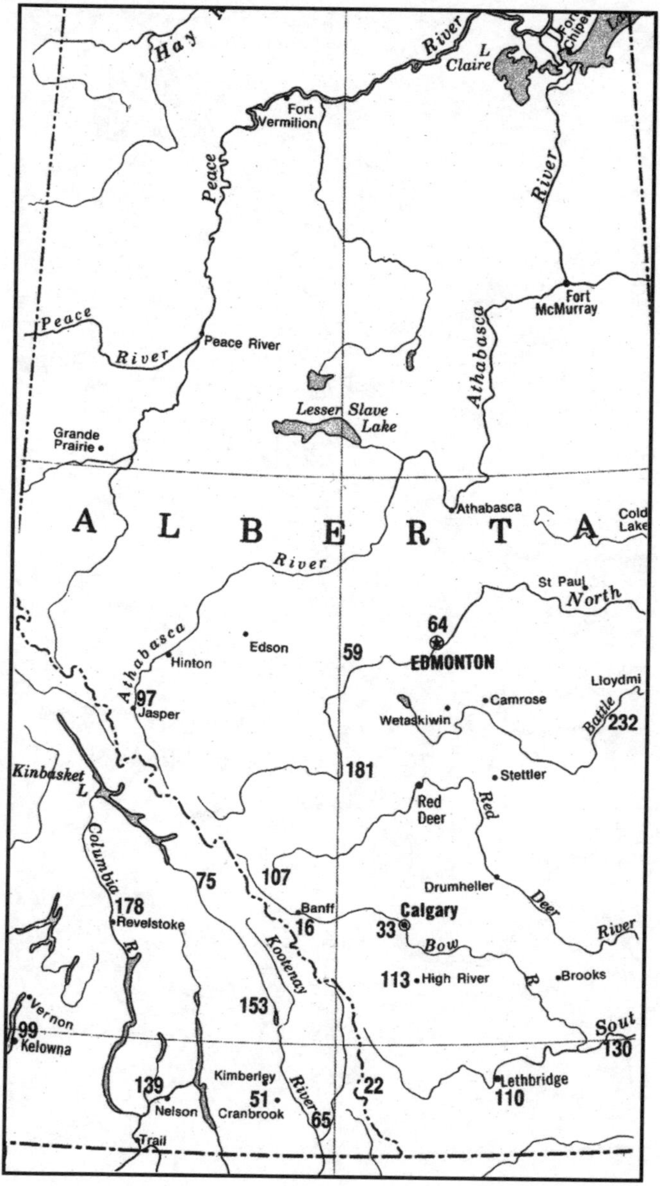
Hay
River
L
Claire
Fort
Vermilion
Peace
River
Fort
McMurray
Peace
River
Peace River
Athabasca
Lesser Slave
Lake
Grande
Prairie
Athabasca
Cold
Lake
A L B E R T A
River
St Paul
North
64
Athabasca
Hinton
Edson
59
EDMONTON
Lloydmi
97
Jasper
Camrose
Wetaskiwin
Battle
232
Kinbasket
L
181
Stettler
Red
Deer
Red
Columbia
75
107
Drumheller
Deer
178
Revelstoke
Banff
16
Calgary
33
Bow
River
R
Kootenay
113
High River
R
Brooks
Vernon
99
Kelowna
153
Sout
130
139
Kimberley
51
River
22
Lethbridge
110
Nelson
Cranbrook
65
Trail

ALBERTA

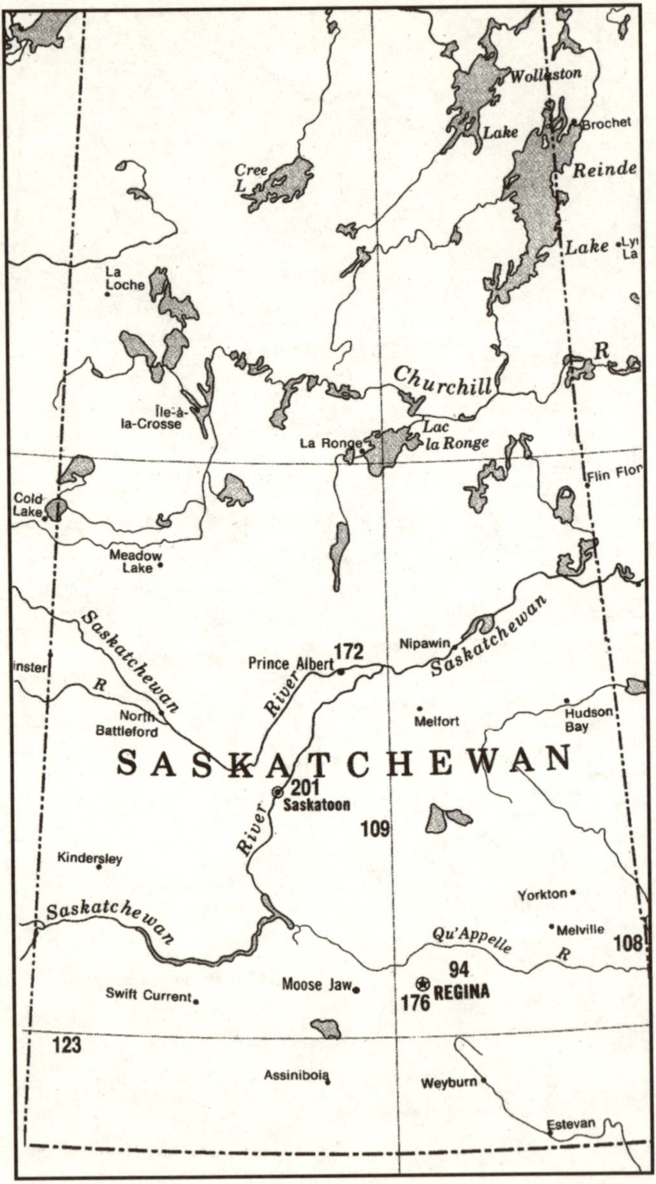

SASKATCHEWAN

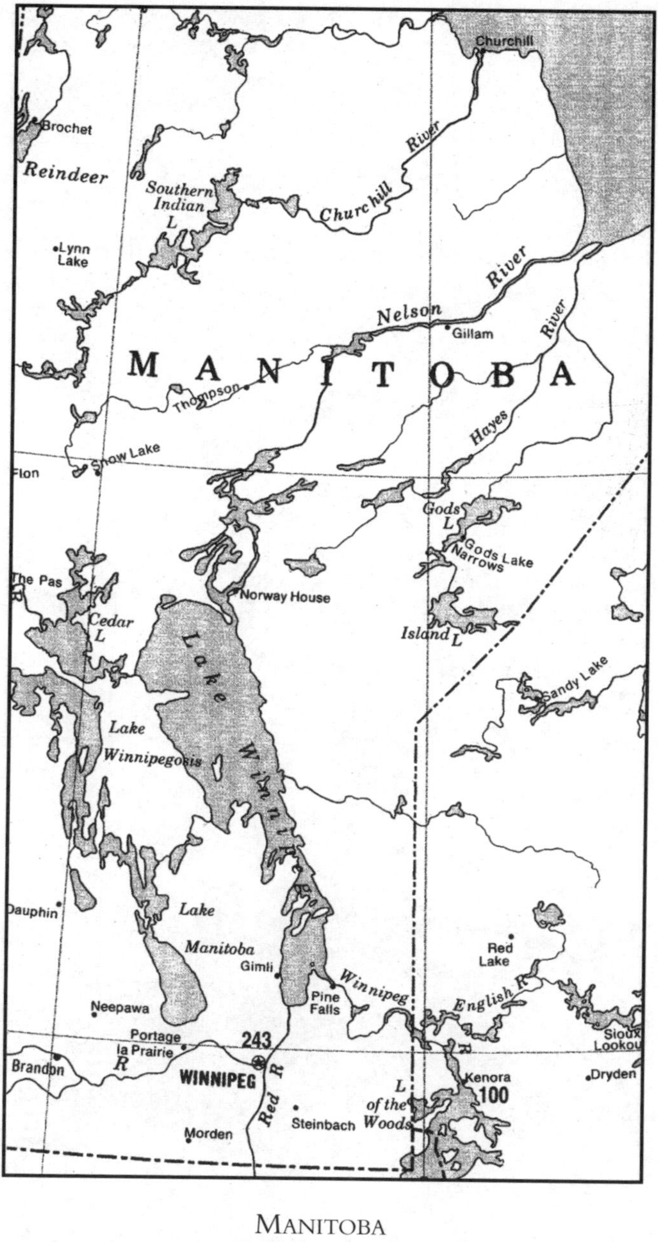
Churchill
Brochet
Reindeer
Southern Indian L
Churchill River
Lynn Lake
Nelson River
Gillam
River
MANITOBA
Thompson
Hayes
Snow Lake
Flon
Gods L
Gods Lake Narrows
The Pas
Norway House
Cedar L
Island L
Sandy Lake
Lake Winnipeg
Lake Winnipegosis
Dauphin
Lake Manitoba
Red Lake
Gimli
Pine Falls
Winnipeg
English R
Neepawa
Portage la Prairie
243
Sioux Lookou
Brandon
R
WINNIPEG
Red R
Kenora
100
Dryden
L of the Woods
Steinbach
Morden

MANITOBA

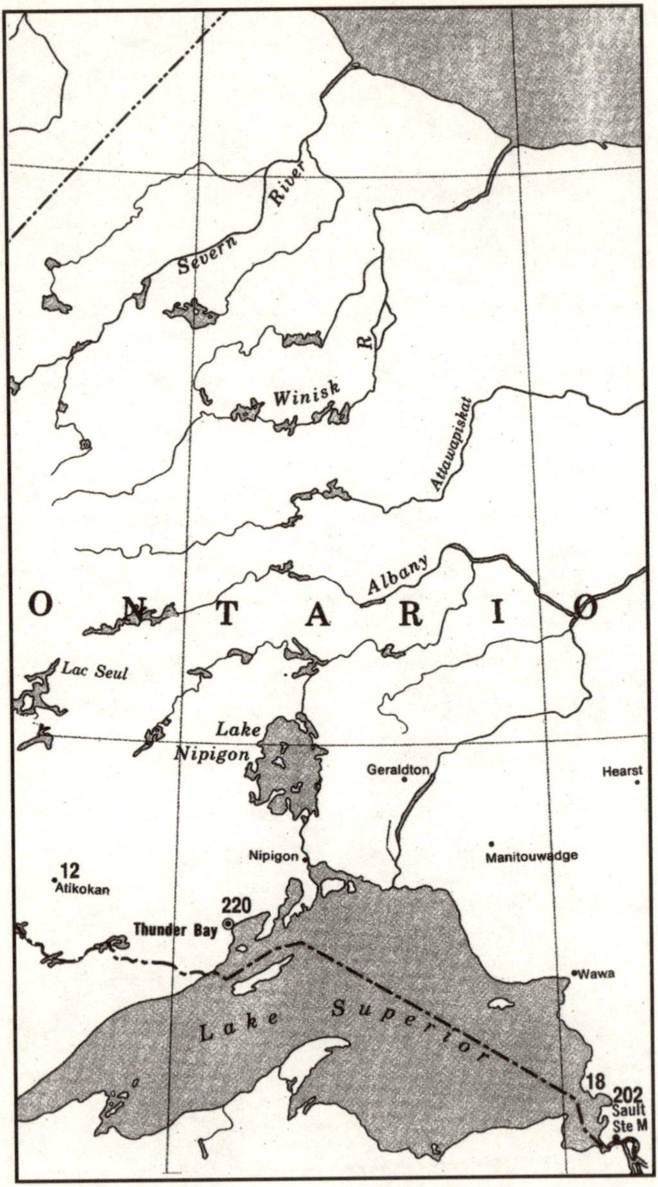

NORTHWESTERN ONTARIO

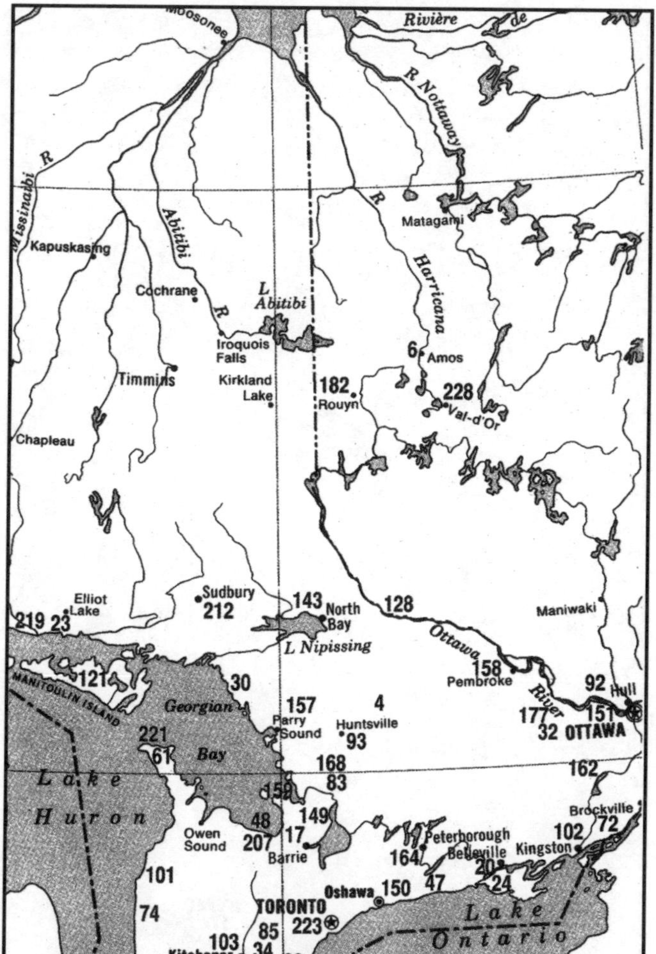

Southern Ontario

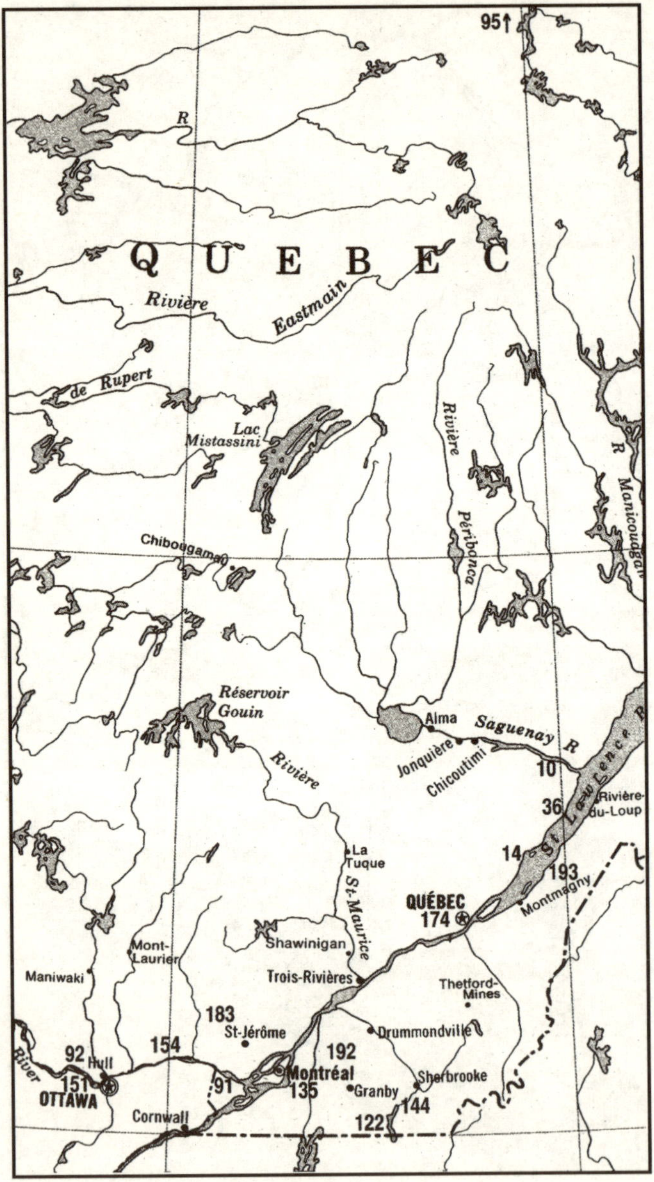

CENTRAL QUEBEC

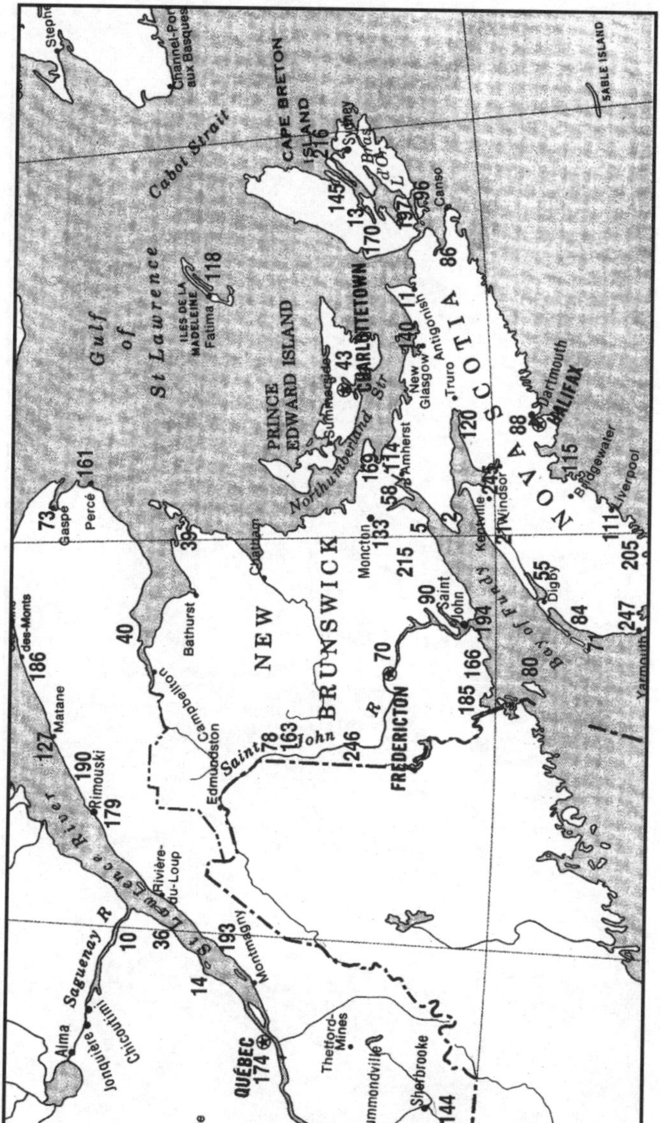

Eastern Quebec & the Maritimes

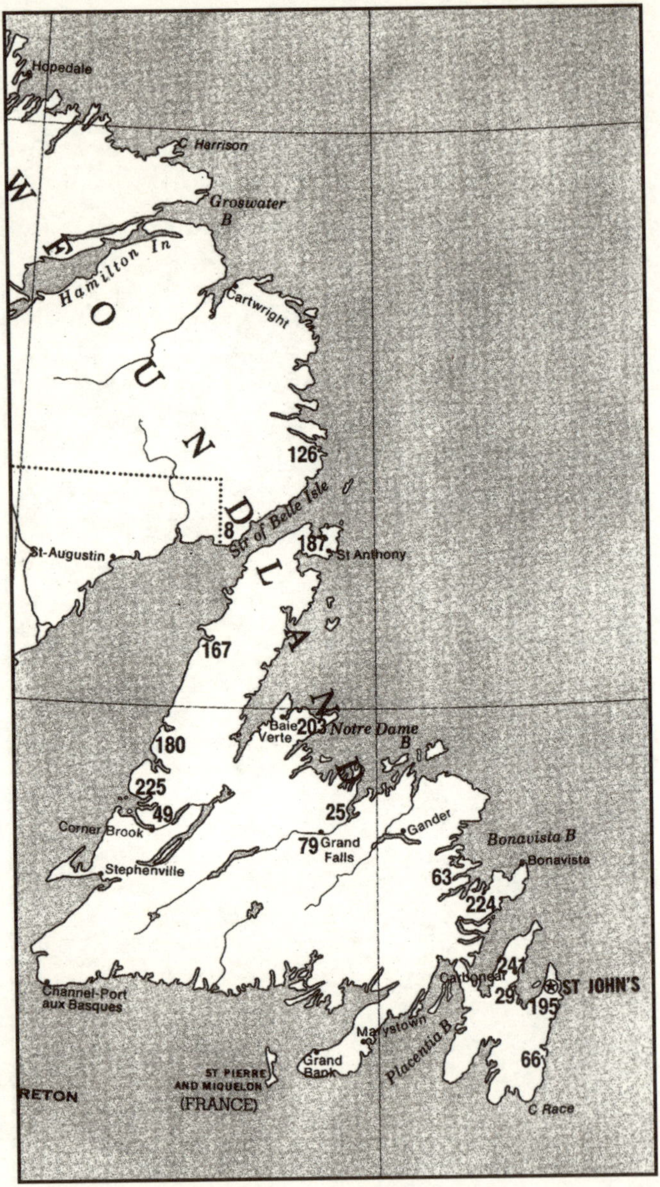

NEWFOUNDLAND & LABRADOR

INDEX TO MAPS

YUKON & NORTHWEST TERRITORIES

87 Haines Junction
240 Whitehorse
248 Yellowknife

BRITISH COLUMBIA

1 Abbotsford
60 Duncan
(60) Cobble Hill
(60) Cowichan Bay
(60) Mill Bay
98 Kamloops
105 Ladysmith
137 Nanaimo
(137) Cedar
156 Parksville
160 Penticton
(160) Oliver
173 Prince Rupert
175 Queen Charlotte Islands
210 Stewart
217 Telkwa
218 Terrace
222 Tofino
(222) Ucluelet
229 Vancouver
230 Victoria
(230) Brentwood Bay
(230) Mayne Island
(230) Saltspring Island
(230) Sidney
(230) Sooke
237 Westbank
238 Whistler

ALBERTA

16 Banff
(16) Canmore
22 Blairmore
33 Calgary
51 Cranbrook
59 Drayton Valley
64 Edmonton
65 Fernie
75 Golden
97 Jasper
99 Kelowna
107 Lake Louise
(107) Castle Junction
(107) Field
110 Lethbridge
113 Longview
130 Medicine Hat
139 Nelson
153 Panorama
178 Revelstoke
181 Rocky Mountain House
232 Wainwright

SASKATCHEWAN

94 Indian Head
108 Langenburg
109 Lanigan
123 Maple Creek
172 Prince Albert
176 Regina
201 Saskatoon

MANITOBA

100 Kenora
243 Winnipeg
(243) Winnipeg Beach

NORTHWESTERN ONTARIO

12 Atikokan
18 Batchawana Bay
(18) Goulais Bay
202 Sault Ste. Marie
220 Thunder Bay

SOUTHERN ONTARIO

4 Algonquin Park
6 Amos
17 Barrie
20 Belleville
23 Blind River
24 Bloomfield
27 Brantford
(27) Paris
30 Britt
32 Calabogie
34 Cambridge
47 Cobourg
48 Collingwood
61 Dyers Bay
68 Fonthill
72 Gananoque
74 Goderich
77 Grand Bend
83 Gravenhurst
(83) Bala
85 Guelph
(85) Morriston
89 Hamilton
(89) Ancaster
(89) Burlington
(89) Waterdown
92 Hull
(92) Chelsea
(92) Wakefield
93 Huntsville
101 Kincardine
102 Kingston
103 Kitchener
(103) Waterloo
112 London
121 Manitoulin Island
128 Mattawa
141 Niagara-on-the-Lake
(141) Welland
143 North Bay
149 Orillia
150 Oshawa
151 Ottawa
157 Parry Sound
158 Pembroke
159 Penetang
162 Perth
(162) Maberly
164 Peterborough
168 Port Carling
177 Renfrew
182 Rouyn
188 St. Catharines
200 Sarnia
207 Singhampton
211 Stratford
(211) St. Marys
212 Sudbury
219 Thessalon
221 Tobermory
223 Toronto
(223) Ajax

(223) Creemore
(223) Kleinburg
(223) Nobleton
(223) Oakville
(223) Whitby
228 Val d'Or
242 Windsor

CENTRAL QUEBEC

10 L'Anse-Saint-Jean
14 Baie-St.-Paul
36 Cap à l'Aigle
91 Hudson
92 Hull
(92) Chelsea
(92) Wakefield
95 Iqaluit
122 Mansonville
135 Montreal
(135) St.-André d'Argenteuil
144 North Hatley
151 Ottawa
154 Papineauville
174 Quebec
183 Ste.-Adèle
(183) St.-Faustin-Lac-Carré
192 St.-Hyacinthe
193 St.-Jean-Port-Joli

EASTERN QUEBEC &
THE MARITIMES

2 Advocate Harbour
5 Alma
10 L'Anse-Saint-Jean
11 Antigonish
13 Baddeck
14 Baie-St.-Paul
21 Berwick
36 Cap à l'Aigle
39 Caraquet
40 Carleton-sur-Mer
43 Charlottetown
(43) Bay Fortune
(43) Brackley Beach
(43) Fortune Bridge
(43) Grand Tracadie
(43) Margate
(43) Montague
(43) Naufrage
(43) North Rustico
(43) Oyster Bed Bridge
(43) St. Peter's Bay
(43) Spry Point
(43) Summerside
(43) Tyne Valley
(43) Victoria
55 Digby
58 Dorchester
70 Fredericton
71 Freeport
(71) East Ferry
73 Gaspé
78 Grand Falls
80 Grand Manan
(80) Deer Island
84 Grosses Coques
86 Guysborough
88 Halifax
(88) Chester
(88) Dartmouth
90 Hampton
96 Janvrin Island
111 Liverpool
(111) Summerville Beach
114 Lorneville

115 Lunenburg
(115) LaHave
(115) Mahone Bay
(115) Martin's Brook
118 Magdalen Islands
120 Maitland
122 Mansonville
127 Matane
133 Moncton
140 New Glasgow
(140) Pictou
144 North Hatley
145 North River
161 Percé
(161) St.-Georges de Malbaie
163 Perth-Andover
166 Pocologan
(166) Dipper Harbour
169 Port Elgin
170 Port Hood
(170) Mabou
174 Quebec
179 Rimouski
185 St. Andrews
186 Ste.-Anne-des-Monts
(186) Cap-Chat
190 Ste.-Flavie
193 St.-Jean-Port-Joli
194 Saint John
197 St. Peter's
205 Shelburne
215 Sussex
216 Sydney Mines
245 Wolfville
(245) Grand Pré
(245) Sheffield Mills
246 Woodstock
247 Yarmouth

NEWFOUNDLAND & LABRADOR

8 L'Anse au Claïr
25 Botwood
29 Brigus
49 Corner Brook
63 Eastport
66 Ferryland
79 Grand Falls
126 Mary's Harbour
167 Port-au-Choix
180 Rocky Harbour
187 St. Anthony
(187) L'Anse-aux-Meadows
(187) Cape Onion
195 St. John's
(195) Mobile
(195) Portugal Cove
203 La Scie
224 Trinity
225 Trout River
241 Whiteway
(241) Dildo

ABBOTSFORD, B.C. **MAP 1**
CLAYBURN VILLAGE STORE ☞
34810 Clayburn Road **$30**
Clayburn
(604) 853-4020

Comfort food is what this place is all about, that and nostalgia. The counters are piled high with biscuit boxes, hat boxes and other memorabilia of the last century. The tearoom is furnished with old kitchen tables and chairs, the tables laid with silver of the sort your grandmother used to have in the kitchen. They serve the only cream tea—scone, Devonshire cream, jam and a pot of tea—this side of Victoria. They also do soups—cock-a-leekie, split-pea, green pea with ham and several lovely chowders, corn, clam and seafood. They have beautiful egg-salad sandwiches, made with tiny Danish roast onions in summer; in winter keep an eye open for the sausage-rolls. Best of all is the sticky toffee pudding, which is always on the menu. The house tea, Tippy Assam, comes from Betty's Tea-Shop in York, and there's a huge assortment of British candies on the candy counter, all sold from big glass jars just as they used to be in the nineteen-thirties. They now have a full liquor licence and sell a lot of Yorkshire ale, including Black Sheep and Monty Python's Holy Grail (tempered over burning witches) as well as Fentiman's botanicals, among them Dandelion and Burdock, Shandy and Victorian Lemonade.
Open Tuesday to Saturday 9 am to 5 pm, Sunday noon to 5 pm. Closed on Monday and from mid-January until mid-February, mid-May until mid-June and from 1 until 30 September. Licensed. Master Card, Visa. No smoking.

ADVOCATE HARBOUR, N.S. **MAP 2**
LIGHTKEEPER'S KITCHEN
Cape d'Or **$60 ($100)**
(902) 670-0534

At the age of 88, Warren Corbin has finally closed his bake-shop. He could turn out a lemon or a wild-

blueberry pie faster than anyone else, and they were first-class pies, every one of them. We'll miss the trim little bakery with its wild rosebushes at the door, and we'll miss Warren Corbin himself. But there are still good reasons to visit Advocate Harbour. The town, one of the oldest in Atlantic Canada, is about 30 miles from Parrsboro on Highway 2. A sideroad just outside the town leads to Cape d'Or and its lighthouse, which stands on a rocky promontory above the Minas Channel, with sheer cliffs rising 500 feet behind it. Struck by the glittering veins of copper (which he mistook for gold) in the rocks, Champlain named the place Cape of Gold in 1604. The lighthouse was built in 1922 and manned for the next 67 years. It now serves as a restaurant, with four guest bedrooms in the old lightkeeper's house. People love everything about the place. Darcy Snell, who is both owner and chef, offers great food at great prices: locally-caught flounder, salmon and lobster, as well as scallops with white wine, sundried tomatoes, spinach and mushrooms. The seafood chowder is one of the best we can remember. There's an abundance of organic vegetables from the Snells' own garden, as well as fruit crisps in season. This summer, Darcy Snell hopes to have a new young chef in the kitchen, but he assures us that nothing will change.
Open daily 11 am to 4 pm, 5.30 pm to 9 pm from 15 May until 31 October. Licensed. No cards. No smoking. ♿

AJAX, Ontario **(MAP 223)**
PENNELLO
15 Church Street S **$85**
(905) 428-7814

This is a fine old house with a traditional Italian menu. The chef starts with a small set *carte* and then adds dishes that he feels like cooking. There's always some pasta (though it's not made in house), as well as steak, chicken, salmon and gourmet pizzas. Everything that comes out of the kitchen is perfectly cooked and presented, and they have an extensive wine-list as well. This is a relax-

ing place with expert service, but you can't reach them by telephone; reservations are made by a central booking office.
Open Tuesday to Friday 11.30 am to 3 pm, 4.30 pm to 9.30 pm, Saturday 4.30 pm to 9.30 pm, Closed on Sunday and Monday. No smoking. Free parking. ♿

ALGONQUIN PARK, Ontario **MAP 4**
AROWHON PINES ☆
Highway 60 **$165 ($550)**
(705) 633-5661

Eugene and Helen Kates took over the Arowhon Pines from Eugene's mother more than 30 years ago and since then they've put their stamp on every inch of the place. Every detail has been carefully thought out. The huge buffet tables piled with salads, fruits and cheeses, for instance, were invented as a way of dealing with the chronic shortage of trained staff. This is a seasonal operation and chefs change between one summer and the next. To deal with this, the Kateses have put all their recipes on a computer, and the chefs follow them to the letter. Menus are planned a week in advance, so no-one is likely to get the same meal twice, even if they stay for several days. The Arowhon Pines is known for their baked ham with maple syrup, their roast beef with Yorkshire pudding, their Ontario lamb with home-grown mint sauce, their pan-fried rainbow trout and their fresh greens, grown outside the kitchen door. Every day there's at least one hot pudding and a variety of cakes and pies. Unless you're staying here, dinner will cost you 70.00 (half that for lunch), plus wine, tax and tip.
Open daily 8 am to 10 am, 12.30 pm to 2 pm, 6.30 pm to 8 pm from late May until Thanksgiving. Bring your own bottle. Master Card, Visa. No smoking. Book ahead. ♿

The price rating shown opposite the headline of each entry indicates the average cost of dinner for two with a modest wine, tax and tip. The cost of dinner, bed and breakfast (if available) is shown in parentheses.

ALGONQUIN PARK **MAP 4**
BARTLETT LODGE
Highway 60 **$130 ($470)**
(705) 633-5543

Bartlett Lodge is said to be the oldest and smallest resort in Algonquin Park. It was built in 1917 and taken over by Kim and Marilyn Smith, who also own Tanamakoon, in 1996. It stands on the shore of Cache Lake, accessible only by water from the mainland. There are 38 guest-rooms and a dining-room that's open to the public. Every evening they offer a five-course *prix-fixe* for 45.00. You start with a homemade soup and go on to sea scallops with mango chips or mixed greens in a cucumber round with plum tomatoes and apple-caramel vinaigrette. Then comes a sorbet and a choice of six or seven entrées: filet mignon with Jack Daniels and black peppercorns, pan-seared Atlantic salmon with asparagus and roast pheasant. Only the pheasant is disappointing. The sweets, said to be the work of Marilyn Smith, are fabulous. There's a sticky toffee pudding, white-chocolate crème brûlée and pecan pie—all equally accomplished. If you call the Lodge when you get to Cache Lake Landing, a water-taxi will appear in minutes.
Open daily at 6 pm and 8 pm (two sittings) from mid-May until mid-October. Bring your own bottle. Master Card, Visa. Book ahead.

ALMA, N.B. ***MAP 5***
TIDES
Parkland Village Inn *$95*
8601 Main Street
(506) 887-2313

Alma is the headquarters of the Fundy National Park, which has forest trails and fine views of the Bay of Fundy. The Village Inn may be right next to the fisherman's wharf, but it's designed for the tourist trade and the dining-room, known as Tides, has a menu that lists nothing but the standard seafoods: fish chowder, mussels, scallops, deep-fried clams, salmon, halibut and lobster. They have a short list of the basic wines and Sawmill Creek by the glass. They're open all day every day from mid-May until mid-October, have a licence and take Amex, Master Card and Visa. No smoking. ♿

AMHERST, N.B.
See LORNEVILLE.

AMOS, Quebec **MAP 6**
LE MOULIN ☆
100 1 Avenue **$120**
(819) 732-8271

Amos is in remote country, 50 miles west of Val d'Or and 75 miles northeast of Noranda. But the Moulin has one of the best kitchens in northern Quebec. Jean-Victor Flingou is a fine cook and he loves his work, even though he has to spend as much time preparing pizza and pasta as rack of lamb and sea scallops. Not that his sea scallops are anything but gorgeous. They're brought in from Montreal, six hours away by truck, and prepared in the French style. He's not interested in pork, but he loves lamb. Sometimes he'll offer an escalope of provimi veal with mushrooms he's gathered himself; when he can't find any fresh mushrooms, he'll offer a traditional blanquette de veau. Veal he also buys in Montreal, like all his fish—salmon, dorade and sushi-grade tuna. He's started doing more and more with shrimps because he knows there's always a demand for it. Duck is served as a maigret or as a confit, or with red currants or homemade grape jelly. Half-chicken is often on the menu because he needs chicken bones for his stock. Every day there's a *menu du jour* priced from 25.00 to 35.00 that starts with soup or snails, goes on to salmon or duck and ends with a raspberry dacquoise or a freshly-made millefeuille.
Open Monday to Friday 11 am to 2 pm, 5 pm to 10 pm, Saturday 5 pm to 10 pm. Closed on Sunday. Licensed. Amex, Master Card, Visa. No smoking. Book ahead. ♿

ANCASTER, Ontario **(MAP 89)**
THE ROUSSEAU HOUSE
375 Wilson Street E **$130**
(905) 648-8863

This comfortable old house has a formal dining-room upstairs and a tapas bar downstairs. The upstairs menu is made up of carefully crafted, slow-cooked dishes based on market-fresh ingredients. The cooking is part traditional, part modern. They're at their best with things like roast loin of haddock on tomato couscous, tenderloin of beef with foie gras in a black-truffle sauce, breast of chicken with ham, mozzarella and spinach, darne of salmon drizzled with lemon grass and chilli oil and loin of wild boar stuffed with a mousseline of ham and leeks. Best of the appetizers is the lobster spring roll with chanterelles and green and yellow tomatoes. On a hot summer evening, when you're dining *al fresco* on the patio, it's a good idea to ask for a green salad made with bocconcini cheese and red and yellow heirloom tomatoes. There are several good things downstairs in the tapas bar, among them steamed clams with diced Westphalian ham, port, scallions and basil. The vegetable samosas are seasoned with garam masala and served with raita and tomato chutney. There are chicken wings Thai-style, lamb sausages and fishcakes with lemon, dill and jalapeno aioli. If you want something sweet, ask for the cold lemon soufflé with lemon curd.
Open Tuesday to Thursday 11 am to 11 pm, Friday and Saturday 11 am to midnight, Sunday 11 am to 10 pm. Closed on Monday. Licensed. Amex, Master Card, Visa. No smoking. Free parking. ♿

L'ANSE AU CLAIR, Newfoundland ***MAP 8***
NORTHERN LIGHTS INN
Labrador
(709) 931-2332 ***$60***

Labrador is no place for a vegetable garden—the season is too short—so at the Northern Lights they fly their vegetables in from the south. Potatoes do grow here, as do the bake-apples and partridge-berries with which they fill their fresh-fruit pies every summer. (They also make a great bread pudding and drown it with rum.) They still bread their scallops before they fry them, but they do poach their cod and their salmon. The Northern Lights is worth knowing about, if only because it's the best place in a town that serves as the point of departure for the ferries that link Labrador to Newfoundland at Bear Cove. For the past few years they've been putting on dinner theatre on Monday and Thursday nights in summer. The show tells the story of a day in the life of a local family half a century ago, and it's followed by a traditional Labrador supper of potted caribou, green-hash stew made with garden vegetables and turnip greens, sliced bread and molasses, pan-fried cod and salmon with pickles, relish and Washington pie. There's potted caribou on the regular menu but no green hash, homemade bread but no molasses, garden potatoes but no Washington pie. The Northern Lights is open all day every day, has a licence and takes Master Card and Visa. No smoking. ♿

L'ANSE-AUX-MEADOWS, Newfoundland **(MAP 187)**
THE NORSEMAN
(877) 623-2018 **$70**

Everybody agrees that the Norseman serves the best food in the area. The mother and daughter who run the place treat the kitchen as if it were their own. They use only the freshest of fruits and vegetables, the freshest of cream and the best extra-virgin olive-oil. Anyone who has taken the long, long drive from Deer Lake—one editor got a deep-vein thrombosis on the way—will be glad of the wonderful lobster and caribou they serve at the Norseman. The caribou is wild and it comes from Labrador. People say it tastes the way it does because it feeds on lichen. The soups—butternut-squash, sweet-potato, asparagus—are good too, and so is the fish chowder, which is made with cod and salmon. When it comes to the sweet course, ask for either the bake-apple cheesecake or the partridge-berry pie. Every Tuesday and Friday evening in summer they put

on an historical pageant accompanied by a live fiddler. The Viking Village, now a world-heritage site, is less than a mile away. The Vikings stayed here only seven years and left nothing behind. The place is very lonely and very still. It's worth a visit.
Open daily 9 am to 10 pm from late May until late September. Licensed. Master Card, Visa.

L'ANSE-SAINT-JEAN, Quebec **MAP 10**
AUBERGE DES CEVENNES
294 rue St.-Jean-Baptiste **$95 ($185)**
(877) 272-3180

Would you expect to find Nunavik caribou on the *menu du jour* in a village on the Saguenay? It's on the *menu du jour* at the Cévennes in L'Anse-Saint-Jean, where the *carte* changes every day. A typical four-course dinner might begin with mushroom soup and follow with a citrus salad or smoked veal with maple vinaigrette. Then there's a choice of at least eight entrées: lamb with sundried-tomato pesto, salmon beurre blanc, fillet of pork with honey and rosemary, scallops with red peppers, goose with maple syrup—and Nunavik caribou. There aren't many important sweets—a cake, perhaps, or crème caramel. But this is a kitchen with a real passion for food. If you stay overnight you'll discover that breakfast is as good as the meal the night before. You'll find L'Anse-Saint-Jean north of Highway 170, just west of Petit Saguenay.
Open daily 6 pm to 9 pm from 1 June until 31 August, daily 7 pm to 9 pm from 1 September until 31 May. Licensed. Master Card, Visa. No smoking. ♿

ANTIGONISH, N.S. **MAP 11**
THE ALCOVE
76 College Street **$105**
(902) 863-2248

The Alcove opened last year in premises once occupied by Fresco. The cooking at the Alcove is better, however, and so is the service. The thin-crust pizzas have their admirers, but if your taste runs more to rack of lamb, say, turn the page. Rack of lamb may be the only expensive dish on the menu, but it's worth it. It's served, simply but eloquently, with rosemary and a demi-glaze of red wine. Chicken is prepared more adventurously with shrimps in tequila marmalade; pork chops come with apple and bourbon, salmon with a coulis of red peppers and pesto. Dinners begin well with mussels, prepared Thai-style with ginger, green curry, garlic and coconut, beef satay with peanut sauce and a tartlet of wild mushrooms in an oxtail marmalade. They end even better with a lemon tart. The wine-list is eccentric and expensive. Ask for a bottle of Gaspereau by Jost. It comes from the Annapolis Valley and it offers better drinking at a more realistic price than anything else on the list.

Open Tuesday and Wednesday 11 am to 2 pm, 4 pm to 9 pm, Thursday to Saturday 11 am to 2 pm, 4 pm to 10 pm, Sunday 4 pm to 9 pm. Closed on Monday. Licensed. Amex, Master Card, Visa. No smoking. Book ahead if you can.

ANTIGONISH **MAP 11**
GABRIEAU'S BISTRO ☆
350 Main Street **$100**
(902) 863-1925

Gabrieau's may look like a bistro at noon, when it hasn't a lot of virtues except an excellent seafood chowder, served with first-class tea-biscuits and a marvellous chocolate soufflé, which lacks nothing but fresh cream. At night, however, everything is different. The chowders and the soufflés are still there, yours for the asking, but there are many other good things too. There are no fewer than nineteen appetizers, among them a well-conceived wilted-spinach salad, a leek tart with warm stilton, candied walnuts and figs and flash-fried squid on a bed of greens. The roasted rack of lamb that follows, napped with sundried tomatoes, brandy and mint, is almost the only expensive thing on the menu at 25.95.

For a lot less there's a charming treatment of grilled breast of chicken glazed with pommery mustard. There's also first-class salmon, plainly roasted in citrus butter. You can spend a lot on a premium wine if you want to—there's a 1998 Mouton Rothschild for 139.95—but you can do almost as well for a lot less. They offer the Moondah Brook chenin blanc from Western Australia for only 28.95, and if you want to experiment there are a couple of single-vineyard wines from Grand Pré for much the same price. The Wynns coonawarra cabernet shiraz costs 10.00 more.

Open Monday to Thursday 11 am to 3 pm, 5 pm to 9.30 pm, Friday and Saturday 11 am to 3 pm, 5 pm to 10 pm. Closed on Sunday. Licensed. Amex, Master Card, Visa. No smoking. ♿

ATIKOKAN, Ontario **MAP 12**

TOWN & COUNTRY

Atikokan Hotel **$85**

(807) 597-2533

Atikokan is on Highway 11 about 140 miles west of Thunder Bay, just north of Quetico Park's million acres of wilderness. The park brings in a lot of Americans every summer, but Highway 11 is busy year-round. The Atikokan Hotel, built in 1938, has been well maintained and has an excellent dining-room. Stephanie Torbiak admits that the name of the game in Atikokan is steak and frozen seafood. But she cooks everything to order, makes all her own soups and all her own pasta. She makes a good quiche and a very good salad. She's Ukrainian and she likes to slip in a few Ukrainian touches here and these. Nobody seems to notice. Nobody noticed either, she'll tell you, when she stopped making her own desserts. She wasn't about to have half a home-baked Black Forest cake left over because people were happier with a bought-in sweet. Besides, cooking three meals a day got pretty tiring. Her barbecued ribs are known all over the county. You can get a half-rack for 18.50, a second half for 11.00. All

dinners come with a salad, a ranch-style potato, baked beans, garlic bread and a cup of coffee.
Open Monday to Saturday 8 am to 9 pm (sometimes later). Closed on Sunday. Licensed. Visa.

BADDECK, N.S. **MAP 13**
THE WATER'S EDGE ☜
22 Water Street **$80 ($215)**
(902) 295-3600

Baddeck has seldom appeared in this guide, but the Water's Edge is something new. It was opened last year by Jeff and Anne Ertel, right on the waterfront in the heart of town. There are six spacious bedrooms, two with cathedral ceilings, and a bright, modern dining-room with capable, friendly service. They start with a first-class seafood chowder, made with fresh cream and delicately spiced. If you're tired of chowders, ask for the chicken-tikka soup, which is full of tender chicken. There's an excellent spinach salad, made with goat-cheese, as well as scallops and bacon. There are wraps (the curried-chicken is the best) and panini sandwiches. Sweets are a strong suit—especially the four-layer carrot cake and the chocolate-soufflé cake. They're interested in coffees (Mexican, Peruvian) and knowledgeable about them. The Water's Edge, with its strong coffee and sensible wine-list, makes a welcome change from the lobster suppers that have plagued Baddeck for years.
Open daily noon to 9 pm from early May until late October. Licensed. All cards. No smoking. ♿

BAIE-ST.-PAUL, Quebec **MAP 14**
LE MOUTON NOIR
43 rue Ste.-Anne **$115**
(418) 240-3030

The Mouton Noir may not be the best restaurant in Baie-St.-Paul, but it's always been our favourite. The spacious deck behind the restaurant overlooks a sleepy

river and all four walls are hung with vines, which turn bright red in the fall. Inside, the place has an authentic charm and a menu most people can afford. The kitchen has always bought everything they could locally and that means all their brie, chèvre and venison. The chef is fond of sweetbreads and recently he's been offering an appetizer of a brioche stuffed with sweetbreads, mushrooms, brandy and cream. He's also known for his chicken-liver parfait flavoured with port and brandy and for his seafood chowder. His lamb shanks are served either on rice or on pasta; his filet mignon comes with brandy, his sauté of red tuna with ratatouille. Meals end with crème brûlée, dark chocolate or chestnut cream en croûte. Forget wine; this is the time to ask for a bottle of Fin du Monde or Maudite, the two great premium beers from Unibroue in Chambly.
Open daily 11.30 am to 2.30 pm, 6 pm to 9 pm from 1 June until late October, Saturday 11.30 am to 2.30 pm, 6 pm to 9 pm from 1 December until 1 May. Closed Sunday to Friday in winter, except for Christmas week and the March break. Licensed. All cards. No smoking. Free parking.

BALA, Ontario **(MAP 83)**
MOON RIVER LOOKOUT
1002 Walker Street **$115**
(705) 762-2393

The big news here is that Derek Walton and Wade Urash have moved to the Moon River Lookout from the Compleat Angler in Port Carling, which closed late in 2004. This has changed everything at Moon River. They've introduced a tapas menu, served between lunch and dinner, where they explore some of their most interesting ideas. This means organic greens in a local cranberry vinaigrette, steamed mussels with garlic and white wine, halibut from the Queen Charlottes with tomato and fennel, scallop sashimi with wasabi and lobster salad in a sesame-scallion vinaigrette. Dinner has changed too. The vocabulary of fusion cuisine has become more prominent. Meals now start with shrimp

tempura with mango, sambal and pea-shoots or a tart of basil and Woolwich goat-cheese. Or maybe with lobster dumplings with smoked bacon and cabbage, or with sashimi of wild Steel River salmon and line-caught Pacific halibut with udon noodles. Nothing quite like this has been seen at Moon River before. Alberta beef is still served with Yukon Gold potatoes, but the kitchen is now more interested in charred sea scallops with shitake mushrooms or barbecued Ontario pork, marinated in soya, honey and ginger and served with soba noodles and bosc pears. The wine-list majors in wines from the Niagara Region, with a number of attractive vintages also from California and Australia. The best buy is the chardonnay from Milpara Park, which is modestly priced at 37.00. The sad fact, however, is that both Derek Walton and Wade Urash cooked better in the old days at the Compleat Angler than today at Moon River, whether because Tiffany and Ken Bol haven't given them their head or because they haven't yet had time to find their feet. Time will tell.
Open daily 11.30 am to 2.30 pm (lunch), 2.30 pm to 5 pm (tapas in summer only), 5 pm to 8.30 pm (dinner). Closed on Wednesday in winter. Licensed. Amex, Master Card, Visa. No smoking. Book ahead if you can.

BANFF, Alberta ***MAP 16***

There are several places in Banff where you can get a casual meal and save money. The Café Soleil at 208 Caribou Street (telephone (403) 762-2090) is a promising newcomer and it's open all day every day. It's a stylish place and so far they're cooking very well. Try the skewers of chicken and figs or the Moroccan lamb with apricots. The Balkan at 120 Banff Avenue (telephone (403) 762-3454) is a Greek place that makes use of old family recipes. They're open all day and have one really great dish, which is arni-psito, a version of lamb Greek-style. The St. James Gate is an Irish pub at 207 Wolf Street (telephone (403) 762-9355). It has 33 beers on tap and 50 single malts. It also has top-notch pub food—meatloaf, shepherd's pie and Guinness-and-cheddar soup. Bumpers at 603 Banff Avenue (telephone (403) 762-2622) is open from 4.30 pm till late seven days a week. They specialize in Alberta beef as well as an all-you-can-eat salad bar. At the other end of the market, you can get an insider's view of the Banff Springs Hotel and enjoy the views from the expansive windows at the Bow Valley Grill (telephone (403) 762-6860). Their broiled flat-iron steak won a gold medal in the Best-of-Alberta beef competition. Adults pay 37.50 for the Sunday brunch and the daily dinner buffet. Kids pay 12.95. All these places are licensed and they all take most cards.

BANFF **MAP 16**
LE BEAUJOLAIS ☆☆
212 Buffalo Street **$175**
(403) 762-2712

The Beaujolais got a new chef last year and so far the kitchen is performing better than it has since the days of Philipp Weingartner. Like his predecessor, Urs Manser offers three set menus every night: a *menu surprise* at 90.00, the classic at 78.00 and the table d'hôte at 55.00 for two courses, 62.00 for three. If you choose the table d'hôte, your meal will probably begin with Ahi tuna sashimi with spiced cucumber and wasabi or with carpaccio of kobe beef. Kobe beef is rare in Canada and it's marvellous. Sea-bass follows, in beurre blanc with thin-sliced purple potato. Sea-bass or tenderloin of beef and venison, the first with confit of shallots and foie gras de canard, the second with quince, apple and calvados. The wine-list, needless to say, has few equals. Albert Moser has collected eight vintages from the Joseph Phelps vineyard, eight from the Eisele vineyard and ten of the blends from Insignia. He has four cabernets from the Gravelly Meadow vineyard of Diamond Creek and three magnificent Caymus cabernets, all special selections—to say nothing of the unusual holdings of beaujolais wines for which the restaurant is named. The presentation is lavish, the service knowledgeable. Nobody leaves the Beaujolais feeling they have been ignored.

Open daily 6 pm to 10.30 pm from 15 April until 14 October, Tuesday to Saturday 6 pm to 10.30 pm from 15 October until 14 April. Closed on Sunday and Monday in winter. Licensed. Master Card, Visa. Book ahead.

BANFF
See also CANMORE.

BARRIE, Ontario **MAP 17**
THE CRAZY FOX
135 Bayfield Street **$125**
(705) 737-5000

Coos Uylenbroek has never been quite the same since he moved to this sumptuous split-level location on Bayfield Street, but he still runs a consistent and surprisingly ambitious kitchen. He likes to start his meals with soft-shell crab with mayonnaise spiked with dijon, squid with sesame-and-lime yogurt or even Ahi tuna with parmesan cheese and truffle vinaigrette. Then perhaps he'll go on to salmon stuffed with crab, veal with serrano ham (a nice touch), pork tenderloin with espresso and rack of lamb with sundried tomatoes and macadamia nuts. This is creative cooking and it usually works. The Crazy Fox is one of the few Ontario restaurants to stock wines from the Okanagan as well as Niagara. Prices on the wine-list aren't high and there's a chardonnay and a syrah from Alice White for only 36.00 a bottle. The coffee is as good as ever.
Open Tuesday to Thursday 11.30 am to 2.30 pm, 5.30 pm to 9.30 pm, Friday 11 am to 2.30 pm, 5.30 pm to 10 pm, Saturday 5.30 pm to 10.30 pm. Closed on Sunday and Monday. Licensed. Amex, Master Card, Visa. Free parking.

Every restaurant in this guide has been personally tested. Our reporters are not allowed to identify themselves to the management or to accept free meals. We accept no advertisements. We accept no payment for listings. We depend entirely on you. Recommend the book to your friends.

BARRIE **MAP 17**
OSCAR'S ☆
52 Bayfield Street **$125**
(705) 737-0522

Everything has changed at Oscar's. Once shabby and bare inside, the interior has now been fixed up and, overnight it seems, the place has become stylish and fashionable. The cooking, of course, has always been stylish. Meals begin with such surprising things as soft-shell crab with a purée of avocado, grilled squid with a warm tapenade and foie gras, perhaps with chicken-of-the-wood mushrooms. (We haven't tried the gravlax with Guinness and cream cheese and aren't sure we want to.) The meal goes on to tuna wrapped in nori with couscous and sesame, rack of lamb with black cardamom and dijon, fillet of ostrich with sweet potato and claret, double-smoked pork tenderloin and local lake trout stuffed with shrimps. Given a few minutes' notice, they'll bring you a molten-chocolate cake, made with valhrona chocolate. The wine-list starts with a beaujolais for 31.00 and ends up with an Opus One for 320.00. Along the way are wines from Italy, France, California, Australia and New Zealand. But the list still needs to be expanded—not long ago there were only two wines from Niagara, both reds. The coffee, however, is good and the balsamic vinegar superb.
Open Tuesday to Friday 11.30 am to 3 pm, 5 pm to 10 pm, Saturday 5 pm to 10 pm. Closed on Sunday and Monday. Licensed. Amex, Mater Card, Visa. No smoking. ♿

BATCHAWANA BAY, Ontario **MAP 18**
SALZBURGER HOF
Highway 563 **$80 ($165)**
(705) 882-2323

Ann Elsigan and her husband bought the Salzburger Hof as an abandoned building back in 1972. They restored the place to look like something out of their native Austria. The cooking may not be quite as good

as it was then, but the view of Lake Superior is as spectacular as ever, the service as cheerful and efficient. Ann's daughter, Karen, has taken over the cooking. She does all her own butchering, smokes all her own bacon and pork and makes everything on the menu from scratch. She buys whitefish and lake trout from local fishermen and puts on an all-you-can-eat fish fry every Friday night. Black Forest cake has always been a specialty of the house, but most readers seem to prefer the apple strudel or the apple dumpling. Visitors from the south may not approve of the old-fashioned menu and old-time cooking, and nobody would recommend the coffee-shop, but local people like the familiar style, and the dining-room is packed on weekends. The Elsigans own 32 acres of land just a few minutes' drive from Pancake Bay and its wonderful white-sand beach. West of Batchawana Bay the scenery is magnificent, but the road is lonely and there's nowhere you can eat. So be prepared.
Open daily 5 pm to 9 pm from 1 May until 31 October (or until the first snow flies). Licensed. Master Card, Visa.

BATCHAWANA BAY
See also GOULAIS BAY.

BAY FORTUNE, P.E.I. **(MAP 43)**
THE INN AT BAY FORTUNE ☆☆
Highway 310 **$180 ($600)**
(902) 687-3745

For years, this has been our favourite place to stay on the Island. The old house and its outbuildings overlook the Fortune River from the top of a grassy slope that rises from the still waters of the bay. The Inn is only an hour's drive from Charlottetown, but chefs seem to feel isolated and they move on—in Michael Smith's case to a successful television show called the Inn Chef. Two years ago, David Wilmer hired Renée Lavalée from the British Virgin Islands. Her style was heartier and less self-conscious than that of her predecessors, but she was

a forceful woman who wasn't given to compromise. In her second year she met a man and left. This year Warren Barr, her sous-chef, has taken over where she left off. He spends his winters in Vancouver's Bistro Pastis (see below), which also has an excellent kitchen. We hope he stays at Bay Fortune and we hope he gets rid of Renée Lavalée's cute menus. He has an enormous kitchen garden at his back door, as well as suppliers who bring him everything from oysters and mussels to local beef. On a good night he's very good indeed, but the dining-room suffers from the fact that David Wilmer tries to cover both Bay Fortune and Spry Point, neither of which has any other maître d'hôtel. The wine-list is one of the best on the Island. It has a number of notable vintages, among them a Caymus conundrum, a gewurztraminer from Malivoire and an Opus One from Mondavi. Only the last is expensive.
Open daily 5 pm to 9 pm from the middle of May until Thanksgiving. Licensed. Amex, Master Card, Visa. Book ahead.

BELLEVILLE, Ontario **MAP 20**
SWEET BASIL
19 Campbell Street **$160**
(613) 961-5000

Shaun Connell says he's grown tired of the California grill. He's now exploring the French idiom, which means a lot more butter and cream. In summer he's interested in seasonal fruit salsas and fruit compotes for use throughout the year. He's also interested in things like ostrich, venison and wild boar, all raised on a nearby farm and available year-round. Connell is very good too with fish. These days, however, lobster thermidor will mean Cuban lobster-tail sautéed in butter, flamed in brandy and finished with cream and romano cheese. Scallops are now pan-seared with smoked bacon, scallions and portobello mushrooms and seasoned with roasted garlic and port. A number of dishes are finished with port, sometimes with port and brandy. Connell is

a persuasive cook and chances are you'll enjoy his beef tenderloin with gorgonzola and red wine, your rack of lamb and your veal marsala. The sweets are rich but convincing. There's a pecan tart with Georgian pecans and Kentucky bourbon in a short-crust pastry and a dark-chocolate pâté in a coulis of blackberries. The wine-list is expensive and you may prefer one of the many open wines, which are cheaper, or perhaps a glass of single malt. They have more than a hundred on offer.
Open Tuesday to Saturday 5 pm to 10 pm. Closed on Sunday and Monday. Licensed. Amex, Master Card, Visa. No smoking.

BERWICK, N.S. **MAP 21**
UNION STREET CAFE
183 Commercial Street **$80**
(902) 538-7787

Jenny McCoy is doing all the cooking at the Union Street Café these days. Her mother and her aunt have retired and her sister is in Africa for a year. Lunch has now become a buffet, featuring a hot dish every day, usually lasagne. Lasagne, handmade with local ricotta cheese, herbs from the garden and organic spinach, is the kitchen's pride and joy. She tries to balance tried-and-true dishes like lasagne and chicken Alfredo with more experimental things, like pan-seared scallops, pan-fried haddock or peanut noodles with chicken or tofu. They use nothing but the best ingredients: organic quinoa and millet for the tabouleh, wild salmon, pork and pork sausage from Meadowbrook Farm and apples from the Annapolis Valley. The sweets change twice a week and they're all gorgeous.
Open Tuesday to Sunday 11 am to 9 pm. Closed on Monday. Licensed. Master Card, Visa. No smoking. ♿

Where an entry is printed in italics this indicates that the restaurant has been listed only because it serves the best food in its area or because it hasn't yet been adequately tested.

BLAIRMORE, Alberta **MAP 22**

MOUNTAIN BAKERY

12849 20 Avenue **$20**

(403) 562-7999

Blairmore is twelve miles from the B.C. border, just east of the Crow's Nest Pass. The Mountain Bakery has been in business here for several years now, though Jean-Pierre Gauthier, the French baker, is having to work a longer day than he used to. He makes sixteen varieties of bread and several superb pastries. Just try his cream puffs, his rum babas or his cinnamon buns. He has six tables, where you can order a hot or cold sandwich made to order. Two new sandwiches are on the menu this year. They're the sunwheat vegetarian and the Montreal smoked meat. Croque monsieur is the best of the hot sandwiches, though he also makes first-class pyrogies in winter. Lunch still costs only 7.95 for soup, a sandwich, a pastry and a cup of coffee.

Open daily 8 am to 6 pm from 1 July until 31 August, Monday, Tuesday and Thursday to Sunday 8 am to 6 pm from 1 September until 30 June. Closed on Wednesday in winter. No liquor, no cards. No smoking.

BLIND RIVER, Ontario **MAP 23**

CHRISTIE'S

Highway 17 **$75 ($125)**

(800) 798-3536

This is a lonely stretch of highway, even lonelier than it used to be. Wayne and Georgina Winterburn are more than ever determined to keep every customer who comes their way. After twelve years on the job, 80% of their business is with repeat customers. So they learned to give people what they wanted. They started by offering Greek salads and Caesar salads with their own homemade dressings, poppyseed and herb vinaigrettes. But they found that customers preferred bottled dressings. Last year they found a farmer who raised his cattle without using chemicals or growth hormones and Wayne uses this beef for all his hamburgers. Fresh vegetables are scarce in the north and in winter there isn't much on the market but green and yellow beans. Things are better in summer, of course, when they get a lot of people from the nearby marina, most of whom ask for the whitefish, dipped in milk and flour and cooked on a flat-top grill. In winter the government travellers and businessmen ask for steak, usually the New York striploin with onions, mushrooms and home-made Tennessee dip. There's generally some chicken on the blackboard and there's always Georgina's raspberry pie. If you stay at Christie's, you get to cook your own eggs for breakfast.

Open Monday to Friday 11 am to 8 pm, Saturday and Sunday 5 pm to 8 pm. Licensed. All cards. No smoking. ♿

BLOOMFIELD, Ontario **MAP 24**

ANGELINE'S ☆☆

Bloomfield Inn **$120**

433 Main Street

(613) 393-3301

Wilhelm Fida has had to work hard all his life, but at least he has the satisfaction of knowing that Angeline's is a success. Prince Edward County is fertile, peaceful country and that's what drew him to Bloomfield in the first place. He refurbished the big, old Victorian house from top to bottom. But when he opened, he found that trained staff was almost impossible to find. Who could forget the confusion of Angeline's early days? But over the years most of the problems have disappeared. Good local produce is now in plentiful supply. They grow their own herbs and vegetables at the door. Local fruit is abundant. Yellow perch comes from the Bay of Quinte. Spring brings local lamb and beautiful asparagus. Fall brings wild game—duckling (served with maple syrup and merlot), pheasant (served with savoury cabbage and cumin), guinea-fowl (in the consommés), quail, squab and, of course, venison, which appears with juniper-berries and mushroom-and-truffle risottos.

Christian Marchsteiner, the *pâtissier*, makes lemon tarts and chocolate confections by the dozen. The wine-list is constantly growing and now includes a fine selection of V.Q.A. wines from Niagara.
Open daily 5.30 pm to 9 pm from 1 July until 30 September, Monday and Wednesday to Sunday 5.30 pm to 9 pm from 1 October until 30 June. Closed on Tuesday in winter. Licensed. Amex, Master Card, Visa. Book ahead.

BOTWOOD, Newfoundland **MAP 25**
DOCKSIDE
243 Water Street **$95**
(709) 257-3355

Timber from the interior used to pass through Botwood every day on its way to waiting ships. The town is just twenty minutes from the Trans Canada Highway and it's still an important distribution centre. The building that houses Dockside began life in the nineteen-thirties as a wholesale warehouse for Wilansky Brothers, and you can still read the old Wilansky price-lists while you wait for a table. The warehouse passed through the hands of several owners before Jim Stuckless took the premises over from a failed pizza parlour, decorated with bars from a demolished jail. Stuckless had until then been a mechanical engineer, but he taught himself how to cook. Now, ten years later, he's in the kitchen most nights because he can't find a chef who can cook as well as he can. He has two rules: he always buys the best of available produce and he always cooks what he himself would like to eat. His beef all comes from Alberta and he has lamb on the menu because he likes lamb. He makes all his own salad-dressings, meat sauces and sweets from scratch, trying a recipe over and over again until he gets it just right. Every summer he goes through at least 50 pounds of mussels a week, turning the left-overs into a lightly-marinated mussel salad. He's particularly proud of his cheddar-baked fillet of cod and of his baked seafood plate—a medley of salmon, shrimps and mussels. Be sure to save space for the sweet course.

There's usually partridge-berry kuchen and Bavarian apple torte, as well as coconut-cream pie, on the menu. Every Sunday after church Jim's mother and aunt put on a roast-turkey and roast-beef dinner with all the trimmings for 6.95. If any senior citizen turns up before they run out, he gets the dinner for 4.95. Who else can match that?
Open Monday to Friday noon to 9 pm, Saturday 5 pm to 9 pm, Sunday noon to 9 pm. Licensed. All cards. No smoking. ♿

BRACKLEY BEACH, P.E.I. **(MAP 43)**
THE DUNES ☆
Highway 15 **$130**
(902) 672-1883

Most visitors to the Island end up sooner or later at the Dunes, if only because there's nothing else quite like it. Peter Jansons, himself a potter, designed the place as a show-room for local art. The gallery, four storeys of wood and glass with decorative inlays, crafted stairways and a Japanese garden, has a café on two levels. The menu combines dishes from East and West and everything is beautifully presented on Jansons' own plates (which are for sale at the front desk). Emily Wells does some quite remarkable things—Asian snow crab with pickled ginger, shrimps and scallops with red peppers, jasmine and fresh vegetables. The roasted rack of lamb is deftly spiced and cooked to order with a medley of vegetables that comes with all the entrées. There are several big, rich sweets, among them a wonderful frozen maple mousse with crystallized ginger. When you book ask for a window table where you can enjoy the view of the garden, with its many grasses and ponds. It's lovely.
Open daily 11.30 am to 9.30 pm from Victoria Day until Thanksgiving. Licensed. Amex, Master Card, Visa. No smoking. ♿

Nobody can buy space in this guide and nobody can buy his way out of it.

BRANTFORD, Ontario **MAP 27**

GED'S

97 Brant Avenue **$135**

(519) 759-1125

When Ged's took over this old house in the heart of Brantford, they were interested, we thought, in casual dining. But they always had a dream, a dream of a serious restaurant, and over the past year or so they've been moving steadily in that direction. Take a look at their wine-list. They have a really deep cellar that offers, among other things, three premier-cru Mouton Rothschilds for 1200.00 to 1400.00 a bottle—as well as a half-bottle of the Henry of Pelham baco noir for 15.00. The menu is seasonal. Last winter you could begin with pan-seared Quebec foie gras with bing cherries and a riesling jelly or sashimi of yellowfin tuna with won-tons and wasabi-lime crème fraîche. After that there was pan-seared fillet of Atlantic salmon with garlic-fried spinach. In the spring there were lamb shanks, lightly smoked, then braised for sixteen hours and served with a forest-mushroom risotto. Their potatoes are whipped with feta, with smoked bacon and cheddar, with garlic or with sweet onions. The sweets aren't exciting, but there are many good wines by the glass, as well as ten for 20.00 or less a bottle.

Open Monday to Thursday 5 pm to 10 pm, Friday 11 am to 2 pm, 5 pm to 10 pm, Saturday 5 pm to 10 pm. Closed on Sunday. Licensed. Amex, Master Card, Visa.

BRANTFORD

See also PARIS.

BRENTWOOD BAY, B.C. **(MAP 230)**

ARBUTUS

Brentwood Bay Lodge **$245**

849 Verdier Avenue

(888) 544-2079

Arbutus is located in a stunning new resort on Brentwood Bay. A soaring glass wall affords diners dramatic sunset views of the harbour. The interior is a crisp blend of Japanese, First Nation and West Coast architectural styles. The cooking is international, but firmly rooted in produce from Vancouver Island and the Gulf Islands. The wine-list is large and expensive and reflects the expertise of the *sommelier*, Brian Storen, formerly of Sooke Harbour House. Alain Leger has three imaginative *prix-fixe* menus, one paired with an interesting flight of wines from Venturi-Schulze. Recent menus featured seared sea scallops, spot prawns, flying squid, pickled lipstick radishes, rock sole, wild sockeye salmon and dungeness crab in a purée of snap peas and sour cream. They also do such game dishes as grilled leg of wild caribou, smoked breast of duckling and local farmed bison. The highlight of the meal is usually the chocolate terrine prepared by the *pâtissier*, Bruno Feldeisen, whose pastries are also sold in the deli in the Brentwood Bay Lodge. *Open daily noon to 3 pm, 6 pm to 10 pm. In summer there's a jazz brunch on Saturday and Sunday from 11 am to 3 pm. Licensed. All cards. No smoking.* ♿

BRENTWOOD BAY **(MAP 230)**
CARDEN STREET WEST
1164 Stelly's Cross Road **$105**
(250) 544-1475

Fairy lights and bright colours make the interior of Carden Street West look like a painting of a country café by Grandma Moses. The little restaurant in the middle of nowhere started out as a vegetable stand and it still features an abundance of local produce. But if the location is remote, the cooking is anything but simple or primitive. In fact, there's no doubt that the chefs have matured in the last year or two. The cooking is still colourful, but no longer quirky. The lobster-prawn-and-scallop cakes, a nice variation on the familiar crab-cake, come with a lively corn-and-black-bean salsa. The smoked scallops appear on a colourful bed of mangoes and strawberries. There's also a lovely adaptation of the traditional Greek spinach pie The pork tenderloin with orange, port and cream is the best of the main courses. In the last several months, the kitchen has developed a new line of African, Malaysian and Thai curries. Breast of duck, for instance, now comes in a tart cherry-coconut curry, prawns in a mango-and-coconut curried salsa. The sweet list is aptly named, running as it does to sticky, syrupy concoctions. If you want something lighter, try the pavlova. The wines are almost more off-beat than the food, but they seem to go together. Remember, Brentwood Bay isn't far from the ferry terminal at Swartz Bay. It's also quite close to the Victoria airport.

Open Tuesday to Sunday 5 pm to 9 pm from 1 March until 31 December, Thursday and Friday 5 pm to 9 pm from 1 January until 28 February. Closed on Monday in summer, Saturday to Wednesday in winter. Licensed. Master Card, Visa. No smoking. ♿

BRIER ISLAND, N.S.

See EAST FERRY, FREEPORT.

BRIGUS, Newfoundland **MAP 29**

THE COUNTRY CORNER

14 Water Street ***$25***

(709) 528-1099

Brigus is an attractive small seaside town, established on the southwest shore of Conception Bay in 1612. It's about an hour's drive from St. John's and is basically a gift shop, with a small café and a covered patio. The food is pretty simple. They have homemade soup, sandwiches and sweets. The specialty of the house is cod chowder, which is more of a bisque than a chowder, in that the fish is puréed and seasoned, as cod usually is, with summer savoury. The chowder is served with what is known as a tea bun in Newfoundland, a biscuit in Prince Edward Island and a scone elsewhere. The pick of the sweets is blueberry crisp with vanilla ice cream and blueberry sauce. They also sell chocolate-chip cookies, brownies, ice-cream cones, sundaes and milkshakes. The Country Corner is open all day every day from Victoria Day until Thanksgiving. No liquor. Master Card, Visa. No smoking.

BRITT, Ontario **MAP 30**
LITTLE BRITT INN ☆
Highway 69 **$95**
(888) 383-4555

Britt is 47 miles north of Parry Sound on Byng Inlet. Surrounded by granite and stunted pine, it lies at the southern end of the Thirty Thousand Islands in the Georgian Bay. The Little Britt Inn stays open year-round, which takes courage, but nobody here is looking for a buyer. On the contrary, Teri McLean is constantly improving her kitchen. She spent time at the Stratford chef's school and she likes to cook as the spirit moves her. Last year she added yellow perch to her fish menu, which already featured pickerel, salmon and catfish, all served with perfectly fresh vegetables and buttermilk-mashed potatoes. Bread-and-butter pudding is usually on the menu, and there are always a number of specials on the blackboard. Adjoining the dining-room there's a raw bar where all summer long they serve fresh oysters, supplied by Rodney's of Toronto and served ice-cold at 35.00 a dozen, as well as mussels and Georgian Bay chowder. The wine-list is built around wines from Reif Estates, which supplies the Inn with four private-label house wines. Markups are unbelievably low, so spend the money you save on one of the better wines. If you want to stay the night (and you probably will), there are four decorator suites. *Open daily noon to 8.30 pm. Licensed. All cards.*

BURLINGTON, Ontario **(MAP 89)**
BLACK TREE ☆
Roseland Plaza **$135**
3029 New Street
(905) 681-2882

Black Tree is a newcomer to the Burlington area, but it's a serious restaurant with an ambitious menu. Matteo Paonessa, the chef, has worked with all the right people—Marc Thuet, Michael Potters, Michael

Stadtländer, Dario Tomaselli and Susur Lee. Last year he opened his own restaurant in the Roseland Plaza. This is a disconcerting address, but pay no attention to that. Inside, the place is at once up-market and artsy—all black and white with brilliant red accents. The menu changes once a month, but everything is made on the premises. Meals begin with a small loaf of freshly-baked bread and homemade butter, followed by an *amuse bouche*, which may be something like an emulsion of walnut. They prepare a different foie gras every day, as well as a soup and a salad. The soups are interesting and unusual. Acorn squash, for instance, is served with an emulsion of black licorice, a play on the name of the restaurant. The best of the main courses is the Alaska black cod with a tempura of bone marrow—that and lamb shanks with gnocchi. Monkfish served osso-buco style with the bone in is a lively alternative. The sweets are good too, especially the sugar-pear turnover, the lemon pudding-cake and the pineapple tart tatin with sweet black-peppercorn crème fraîche. Black Tree has made an impressive start.

Open Tuesday to Saturday 6 pm to 10.30 pm. Closed on Sunday and Monday. Licensed. Master Card, Visa. No smoking. ♿

BURLINGTON **(MAP 89)**

MIZUNA'S

399 John Street **$100**

(905) 639-8860

Mizuna's is one of two restaurants (Black Tree is the other) that look ready to fill the gap created by the closing of Collet's several years ago. It's run by Robert and Marie Dickson, with Robert in charge of the kitchen and Marie in charge of the front of the house. They change their menu several times a year, but in any season the crab-cakes are their best dish. They also do first-class ravioli stuffed with duck and garnished with roasted mushrooms and grilled leeks. Sea scallops are served with baby spinach, red onions and toasted

macadamia nuts tossed in sherry vinaigrette. Atlantic salmon comes with caramelized onions, pork tenderloin with gingered apricot in a reduction of port—a splendid dish. Better still is the squash gnocchi, though it's not often on the menu. There's a decent, small wine-list, but no choice of open wines. Usually, however, Marie can be persuaded to open one of the bottled wines if she can be sure of selling a couple of glasses. Sweets are not a strong suit. Settle instead for a cup or two of coffee—it's great.
Open Monday to Friday 11.30 am to 3 pm, 5 pm to 9.30 pm (later on Friday), Saturday 5 pm to 10 pm, Sunday 5 pm to 9 pm. Licensed. All cards. No smoking.

BURLINGTON **(MAP 89)**
PANE FRESCO
414 Locust Street **$25**
(905) 333-3388

Pane Fresco is a new bakery café in downtown Burlington, not far from the lakeshore. A huge variety of breads and pastries are on display on the counter and they're all of very high quality. There's twelve-grain and sourdough bread as well as baguettes and such unusual things as porcini-and-shitake ciabattas, sundried-tomato-and-asiago bastones, white-and-dark-chocolate panetones and sesame-cheddar twists. The hand-made artisan breads are spectacular. The pastries include apricot-custard Danishes, chocolate panes, Sicilian canolis and Belgian waffles. They also offer several homemade gelatos and five different paninis. For lunch there are salads and gourmet pizzas made with mozzarella, goat-cheese, sun-dried tomatoes, sausages and black olives. Every day there are two homemade soups. One might be a lobster bisque, the other a cream of wild mushrooms and goat-cheese.
Open Tuesday to Saturday 7.30 am to 6 pm, Sunday 7.30 am to 4 pm. Closed on Monday. No liquor, no cards. No smoking. ♿

CALABOGIE, Ontario **MAP 32**
THE DUCK ☆
729 Mill Street **$125**
(613) 752-0888

The approach to Calabogie on Highway 511 is very beautiful and the Duck has a lovely setting. It also has an ambitious kitchen and an elaborate menu that changes once or twice a week. Presentation is spectacular, portions ample. You can start with something as simple as a leaf salad with breast of duck in a raspberry vinaigrette and be surprised by the brilliant flavours. Or you can ask for smoked salmon with salmon pâté or grilled sea scallops. The scallops are served in a squash beurre blanc with curried couscous—an unusual and highly imaginative treatment. They have fresh fish at the Duck year round and their rainbow trout with saffron is a delightful dish. The rack of lamb starts as a cliché of mustard and green herbs and ends with such fresh ideas as black-bean stew and sun-dried-tomato bread. The almond crust is too dry for the tenderloin of pork, but the signature duck goes well with its red cabbage and crabapple gravy. The sweets are disappointing (especially the lime cheesecake), but the coffee is wonderful. There are only six Italian wines, seven from California and eight from Australia. Of the dozen or so wines from Niagara two are from East Dell and neither is of much interest. France, however, is another story. They have a Château Latour in the cellar as well as a Mouton Rothschild and an Haut Brion. They have the beautiful gewurztraminer from Dopff & Irion and an immaculate pinot blanc from Trimbach. They even have a grand-cru Echezaux from Faively (for 195.00). At the Duck, you drink French.
Open Wednesday to Sunday 5 pm to 9 pm. Closed on Monday and Tuesday. Licensed. Master Card, Visa. No smoking. ♿

If you use an out-of-date edition and find it inaccurate, don't blame us. Buy a new edition.

CALGARY, Alberta **MAP 33**
THE BELVEDERE ☆☆
107 8 Avenue SW **$195**
(403) 265-9595

The Belvedere, with its dark wood, tall mirrors and soft lighting, is designed to look and feel like a gentleman's club. This year they've decided to shake up the menu and to hire a Canadian chef, an Albertan, as it happens, by the name of Alain Chabot. Prices are still as high as ever and there's still a lot of foie gras on the menu. The pan-seared foie gras with poached quail eggs and truffled soldiers is a bit over the top. It's better to ask for the terrine de foie gras with quince jam or, better still, the pan-seared side-stripe prawns with an emulsion of yuzo-lemon brown butter. But there are other things as well, things that celebrate Alberta instead of France. There's beef tenderloin with madeira, Alberta lamb cooked in two ways, pork chops with oyster mushrooms and grainy mustard. The Alberta elk with a reduction of vintage-port is still on the menu, though without the strawberries and geraniums that used to come with it. There's also Alberta white-tail deer with a caramelized-parsnip purée and buckwheat spaetzle. The appetizers are varied and imaginative, but there's nothing imaginative about the sticky-toffee pudding that ends the meal. It's been on the menu from the beginning and it's still wonderful. For three straight years the Belvedere has been honoured by the *Wine Spectator* for its wine-list and there are great wines too numerous to mention. Prices are high and if you want an open wine ask for a glass of the Whitehall Lane Bommarito for 14.00.
Open Monday to Friday 11.30 am to 2 pm, 5 pm to 10 pm, Saturday 5 pm to 10 pm. Closed on Sunday. Licensed. Amex, Master Card, Visa. No smoking. Book ahead. ♿

This is a guide to Canadian restaurants from coast to coast—the first ever published and the only one of its kind on the market today.

CALGARY **MAP 33**
BRAVA
723 17 Avenue SW **$135**
(403) 228-1854

Brava opened about three years ago to almost universal acclaim. They had a *wunderkind* in the kitchen who had no sooner been voted the best new chef in town than he left. His place was taken by Kevin Turner, who is still on the job today. Inevitably, some of the original gloss has worn off, but the menu is still much as it was and they still do some things very well indeed. Try their seared scallops with buttered spinach or their lobster gnocchi with mushy peas and see for yourself. Their osso buco, braised in white wine with saffron risotto, is an unusual treatment that turns out to be everything it should be—and it costs only 28.00. Fresh tomatoes make the most of the Ahi tuna and the Atlantic salmon goes particularly well with its ragoût of asparagus, peas and potatoes. The gingerbread cake is still Brava's most remarkable achievement. Drenched with hot melted butter and scotch, it has no equals anywhere that we know of. The wine-list has no big Italian reds to boast of, still less any of the leading French clarets. It concentrates instead on chardonnays and cabernets from Australia and California, all of them well chosen and fairly priced.
Open Monday to Thursday 11.30 am to 3 pm, 5 pm to 11 pm, Friday and Saturday 11.30 am to 3 pm, 5 pm to midnight. Closed on Sunday. Licensed. All cards. No smoking. ♿

CALGARY **MAP 33**
CATCH ☆☆
100 8 Avenue SE **$185**
(403) 206-0000

Last year Catch lost its chef and was sold. This year it has new owners and a new chef, Brad Horen, who's winning praise from all comers. The previous owners spent six million dollars renovating the old Imperial

Bank building and fitting it up with an oyster bar downstairs and an open kitchen upstairs. The oyster bar is a casual place that offers a variety of Atlantic and Pacific oysters from Cortes Island and Gorge Inlet in B.C. and from Neguac in New Brunswick, Stanley Bridge in Prince Edward Island and St. John's in Newfoundland. The formal dining-room has an elaborate menu that features Digby scallops, halibut from the Queen Charlottes, roasted Nova Scotia lobster and several choice cuts of Galloway beef with madeira. (The beef is raised and aged expressly for Catch by the Foehler family of Strome, Alberta.) The presentation and service are outstanding, both in the oyster bar and the formal dining-room, but it's too soon to say how Catch will perform over the long haul.

Open Monday to Friday 11.30 am to 1.30 pm, 5.30 pm to 9.30 pm, Saturday 5.30 pm to 9.30 pm. The oyster bar is open Monday to Friday 11.30 am to 10 pm, Saturday 5 pm to 10 pm. Both are closed on Sunday. Licensed. All cards. No smoking. ♿

CALGARY **MAP 33**
DIVINO ☆
113 8 Avenue SW **$140**
(403) 410-5555

With its period setting and smart interior, Divino is a place worth seeing. Of course, it has other virtues as well. It's cheap as these things go. It's open all day. It offers sandwiches, not only at noon, but in the evening as well. It has a cheese-bar and a remarkable one at that. And it has a good kitchen that tosses off things like a ballotine of figs and a tarte tatin of portobello mushrooms and marinated goat-cheese with a flick of the wrist. There's a long list of appetizers that are meant to be eaten like tapas: mussels with fries, foie gras with candied rhubarb, sweetbreads with mushrooms and endive, shrimps with a beet salad, as well as the ballotine and the tarte tatin. The main courses, on the other hand, are a bit thin on the ground. Apart from Pacific

salmon, there's only roast breast of chicken and a couple of steaks. That's because you're meant to order from the cheese-bar, where they have 30 cheeses on offer, all of them in peak condition. Things like taleggio, pecorino, drumloch, brie de Meaux, caprice des dieux, tête de moine, even boursault. Like everything else, the wine-list has an offbeat excellence. As for the service, it's beyond compare.
Open Monday to Friday 11 am to 11 pm, Saturday and Sunday 5 pm to 11 pm. Licensed. All cards. No smoking.

CALGARY **MAP 33**
FLEUR DE SEL
2015 4 Street SW **$125**
(403) 228-9764

Fleur de Sel is a small French bistro with a high ceiling brightly painted in reds, yellows and blues. There are only about a dozen tables, and every one of them is full six nights a week. Conversation is impossible and if you want to talk it's best to come for lunch. If you come here and order rack of lamb, rib-eye of beef or maigret of duck, chances are you'll be disappointed. The kitchen does much better with its signature dishes, and that means cassoulet de Toulouse and Alsatian choucroute. You can begin more conventionally with oysters or mussels dijonnaise or smoked Atlantic salmon with pickled ginger. (Don't be tempted by the escargots des charentes, which are merely curious.) The wine-list is small and eccentric, but there are some notable wines. There's a Guy Saget vouvray for 45.00, a Guigal gigondas for 55.00 and a Stag's Leap cabernet sauvignon for 125.00. Meals are inexpensive if you choose the cassoulet or the choucroute and avoid the Stag's Leap.
Open Tuesday to Friday 11 am to 2 pm, 5 pm to 10 pm, Saturday and Sunday 5 pm to 10 pm. Closed on Monday. Licensed. Amex, Master Card, Visa. No smoking. ♿

Our web site is at www.oberonpress.ca Readers wishing to use e-mail should address us at oberon@sympatico.ca

CALGARY **MAP 33**
RIVER CAFE ☆
Prince's Island Park **$150**
(403) 261-7670

The River Café has every advantage—except convenience of access. They use nothing but fresh local produce, supporting local farmers and coastal fishermen. They raise many of their own organic vegetables. They have a lively, ambitious menu (halibut, pickerel, Arctic char and, best of all, Alaska black cod). They maintain a magnificent list of clarets (among them Haut-Brion) and a splendid list of wines from the Napa Valley (Spottswoode, Joseph Phelps). They're comfortable with such Canadian wines as the Malivoire chardonnay and the Blasted Church pinot blanc. They support breweries like the Fish Brewing Company of Olympia in Washington and Unibroue in Quebec, whose Maudite and Fin du Monde make most other beers look pale by comparison. They make their chocolate torte with the best Callebaut chocolate and buy the best unpasteurized cheeses for their cheese-plate. Unfortunately, however, they no longer have a two-star kitchen. The cooking lacks excitement, the execution lacks polish. It remains to be seen whether or not they will regain their old form this summer.
Open Monday to Friday 11.30 am to 2.30 pm, 5.30 pm to 10 pm, Saturday and Sunday 10 am to 3 pm (brunch), 5.30 pm to 10 pm. Licensed. Amex, Master Card, Visa.

CALGARY **MAP 33**
SUGO CAFFE ITALIA ☆
1214 9 Avenue SE **$120**
(403) 263-1115

Sugo is small, elegant and loveable. It's very well served and reasonably priced—if noise bothers you, ask for a table by the window. They change the menu every day, so you'll just have to hope that the garden-vegetable crostinis with grilled prawns are on offer when you get

there. They're marvellous. There's apt to be too much mozzarella on the grilled portobello mushroom, but the wild-mushroom bruschetta is lovely. There are two or three pastas every evening—handmade gnocchi with shrimps, egg-noodle fettucine with grilled chicken, goat-cheese and basil pesto. Buffalo rib-eye is the most expensive of the meats, wild spring salmon the cheapest of the fish. The salmon is served with goat-cheese and tomatoes, the sea-bass with almonds and frangelico. The breast of duck is overwhelmed by its port-and-blueberry sauce, but the venison chops go beautifully with their spicy pepperonata. We admire the tiramisu; others go for the lemon soufflé. But everyone likes the capuccino, which they serve with homemade biscotti. The wines, naturally enough, are mostly Italian and come from every important region, from Toscana to Abruzzi. There are also a few big red wines from Australia and California. The whole list is priced to sell, even the two brunellos.
Open Tuesday 5.30 pm to 9.30 pm, Wednesday to Friday 11.30 am to 2 pm, 5.30 pm to 9.30 pm, Saturday 5.30 pm to 9.30 pm. Closed on Sunday and Monday. Licensed. All cards. No smoking. Book ahead if you can. ♿

CALGARY **MAP 33**
TEATRO ☆☆
200 8 Avenue SE **$275**
(403) 290-1012

Teatro is very, very expensive. In Calgary, it appears that this is no handicap, especially if you have, like Teatro, a really good kitchen. Dominique Moussu is more than usually addicted to foie gras, serving as he does things like foie-gras torchon and beef tenderloin with foie-gras ravioli. But his signature dish isn't foie gras at all; it's scallop-and-lobster lasagne, which is on the menu every day at both lunch and dinner. (Ravioli also comes with dungeness crab and venison.) He's offered roast bison and pan-roasted Arctic char for years, but this year one or two new things—rack of lamb with polente and grilled vegetables and quail from Quebec with spaghetti squash, mushrooms and maple syrup—have appeared on the dinner menu. The wine-list is extraordinary. There are dozens of pauillacs, dozens of barolos and super-Tuscans. From California there are three wines from Caymus, three from Spottswoode and three Insignia blends from Joseph Phelps. There are five Penfolds grange shiraz from Australia. The selection of wines from the Okanagan, however, is thin, though they do have the Note Bene from Black Hills. The lovely thing about Teatro is that it's right across the street from Theatre Calgary and doesn't close its doors until 11 pm or later. *Open Monday to Thursday 11.30 am to 2.30 pm, 5 pm to 11 pm, Friday 11.30 am to 2.30 pm, 5 pm to 11.30 pm, Saturday 5 pm to 11.30 pm, Sunday 5 pm to 10 pm. Licensed. All cards. No smoking.* ♿

CALGARY **MAP 33**
TOWA SUSHI
2116 4 Street SW **$75**
(403) 245-8585

This exciting new restaurant in downtown Calgary has been crowded since the day it opened. They have an enormous variety of sushi and the presentation is spectacular. They declare on the menu that their sushi is large, and that's true. The duck salad maison is also generously served and comes with an abundance of sweet duck. The best of the sushi, we think, is the unagi roll (unagi means barbecued eel) and the spicy tuna roll. Aside from sushi, they also have a number of noodle dishes, salads, raw oysters, teriyaki and even a sushi pizza.
Open Tuesday to Thursday 11.30 am to 1.45 pm, Friday 11.30 am to 1.45 pm, 5 pm to 10.45 pm, Saturday 5 pm to 10.45 pm, Sunday 5 pm to 9.15 pm. Closed on Monday. Licensed. All cards. No smoking.

Nobody can buy space in this guide and nobody can buy his way out of it.

CALGARY **MAP 33**
WILDWOOD ☆
2417 4 Street SW **$130**
(403) 228-0100

Downstairs at Wildwood there's a pub where they sell local beers, including one that's brewed on the premises. They have a late-night menu and live music. Upstairs there's a restaurant, where there's a lot of dark wood, soft lighting and expert service. There they have an abundance of game: bison carpaccio, seared buffalo steak with a salad of mango and red chilli, a wild-boar pizza, buffalo liver crusted with wild mushrooms and elk medallions with toasted pistachio nuts. The rest of the menu is more familiar. There's lamb with rosemary, orzo with roasted tomatoes, breast of chicken with grapes and vermouth and grilled Arctic char with green-pea sauce and an asparagus risotto. Some of these dishes are really remarkable, but it's probably more fun to order one of the game dishes. Where else can you get buffalo liver or elk with pistachio nuts? There's a good, strong wine-list and reasonable prices across the board.
Open Monday to Thursday 11.30 am to 2 pm, 5 pm to 10 pm, Friday 11.30 am to 2 pm, 5 pm to 11 pm, Saturday 11 am to 2 pm (brunch), 5 pm to 11 pm, Sunday 10.30 am to 2 pm (brunch), 5 pm to 9.30 pm. Licensed. All cards. No smoking. ♿

CAMBRIDGE, Ontario **MAP 34**
LANGDON HALL ☆☆
1 Langdon Drive **$195 ($395)**
(800) 268-1898

Langdon Hall occupies a stately brick mansion in a setting of woods and gardens. You can stay for the night (at a price) in one of its luxurious guest-rooms or in one of the new stable suites. Or you can spend the inside of 200.00 on dinner for two in the splendid dining-room overlooking the garden. This is one of Canada's

few Relais & Châteaux, which shows in every detail of the ambience and service. Lunch begins in stately fashion with foie gras and chicken-liver brûlée with sweet-and-sour bing cherries and goes on to wild lake trout, Ontario lamb with sweet corn and rosemary polente, onion rings and sweet peppers or dry-aged beef tenderloin with goat-cheese and fingerling potatoes. The kitchen treads softly and makes few mistakes. In the evening they take more chances, starting with foie gras with cippolini and kumquat jam or scallops with parsnip, mascarpone and thyme ravioli in vanilla vinaigrette. The most interesting of the main courses is the steamed suet pudding of braised lamb and capers, paired with lamb-and-lentil boudin in eggplant purée and garlic-mint jus. (Almost everything on the menu is paired with something else—breast of Brome Lake duck with confit of duck leg, braised Ste.-Agathe rabbit pie with roasted shank of rabbit. After such an entrée, citrus panna cotta with champagne and pink grapefruit may come as a welcome surprise. The wine-list tries to be all things to all men and it succeeds. The list of cabernets and chardonnays from the Niagara Region has few peers. Prices are, of course, extremely high, but there is one fabulous bargain, a bottle of the 2003 Caymus conundrum for 55.00. Perhaps it was a misprint.
Open daily noon to 2 pm, 6 pm (5 pm in summer, when the Stratford Festival is on) to 9 pm. Licensed. All cards. ♿

CAMBRIDGE **MAP 34**
MIMOSA ☆
121 Ainslee Street N **$135**
(519) 624-2023

Mimosa is still the most innovative restaurant in the Cambridge area. Dinners run to ten appetizers, a couple of pastas and twelve entrées. This is a tiny place with only a few tables to support such luxuries as truffle oil, shitake mushrooms and foie gras, so prices have to be quite high. We for our part have enjoyed the truffle oil with wild mushrooms, fresh greens and goat-cheese and

the foie gras on polente with a port-and-fig glaze. The main courses are rather less adventurous. If you don't feel like veal marsala or saddle of rabbit with rosemary and madeira, ask for fresh seafood on basmati rice with ginger, coconut, lime and sambal. The lunch menu is broadly similar, though at noon there are also one or two sandwiches (pork tenderloin with dijon, grilled veal on focaccia with camembert), a risotto and chicken and seafood crêpes—all a far cry from the usual businessman's lunch. There are only a few sweets, all made on the premises. The modest wine-list is well chosen and there's a generous choice of wines by the glass. On gourmet evenings they have a fixed-price menu with selected wines supplied by their Toronto importer.
Open Tuesday to Friday 11 am to 2.30 pm, 5 pm to 9 pm, Saturday 5 pm to 10 pm. Closed on Sunday and Monday. Licensed. All cards. No smoking. Free parking.

CANMORE, Alberta **(MAP 16)**
THE COPPER DOOR ☆
926 9 Street **$100**
(403) 678-5233

A few years ago, Chris Dmytriv, the co-owner of Zona's, bought the Peppermill. and renamed it the Copper Door. Dmytriv doubles as an artist and designer and the artwork on the walls, the table settings and the handmade pottery are all his. Last spring the chef left and since then Dmytriv has been in charge. He spends most of his time here now, perfecting a traditional Franco-Italian cuisine, which is a far cry from the eclectic cuisine he developed at Zona's. He makes everything from scratch, changing his menu twice a year. The cooking is extremely consistent and there are no more off nights. Dmytriv has always been good with fish. Last summer that meant halibut, which is now hard to get. This year it means Atlantic salmon, perhaps baked in a maple-whisky sauce. There's an excellent bouillabaisse, made with fresh mussels, halibut cheeks, black tiger prawns and scallops, cooked in a broth of tomato and

fennel. A lot of people still remember the lamb shanks at Zona's. At the Copper Door Dmytriv does a slow-roasted leg of lamb, which is removed from the bone and sautéed with roasted garlic and port-thyme jus. The sweets—Callebaut chocolate, ginger-truffle tart—are as good as ever. The wine-list is small, but almost every wine is the best of its kind. There are several dessert wines as well and three tawny ports.
Open daily 5 pm to 11 pm from 1 June until 30 September, Wednesday to Sunday 5 pm to 10 pm from 1 October until 31 May. Closed on Monday and Tuesday in winter. Licensed. Amex, Master Card, Visa. No smoking. ♿

CANMORE **(MAP 16)**
THE CRAZY WEED ☆
626 Main Street **$125**
(403) 609-2530

This used to be a funky little place, but that's all history now. The restaurant has been completely redecorated and the inside is bright and cheerful, the prices reasonable. The wine-list is full of unusual ideas. (If you're tired of Wente chardonnay, no longer a buy at 39.00, ask for a bottle of Louis Sipp gewurztraminer and see what we mean.) Lunch is a matter of pizzas, panini sandwiches and chicken curry—the lamb is too expensive at 20.00. Jan Hrabec cooks a more ambitious menu in the evening, when there's always a good homemade soup (offered also at noon), as well as things like Alaska black cod with soy and wildflower honey and locally-picked chanterelles with hand-cut pasta. Best of the sweets this year is the Callebaut-chocolate cake with sundried cherries. But remember, they don't take reservations.
Open Monday to Saturday 11.30 am to 4 pm, 5 pm to 8.30 pm, Sunday noon to 6 pm. Licensed. Master Card, Visa. No smoking. No reservations. ♿

The map number assigned to each city, town and village gives the location of the centre on one or more of the maps at the start of the book.

CANMORE **(MAP 16)**
SUNFOOD
743 Railway Avenue **$65**
(403) 609-2613

This is a small vegetarian café where the food is so fresh one can hardly believe it. Christian Lendi, the owner and chef, trained in Switzerland, but his menus come from all over. He has an excellent tabouleh and a very good spinach salad. His mushroom ravioli is *al dente* without being heavy, and his teriyaki tofu steak is full of flavour and rich in texture. He also has several Thai-style vegan and gluten-free dishes, but his sweets are on the whole less interesting. There's also a Sunfood Café on the second floor of the Sundance Mall at 215 Banff Avenue in Banff (telephone (403) 760-3933).
Open daily 9.30 am to 9 pm. Licensed. Master Card, Visa. No smoking. ♿

CANMORE **(MAP 16)**
ZONA'S
710 9 Street **$75**
(403) 609-2000

A year or so ago, Chris Dmytriw turned the kitchen at Zona's over to Carrisa Tkachyk so he could spend more time at the Copper Door. Zona's was his creation: a funky little tapas bar in an old log house left over from the days when Canmore was a coal-mining town. First it became a full-service restaurant, then a late-night bistro. Dmytriw was a creative chef with a lot of intriguing ideas. The menu keeps changing, but the Moroccan lamb curry, which dates back to the opening day, is still here and so is the green Thai curry of chicken and coconut. The fish is all fresh. Keep an eye out for the red snapper with tandoori spice and a salsa of fennel. You can finish off with a chocolate pâté spiced with cayenne pepper or, more cautiously, with a warm gingerbread-pear cake.
Open daily 5 pm to 10 pm, 10 pm to midnight (tapas only). Licensed. Visa. No smoking. ♿

CAP A L'AIGLE, Quebec **MAP 36**
AUBERGE DES PEUPLIERS ☆☆
381 rue St.-Raphael **$160 ($330)**
(888) 282-3743

The Auberge des Peupliers, the creation of Ferdinand Tremblay and now owned by Claude Dufour, is still as attractive as anything in the Charlevoix, but Dominique Truchon, who has been in charge of the kitchen for more than twenty years, hasn't as many surprises up his sleeve as he used to have. He serves a five-course *prix-fixe* dinner for 48.00 a head, plus wine, taxes and service. The meal may start with a tartar of yellowfin tuna and go on to an earthy soup—zucchini, say, or broccoli. He likes Charlevoix lamb, which he often serves with a warm salad. His beef comes to the table wrapped in pancetta, his veal is served with pleurotes and basil. Breast of duck is marinated with coffee and served with couscous, salmon is pan-fried on one side and served in a reduction of red wine, scallops are crusted with shitake mushrooms and trimmed with asparagus. The sweets are more pedestrian than we remember—crème brûlée with rhubarb and poached pears with blue cheese from Baie-St.-Paul. We prefer the cheese course, which features the local migneron de Charlevoix. There are still some great wines in the cellar—two Lafites and a Mouton Rothschild, three Caymus and two Opus One from California and three tignanellos from Tuscany.
Open daily 7.30 am to 10.30 am, 6 pm to 9 pm. Licensed. All cards. No smoking. ♿

CAP-CHAT, Quebec **(MAP 186)**
LE FLEUR DE LYS
184 route 132 e **$105**
(418) 786-5518

This roadside restaurant, which is now the best in Cap-Chat, expanded last year and the dining-room is now a lot more spacious and comfortable than it used to be.

Chef Yvan Belzile specializes in products of the Gaspé: bouillabaisse with pastis and saffron, shrimps en croûte, scallops with pistachios and red peppers, noisettes of local venison with pink peppercorns, turbot with graine de moutarde and home-smoked salmon. At noon there's a three-course table d'hôte priced at 21.00. In the evening the *menu du jour* costs more —38.95 for the entrecôte, a dollar more for the venison. The so-called capriccio of chocolate is the best of the sweets. The wine-list still needs to be improved.
Open daily 5.30 pm to 8.30 pm from mid-May until mid-October. Licensed. Diner's Club, Master Card, Visa. No smoking. ♿

CAPE ONION, Newfoundland **(MAP 187)**
TICKLE INN ☞
Highway 437 **$60 ($130)**
(709) 452-4321

Cape Onion is as far north as you can go in Newfoundland. It's at the very end of Highway 437 and from the garden of the Tickle Inn you can see the coast of Labrador across the Strait of Belle Isle. Except in high summer, when David and Barbara Adams are in charge, Sophie Bessy is alone in the kitchen, which gives her warm and gentle welcome at the door its special value. The house was built more than a century ago by William Adams, David's great-grandfather, and four generations of the Adams family have lived here. The Tickle Inn has four bedrooms and two bathrooms. Downstairs, the front parlour is much as it always was. Meals are served around a single big table, where everyone sits together for breakfast and dinner. Breakfast means homemade muesli, wholewheat toast and one of several local jams, with tea or coffee. Dinner means a spicy tomato or carrot soup, fresh cod or fresh trout and something like blueberry gingerbread or partridge-berry pudding.
Open daily at 7.30 pm by appointment only from 1 June until 30 September. Licensed. Master Card, Visa. No smoking. You must book ahead. ♿

CARAQUET, N.B. **MAP 39**
HOTEL PAULIN
143 boulevard St.-Pierre o **$100 ($250)**
(866) 727-9981

Caraquet makes an ideal base for anyone interested in either the Acadian Village or the unspoiled beaches of Miscou Island. You won't do better than the Hôtel Paulin anywhere along this shore. The Paulin, built in 1891, is a picturesque building with snug bedrooms and a dignified dining-room. But you must book: "I have twelve bedrooms," Gérard Paulin likes to say, "and twelve tables." The kitchen is at its best with seafood—lobster, crab, shrimps and scallops are all at their peak from May to October. The service may be slow, but the hotel is long on charm.
Open daily 5.30 pm to 9 pm from early May until Thanksgiving. Licensed. Master Card. Visa. No smoking. You must book ahead. ♿

CARLETON-SUR-MER, Quebec **MAP 40**
LE MARIN D'EAU DOUCE
215 route du Quai **$100**
(418) 364-7602

When Jacques Cartier stopped here in1534, he called it the *Baie des Chaleurs.* Four centuries later people still flock here to enjoy the warm-water beaches. The route du Quai is thick with shorebirds who summer nearby. No. 215 is the address of the Marin d'Eau Douce, an old house built in 1820 overlooking the beach. There's a big deck at the back and inside there's an attractive, modern dining-room where they prepare local seafood in unfamiliar ways. You can expect marinated Gaspé herring, scallops beurre blanc, cods' tongues in lemon butter, pré-salé lamb and grilled or boiled lobster. Mustapha Benhamidou may not be as original or surprising as he thinks, but he's a real cook with a genuine respect for local produce.

Open daily 11 am to 10 pm from mid-June until mid-September, daily 11 am to 2 pm, 5 pm to 10 pm from mid-September until mid-June. Licensed. All cards. No smoking.

CARLETON-SUR-MER **MAP 40**
LA ROCHELLE
536 boulevard Perron **$80**
(418) 364-3611

La Rochelle is a lovely, wide-verandahed house right on Highway 132. Inside it's surprisingly small and so you should take care to book ahead. Mussels are the specialty of the house, mussels prepared in 21 different ways, all of them served with homemade fries and a big bowl of homemade soup. There are mussels with pimento, onions, leeks, parsley and butter, mussels with smoked salmon, white wine and tomatoes, mussels with cheese and ham, mussels with maple syrup. Real mussel lovers can have a giant casserole of mussels in white wine with fries and a pitcher of Molson's Export for 29.95. If you don't like mussels, you can have linguine with shrimps in a rosé sauce, poached salmon with spinach—or an entrecôte. When you've finished your mussels you should ask for the maple-syrup mousse or the apple pie glazed with maple syrup. The service, you'll find, is charming.
Open daily 11 am to 2 pm, 5 pm to 9 pm from early June until the middle of October, Friday to Sunday from the middle of October until early June. Closed Monday to Thursday in winter. Licensed. All cards. No smoking. Book ahead.

CASTLE JUNCTION, Alberta **(MAP 107)**
STORM MOUNTAIN LODGE ☆
Highway 93 S **$160**
(403) 762-4155

A lodge was first built on this site in 1922. In the early nineties Storm Mountain was owned and run by the Schwartz brothers of the Post at Lake Louise (see below). Eventually the logistics of supply became too much for them and they closed the place. Two years ago it reopened with new owners. The Lodge is five miles south of the Trans Canada Highway at the heart of the Banff-Lake Louise-Radium triangle. From this sub-Alpine forest there are panoramic views of Storm Mountain, Castle Mountain, the Sawback Range and the Bow Valley. The kitchen is run by Corey Fraser, who is dedicated to organic fruits and vegetables and organically-raised meat and fish. Meals begin with something like Brome Lake duck on heirloom greens or baked phyllo rolls with goat-cheese, smoked salmon and shallots on a bed of marinated spinach. There are usually five or six entrées, among them Alberta buffalo tenderloin with wild mushrooms, organic salmon with charred summer tomatoes and rack of Alberta lamb roasted with rosemary and served with a reduction of raspberry and port. The breads and the sweets are all made on the premises and they have an extensive list of Okanagan wines, among them a summit reserve from Boucherie priced at just 44.00 a bottle. Every day in summer they have a wine-tasting event, where you can sample the best of these wines with local cheeses and terrines.

Open daily noon to 3.30 pm, 5 pm to 10 pm. Licensed. Master Card, Visa. No smoking.

CEDAR, B.C. **(MAP 137)**
THE MAHLE HOUSE ☆
2104 Hemer Road **$110**
(250) 722-3621

Most restaurants, however good, lose their edge after a few years. But Maureen Loucks, the chef at the Mahle House, and Delbert Horrocks, the *sommelier*, have never lost their first enthusiasm. Maureen has tracked down all the best local suppliers of game, seafood and poultry. She tries a lot of new recipes and discards most of them. What she's left with are the staples of her menu: rack of lamb with cassis or a mustard-and-bacon demi-glaze, local free-range chicken or duck, a mixed grill

that includes rib-eye steak, chai-seasoned lamb chops and Moroccan sausages and her signature dish, porcupine prawns. There's always plenty of local seafood, as well as a marvellous vegetarian tower—a portobello mushroom stuffed with goat-cheese and served on a lentil loaf with grilled vegetables, olive tapenade and a red-pepper purée. Dinners typically begin with a creamy carrot-and-ginger soup, a tangy romaine salad with pecans, blue cheese and beets or deep-fried havarti with a pecan-and-blueberry chutney. With luck, you can finish up with either a lemon-tart in a coulis of raspberries or fontina-cheese ice cream with poached figs in red wine. The wine-list moves quickly up to high-end vintages, but if you're looking for a good buy you won't do better than the Concannon syrah. As the vines age, Delbert is adding to his holdings of Okanagan reds, which now compare favourably with the best red wines from California. If you arrive in July, you can enjoy an outdoor wine-tasting party with an *al fresco* lunch.
Open Wednesday to Sunday 5 pm to 9.30 pm. Closed on Monday and Tuesday. Licensed. Master Card, Visa. No smoking. Book ahead if you can.

CHARLOTTETOWN, P.E.I. — *MAP 43*

Every year we urge readers to go to the Farmer's Market, which is held every Saturday in Charlottetown. There are lots of things to eat: Chinese dumplings, beignets, pyrogies, Kim Dormaar's smoked salmon on a bagel, the best sausages on a bun we've ever tasted and excellent coffee from the espresso bar by the south door. Beanz at 38 University Avenue (telephone (902) 892-8797 is another espresso bar, but it also makes soups, sandwiches and salads to eat in or take out. Their squares, cookies and cheesecakes are all wonderful. They're open Monday to Friday 6.30 am to 6 pm, Saturday 8 am to 6 pm, Sunday 9 am to 5 pm. You'll find Piece a Cake at 119 Grafton Street (telephone (902) 894-4585) upstairs in the Confederation Centre and it can be reached either by an escalator in the Mall or by a steep flight of stairs from Grafton Street. It's a useful place to know about if you want a quick lunch before taking in a matinée of Anne of Green Gables. They have a lot of Asian spices—try the so-called penne on fire with charred onions. They have an espresso machine and all the usual sweets, and they're open daily 11 am to 10 pm all year. There are two good Lebanese restaurants in the city. One is Shaddy's at 44 University Avenue (telephone (902) 368-8886). They have the only upright broiler on the Island. The shawarma with tabouleh is a meal in itself and it's very good value. The shankleesh is hard to find elsewhere, but we actually prefer the kebabs of lamb—ask for them rare. The pastries all come from Montreal, where the chef spent ten years before moving to the Island. Cedars at 81 University Avenue (telephone (902) 892-7377) is the other. It's been around forever and it's really just a diner, but there's good draught beer and they stay open until 3 in the morning—Shaddy's closes at 11. It's a lively place in the evening, when it's full of students. They seem to like the homous, the abrak (stuffed vine-leaves) and the shawarma, which in this case means pita bread stuffed with beef or chicken and served with a hot sauce. But the rice is no match for Shaddy's.

CHARLOTTETOWN **MAP 43**
THE GRIFFON ROOM
Dundee Arms Inn **$130**
200 Pownal Street
(902) 892-2496

It's many years since we thought we had any reason to recommend the Dundee Arms. The hotel was built as a private house in 1903 and turned into a hotel in 1972. Recently it's been restored again, this time to what the proprietor likes to call its original Victorian grandeur. Patrick Young has been in charge of the kitchen for several years and he has the largest and most ambitious menu in town. We suggest you choose something relatively simple, because the more complicated the dish the richer it is. Better the salmon trio, for instance, than the lobster seafood cake in chive crème fraîche. The roasted tenderloin of pork is well prepared and handsomely presented, and all the fish is fresh. The sweets, however, appear on a trolley, something we thought had disappeared in the middle of the last century. But the Griffon Room has one great virtue: unlike most Island restaurants, it's open year-round and it's always very well served.

Open Monday to Friday 11.30 am to 2.30 pm, 5 pm to 10 pm, Saturday and Sunday 9 am to 11.30 am (brunch), 11.30 am to 2.30 pm (lunch), 5 pm to 10 pm from 1 June until 30 September, Monday to Friday 11.30 am to 2.30 pm, 5 pm to 9 pm, Saturday and Sunday 9 am to 11.30 am (brunch), 11.30 am to 2.30 pm (lunch), 5 pm to 10 pm from 1 October until 31 May. Licensed. All cards, No smoking. Free parking. ♿

CHARLOTTETOWN

See also BAY FORTUNE, BRACKLEY BEACH, GRAND TRACADIE, FORTUNE BRIDGE, MARGATE, MONTAGUE, NAUFRAGE, NORTH RUSTICO, OYSTER BED BRIDGE, ST. PETER'S BAY, SPRY POINT, SUMMERSIDE, TYNE VALLEY, VICTORIA.

CHELSEA, Quebec (MAP 92)

LES FOUGERES
783 route 105 **$135**
(819) 827-8942

If you order à la carte, Les Fougères is an expensive place to have dinner. The thing to do is to ask for the table d'hôte, which offers three courses and coffee for 39.00. The cooking, naturally enough, has the same virtues and the same vices as on the à la carte. For instance, a recent *menu du jour* began with home-smoked lake trout served on a salad à la crème with radishes, puy lentils, peas and dill. Next came—believe this—pan-fried veal and veal-kidney trifolati, served on egg noodles tossed with cherry tomatoes, asparagus tips and basil. The meal ended with passion-fruit-and-chocolate mousse served on a chocolate macaroon. The kitchen never knows when to stop, though one has to admit that the cooking is vigorous, the flavours intense. The wine-list is concentrated on Italian reds and Alsatian whites and, though there's no choice of wines by the glass, they'll open almost any wine on the list for the price of a couple of glasses. Les Fougères is a friendly, happy place. *Open Monday to Friday 11 am to 10 pm, Saturday and Sunday 10 am to 4 pm (brunch), 4 pm to 10 pm (dinner). Licensed. Master Card, Visa. No smoking. Book ahead.* ♿

CHESTER, N.S. **(MAP 88)**
JULIEN'S ☜
43 Queen Street **$35**
(902) 275-2324

There are several Julien's now, but this is still the best. Julien's started out in Chester as a bake-shop, serving bread (and cheese), as well as muffins, cookies, brownies, tarts and cakes. Then they added soups (a squash soup, perhaps) and a hot special like shepherd's pie—the specials available only at noon. There are always first-class sandwiches made with lovely homemade bread—we particularly like the light seven-grain loaf. The lobster sandwich is so good it's usually sold out. They also have a useful deli counter where you can buy imported cheeses of all sorts. The espresso, capuccino and filter coffee are very cheap and they're as good as you can buy at any price. They have a licence for beer and wine, but why bother with wine when the coffee is this good and this cheap.
Open daily 8 am to 5 pm from Victoria Day until Labour Day, Tuesday to Saturday 8 am to 5 pm, Sunday 8 am to 4 pm from Labour Day until Victoria Day. Closed on Monday in winter. Licensed for beer and wine only. Amex, Master Card, Visa. No smoking.

CHESTER **(MAP 88)**
KIWI ☜
19 Pleasant Street **$60**
(902) 275-1492

The chef at Kiwi comes from New Zealand and that's, no doubt, why they offer Banrock Station as their house

wine. Of course, the place has other virtues as well. There are two or three homemade soups every day (perhaps carrot or cauliflower-and-bacon). There are several salads and sandwiches. There's a hot dish (perhaps hell's-kitchen chili) and a number of fresh-fruit sorbets (lemon, say, or raspberry or mango-kiwi). Best of all, they make some of the world's best brownies and some of the world's best coffee.
Open Monday to Saturday 8 am to 4 pm. Closed on Sunday. Licensed. Master Card, Visa. No smoking. ♿

COBBLE HILL, B.C. (MAP 60)
LA POMMERAIE
Merridale Cidery **$100**
1230 Merridale Road
(250) 743-4293

If you come to the Pommeraie, try to get a table on the verandah, overlooking the orchards. Simon Manville of Dock 503 in Sidney took over as chef earlier this year. The only holdover on the menu is the very popular ploughman's platter, which combines purée of quash, goat-cheese, candied sockeye salmon, chicken sausage, hard-boiled eggs, mustard and house-made pickles. It's twice as filling as it sounds. Manville's new menu features Basque-style tapas, as well as Saltspring cheese and fish, water-buffalo and duck from the Cowichan Valley and fresh local chanterelles. In the evening he adds local poussin with black-olive rostii and asparagus, sockeye salmon poached in Merridale cider and venison sirloin with a pavé of Yukon Gold potato. There are a few local wines and a number of local ciders.
Open Monday to Thursday 11.30 am to 4 pm, Friday and Saturday 11.30 am to 4 pm, 5 pm to 8 pm, Sunday 11.30 am to 4 pm. Licensed. Master Card, Visa. No smoking. Free parking.

We accept no advertisements. We accept no payment for listings. We depend entirely on you. Recommend the book to your friends.

COBOURG, Ontario **MAP 47**

WOODLAWN INN

420 Division Street **$125 ($295)**

(800) 573-5003

Few of Ontario's old stone towns have a restaurant you'd be likely to enjoy. Cobourg is different. The Woodlawn Inn is a credit to the town. The oldest part of the building dates from 1835. Today it has a big, comfortable dining-room and a well-stocked wine-cellar. As for the kitchen, it buys as much fresh local produce as it can. That means Northumberland County fresh-water trout, free-range Ontario lamb and fine, properly-cooked local vegetables. They bring in foie gras from Quebec, sauté it and serve it with caramelized pears and pan juices. The roasted breast of local duck is prepared with a five-spice rub and sour cherries. Duck is something they do especially well, but if you order beef you'll find that it's certified Black Angus, served rare if you ask. There may be a whisky-pecan tart for sweet, or perhaps a Northumberland County apple pie with a lattice crust. There's a good selection of Niagara chardonnays in the cellar, as well as a number of good cabernets from Australia.

Open Monday to Friday 11.30 am to 2 pm, 5.30 pm to 9 pm, Saturday 5.30 pm to 9 pm, Sunday 11.45 am to 2 pm (brunch), 5.30pm to 8.30pm. Licensed. All cards. No smoking. ♿

COLLINGWOOD, Ontario **MAP 48**

BETWEEN FRIENDS

188 1 Street **$125**

(705) 446-3337

Between Friends occupies the old house that once housed Georgian Renaissance. Unfortunately, the new owners haven't inherited Alan George's amazing wine-cellar, but Andi Furrer is a trained Swiss chef. His menu is essentially contemporary with a scattering of Swiss specialties and Japanese dishes (Furrer's wife, Nancy, is a

Canadian of Japanese origin). The cooking is outstanding. One traveller writes that he spent four nights at Between Friends, knowing he'd have had to pay three times as much for a meal in Paris. You can begin with six-onion soup, lentil-and-tomato salad, crab-cakes with rostii and horseradish or oyster mushrooms mousseline and go on to grouper on green lentils and stewed tomatoes, duck confit with red wine and new potatoes, rack of lamb with mustard and jalapeno mint and Alberta beef with caramelized onions and stilton. For sweet you won't do better than the Swiss carrot torte or the Swiss apple pie, which means shredded apples with custard.
Open Tuesday to Friday 11.30 am to 2 pm, 5 pm to 10 pm, Saturday 5 pm to 10 pm. Closed on Sunday and Monday. Licensed. All cards. No smoking.

COLLINGWOOD **MAP 48**
SAN DIEGO ☆
72 1 Street **$85**
(705) 445-9876

Emilio and Jana Dodaro are a warm couple and they run the kind of restaurant you'd like to make a habit of. They settled in Collingwood because they liked to ski. They stayed because they like to cook and because they like people. They do everything themselves, Emilio cooking the main courses, Jana the soups and the sweets (pavlovas, chocolate tortes, opera cakes with meringue and fresh cream). If you think we've talked about these dishes before it's because we have. The menu never changes, except for the occasional daily special, such as veal marsala or veal sorrentino with eggplant. Emilio's lasagne is made with homemade crêpes, which are much lighter than the customary noodles. The penne has a rose sauce with a hint of vodka, the chicken is sautéed with white wine and lemon. They have wonderful espresso and very good biscotti. The wine-list has all the usual Italian reds at astonishing prices. There may be a Masi amarone at 69.95, but there's also a Masi valpolicella at 26.95 that goes well with most of the food.

Open Monday and Thursday to Sunday 5.30 pm to 9 pm. Closed on Tuesday and Wednesday. Licensed. Visa. No smoking. Book ahead if you can. ♿

COLLINGWOOD **MAP 48**
SIMCOE COUNTY ☆
206 Hurontario Street **$120**
(705) 445-6957

Doug Porter and Carla Carbone both apprenticed in Switzerland and worked at a number of well-known restaurants in Canada before settling down in Collingwood to open their own place. Simcoe County used to be a diner and it still has its booths and an open kitchen. But there's more to this place than booths and an open kitchen. They have a lot of organic produce raised by local suppliers. Porter buys his beef by the quarter or half-steer and butchers it himself. In summer, he gets trout from the last licensed fisherman working out of Collingwood. His pork comes from a farm near Barrie, his vegetables from neighbouring counties. If you go with the small daily menu you can order a burger made with freshly-ground organic beef or lamb, a vegetable hush-puppy or hand-cut veal liver. In the evening, dinners start with a warm mushroom salad with sesame vinaigrette, baked brie en croûte with raspberry chilli or a blue-crab cake in a pepper-and-tomato purée. A ragoût of venison and root vegetables might come next, or black cod provençal or a Cajun seafood stew. Sweets run to exotic cheesecakes, a seasonal-fruit crumble or a molten-lava cake. The wine-list is made up of bin-ends they pick up on trips to Toronto. There's no room for a proper wine-cellar.
Open Tuesday to Saturday 11.30 am to 2 pm, 5 pm to 9 pm. Closed on Sunday and Monday. Licensed. Master Card, Visa. No smoking.

Every restaurant in this guide has been personally tested. Our reporters are not allowed to identify themselves or to accept free meals.

COLLINGWOOD **MAP 48**
TWENTY-SEVENTH ON FOURTH ☆☆
27 4 Street E **$130**
(705) 444-8322

Twenty-Seventh on Fourth has lived up to its initial promise and taken over where the Georgian Renaissance left off. Michael Steh is gone and been replaced by his old sous-chef, Andrew Lacharity. Lacharity has kept at least one dish from the original menu, the grilled provimi-veal liver with jumbo roquefort gnocchi, baby spinach and pork belly. Sometimes he seems less innovative than his predecessor, at other times he seems more playful, as with his mussels in Creemore lager with apricots and pumpkinseeds and his snails in a garlic brioche with paprika sausage and thyme. He serves Atlantic salmon with a scallion pancake and lemon-ginger aioli, pork tenderloin with a shitake ragoût and blackberries and free-range chicken with caramelized pineapples and sweet ginger. Abbey Ewing, the *pâtissière*, has created several memorable sweets: a caramel box filled with caramel and chocolate mousse, rice pudding with butterscotch and lemon-curd tart with a compote of winter fruit. On Sunday evening she offers a Valhrona-chocolate buffet. If you haven't got a sweet tooth, ask for a selection of cheeses and a glass of twenty-year-old port.
Open Tuesday to Sunday 5.30 pm to 10 pm. Closed on Monday. Licensed. All cards. No smoking. Book ahead.

CORNER BROOK, Newfoundland ***MAP 49***
THISTLEDOWN FLORIST CAFE ☞
Millbrook Mall ***$40***
2 Herald Avenue
(800) 469-4389

Over the years, Corner Brook has had some first-class restaurants, but one by one they've all worn down and closed. If you're looking for a simple, straightforward lunch or supper, the best place we know of right now is the Thistledown. It's really a flower shop and you wouldn't look twice if you hadn't been told that they know how to cook. There are good homemade soups every day and good wraps and very good panini. Their fishcakes, it's true, have more potato in them than fish, but everybody likes the homemade sweets, especially the carrot cake. They're open all day every day except on Saturday and Sunday, when they close early. They have a licence and take all cards. ♿

COWICHAN BAY, B.C. **(MAP 60)**
THE MASTHEAD ☆
1705 Cowichan Bay Road **$110**
(250) 748-3714

The Masthead is one of the very few good dockside restaurants in British Columbia, It was built right on the water in 1868, and it's the oldest building in the village. This year they have a new chef, Andrew Stevens, who came here from the Aerie in Mill Bay. The Masthead has always made full use of the plentiful organic fruits and vegetables and free-range meats raised in the Cowichan Valley. Their fish is outstanding too, from Fanny Bay oysters and Saltspring mussels to pan-seared halibut and sea scallops from Comox. The Alberta beef tenderloin is something of a surprise. It's as good as the Cowichan Bay duck, which comes with roasted shallots in a purée of corn and ginger. The Caesar salad made at your table is one of the best on the Island. All the main courses come with a pot of perfectly-prepared vegetables. They have most of the best wines from the Cobble Hill area, notably those from Venturi-Schulze and Alderlea.
Open daily 5 pm to 10 pm (shorter hours in winter). Licensed. All cards. No smoking. ♿

This is a guide to Canadian restaurants from coast to coast—the first ever published and the only one of its kind on the market today. We accept no advertisements. Nobody can buy his way into this guide and nobody can buy his way out.

CRANBROOK, B.C. **MAP 51**
CANCUN
303 Cranbrook Street N **$65**
(250) 426-7525

You don't go to Cranbrook expecting to find a great restaurant, but this Mexican diner is good enough for anyone. It's bright, clean and cheerful and has friendly service and very low prices. The menu has most of the standard dishes—quesadillas, enchiladas, burritos and chimichangas. Everything is made on the premises and everything is fresh. Our favourite dish is the chillis relenos, and not just because it costs less than 10.00. There's one dish you aren't likely to find elsewhere and that's the so-called coctel de aguacate, which is made from diced avocado mixed with onion and tomato and dressed with olive-oil and orange-juice. The sweets are disappointing, as they are in most Mexican restaurants. At lunchtime there's no set menu and the chef will make you just about anything you want. The best thing to drink at any hour of the day is one of the blond Mexican beers. *Open Monday to Saturday 11 am to 2.30 pm, 4.30 pm to 10 pm, Sunday 4.30 pm to 10 pm. Licensed. No cards. No smoking.* ♿

CREEMORE, Ontario **(MAP 223)**
CHEZ MICHEL ☆
150 Mill Street **$130**
(705) 466-3331

It's three years now since Michel Masselin moved from Craigleith to Creemore, and to all appearances the move has been a great success. For all its warmth and charm, the restaurant in Craigleith was seldom full. Creemore, on the other hand, is always crowded. Not that it's cheap. Red-and-yellow beet salad, a new idea, costs 12.80, smoked salmon and squid with mango and cilantro crème fraîche both cost 14.50. There's still a lot of fresh seafood and the *carte* always offers paupiettes of salmon stuffed with salmon mousse and coquilles St.-

Jacques à la Parisienne. Calf's liver is prepared à la Lyonnaise. Masselin thinks of his restaurant as a touch of France in the village of Creemore, which is why he uses Paris and Lyon to name his sauces. The wine-list, however, is disappointing. There are only a couple of dozen wines on the list, most of them familiar old chestnuts. Ostensibly, there's no choice of open wines, but if you ask you'll find that they keep several, some of them excellent, under the counter. Knowing this gives you a real sense of belonging.
Open Wednesday to Sunday 11.30 am to 2 pm, 5 pm to 9 pm. Closed on Monday and Tuesday. Licensed. Amex, Master Card, Visa. No smoking. Book ahead. ♿

DARTMOUTH, N.S. **(MAP 88)**
JOHN'S LUNCH ☞
352 Pleasant Street **$30**
(902) 469-3074

John's Lunch hasn't changed since it opened in 1969 and that's a big part of its charm. Local people are stoutly loyal to the place, which occupies a small, unpretentious building in an industrial district of Dartmouth not far from the Halifax ferry terminal. Inside, there are photographs of the owner, Fortis Fatouris, with former Governor General Adrienne Clarkson, competing for space with postcards from admirers around the world. They serve pizzas and sandwiches with fries and coleslaw, as well as local seafood of all sorts. We usually go for the clams, which have to be the best in the province, if not the world. The fish and chips are good too at half the price—the secret of it all is in the fresh oil and the timing of the fryer, though they really should use hand-cut fries instead of the commercial product. On the whole, it's best to forget the sandwiches and the pizzas and order the fish. Helpings are enormous and you can share almost anything on the menu. No wonder John's has become a Dartmouth institution.
Open Monday to Saturday 10 am to 9 pm, Sunday 11 am to 9 pm. No liquor, no cards. No smoking. No reservations. ♿

DEER ISLAND, N.B. **(MAP 80)**

SPIRIT OF THE ISLAND

Butler's Point **$60**

(506) 747-0101

There's nowhere to eat closer to the ferry terminal than Butler's Point. The Spirit of the Island is basically a gift shop with four or five tables and a small outdoor patio. It's run by a couple from Quebec, who keep the restaurant open all year. If you ask them why, they'll tell you that Deer Island is so beautiful they never want to leave. The ferry runs year-round and if there aren't many people on board that means that they have more time to dream up new recipes. One day last January they had just picked some fresh parsley from the garden and were preparing to make pork osso buco, thinking that pork might do just as well as veal. That's when pork osso buco first appeared on the menu. Everything they serve is made in the kitchen. There are fresh flowers on every table and edible flowers in the salads. Vegetables come fresh from the garden; cheeses come from the City Market in Saint John. They use no margarine—nothing but fresh butter—and make their milkshakes in the old-fashioned way. Every day there are specials that don't appear on the menu; regulars like to ask for them and often do. In the winter there's a lot of comfort food like roast turkey with gravy, baked ham, cannelloni and even pizza. Pan-fried haddock is on the menu all year and so is soup. There are at least two grand sweets: a vermouth cake that's filled with butter and eggs and drenched with vermouth and a three-layer chocolate cake that's called a weir cake because, like a weir, it needs stakes to hold it up.

Open Tuesday to Sunday 9 am to 8 pm from 1 June until 30 September, Wednesday to Sunday 9 am to 8 pm from 1 October until 31 May. Closed on Monday in summer, on Monday and Tuesday in winter. No liquor. Master Card, Visa. No smoking.

If you use an out-of-date edition and find it inaccurate, don't blame us. Buy a new edition.

DIGBY, N.S. **MAP 55**
BOARDWALK CAFE
40 Water Street **$60**
(902) 245-5497

Digby may be a leading supplier of scallops, but it's a tiny place with a population of only 2500. Esther Dunn opened a tiny café here and later moved to a better location on the Boardwalk. It's not a stylish place and the food isn't very stylish either, but most people would rather eat here than anywhere else in the vicinity. If you don't feel like fishcakes or baked beans, try the seafood chowder, which is chock full of fish and shellfish, or the shrimp-and-avocado salad. The scallops are always perfectly cooked and there's also some good chicken (maple chicken curry, chicken pot-pie). The sweets are made fresh every day and they're spectacular, especially the blackberry cheesecake and the blueberry pie. There's also an espresso bar, but, frankly, we'd rather spend our money on a second helping of the blueberry pie.
Open daily 11 am to 8 pm from 1 May until 30 September, 11 am to 2 pm from 1 October until 30 April. All cards. No smoking. ♿

DILDO, Newfoundland **(MAP 241)**
INN BY THE BAY
78 Front Road **$95 ($205)**
(888) 339-7829

The Inn by the Bay and the nearby George House Bed and Breakfast were both built in the eighteen-eighties and both are now owned and managed by Todd Warren. The dining-room overlooks Trinity Bay, as the name implies. The menu is quite limited, but everything is well prepared and attractively presented. The only appetizer is a garden salad and it's served with cruets of oil and vinegar. The main course might be Atlantic salmon with lemon-pepper and dill or local cod pan-fried with onions and spices. Both come with a selec-

tion of fresh vegetables. There's usually only one sweet, which in season might be blueberry butter-cake with caramel sauce. It's fabulous. The tiny wine-list features a Kissing Bridge merlot from Australia and a Fat Bastard shiraz from France, as well as four beers from the Quidi Vidi Brewing Company. If you want to spend the night, the bed and breakfast has several pretty bedrooms.
Open daily 6 pm to 8 pm from 1 May until 23 December. All cards. No smoking.

DIPPER HARBOUR, N.B. (MAP 166)
FUNDY HAVEN
66 Highway 790 **$45**
(506) 659-2231

Dipper Harbour is on the coast just west of Saint John, eight miles or so from Highway 1. The Fundy Haven is a small, unpretentious place across the road from the fish plant. The menu is short and simple and there's almost nothing on the wine-list. But we've had nicely sautéed scallops here, with good fries and excellent hot bread-rolls. The seafood chowder is good too and so is the carrot soup. There are some quite surprising sweets, things like maple cake and blueberry pie. The service is friendly and attentive, the sea-views great.
Open daily 8 am to 8 pm from early May until late September. Licensed for beer and wine only. Master Card, Visa. No smoking.

DORCHESTER, N.B. MAP 58
THE BELL INN ☞
3515 Cape Road **$45**
(506) 379-2580

You'll find Dorchester a few miles west of Sackville on Highway 106. Built in 1810, it was restored by David McAllister twenty years ago. Inside it's filled with comfortable Victoriana. The service is friendly and efficient. They prepare a homemade soup every day (split-pea,

perhaps), a number of salads and sandwiches and several hot dishes (roast turkey with cranberry sauce, calf's liver with bacon, grilled ham with pineapple. On the blackboard they list such daily specials as grilled chicken and meat-loaf, apple crisp and pumpkin pie, both served with real whipped cream, which is something of a rarity these days. Their ice cream is all homemade, as are the scones that come with the soup. There's nothing to drink but good, strong coffee. However that may be, the Bell Inn has many friends. We know of a person who came here for lunch on 132 occasions in one year. They counted.
Open Wednesday to Sunday 11 am to 7 pm from 1 April until 15 November. Closed on Monday and Tuesday. No liquor. Master Card, Visa. No smoking. Free parking.

DRAYTON VALLEY, Alberta ***MAP 59***
DRAYTON'S ☞
5119 51 Avenue ***$50***
(780) 542-2286

Nothing is going to change at Drayton's as long as Nick is in the kitchen. He does everything himself except the cheesecakes. Why should he make cheesecakes, he asks, when he can buy twenty different varieties from the cheesecake factory any time he wants? Every day he has hot specials at both lunch and dinner. One of them is usually some form of pasta—lasagne, perhaps, or fettucine Alfredo or fettucine with Cajun chicken. Everything is cheap: a bowl of homemade soup and a grilled ham-and-cheese sandwich cost less than 6.50. Though he makes good barbecued ribs as well, mostly what he sells is steak. He buys the best Alberta beef and he knows just how to prepare it. And, like everything else, he sells his steaks for rock-bottom prices. Drayton Valley is 80 miles southwest of Edmonton on Highway 22, in the middle of nowhere. Drayton's is open every day but Sunday (when they open at 4 o'clock) from 11 am to 10 pm. They have a licence and take Amex, Master Card and Visa. ♿

Nobody can buy space in this guide and nobody can buy his way out of it.

DUNCAN, B.C. **MAP 60**

GOSSIPS

161 Kenneth Street **$90**

(250) 746-6466

Gossips, as its name suggests, is a casual place to hang out. But it's more than that. The premises extend back from a shady street-side terrace to two small rooms decorated with local art. Breakfasts are a feature, especially on Saturday when they last until 3 o'clock. The English breakfast doesn't offer fried bread, but it does include baked beans and fried tomatoes. At noon there are soups and salads full of olives, asiago cheese and an orange-and-ginger dressing. There's also a good croque monsieur and a croque madame. At night they add Moroccan lamb with apricot chutney and a seafood Tom Yum with lemon grass, kaffir lime, cilantro and Thai basa fish. There's always some kind of chocolate cake on the menu and there's a wine-list with several local beers and a number of Cowichan Valley wines. Keep an eye open for the Blue Grouse gamay noir.

Open Tuesday to Friday 10 am to 9 pm, Saturday 9 am to 9 pm. Closed on Sunday and Monday. Licensed. Amex, Master Card, Visa. ♿

DUNCAN **MAP 60**

RIVERWALK

200 Cowichan Way **$85**

(877) 746-8119

Beverley Antoine, the chef at Riverwalk, is influenced both by her training as a chef and her First Nations heritage. What this means is a new slant on fusion cuisine—indigenous ingredients crossed with Latin America, Asian and European cooking styles. The lunch menu offers sandwiches and burgers of a kind you'll get nowhere else: bison-rib sandwiches, alder-grilled venison burgers and grilled wild salmon served on focaccia with chipotle aioli. The dinner menu is quite limited. Buffalo ribs are served with white-cheddar pasta, ader-grilled wild sockeye salmon comes with white wine, garlic and wild ginger, pan-seared venison with wild berries. As a take-off on the tea served at the Empress Hotel in Victoria, Riverwalk has a signature high tea First Nations style, featuring traditional scow bread, wild-blackberry tarts, smoked and candied local salmon with indigenous herbal tea. The wine-list is very limited, but features several award-winning vintages from the nearby Cherry Point winery.

Open Monday to Thursday 11 am to 4 pm, Friday and Saturday 11 am to 8 pm, Sunday 11 am to 4 pm from early June until mid-September. Licensed. Master Card, Visa. No smoking. Book ahead if you can. Free parking. ♿

DUNCAN **MAP 60**

VINOTECA ZANATTA
5039 Marshall Road **$110**
(250) 709-2279

You get to Vinoteca Zanatta from Duncan by way of Allenby Road and Indian Road. Ileana Zanatta has taken over her family's century-old farmhouse and turned it into a restaurant. Her husband, Vigneti Zanatta, is in charge of the surrounding vineyards. Zanatta's makes a charming place for lunch. Fatima DaSilva is the chef here and at Gossips and her menu features cheeses from Cowichan Bay and Cherry Point, fish and shellfish from the Saanich Inlet and herbs and vegetables from the farm itself. The most popular choice at noon is the roast-vegetable sandwich on ciabatta. The salads are all made with organic baby greens, the crab-cakes with saffron aioli. In the evening people look for such familiar Italian dishes as veal scaloppine, mushroom risotto and angel-hair pasta with shrimps. The wines come from the family vineyards, many of them made from the Ortega grape, which grows here in abundance.

Open Wednesday to Saturday noon to 5 pm (lunch), 5 pm to 9.30 pm (dinner), Sunday noon to 5 pm from 1 March until 31 December. Closed on Monday and Tuesday. Licensed. Master Card, Visa.

DUNCAN
See also COBBLE HILL, COWICHAN BAY, MILL BAY.

DYERS BAY, Ontario **MAP 61**
ROCKY RACCOON CAFE ☆
967 Dyers Bay Road **$75**
Miller Lake
(519) 795-7586

Gore Bay on Manitoulin Island is just twenty minutes away from Dyers Bay by seaplane—by ferry it takes longer. This means that Robin Pradham and Shelley Beniz can run both restaurants, at least until a sous-chef is trained at Gore Bay. Pradham is Nepalese and there are a number of Nepalese dishes on the menu. He likes to think of the Rocky Raccoon as a Tibetan teahouse. Each year Robin and Shelley choose a cuisine they want to explore and then build their menus accordingly. Last year they were doing a lot of seafood and a lot of French crêpes. Now that Robin's brother, Sunam, has joined them, they're making the most of his knowledge of Bengali, Vietnamese and Burmese curries. Spices are introduced carefully. "Canadians don't want to be overpowered," they say. Shelley herself makes a terrific baba ghanoush. Last year they bought 150 acres of farmland and this summer they'll be growing their own organic herbs and vegetables. A local supplier has been found for their baked goods and another for their fresh-caught fish. They can get fresh Arctic char on a week's notice and Fundy lobster is available in season. The service is lively and prompt. Look for Dyers Bay on the east coast of the Bruce Peninsula, not far from Tobermory.
Open daily 11 am to 10 pm from 1 April until 31 December. Licensed. All cards. No smoking.

This is a guide to Canadian restaurants from coast to coast—the first ever published and the only one of its kind on the market today. Every restaurant in the guide has been personally tested. Our reporters are not allowed to identify themselves or to accept free meals.

EAST FERRY, N.S. **(MAP 71)**

PETITE PASSAGE CAFE ☞

East Ferry General Store **$30**

3450 Highway 217

(902) 834-2226

East Ferry is 30 minutes by car west of Digby on Digby Neck. From the Petite Passage Café you can sit on the patio and watch the ferry on its way back and forth between East Ferry and Long Island. The proprietor has a son who runs whale-watching expeditions out of Petite Passage, and she always stays open until the last boat comes in. She's not about to cook dinner until she can find someone to help her in the kitchen, but she offers a full breakfast and lunch all day long. People speak of the seafood chowder as being one of the best of its kind. It's crammed with lobster, scallops and haddock, served in milk laced with 18% cream and served with a homemade dinner roll. The lobster rolls were so popular that there often wasn't enough lobster left for the chowders. But they're still offering scallop rolls, which are made with lemon pepper and homemade tartare sauce. The sandwiches are good too and they're very proud of their apple crumble, their fresh berry strudel and their great big chocolate-chip cookies.
Open daily 8.30 am to 7 pm from mid-May until mid-October. No liquor. Master Card, Visa. No smoking. ♿

EASTPORT, Newfoundland ***MAP 63***

When you're travelling in Newfoundland you're probably looking for dramatic scenery, not great restaurants. But if you follow the road from the Eastport turnoff for Glovertown, you'll find Whimsicals at 200A Main Street N (telephone (709) 533-1024), a pretty little café right on the water. The menu is very small, but the sandwiches are good and the chowders, made with fresh fish and shellfish, very good. You can eat inside or out, and either way the service is prompt and friendly. The adjoining craft shop is well worth your time. We can also recommend the Bosun's Whistle in Happy Adven-

ture, which is just outside Eastport (telephone (709) 677-2109). They offer afternoon tea on a deck built out over the sea, from which you can watch whales spouting. You come here for the cakes: carrot cake, rhubarb cake, partridge-berry cake and, best of all, the East Wind cake with pecans. If you come in crab season, the crab sandwiches at the Killick in Salvage (telephone (709) 677-2440) are, as one visitor put it, "heavenly." Salvage (pronounced to rhyme with rage) is one of the prettiest of the outports, and the place where everything on the Eastport Peninsula started. All three places are open all day every day in summer, have no liquor and take no cards. No smoking.

EDMONTON, Alberta **MAP 64**
THE BLUE-PLATE
10145 104 Street **$55**
(780) 429-0740

For almost ten years John Williams and Rima Devitt worked at Zenari's Across the Street. Then, in the fall of 2004, they opened a small diner a few blocks to the west, with the idea of making and selling food just like Mother used to make. Some of their cooking is true to the nineteen-fifties, but some is not. Last Christmas they were serving roast turkey with all the trimmings. Well and good. But you could also get acorn squash stuffed with quinoa, mushrooms, pine-nuts and red peppers, with side orders of grilled vegetables and cranberry-walnut stuffing. Nobody in the nineteen-fifties had ever heard of acorn squash stuffed with anything, let alone with quinoa and pine nuts. Williams and Devitt are at their best with vegetables. Try their gluten-free beet burger with zucchini, carrots and sweet-potato fries. Or their sensational bread pudding, made with brown sugar, cinnamon and vanilla. If that's too sweet for you, ask for the cornbread, which is grilled and glazed with maple syrup.
Open Monday to Friday 11 am to 10 pm, Saturday 9 am to 1 pm (brunch), 1 pm to 10 pm, Sunday 9 am to 2 pm (brunch), 2 pm to 10 pm. Licensed. Amex, Master Card, Visa. No smoking.

EDMONTON **MAP 64**

BOULEVARD
10072 Jasper Avenue **$140**
(780) 486-5802

At Via Vai, Patrizio Sacchetto offered the most exciting cooking in town, and the most beautiful presentation, all in a gorgeous setting. The trouble was that Via Vai was in a remote industrial suburb. So we weren't surprised when Sacchetto moved to Jasper Avenue and reopened in Scotia Place under a new name. Boulevard has an open kitchen of copper and glass, surrounded by three or four dozen tables. The dining-room is softly lit and inviting, the service professional and attentive. They started out well, offering things like Alaska black cod baked in the oven with a crust of sea-salt and served with a stuffing of citrus fruit. Before long, however, Sacchetto had left, ending up (so we are told) in San Francisco. Boulevard is still a good restaurant, but it's also extremely expensive. For this sort of money, people have the right to expect transcendent cooking, which they don't get here except with the sweets. You won't go far wrong, however, with the roast duck glazed in Acacia honey, the rack of lamb with a dijon-panko crust or the Black Angus beef with mushrooms in a reduction of shiraz. Unfortunately, the same vegetables come with every entrée and the only really interesting appetizer is the potato gnocchi with four cheeses. There are a number of super-Tuscans in the cellar, as well as a good selection of wines from the Okanagan.
Open Tuesday to Friday 11.30 am to 2 pm, 5.30 pm to 10 pm, Saturday 5.30 pm to 10 pm. Closed on Sunday and Monday. Licensed. All cards. No smoking. Book ahead if you can. ♿

This is a guide to Canadian restaurants from coast to coast—the first ever published and the only one of its kind on the market today. Every restaurant in the guide has been personally tested. Our reporters are not allowed to identify themselves or to accept free meals.

EDMONTON **MAP 64**
HARDWARE GRILL ☆
9698 Jasper Avenue **$150**
(780) 423-0969

Larry Stewart took over this corner site in 1996. Until then it had been occupied by a hardware store, and next door there's still a cheap hotel and a diner or two. He turned the site into a spacious, well-served restaurant with an open kitchen where the cooking was both lively and up-to-the-minute. Over time, however, the cooking has become more and more pedestrian. The menu offers things like venison with beef short ribs and "really big" (their words) New York steaks with goat-cheese. They crust their sea-bass with porcini and serve cedar-planked salmon, a presentation that was à *la mode* a generation ago. Their breast of duck is cut much too thick, as if it was meant to be a steak—though it's certainly well served by its maple parsnip garnish with apples and burnt orange. Larry Stewart is still deft with his small plates—his Ahi tuna, served rare with a tomato tart, his applewood-smoked salmon, served with graine de moutarde and salmon roe and his foie gras, served with onion marmalade and blackberries. And last winter there were at least two outstanding sweets: triple-cream brie with warm figs and gingerbread cake with warm caramel. You could do worse than ask for an appetizer and one of the sweets, with a good wine, of which there are many. Unless you want a big claret—there's a Latour for 1850.00 and a Pétrus for 3000.00—look for one of the private-reserve wines from Don Melchior. There are eight of these Chilean wines on the list, as well as a number of the top wines from California.
Open Monday to Friday 11.30 am to 2 pm, 5 pm to 9.30 pm, Saturday 5 pm to 9.30 pm. Closed on Sunday. Licensed. Amex, Master Card, Visa. No smoking. Book ahead if you can. ♿

Our web site is at www.oberonpress.ca Readers wishing to use e-mail should address us at oberon@sympatico.ca

EDMONTON **MAP 64**

TASTE OF INDIA
6 Blackfoot Road **$65**
Sherwood Park
(780) 449-2794

Taste of India is a hybrid, one side Mexican, the other side Indian. An Indian family had owned Amigo's, a Mexican café, for some years when they plucked up the courage to offer an Indian dish or two. They then hired a third-generation Indian chef who was working at Haveli at the time, and gave him the run of the kitchen. The Taste of India is the result. His karai chicken is a heady experience of shredded ginger, sweet peppers, onions, tomatoes and garam masala. His baingin bartha is notable for its rich, sweet flavour. Fish is always plentiful on his menu, which lists fish dum masala with tomatoes, marinated and deep-fried Punjabi fish, shrimp vindaloo and lightly-seasoned Bombay fish. Vegetarians eat well here too. There's vegetable biryani, spinach and soft-cheese saag panir and mutter panir with peas. There's excellent nan as well as a number of stuffed parathas. And there's one superb sweet—carrot halva, sweet, laden with pistachios, simmered in milk and finished with a grating of cheese. But you must book ahead if you want it.

Open Monday to Saturday 11.30 am to 10 pm, Sunday 4 pm to 9 pm. Licensed. Amex, Master Card, Visa. No smoking.

EDMONTON **MAP 64**

THE UNHEARDOF ☆
9602 82 Avenue **$155**
(780) 432-0480

The Unheardof is still by far the most comfortable place to eat in Edmonton. The menu is interesting, the service reassuring, the cooking reliable. The stuffed portobello mushroom and the tomato soup spiked with gin have both been around for a long time, but the so-called butter and blue is probably better than either. It's made with butter lettuce and grated blue cheese and it's light and very fresh. The beef tenderloin, now made with honey, mustard and hollandaise (not a good idea), isn't what it used to be. This is probably a good time to experiment with bison or caribou, or, perhaps, with the pork tenderloin or the rack of lamb. You won't go wrong with the roast chicken with lemon grass either. After that, ask for the orange pot de crème—it's beautiful. The wine-list is large and fairly priced. There's a Greg Norman chardonnay, for instance, for just 55.00 and, if money is no object, a Wolf Blass black label cabernet sauvignon for 95.00. The most extraordinary thing about the Unheardof is its tea-list. They have white teas and green teas from China, oolong teas from Taiwan and black teas from Sri Lanka and India. They also have four estate teas, all black, two from India and two from Sri Lanka. It's almost like sampling a collection of Lafites.

Open Tuesday to Sunday 5.30 pm to 8.30 pm (later on weekends). Closed on Monday. Licensed. No smoking. Book ahead. Amex, Master Card, Visa. ♿

EDMONTON **MAP 64**

WILD TANGERINE ☞

10383 112 Street **$80**

(780) 429-3131

Wild Tangerine is all about snacks, the kind of snacks you've never had before. For instance, you can sample an appetizer of shrimp lollipops, implausibly served with a swab of wasabi yogurt. You can ask for an Asian-style Caesar salad and wonder why you've never before had greens with sugared walnuts, pork-filled spring-rolls and a dash of cabernet sauvignon. Or you can try a tiramisu in a reduction of barolo and puzzle over the combination of sticky rice and green tea with pomegranate seeds and a hint of guava. Maybe you'll wonder just how far the brother-and-sister team of Judy and Wilson Wu can go when left to play with food and wine. They spent ten years at Polos Café, where they were known for Judy's fusion cuisine and Wilson's bizarre wine selections. They opened Wild Tangerine in the summer of 2004 and jazzed it up with multi-coloured tiles. People liked their playful style and their interest in health. Their shrimp lollipops are rolled in shredded phyllo and deep-fried, but contain almost no oil. Their marsala-masala lamb has a suitably long finish with sweet Indian spicing. Their fork-tender cubes of spiced beef are gently perfumed with five-spice hoisin. The helpings aren't big, but everything is very cheap. The only trouble with Wild Tangerine is that they don't take reservations, which means that nobody can risk a visit except at off-peak hours.

Open Monday to Thursday 11.30 am to 10.30 pm, Friday 11.30 am to 11.30 pm, Saturday 5 pm to 11 pm. Closed on Sunday. Licensed. All cards. No smoking. No reservations.

EDMONTON — MAP 64

ZENARI'S
Manulife Place
10180 101 Street
(780) 423-5409

$30

Zenari's is a beautiful place and it's no wonder that everyone within walking distance of Manulife Place comes here for a quick lunch. Zenari's is many things: a supplier of gorgeous kitchenware, a deli supplying coffees, cheeses and prepared meats of all sorts and a restaurant with high chairs and tall tables where you can stop for a sandwich and a glass of wine six days a week. The deli deals in corned beef, pastrami, mortadella and Italian sausage. It stocks coffee from Brazil, Costa Rica, Panama, Columbia and France. They have asiago, fontina and provolone cheese as well as brie and Danish blue. If you don't feel like a sandwich, there are a number of daily specials—a soup or two, a quiche, lasagne and a variety of pastas. Or you can settle for a cup of macciato and a muffin or a scone, a wedge of cake or a piece of pie. Every Thursday evening, a grand

dinner is prepared by a guest chef. On one recent occasion, diners were served with chilled corn chowder, followed by bison carpaccio and pork tenderloin stuffed with elk sausage. Last summer Zenari opened Zenari's on First across the street at 10117 101 Street (telephone (780) 425-6151). They major in salads, sandwiches, risottos and crostonis. There's a nice seafood salad on a bed of pea-shoots. The sandwiches, all made on focaccia, are first class, but what the restaurant is really about is its crostonis. They have smoked salmon, Italian sausage, chicken with mushrooms and, the best of all, gorgonzola with onions and rosemary. The wine-list is still very small, but everything is sold by the glass as well as the bottle.
Open Monday to Wednesday 7.30 am to 5.30 pm, Thursday 7.30 am to 9 pm, Friday 7.30 am to 8 pm, Saturday 8.30 am to 6 pm. Closed on Sunday. Zenari's on First is open Monday to Thursday 11 am to 4 pm, Friday 11 am to 11 pm. Closed on Saturday and Sunday. Both are licensed and both take Amex, Master Card and Visa. No smoking. ♿

FERNIE, B.C. **MAP 65**
THE CURRY BOWL ☞
931 7 Avenue **$70**
(250) 423-2695

This is a small, comfortable place that was once owned by a local coal miner. It's now a Japanese restaurant with an assortment of curries and hot-pots made with chicken, fish, noodles and assorted vegetables. Everything is artfully prepared and presented. Their signature dish, Vietnamese summer rolls, is prepared with shrimp, cucumber, red pepper and bean-sprouts, wrapped in rice paper and served with an aromatic chilli sauce. They also have a good Japanese curry, made with thinly-sliced pork and potatoes, carrots, onions and green beans, as well as a first-class nasi goreng. The best of the sweets is the banana bati (banana and pineapple wrapped in pastry and dipped in icing sugar), though the hazelnut-caramel square also has its admirers. There are only a few wines, but beer is the name of the game.

They have more than 30 imported beers, ten of them from local micro-breweries. They also have three sakes on draught, all served cold.
Open Tuesday to Sunday 5 pm to 10 pm. Closed on Monday. Licensed. Master Card, Visa. No smoking. ♿

FERNIE **MAP 65**
THE WOOD KITCHEN ☆
5369 Ski Hill Road **$100**
(250) 423-4597

The Wood Bistro has a new name this year and a new location at the foot of the ski hill. Corey Sullivan is still the chef, and his two most successful dishes are still on the menu—steamed mussels in a diced-tomato sauce and Alberta beef tenderloin, marinated for five days until it's fork-tender and ready to serve with roast vegetables, a wedge of straw-potato cake and rosemary jus for just 24.00. Pan-seared red trout, coated with lemon and poppyseed and served with fresh asparagus and potato purée is another outstanding dish. Sullivan learned his trade in the classical French cuisine and he uses a lot of butter and cream. Some people, for instance, might find his braised rabbit too rich for their taste. There has always been a tapas bar at the Wood Kitchen and there still is. Over time we've sampled the tomato tart on puff pastry, the warm braised octopus with pan-fried potatoes, the caramelized onions baked in a short-crust pastry with celery root and roasted beet remoulade. The tempura dishes are better avoided, but the sweets are hard to resist. They prepare everything from scratch here—the breads, the pastries, the ice creams. We were sorry that the sticky-date pudding is gone, but there's a fine chocolate bread pudding with caramel ice cream and a first-class lemon pudding-cake with slices of persimmon and crème anglaise. The wines all come from small local wineries, the beers from nearby cottage breweries.
Open daily noon to midnight from mid-June until mid-October, daily noon to midnight from mid-December until mid-April. Licensed. Master Card, Visa. No smoking.

FERRYLAND, Newfoundland **MAP 66**

LIGHTHOUSE PICNICS

Highway 10 **$25**

(709) 363-7456

Lighthouse Picnics has survived for two years now and by all accounts it's flourishing. People thought that Jill Curran and Sonia O'Keefe had taken leave of their senses when they proposed to open a gourmet kitchen in the wind-swept ruins of a lighthouse built in 1869. It's 25 minutes by foot from the nearest road, an hour's drive from the nearest city. But if you build it, they will come—sometimes that's true. Both women have Irish dreams and this is the Irish coast. Waves break, whales surface and dive, the fog rolls in and out again. To explore this country you need a picnic, and picnics are their stock-in-trade. That means leek-and-potato soup, chutney-glazed ham sandwiches with emmenthal cheese and wild-berry muffins. That's just for starters. They also offer crab-cakes, cheese-and-mushroom tarts, organic salads and a variety of squares, cakes and fools. There's fair-trade coffee to drink, as well as home-made lemonade. And if you like you can eat your picnic indoors—the lighthouse has tables.

Open Tuesday to Saturday 1.30 pm to 6 pm from 1 May until 30 September. Closed on Sunday and Monday. No liquor, no cards. Master Card, Visa.

FIELD, B.C. **(MAP 107)**

TRUFFLE PIGS CAFE

318 Stephen Avenue **$95**

(250) 343-6462

Truffle Pigs has the flavour of the West (or the West as easterners imagine it to be) like no other place we know of. It's a delicatessen, a liquor store and a general store. They carry prosciutto, Black Forest ham, a broad selection of Okanagan wines as well as such local beers as Black Tusk, Rainforest Amber, Kokanee, and Kootenay Mountain. In summer they barbecue organic buf-

falo burgers, Alberta beefsteaks and maple-whisky teriyaki salmon on an outside grill. Summer lasts from Victoria Day until the end of September and the barbecue is running every day from 5.30 pm to 10 pm. After that the Café has only two or three indoor tables, where they serve beef bourguignon, various fondues and wild morels sautéed in port every evening but Sunday. In the morning they offer breakfast and, later, soup and sandwiches made with multi-grain bread, cheese and any of the deli meats. They sell dark-roast coffee beans to take away, as well as espresso and capuccino to drink on the premises.
Open daily 8 am to 11.30 am (breakfast), 11.30 am to 3 pm (lunch), 5.30 pm to 10 pm from Victoria Day until 30 September, Monday 8 am to 5 pm, Tuesday to Thursday 8 am to 8 pm, Friday and Saturday 8 am to 9 pm from 1 October until Victoria Day. Closed on Sunday in winter. Licensed. Amex, Master Card, Visa. No smoking.

FONTHILL, Ontario **MAP 68**
ZEST ☆
1469 Pelham Street **$135**
(905) 892-6474

From time to time, *Where to Eat in Canada* makes an important discovery. Frankie's in Orillia was one—we discovered that place ten years ago. Last year, it was Glow in Nanaimo. This year, it's Zest in Fonthill, the town made famous by Marlene Stewart, the golfer. To get to Zest, turn south from the Queen Elizabeth on Highway 406 in St. Catharines, then west on Highway 20 and finally left on Pelham Street in Fonthill. Zest occupies a fine old house with deep black-leather chairs, dark bare tables and an open kitchen. The hostess dresses like something out of *Vogue*. All this in a small country town not far from Welland? All this and more. If you come for lunch you can expect mesclun greens, crispy squid with a Vietnamese dip or a Thai beet salad with peanut sauce and pineapple sambal, followed by a mushroom stir-fry in coconut milk. If you come for dinner you'll be offered salmon with maple syrup and sake, Ontario lamb grilled with chipotle corn and eggplant and Vietnamese chicken curry in a yellow coconut sauce. Zest is a new restaurant and the wine-list is still quite small. There are nine reds and nine whites, most of them sold by the glass as well as the bottle, almost all from the Niagara Region. If you like oak, ask for the Legends chardonnay, which sells for 33.00 a bottle, 7.00 a glass.

Open Tuesday to Friday noon to 3 pm, 5 pm to 9 pm, Saturday 5 pm to 9 pm (later on weekends). Closed on Sunday and Monday. Licensed. Master Card, Visa. No smoking. Free parking. ♿

FORTUNE BRIDGE, P.E.I. **(MAP 43)**

SHELTERED HARBOUR CAFE

2065 Highway 2 **$45**

(902) 687-1997

This is not the sort of place that travellers from central Canada know about. But local people do and they love it. We were last there on a rainy Sunday in late September and we had to wait for more than twenty minutes before we could find a place to sit. The Café is attached to a convenience store and gas-station. Ed and Mary Steele, who own it, are always in the kitchen, whatever the time of day. The menu is pretty simple, but everything on it, or almost everything, comes from the neighbourhood. The menu is the same for lunch and dinner, which means that you can always start with a seafood chowder, a garden salad, a spinach salad or a side order of onion rings. The hamburgers and cheeseburgers taste the way they did 50 years ago. The clams are breaded, which may offend the purists, but they taste as good as the fish and chips. If you don't like fish, you can ask for a roast-turkey dinner. People come from as far away as Summerside for the best breakfast on the Island. They have ten kinds of omelette as well as fishcakes with homemade beans and Sea Biscuit or scrambled eggs on a scone. All this for 6.00 or 7.00.

Everything, however, is cooked in an open kitchen. The windows are always shut and the air-conditioning can't keep up. In summer it's pretty hot.
Open daily 6.30 am to 10 pm from early June until Labour Day, Monday to Saturday 6.30 am to 8 pm, Sunday 8 am to 8 pm from Labour Day until early June. Licensed. Visa. No smoking.

FREDERICTON, N.B. **MAP 70**
THE PALATE
462 Queen Street **$75**
(506) 450-7911

The Palate used to be hidden away from public view on Piper's Lane. Last year it moved to a much larger dining-room on the main street, where it's serving the best food in town. The menu is large, perhaps too large, and changes twice a year. Local people are impressed with the smoked salmon wrapped in phyllo with brie, the Digby scallops, the salmon, the ocean perch, the halibut and the rack of lamb. If snow crab is on the menu be sure to ask for it. Usually there are four or five sweets on offer, the best of which is the pumpkin-harvest carrot cake, very rich but very light. People speak more harshly, however, of the rice and the crème brûlée. The wine-list has greatly improved in the past year and so has the service.
Open Monday to Wednesday 11 am to 3 pm, 5 pm to 8 pm. Thursday and Friday 11 am to 3 pm, 5 pm to 9 pm, Saturday 10 am to 3 pm, 5 pm to 9 pm from Mother's Day until Thanksgiving, Closed on Sunday. Licensed. All cards. No smoking. Book ahead if you can. ♿

FREEPORT, N.S. **MAP 71**
LAVENA'S CATCH ☞
Highway 217 **$60**
Long Island
(902) 839-2517

Freeport is a picturesque village at the far end of Long Island. You can stay at Brier Island if you like, and take

the five-minute crossing on the *Joe Casey* for dinner at Lavena's Catch. The kitchen at Lavena's specializes in seafood, which is all carefully cooked. We remember a huge, beautiful fillet of pan-fried haddock. Others speak of fine Digby scallops, served with boiled new potatoes and young carrots. Lovely molasses rolls come with every meal. Aside from fish and fish chowders, there are sandwiches, nachos, burgers, fajitas, guacamole and Solomon Gundy from the Acadian shore. If you're over 60 and come in between 5 and 8 pm, she'll give you a discount on the price of your meal. Last year Lavena started opening for breakfast too, and her breakfasts are as good as everything else she does. This year the service has greatly improved too and is now as reliable as the coffee.
Open daily 9 am to 9 pm. Licensed. Visa. No smoking.

FREEPORT
See also EAST FERRY.

FROBISHER BAY, Nunavut
See IQALUIT.

GANANOQUE, Ontario **MAP 72**
CASA BELLA ☆
110 Clarence Street **$145**
(613) 382-1618

Casa Bella occupies an old Victorian house in Gananoque, a few miles east of Kingston. It's run by Stev George and Deanna Harrington. Both are graduates of the Stratford Chef's School and both spent a year in the kitchen of Sooke Harbour House (see below). Both are wonderfully sensitive to tastes and textures, though their presentation isn't always up to the importance of the dishes. They have a table d'hôte for 38.00 that starts with asparagus soup with tarragon and goes on to grilled pork tenderloin with rhubarb and a vanilla-bean crème brûlée. The tasting menu, which costs 65.00 (90.00 with wine) has six courses, either all meat

(sweetbreads with porcini mushrooms, wild caribou with elderberry and potato gnocchi) or all fish (sea-bass with wild arugula and leeks, sea-bream with asparagus risotto). Sweets are all prepared in house, whether it's pavlova with passion fruit or molten chocolate cake with mascarpone cheese. The bread is excellent, the wine-list large and fairly priced.
Open Tuesday to Saturday 6 pm to 9 pm from 1 May until 31 October (in winter by appointment only). Closed on Sunday and Monday. Licensed. Amex, Master Card, Visa. No smoking. Book ahead if you can.

GANDER, Newfoundland
See BOTWOOD.

GASPE, Quebec **MAP 73**
CAFE DES ARTISTES
249 rue de Gaspé **$105**
(418) 368-2255

Every day in season the Café des Artistes opens at 6 o'clock with a small à la carte and a table d'hôte, priced at 40.00, that starts with a garden salad and a millefeuille of smoked fish and goes on to Portuguese-style fillet of cod, loin of park in mango purée and mussels with fries. There's a nice short list of French wines, as well as a small selection from California and Chile. Out of season, head for the Brûlerie at 101 rue de la Reine (telephone (418) 368-3366). It's a picturesque little place just up the hill from the bridge. They roast their own coffee on the premises, and it's great. So is the Belgian-chocolate truffle-cake. They make their own pasta and their own tomato sauce to go with it. (You can save 2.00 for the soup if you ask for butter or olive-oil instead of the tomato sauce.) Fresh shrimps are a rarity, but here they come in fresh from Rivière-au-Renard and appear in both the salads and the sandwiches.
The Café is open daily 6 pm to 10 pm from mid-June until early September, the Brûlerie Monday to Saturday 7 am to 10.30 pm, Sunday 8 am to 10.30 pm. Licensed. Amex, Master Card, Visa. No smoking.

GODERICH, Ontario **MAP 74**
BAILEY'S ☆
120 The Square **$110**
(519) 524-5166

Bailey's doesn't look much from the outside. It's been sandwiched between a real-estate office and a Chinese restaurant for twenty years now, so they must know how to cook. And in fact they do. Ben Merritt started cooking at the Church in Stratford and then moved on to the Benmiller Inn before opening his own restaurant in Goderich. Here he writes up his menu, which changes every day, on a whiteboard. He always has four or five appetizers and three or four main dishes. He knows what he does best and what his customers expect of him, and that means seafood chowder, chicken-liver pâté with brandy, goat-cheese in feather-light phyllo and, best of all, Thai shrimp, a dish for which Bailey's is famous. The lamb is imported fresh from New Zealand, the steak au poivre is well hung and tender, the roast chicken is oven-crisp and moist. The fries are cut from sweet potatoes and they're great. They make their own cheesecake with Bailey's Irish Cream, or if you like you can ask for bread-and-butter pudding. The wine-list is well planned and fairly priced.
Open Monday 11.30 am to 2 pm, Tuesday to Saturday 11.30 am to 2 pm, 5.30 pm to 8 pm (later on Friday and Saturday). Closed on Sunday. Licensed. Master Card, Visa. No smoking. ♿

GOLDEN, B.C. **MAP 75**
THE CEDAR HOUSE ☆
735 Hefti Road **$145**
(250) 344-4679

The Cedar House has everything: a compelling view, a beautiful building, all the right ideas and first-class suppliers. The cooking lost its excitement for a time last year, but this year the kitchen seems to have regained its footing. Diners mention the pork tenderloin with

figs, thyme and sherry, the warm feta-and-raspberry phyllo on mixed greens with asparagus and pine-nuts, the linguine with shrimps and scallops in white-wine-and-lemon-butter and the baked pears with a red-onion-and-cheese strudel. The Cedar House is sited in ten acres of wooded land, just south of Golden off Highway 95. Inside it's all raw wood and squared timbers, and there's an open kitchen. Scott Belton and Caroline Green are firm believers in organic fruit and vegetables; in fact they grow many of their vegetables in the planter boxes at the door. Their fish all comes from wild sustainable stock, their meats are all steroid-free. The presentation is lovely, the helpings almost too large. Most of the wines come from the Okanagan and many of them are also organically grown. They're all fully priced, though they still offer the Caymus conundrum for 75.00, the Burrowing Owl merlot for 52.00.
Open daily 5 pm to 10.30 pm from Victoria Day until 31 October and from 1 December until 31 March. Licensed. Master Card, Visa. No smoking. ♿

GOLDEN **MAP 75**
EAGLE'S EYE ☆☆
Kicking Horse Mountain Resort **$160**
(250) 439-5400

To get to the Eagle's Eye you have to spend half an hour in a gondola. The gondola is accessible to wheelchairs and once you get to the top the scenery is stunning. This is the highest restaurant in Canada, towering over the Kicking Horse Resort, and it has amazing views of the Purcell, Selkirk and Rocky Mountain ranges. The kitchen is mainly interested in game, though it does offer fresh Alberta lamb and fresh seafood, which they bring in on ice. The bison are pastured just outside Radium, the caribou comes from Nunavut. The caribou is grilled and served with confit of cabbage, sweet-potato gnocchi and port-and-juniper jus. It's lovely, but if the venison osso buco is on the menu, ask for it. Otherwise, there's Rocky Mountain buffalo, Arctic

char with littleneck clams and grilled B.C. salmon with butternut blinis and loganberry chutney. House-cured salmon is also served as an appetizer with lovely beets and a poppyseed vinaigrette; foie gras from Quebec comes with a beautiful fig marmalade. Sweets, however, are not a strong suit, with the exception of the chocolate torte with hazelnuts, candied ginger and orange. The wine-list is extensive and there are a lot of high-end wines to choose from. The best buy is the Black Hills Nota Bene, which costs 59.00.
Open Monday to Thursday 11.30 am to 3 pm, Friday to Sunday 11.30 am to 3 pm, 5.30 pm to 8.30 pm from 26 June until 6 September (shorter hours in winter). Licensed. All cards. No smoking. ♿

GOULAIS BAY, Ontario **(MAP 18)**
SCHNITZEL HOUSE
Buttermilk Alpine Ski Village **$70**
(705) 649-3124

The Elsigan family know their market. They've tried new dishes and the customers ask for the old ones. Once the first snow comes Karen Elsigan leaves Batchawanna Bay (see above) to join her sister, Sylvia, who, with her husband, Armando Tempesto, runs the Schnitzel House in Goulais Bay. They've made a few changes here in the last year or so. They now have a barbecue plate—spareribs, sausage and chicken—every night instead of the old barbecue on Saturday. They also have a fish fry every Friday, Saturday and Sunday night. Fresh whitefish and fresh lake trout are on the menu year round, and in summer smoked pork loin and smoked bacon come in regularly from the smokehouse at Batchawanna Bay. Everything else is made in the kitchen. They have seven varieties of schnitzel, as well as sauerbraten, rouladen, bratwurst and weisswurst with spaetzle. The sweets change daily: apple strudel, cheesecakes and pies filled with whatever fruit is in season. Look for Goulais Bay 25 miles north of the Sault on Highway 563.

Open Friday to Sunday 5 pm to 9 pm. Closed Monday to Thursday. Licensed. Master Card, Visa.

GRAND BEND, Ontario **MAP 77**

LAKEVIEW CAFE

85 Main Street **$110**

(519) 238-2622

Grand Bend is a resort town on Lake Huron, at the mouth of the Ausable River. The Lakeview Café is at the bottom of the main street, which is lined with souvenir shops and fast-food outlets. Summers are busy here, but winters can be pretty quiet. They didn't let this get them down. Instead they expanded. There were two houses on their lot, so they renovated the one at the back and fitted it up as a bar and grill. Then they built a kitchen that linked the two buildings. In the grill you can get shepherd's pie with corn-whipped mash, fish and chips made with halibut, lamb shanks with fingerling potatoes and whole soft-shell crab with a remoulade sauce. In the café they serve things like rack of lamb with ratatouille and caramelized-onion couscous, a seafood sampler of shrimps, scallops and mussels, vegetable strudel with rostii potatoes and butternut-squash ravioli with hazelnut-sage butter. In hot weather they sell a lot of homemade sorbets; in winter people tend to ask for the chocolate cake or the warm gingerbread with butterscotch and caramelized apples.

Open Tuesday to Saturday 5 pm (9 am in the grill) to 9.30 pm from 1 April until 30 June, daily 5 pm to 9.30 pm (9 am in the grill) from 1 July until Labour Day, Tuesday to Saturday 5 pm (9 am in the grill) to 9.30 pm from Labour Day until 31 December. Closed on Sunday and Monday in the spring and fall. Licensed. Master Card, Visa. No smoking. Book ahead if you can.

This is a guide to Canadian restaurants from coast to coast—the first ever published and the only one of its kind on the market today.

GRAND FALLS, N.B. **MAP 78**

KARL'S

Lakeside Lodge **$60**

596 Gillespie Road

(506) 473-6252

Karl's isn't easy to find. Look for the signs on Highway 2 about ten miles south of Grand Falls. They have 70 acres of land on a private lake close to the American border, with hiking trails and canoes for hire. Karl's is the only German-style restaurant that we know of in this part of the country. The cooking is excellent, though the menu seldom changes. There's shrimp cocktail, garlic bread, rib-eye steak and every conceivable kind of schnitzel. You can begin with home-smoked ham and homemade bread and then go on to bratwurst, sauerbraten or one of the schnitzels. They make a first-class Black Forest cake (to the original recipe, with liquor), as well as a chocolate-cream torte and a Bavarian torte with hot raspberries. Karl has only a few wines, but they're cheap.

Open Friday and Saturday 5 pm to 9 pm, Sunday 5 pm to 8 pm from the beginning of April until the middle of June, Tuesday to Sunday 5 pm to 9 pm from the middle of June until Labour Day, Friday and Saturday 5 pm to 9 pm, Sunday 5 pm to 8 pm from Labour Day until the middle of November. Closed on Monday in summer, Monday to Thursday in the spring and fall. Licensed. Master Card, Visa. No smoking. ♿

GRAND FALLS, Newfoundland ***MAP 79***

MOUNT PEYTON HOTEL

Trans Canada Highway ***$70***

(709) 489-2251

The people here will tell you that this is one of the best steak houses in Canada, and that could be true. It was built over an abandoned swimming-pool and they serve well-hung Alberta beef, romaine salads and a selection of sweets prepared in the main dining-room. This year they've added fresh cod to the menu as well. The wild-berry tarts are all lovely—bake-apples are scarce this year, so they're using more partridge-berries and wild blueberries. The Mount Peyton is open Monday to Friday 5 pm to 11 pm, has a licence and takes all cards. No smoking.

GRAND MANAN, N.B. **MAP 80**
THE INN AT WHALE COVE
North Head **$100 ($240)**
(506) 662-3181

No sooner had the improved ferry service made Grand Manan a viable destination than the Americans stopped coming to Canada. Last year wasn't an easy one for the Inn at Whale Cove. But, if you're looking for some feeling for the Island as it used to be, it's still the place to go. Visitors have been coming to this cluster of weathered buildings for more than a century. The main house was built in 1816, and Willa Cather once owned one of the cottages. Laura Buckley and her late mother, Kathleen, renovated the kitchen and the bedrooms and filled the lounge with antique Shaker furniture. For five months of every year, Laura cooks seven days a week. If she's not always in top form, who can blame her? She doesn't cook her Saturday-night table d'hôte very often now, but when Michael Smith, the Inn Chef, came to cook for a night, she found the time and strength to pick twenty pounds of the local chanterelles for him. If you come in lobster season, you can have your bouillabaisse made with lobster. Later on, there's a warm scallop salad, oven-roasted salmon with a red-pepper-and-chipotle relish, rack of lamb provençal and pork tenderloin with rhubarb. Dinners usually begin with a roasted-beet salad, a Thai shrimp spring roll, or Oven Head smoked salmon. There's a different sweet every day, often a hazelnut crème caramel. If you want to settle in, there are several cottages, all of them different and all attractive.
Open daily 6 pm to 8 pm from early June until early October. Licensed. Master Card, Visa. No smoking. Book ahead.

GRAND MANAN
See also DEER ISLAND.

GRAND PRE, N.S. **(MAP 245)**
EVANGELINE ☞
Highway 1 **$30**
(888) 542-2703

They got a new menu at the Evangeline a year or so ago and also a new parking-lot. You can still start with a cup of homemade soup or a bowl of fish chowder, properly made with milk (not cream), crammed with fresh haddock and new potatoes and served with a hot homemade scone. A daily special now comes next—salmon fishcakes, say, with scrambled eggs—followed by a wedge of homemade pie. The lemon-meringue and the peach are too sweet, but the cherry (in spring) and the gravenstein-apple (in the fall) are as wonderful as ever. There's good coffee on hand, and milkshakes made in the old-fashioned way. Breakfast means pancakes or bacon and eggs with toast and homemade ginger-pear marmalade.
Open daily 8 am to 7 pm from early May until late October. No liquor. Amex, Master Card, Visa. No smoking. ♿

GRAND TRACADIE, P.E.I. **(MAP 43)**
DALVAY-BY-THE-SEA ☆
Covehead **$145 ($300)**
(902) 672-2048

Andrew Morrison is in his fourth season as chef at Dalvay and he's good. So far this year the dining-room has been full, though business has been slow on the Island. The setting, of course, is splendid and the service is now everything it should be. The wine-list is probably the best on the Island and they have a sophisticated selection of cocktails. The menu, in what used to be known as the modern Australian style, is both interesting and provocative. Spring greens with caramelized pears, gorgonzola and spiced pecans in a lemon-maple vinaigrette

may sound over the top but in fact it's a lovely dish. The yellowfin tuna dusted with coriander is seared rare and beautifully presented in a gingered vegetable spring-roll with wasabi and pea-shoots. They offer local mussels, lobster and Malpèque oysters as a matter of course. They serve their filet mignon with rock crab and black truffles in a purée of cauliflower. The sticky toffee pudding may have been featured in *Gourmet* magazine, but we still think it's too sweet. Better the espresso ice cream with butterscotch. Breakfast is a splendid meal and so is afternoon tea, which comes with dainty sandwiches and scones with jam and clotted cream.
Open daily 8 am to 9.30 am, noon to 1.30 pm, 2 pm to 4 pm, 5.30 pm to 9.30 pm from the middle of June until the middle of September. Licensed. Amex, Master Card, Visa. No smoking. Book ahead. ♿

GRAVENHURST, Ontario **MAP 83**
TABOO ☆☆☆
Muskoka Beach Road **$195**
(705) 687-2233

At the end of last season, Jay Scaife took over the Culinary Theatre at Taboo from Michael Pateran. The Culinary Theatre occupies the heart of the dining-room, which has a dramatic view of the lake through a screen of trees. Scaife, who used to work with Pateran, now cooks alone for the twenty guests who have booked seats at the bar and maintains a running conversation with anyone more interested in cooking than their girlfriend or mother-in-law. There's no menu. Diners can choose three, five or even seven courses, each with an optional wine service. Pateran used to cook, broadly speaking, in the Asian style; Scaife used to cook in the modern French style with a Mediterranean accent. Now Scaife does both—preparing exquisite morsels of bison, caribou, sablefish, king salmon, chiogga beets and beautiful chawan mushi or custard soup. He makes full use of fresh local produce—many of the vegetables, for instance come from Mrs. McBride of the Gravenhurst Farmers' Market. Scaife is an elegant, original and entirely convincing chef. He doesn't cook the sweets, which are much less interesting, but he does choose the wines that come with each course and he chooses extremely well. He's equally at home with sake and has four from Japan and one from California to choose from, priced at up to 140.00 a bottle. (If you want something cheaper, ask for Tsingtao beer from China, Asahi from Japan or Mcauslan apricot wheat from Quebec.) Taboo is an adventure you shouldn't miss, whatever the cost.

Open Wednesday to Sunday 5 pm to 9.30 pm from Victoria Day until Thanksgiving. Closed on Monday and Tuesday. Licensed. Amex, Master Card, Visa. Book ahead. ♿

GRAVENHURST

See also BALA.

GROSSES COQUES, N.S. **MAP 84**

CHEZ CHRISTOPHE ☞

2655 route 1 **$60**

(902) 837-3817

It's almost ten years since we discovered this unlikely little place, but nowadays it's in all the guide-books. This year they've opened a bed-and-breakfast across the street. They have live entertainment every evening in summer. And they have a brand-new kitchen. "Will table-cloths be next?" asked one regular, who regrets the passing of the old ways. Paul Comeau always was a real cook. His seafood chowder, made with haddock, lobster and scallops, is as good as any we know of. His pan-fried scallops and haddock are beautiful. His rappie pie, made with clams and grated potatoes baked to a golden brown, is irresistible. His fresh-fruit pies follow the seasons—rhubarb, strawberry, blueberry—and they're all lovely. If you stay across the street you can come in next morning for a big breakfast of fishcakes made with salted pollock or, in lobster season, of lobster with scrambled eggs.

Open Tuesday to Sunday 6 am to 10 pm. Closed on Monday. Bring your own bottle. Master Card, Visa. No smoking. ♿

GUELPH, Ontario **MAP 85**
BISTRO SIX ☆
35 Harvard Road: Unit 13 **$105**
(519) 837-5754

The Bistro Six doesn't look much from the outside. It's in a small suburban shopping-centre and there's plenty of parking. The interior, however, is suave and stylish. There's a lot of old brick and mirrors and a bed of dried allium plants along one wall. It's called Bistro Six because it's the sixth place that Alvin and Glenna Rebick have made their own. They last worked at the Bookshelf Café, where Alvin never had time for his garden and Glenna never had time to paint. Here they have time for both, though you'd never guess it from the menu or the cooking. The chicken sesame with basmati rice and Asian vegetables no longer seems quite so magical as it once did. These days you look for fresh Atlantic salmon in lemon-feta vinaigrette, shrimps provençale with wild-mushroom ravioli or, perhaps best of all, pork tenderloin with rhubarb chutney and horseradish mash. There's a home-cooked soup every day, as well as steamed mussels with tomatoes, garlic and basil and vodka-cured salmon with crème fraîche and dill. They make a good chocolate pâté, using the best Belgian chocolate and first-class crème anglaise. The coffee is excellent and the wines—from Niagara, California, Australia and New Zealand—all very cheap. Only the list of chardonnays from California needs to be expanded.
Open Tuesday 5 pm to 10 pm, Wednesday to Friday 11.30 am to 2 pm, 5 pm to 10 pm, Saturday and Sunday 5 pm to 10 pm. Closed on Monday. Licensed. Amex, Master Card, Visa. No smoking.

Nobody can buy space in this guide and nobody can buy his way out of it.

GUELPH
See also MORRISTON.

GUYSBOROUGH, N.S. **MAP 86**
DESBARRES MANOR
90 Church Street **$95**
(902) 533-2099

Guysborough is a pretty little town, left behind by history and ignored by tourists. The DesBarres Manor is a grand old house, built in 1830 by W.F. DesBarres, a lawyer and judge. His family lived here until 1991, when the property was acquired by Michael and Gisela Rankl, who restored the building and opened an upscale dining-room. The venture soon came to grief. New owners have now installed a first-class chef, but local people seem to find the prices high and so far the tourists haven't arrived. But the Manor also owns the Rare Bird (telephone (902) 533-2128), a pub in the waterfront complex in Guysborough. It has a big deck at the back overlooking the bay and a good pub menu emphasizing local seafood. They brew their own beer and their pizzas and bruschettas are both proving popular. They cook their fish well too and the same is true of their vegetables. One hopes that the Pub will give the Manor the support it needs. It's certainly a lot cheaper.
Open daily 4 pm to 9 pm from 15 May until Thanksgiving. The Pub is open Sunday to Thursday 11 am to 4 pm (lunch), 4 pm to 10 pm (dinner), Friday and Saturday 11 am to 4 pm, 4 pm to 1 am from 15 May until 31 October. Both are licensed. Amex, Master Card, Visa. No smoking. ♿

HAINES JUNCTION, Yukon **MAP 87**
THE RAVEN ☆☆☆
181 Alaska Highway **$165 ($300)**
(867) 634-2500

Most of the people who come to Haines Junction come from a distance. A surprising number drive all the way from Alaska, though it's four hours by ferry and three by car from Juneau, which means that the trip from Anchorage to Haines Junction takes a whole day. The Kluane National Park has some of the grandest mountains in Canada, and the Raven has a magnificent view of the St. Elias range from its wide-windowed second-floor dining-room. Apart from that, it's become a destination for gourmets. Christine Nelles now does all the cooking herself, and like her husband, Hans, she's a perfectionist. When she and Hans found themselves working sixteen hours a day, they decided to offer a continental breakfast instead of the huge German-style breakfasts they'd been offering before. But the guests complained. People settle in here, sometimes for a month, and breakfast is important to them. In a new effort to conserve Christine's energy, they decided to limit their dinners to three dishes in each course. The menu changes nightly. They have their own vegetable garden and their own herb-and-edible-flower garden. Christine has a genuine feel for vegetables. She makes her own pasta every morning and her own wholewheat bread-rolls, as well as two kinds of bread. Dinners feature a lot of fish and game. As well as the magnificent loin of lamb, there's often tenderloin of caribou and medallions of elk on the menu. Both are supplied by a Vancouver game specialist. There's almost always red spring salmon, Alaska black cod and pan-seared halibut, crusted with ground nuts, finished in the oven and presented with a sweet red-pepper mousse. Christine makes her own Italian gelato with fresh guava, mango and raspberries. The hazelnuts and pistachios in the gelato are peeled, then soaked in milk, roasted and ground. The coffee is beautiful. Christine and Hans buy their white wines from Okanagan wineries, their reds from organic vineyards in Chile. If you decide to settle in, there are twelve immaculate bedrooms downstairs. *Open daily 5.30 pm to 9 pm from 1 May until 30 September. Licensed. All cards. No smoking.* ♿

If you use an out-of-date edition and find it inaccurate, don't blame us. Buy a new edition.

HALIFAX, N.S. **MAP 88**

BAAN THAI ☞

1569 Dresden Row: Floor 2 **$65**

(902) 446-4301

Baan Thai is a very different kettle of fish from Scanway, the previous occupant of this space. But a Thai restaurant is much more likely to succeed than a Scandinavian one, if only because the prices are so much lower. Baan Thai has acquired a large following in the last few years and nowadays it's always full during peak hours. Victor and Sue Woo run a well-organized operation and they both cook well, especially when it comes to fish. Five Flame Fish is a good example. They grill a whole fish until it's crisp and season it with the hottest of hot chilli. It's amazing. The shrimp chios may seem pretty ordinary until you dip the shrimp in the peanut sauce and then you'll think you're in Bangkok. The tom-yum soup warms up the coldest winter evening, but if you're not used to Thai cooking it may be better to begin your meal with a lettuce wrap, which is a roll-your-own wrap filled with pork or tofu and Thai noodles. Pad Thai has now become a cliché, but this version is a lot better than most. The best of the curries is probably the yellow curry, which comes with potato, peanuts and your choice of meat or vegetables. As a matter of fact, there's no better vegetarian cooking in town than at Baan Thai, though the same cannot be said of the sweets. As for wine, Thai beer is the thing to drink.

Open Tuesday to Thursday 5 pm to 10 pm, Friday and Saturday 5 pm to 11 pm, Sunday 5 pm to 10 pm. Closed on Monday. Licensed. All cards. No smoking. No reservations.

Every restaurant in this guide has been personally tested. Our reporters are not allowed to identify themselves to the management or to accept free meals. We accept no advertisements. We accept no payment for listings. We depend entirely on you. Recommend the book to your friends.

HALIFAX **MAP 88**
CHEELIN ☆
Brewery Market **$80**
1496 Lower Water Street
(902) 422-2252

Fanny Chen spent a month in China four or five years ago and came back full of new ideas. For a time, the cooking at Cheelin was better than ever. Then the kitchen seemed to lose its footing and standards slipped. The restaurant disappeared from this guide. Now, after a couple of years in the wilderness, it's back once again. You can make a whole meal of the seafood soup, which comes with fresh haddock, scallops, shrimp and whatever vegetables are to hand. Chinese eggplant is stuffed with shrimp and pork sautéed with homemade yusing sauce, rice vinegar, ginger, garlic and soy. You can have moshi pork or chicken either as an appetizer or as a main course: shredded pork or chicken is mixed with egg and vegetables (bok choy, nappa cabbage and green onions) and served with pancakes in hoisin sauce. For the crispy seafood haddock is cut into small pieces, along with scallops, shrimps, green onions, ginger and garlic, marinated in egg, fried until crisp in a deep fryer and finished in a wok. Fanny and her husband are in the kitchen every day and make all the sauces themselves. It shows.
Open Monday 11.30 am to 2 pm, Tuesday to Saturday 11.30 am to 2 pm, 5 pm to 10 pm, Sunday 5 pm to 10 pm. Licensed. All cards. No smoking. ♿

HALIFAX **MAP 88**
CHIVES ☆
1537 Barrington Street **$105**
(902) 420-9626

Craig Flinn cooked in London, Switzerland and New York before settling in Halifax, where he continues to perform miracles. At Chives his menu is seasonal and changes at least six times a year. It's designed for people who like to eat well but can't always afford to. Flinn makes a practice of taking his chefs and waiters on visits to local suppliers, so they all know what he's looking for. Warm sourdough bread is brought to the table while you read the menu. The kitchen, you'll find, is at its best with soups, either purée of squash or the hotpot of the day. The heirloom-tomato salad is made from a variety of local field tomatoes, served with lamb's lettuce and fresh mozzarella cheese. There's always Nova Scotia beef to follow, perhaps served with graine de moutarde or butter-poached fingerling potatoes. Lamb shanks are seasoned with chestnuts and mint, spice-rubbed pork tenderloin with apple and cranberries. Fresh seafood may come with garlic and fresh herbs in a risotto filled with shrimp, snow crab and mussels. Lemon tart will end the meal or perhaps a pumpkin crème brûlée. The wine-list has been greatly improved since last year. There are now half a dozen reds and half a dozen whites available by the glass, as well as a substantial list of Australian cabernets by the bottle. If you want a lighter wine, look for the Tim Adams shiraz. It's lovely.

Open Monday to Saturday 5 pm to 9.30 pm. Closed on Sunday. Licensed. All cards. No smoking.

HALIFAX **MAP 88**
EPICURIOUS MORSELS ☆
5529 Young Street **$110**
(902) 455-0955

This is our favourite neighbourhood restaurant in Halifax. The Hydrostone District, which was rebuilt after the Halifax explosion, is just five minutes from downtown, but it took a while for people to discover Jim Hanusiak and Linda Baldwin's great little restaurant on Young Street. Jim worked for twenty years in the fish-farming business before opening his own restaurant, and he really understands seafood. He smokes his own salmon and cures his own gravlax. Fresh Atlantic salmon appears every which way: oven-roasted with sorrel, in a salad, in a quiche with broccoli and baked in phyllo with fresh grated ginger. He's also good with scallops, flounder and monkfish. All his sauces are robust, his salads and sweets are all exciting. Epicurious Morsels isn't cheap: entrées cost 18.00 to 20.00, appetizers half that. But, after all, this would be a two-star restaurant if it had a better wine-list. Meanwhile, it's offering Banrock Station as a house wine for 6.95 a glass and a bottle of Houghton burgundy for 29.70. The weekend brunches are fabulous.

Open Tuesday to Friday 11.30 am to 3 pm, 5 pm to 8 pm, Saturday 10.30 am to 11.30 am (brunch), 11.30 am to 2.30 pm (lunch), 5 pm to 8 pm, Sunday 10.30 am to 11.30 am (brunch), 11.30 am to 2.30 pm (lunch). Closed on Monday. Licensed. All cards. No smoking. ♿

HALIFAX **MAP 88**

FID ☆

1569 Dresden Row **$130**

(902) 422-9162

Dennis Johnston has regained his footing this year and Fid is now once again as good as any restaurant in Halifax. He's imaginative and his execution is faultless; his partner, Monica Bauche, runs the front of the house with smooth efficiency. Several Thai dishes—pad Thai, coconut-and-galangal soup, green-curry chicken with sticky rice—have reappeared on the lunch menu. The warm mushroom tart and the snow-crab salad with avocado in a coulis of yellow beets are both now back on the dinner menu. We've always liked Johnston's beef tenderloin and his breast of chicken with potato gnocchi and Russian kale. All the fish is impeccably prepared: try the salt-and-pepper black-tiger shrimp with wok-fried vegetables. The sweets are lovely, though they seldom seem to change. There's still ginger crème brûlée, chocolate moelleux and Jonagold-apple tatin with fresh Tahitian-vanilla ice cream. The wine-list, like the menu, is short and it needs to be expanded.

Open Tuesday 5.30 pm to 9.30 pm, Wednesday to Friday 11.30 am to 2 pm, 5.30 pm to 9.30 pm (later on Friday), Saturday 5.30 pm to 10 pm, Sunday 5.30 pm to 9.30 pm. Closed on Monday. Licensed. All cards. No smoking. Book ahead if you can.

HALIFAX **MAP 88**
JANE'S ON THE COMMON
2394 Robie Street **$80**
(902) 431-5683

Jane's is a suave, stylish little bistro across the street from the Common on Robie Street. The place is all black and white and decorated with a full-length portrait of the naked Eve by Lucas Cranach. The menu, however, is small and simple. At noon there's a baby-spinach salad and a seafood chowder, followed by cornbread-crusted haddock and a number of burgers. In the evening they usually add something like sesame-crusted salmon, loin of pork with szechuan-style black beans and roasted breast of chicken with maple and cracked-pepper butter. The bread pudding and the flourless-chocolate cake are both inclined to be heavy and there aren't many wines. For 9.95, however, they offer a small bottle of vidal icewine from Jost and that's pretty hard to beat.
Open Tuesday to Thursday 11 am to 2.30 pm, 5 pm to 9 pm, Friday 11 am to 2.30 pm, 5 pm to 10 pm, Saturday 9.30 am to 2.30 pm (brunch), 5 pm to 10 pm, Sunday 9.30 am to 2.30 pm (brunch), 5 pm to 9 pm Closed on Monday. Licensed. All cards. No smoking. No reservations. ♿

HALIFAX **MAP 88**
DA MAURIZIO ☆☆
Brewery Market **$160**
1496 Lower Water Street
(902) 423-0859

Da Maurizio is a spectacular restaurant. It has a spectacular setting and spectacular presentation, cooking and service. The dishes all come from the north of Italy,

but the north of Italy was never like this. Chances are you'll be given a morsel of foie gras when you sit down. The menu itself is full of glorious surprises. Scampi baked with garlic and brandy—maybe the brandy is a good idea, maybe it isn't. Chilled poached lobster with avocado aioli. Grilled eggplant with prosciutto and bocconcini. The pasta is all handmade and served, in the Italian manner, as an appetizer. There are only two veal dishes—saltimbocca and lombardo. Perhaps they need another—piccata limone, perhaps. The braised lamb shanks are served in an intense, dark reduction of red wine, and they might have been better in a paler, less intense sauce, though many would disagree. Sea-bass is sautéed with extra-virgin olive-oil, sea scallops pan-seared with chilli, chives and port. Best of the sweets is the crostata al limone—lemon zabaglione custard served in a crust of roasted pine-nuts. You expect a big, important list of Italian reds, but what you get is a provocative selection of the better wines from Australia, California, France and Italy. So two wines from Caymus appear next to a cabernet sauvignon from sassicaia. For these all you need is money.
Open Monday to Saturday 5.30 pm to 10 pm. Closed on Sunday. Licensed. Amex, Master Card, Visa. No smoking. Book ahead if you can. ♿

HALIFAX **MAP 88**
MILAMODO
30 Farnham Gate Road **$80**
(902) 446-6888

No matter that the Sushi Shige has opened on Spring Garden Road in the last year. Milamodo is still the best place for sushi in Halifax. Clayton Park, where it's located, is a fifteen-minute drive from downtown Halifax, so you may prefer to settle for Sushi Shige. But if you have a car, you'll find that Milamodo has unequalled quality and presentation. Sushi and sashimi are, of course, the name of the game, but the soft-shell crab with ponzu sauce is an exciting dish too. If you come with a large party, it's a good idea to order one of the combination plates, both of which offer a huge variety of sushi and sashimi. Aside from the usual tuna, shrimp and salmon, there's squid, mackerel, octopus, clams and flying-fish roe. Finish with a dish of banana tempura sprinkled with icing sugar. Sake is the thing to drink, and this year they've added several premium vintages to the list.

Open Monday to Saturday 11.30 am to 2.30 pm, 4.30 pm to 10 pm. Closed on Sunday. Licensed. All cards. No smoking. ♿

HALIFAX **MAP 88**

ONYX ☆☆☆

5680 Spring Garden Road **$150**

(902) 428-5680

Onyx is a newcomer to the restaurant scene in Halifax, but already we think it's the best restaurant in the city. Not that it's the place for a quiet, romantic evening. But for the young and the wannabe young, it's the place to see and be seen. The Pakistani chef, Tahir Salamat, has an impressive international background. Everything his kitchen turns out is a complex arrangement of flavours, like a good wine. None is ever allowed to dominate. Every few weeks he designs a new *prix-fixe* menu, which he offers at 42.00 for three courses, 34.00 for two. Not long ago, he was starting with diver scallops prepared in three ways—tartar with sake-and-mirin vinaigrette, pan-seared with a kaffir lime-curry emulsion and shiso in a purée of soy-beans—followed by spice-rubbed Arctic char and herb-crusted local lamb with périgourdine sauce. The sweets are all suitably elaborate: baked Alaska with port-infused figs and a kumquat-cranberry compote, On Wednesday night they offer a 50% discount on their sharing platters. We particularly liked the burgundy platter, which costs just 13.00 for two. Onyx is the only restaurant in Halifax to serve their wines in Riedel varietal-specific wineglasses, and they have a dazzling wine-list.

Open Monday to Wednesday 4.30 pm to 11 pm, Thursday to Saturday 4.30 pm to 1 am. Closed on Sunday. Licensed. All cards. No smoking. Book ahead if you can. ♿

HALIFAX **MAP 88**
SAEGE ☆☆
5883 Spring Garden Road **$75/$110**
(902) 429-1882

This is Unni Simensen's latest venture. She started out many years ago at Scanway and still operates Cheapside in the Art Gallery and Sweet Basil on Upper Water Street near the ferry terminal. Saege has everything they have and much more. It occupies the ground floor of a new condominium next to the public gardens on Spring Garden Road, a few blocks from the retail district. It's been open for less than a year but already most of the bugs have been eliminated and the place is booming. The chef is Unni's son, Geir, who works in an open kitchen and maintains a huge menu that begins with breakfast, a stylish meal that features huevos rancheros with cilantro. For lunch there are soups, salads, pastas (butternut-squash gnocchi with tarragon and maple cream), pizzas, brochettes, Thai rolls with pickled ginger and pepper latkes with mustard and dill. For dinner there's mojhito salmon with rice noodles, halibut with a cumin-and-cardamom rub, coconut and lime. The chef is at his best with fish and the salmon and halibut are both splendid dishes, as are the rack of lamb with sage and mint and the breast of chicken stuffed with oka and roasted corn. The sweets are all impeccable and you can take your pick among the tarte tatin with cinnamon ice cream, the prickly-pear parfait with peaches and blackberries and the lemon flan with mint jelly. The wine-list is full of bargains. The Kim Crawford sauvignon blanc costs only 45.00, the See Ya Later chardonnay from Hawthorne Mountain only 43.00, the old-vines Foch from Quail's Gate only 46.00. Overall, Saege is a good buy.

Open Tuesday to Sunday 7 am to 10 am, 11.30 am to 3 pm, 5 pm to 10 pm. Closed on Monday. Licensed. All cards. No smoking. Book ahead if you can. ♿

HALIFAX **MAP 88**

SALVATORE'S
5541 Young Street
(902) 455-1133

☞ **$35**

Salvatore still makes the best pizzas in town, bar none. What makes them so good is the artful combination of flavours—no single flavour is ever allowed to dominate the others. One could wish, however, that Salvatore would expand his menu by adding two or three new things. Meanwhile, about all we can do is to recommend (once again) the thin-crust Miguel, though it may come with an excess of raw garlic. If you feel strongly about raw garlic, ask for the four-cheese pizza, which is made with ricotta, parmesan, mozzarella and romano. It goes particularly well with the splendid Greek salad. At lunchtime, they sell one or two of their pizzas by the slice, which is enough for most people. If you don't feel like a pizza, ask instead for the meatball hero. It's good too. If you need something sweet to follow, head next door to Epicurious Morsels (see above).
Open Monday 4 pm to 10 pm, Tuesday to Saturday 11.30 am to 11 pm, Sunday 4 pm to 10 pm. No liquor. All cards. No smoking. ♿

HALIFAX **MAP 88**

SEVEN
1579 Grafton Street
(902) 444-4777

$145

Seven is a suave, contemporary restaurant that opened in the spring of 2004. In the two years since then, however, it has lost much of its original gloss. The menu still reads well. There's bison carpaccio, Quebec foie gras, mushroom terrine, goat-cheese galette, honey-cured salmon with succotash, rack of lamb with potato mash and brown butter and Brome Lake duck with blueberry jus. But, with a few exceptions (like the bison carpaccio), the dishes that come to your table lack excitement. Some (like the rack of lamb) are downright

disappointing. The wine-list, of course, is as brilliant as ever—kitchens freeze over before their wine-lists—and there are probably more outstanding wines per square inch at Seven than anywhere else in the city.
Open Monday to Wednesday 11 am to 10 pm, Thursday to Saturday 11 am to 11 pm, Sunday 4 pm to 10 pm. Licensed. All cards. No smoking. ♿

HALIFAX **MAP 88**
TAREK'S
3045 Robie Street **$70**
(902) 454-8723

Tarek is a friendly immigrant from Syria, who came to Canada as a sailor when he was nineteen. Having learned his trade under a variety of hotel chefs in Vancouver and Toronto, he's been cooking now for more than 30 years. He ended up at La Scala in Halifax and then opened his own place. It's tucked away in a small strip mall in the North End of the city, and it has just eight tables and ten seats at the counter. Though it's surrounded by fast-food outlets, Tarek's is always busy. The key to its success is high-quality ingredients—fresh herbs, fresh vegetables and hand-chopped garlic. You order at the counter, where you're usually greeted by the proprietor himself, then wait in line for the meal to be prepared for you from scratch. Tarek's is a great place for vegetarians—the fellafel is about the best we can remember. We also like the chicken kebabs and the Mediterranean salad. As for the soups, they're all made fresh every morning. Tarek's is a likeable place.
Open Monday to Friday 8 am to 7.30 pm, Saturday 11 am to 7 pm. Closed on Sunday. No liquor, no cards. No smoking. ♿

HALIFAX
See also CHESTER, DARTMOUTH.

Our web site is at www.oberonpress.ca Readers wishing to use e-mail should address us at oberon@sympatico.ca

HAMILTON, Ontario **MAP 89**

LAS AGUAS

1375 King Street E **$110**

(905) 545-5567

Las Aguas is an attractive place, with fresh flowers and crisp, white table-cloths on every table. It looks smart without being stuffy. In the last year or two the kitchen has changed its focus and now concentrates on Mediterranean cooking, its vocabulary borrowed from Greece and Morocco as well as Italy and Spain. Typically, there are four or five appetizers, one of which is always a soup. Everyone admires the date-and-orange salad and the pan-seared foie gras with goat-cheese custard and a reduction of wild mushrooms. Main dishes start with a Spanish-style paella and continue with a flat-iron steak on drunken risotto, stuffed breast of chicken and lamb chops. In another mood, they'll offer things like grilled halibut, pesto salmon and grilled red snapper with wild-mushroom polente and a fresh tomato sauce. The kitchen is probably at its best with its sweets: chocolate soufflé, peach cobbler, strawberry shortcake, lemon tart with ginger ice cream and spiced plums on oatmeal scones. The wine-list is carefully chosen and fairly priced.

Open Tuesday to Thursday 5 pm to 9 pm, Friday and Saturday 5 pm to 10 pm. Closed on Sunday and Monday. Licensed. Amex, Master Card, Visa. ♿

HAMILTON **MAP 89**

LA CANTINA

60 Walnut Street S **$105/$70**

(905) 521-8989

It was true last year and it's truer than ever this year. You don't come to La Cantina for its upscale restaurant, Vicolo 54; you come for the wood-burning pizza oven, the bar and the outside patio at La Spiga, which is essentially a pizzeria and nothing more. True, at Vicolo 54 you can get conservative treatments of loin of lamb,

breast of chicken, fillet of salmon, ostrich and even surf 'n turf. It's also true that they're good with pasta, especially the scallops with tagliatelle, porcini and crimini mushrooms, onions and garlic. They make one or two good risottos, especially the risotto pescatore with shrimps, squid, mussels and scallops in garlic rosé. And their daily specials are usually worth looking at. If Arctic char in a purée of sundried tomato and pesto is on offer, settle for it. But, day in and day out, you'll do better with one of the thin-crust pizzas at La Spiga, which are better than ever this year. Our favourites are the so-called San Marco (chicken with hot and sweet peppers, red onions, mozzarella and capers) and the Marinara (shrimps, squid and mussels). Sweets aren't what they used to be and the tiramisu is dry and rather tasteless. The wine-cellar, however, is very well stocked and they offer a different V.Q.A. wine from Niagara every month—by the glass as well as the bottle.
Open Tuesday to Thursday 11.30 am to 2.30 pm, 4.30 pm to 10 pm, Friday 11.30 am to 2.30 pm, 4.30 pm to 11 pm, Saturday 4 pm to 11 pm. Closed on Sunday and Monday. Licensed. Amex, Master Card, Visa.

HAMILTON **MAP 89**
ROOM 41
41 King William Street **$120**
(905) 524-2777

Room 41 occupies the premises that once belonged to La Costa in downtown Hamilton. They have an ambitious menu and at first seemed to be trying too hard. But the place has been open for almost a year now and the cooking and service have both settled down. They serve a lot of salads (bocconcini with tomato and campari) and one or two soups (gazpacho with three-year-old cheddar), but the best of the appetizers is the butternut-squash-and-ginger flan with pecans and a reduction of balsamic vinegar—the sweetness of the balsamic vinegar nicely balanced by the bitterness of the pecans and the squash. Then there's a choice of bouillabaisse with chorizo and saffron, seared rack and slow-cooked leg of lamb and steak with fries and soft blue cheese. At noon they sometimes do gnocchi as a daily special. The gnocchi is tender and perfect and served with scallops, wild mushrooms and oil of white truffles. The sweets (dark-chocolate mousse, white-chocolate crème brûlée) are all made in-house. The cheapest open wines, however, cost between 10.00 and 15.00, which is too much for the average single diner.

Open Monday to Thursday 11 am to 10 pm, Friday 11 am to 11 pm, Saturday 5 pm to 11 pm, Sunday 5 pm to 9 pm. Licensed. All cards. No smoking.

HAMILTON

See also ANCASTER, BURLINGTON, WATERDOWN.

HAMPTON, N.B. **MAP 90**

HOLLY'S

454 Main Street

(506) 832-5520

☜

$60

Holly was busy revising her menu when this edition went to press, so all we can do is to tell you what she was doing last winter. Hampton is a pretty little town in lovely country, halfway between Saint John and Sussex. Holly does all her own baking and her cheesecakes are famous. She regularly brings in fresh haddock (three-ounce cheeks), mussels and salmon. The salmon, served with a maple glaze, comes in fresh, but is then filleted and flash-frozen. The battered haddock is very popular, as are the Thai salad and all the stir-fries. This year she started making what she calls a New Orleans salad, which is like a Thai salad except that it's made with Cajun spices. She's also experimenting with fajitas, which are excellent, and with bruschettas made with homemade French bread. In summer she serves raspberry crumbles to all comers and freezes whole strawberries to use in her pies all winter long. On weekends she serves buffet suppers for only 16.95 a head and on Sundays there's a big breakfast brunch.

Open Monday to Friday 8 am to 10 pm, Saturday 9 am to 10 pm, Sunday 9 am to 9 pm (shorter hours in winter). Licensed. All cards. No smoking. ♿

HUDSON, Quebec **MAP 91**

CLEMENTINE
398 rue Principale **$130**
(450) 458-8181

Clémentine occupies a charming old house on the main street of Hudson, three miles north of Highway 40 just west of Montreal. The kitchen is run by Michel Beaulne; his wife, Louise, is the *pâtissière*. We used to think Louise much the better cook of the two, but this year we're not so sure. Michel may still be offering things like filet mignon with brandy and black peppercorns and deer with red currants, but there are other, more interesting things to be had as well—snow crab with Thai chilli, for instance, or scallop-and-shrimp tandoori, quail with five spices or foie gras de canard with honey and apples. His braised lamb shank is a great buy at 19.00 and his sweetbreads with balsamic vinegar is a splendid dish. The wine-list isn't what it used to be, but there's a useful selection of French wines, along with a few Italians and a few from each of California and Australia. Louise is rightly proud of her tea-list, which includes three vintage teas from Russia. And if her crème-brûlée pie now seems altogether too heavy, she's a warm and friendly hostess who insists on keeping the salt-cellar on every table full of the best sea-salt money can buy.
Open Tuesday to Saturday 5.30 pm to 10 pm. Closed on Sunday and Monday. Licensed. Amex, Master Card, Visa. No smoking. ♿

This is a guide to Canadian restaurants from coast to coast—the first ever published and the only one of its kind on the market today. Every restaurant in the guide has been personally tested. Our reporters are not allowed to identify themselves or to accept free meals.

HULL, Quebec **MAP 92**

LE BACCARA ☆☆

Casino de Hull **$200**

1 boulevard du Casino

(819) 772-6210

Baccara is the top-of-the-line restaurant at the Casino de Hull, reached by a bridge over the great hall where people by the hundred are gambling away their paycheques. The place is the last word in comfort and luxury. The service is impeccable, the menus stunning. There are four: a vegetarian menu, a menu gourmand, a grand menu dégustation and a menu gastronomique, the most expensive of the four at 115.00. There's also a regular à la carte. You begin by choosing your water from a water-list—Hildon, Evian and Voss (Voss comes from Norway and is the best.). You help yourself to twelve-grain bread, served with house-churned butter. You can start your meal, if you like, with consommé, but consommé is hardly the point of Baccara. For twice the money, you have your choice of grilled tuna with mustard sprouts, fondant of pheasant with goat-cheese, warm foie gras in asparagus vinaigrette and snow crab with fennel and cucumber. (The tuna has a rather crisp texture, perhaps from having been seared and then chilled.) Fish may not be their strong suit: the Arctic char, for instance, is habitually overcooked, the roasted lobster and scallops overwhelmed with brandy. The meats are often better—they made their reputation, after all, with their caribou. But it has to be admitted that the Quebec lamb lacks flavour and profits little from the sweetbreads that come with it. The wine-list is at its best with its Latours and Lafites and Rothschilds—they offer a 1959 Mouton Rothschild for 7237.00. The low end is pretty hard to find. There's a vouvray sec from Huët for 77.00 and a cru-bourgeois médoc from Haut-Cassan for the same price, and you probably won't do better than either. The coffee is Jamaican Blue Mountain—a rare delicacy. As for the so-called chocolate délice—a dry meringue covered with praline and gianduja chocolate—it's marvellous.

Open daily 5.30 pm to 10.30 pm. Licensed. All cards. No smoking. Book ahead. You must be over eighteen and wear a jacket and tie. ♿

HULL
See also CHELSEA, WAKEFIELD.

HUNTSVILLE, Ontario **MAP 93**
THE NORSEMEN ☆
Limberlost Road **$120**
(705) 635-2473

As long as Ursula Uetz is in the kitchen, the Norsemen will remain a significant destination. The Walker Lake resort where she works doesn't belong to the new Muskoka, where cottages sell for eight million dollars or more. For all we know, Goldie Hawn has never even heard of the place, which is hidden away on a back road northeast of Huntsville. The dining-room has a home-spun, old fashioned air, but the menu is up to the minute. Meals start with such things as tartar of gravlax with passion-fruit crème fraîche, terrine of duck with apple-and-cranberry chutney, smoked pickerel with grated daikon and one or two homemade soups—wild-mushroom, perhaps, and carrot-and-squash. True, these dishes don't all work equally well. Pears don't go particularly well with onions and thyme and lobster doesn't do much for breast of chicken. Pan-fried pork tenderloin, on the other hand, makes the most of its garnish of apricots and lavender, as do the Atlantic salmon (with sesame and mango), the breast of pheasant (with blueberries and scotch) and the venison chop (with cranberries and red wine). The cooking can at times be a bit rough—the salmon and the pickerel are both apt to be overcooked—but this is an adventurous kitchen and it's full of good ideas. The ingredients are all first class—the fish is fresh, the beef tenderloin beautifully tender and full of flavour. The pastry, once impeccable, is no longer what it used to be, but where else in Muskoka, except perhaps at Taboo, could you expect to be offered a lemon-curd tart? The wine-list isn't large, but they'll open almost any wine on the list for you if you want to drink by the glass. A glass of Wente chardonnay, for instance, can be had for less than 9.00.

Open Wednesday to Sunday 6 pm to 9.30 pm from Victoria Day until 30 June, Tuesday to Sunday 6 pm to 9.30 pm from 1 July until 31 August, Wednesday to Sunday 6 pm to 9.30 pm from 1 September until Thanksgiving, Thursday to Sunday 6 pm to 9.30 pm from Thanksgiving until Victoria Day. Closed on Monday and Tuesday in the spring and fall, on Monday in summer, Monday to Wednesday in winter. Licensed. Amex, Master Card, Visa. Book ahead if you can. ♿

ILES DE LA MADELEINE, Quebec

See MAGDALEN ISLANDS.

INDIAN HEAD, Saskatchewan **MAP 94**

SANDPIPER'S ☆

Katepwa Beach Hotel **$125**

Highway 56

(306) 332-4696

Some people come to Indian Head for the agricultural research centre. Others come for the Katepwa Beach Hotel. Katepwa, a tiny village ten miles north of Indian Head, overlooks Katepwa Lake, which is one of a chain of lakes in the Qu'Appelle Valley. The big attraction at the Katepwa Beach is Sandpiper's, where most people would rather eat than play golf. Winter and summer, they come from as far away as Calgary for a taste of John McKenzie's cooking. He offers all the usual steaks, as well as things like blackened chicken with Cajun spices. But, what's more unusual in this part of the world, he also offers a surprising variety of fresh fish and shellfish. Lately McKenzie has been using a lot of Diefenbaker Lake trout, crusted with sesame, garnished with slivered carrots and glazed with maple syrup and lime. He's also using tiger shrimps, wrapped in prosciutto and served on a timbale of couscous. Every so often, he does a theme night, of which the most interesting is the

Canadian-Asian fusion night. Quite often, he puts on a seafood night, when you may be offered such things as lobster thermidor, as well as a variety of fresh oysters. There's at least one outstanding sweet, the so-called chocolate explosion, and it's almost always on offer. There are wines from all over the world in the cellar and house wines are by Mission Hill.

Open daily 5 pm to 10 pm from early May until late September, Friday to Sunday 5 pm to 9 pm from late September until early May. Closed Monday to Thursday in winter. Licensed. Master Card, Visa. No smoking. ♿

INVERMERE, B.C.
See PANORAMA.

IQALUIT, Nunavut **MAP 95**
THE GRANITE ROOM ☆
Discovery Hotel **$135**
(867) 979-4433

The Granite Room is still the best place to eat in Iqaluit. The Discovery takes both cooking and service seriously and they hire good people, the best they can get. The two chefs, Martin and Max, have been here forever. You should always book a table before you come, because the Granite Room is always packed, morning, noon and night. The Sunday brunch is so popular that they have two sittings, 50 at a time. The airport is on the Great-Circle route, so fresh fish, fresh meat and fresh vegetables come in year-round from the south. They get Arctic char and Arctic halibut (cooked in white wine and topped with crabmeat) from Pangnirtung. The char is frozen as soon as it's caught, but it's a great dish anyway, whether it's grilled or poached in a saffron cream sauce. Sometimes they have caribou—whenever a hunter brings some to the door. Their other great dish is Grade A Alberta beef, which tastes the way beef used to taste 25 years ago. The soups change every day and they make all their own ice cream—raspberry, black cherry, chocolate, caramel. The Granite Room is expensive and if that's a problem take a look at one of the daily specials—pork tenderloin dijonnaise, scallops Cajun-style or beef with blue cheese. They're all quite cheap.

Open Monday to Saturday 11.30 am to 2 pm, 6 pm to 9 pm, Sunday 11 am to 2 pm (brunch), 6 pm to 9 pm. Licensed. All cards. Book ahead. ♿

JANVRIN ISLAND, N.S. — MAP 96

VOLLMER'S ISLAND PARADISE
St. Mary's Road — **$85 ($195)**
Cape Breton
(902) 226-1507

This place has the feel of the old rural Canada. There's a frame house with bedroom cottages scattered across the lawn and delightful watery views beyond. People come here to see the birds, to paddle a canoe, to walk or fish. Mrs. Vollmer changes her menu every day and cooks everything from scratch. She buys her sole, haddock, salmon and scallops locally and drives twenty miles to Port Hawkesbury for organic fruits and vegetables. There's always something for vegetarians—perhaps fennel in a coulis of tomato, a casserole of mixed mushrooms and vegetables, wholewheat spaghetti with sundried tomatoes. She does her best to find organic lettuce for her salads, which she dresses in maple-syrup vinaigrette. Needless to say, she makes all her own sweets. In summer she likes to serve flambéed peaches or pineapple over ice cream; in winter there's rumtopf, or fruits and berries marinated in rum. Both go well with her rich, dark German coffee. Arthur Vollmer has his own recipe for fillet steak and it's pretty hard to beat. Janvrin Island is just off Ile Madame, overlooking Chedabucto Bay and the distant shores of Guysborough County. Take Highway 104 from Port Hawkesbury and turn south on Highways 320 and 206, then follow the signs. Remember to make a booking before you come.

Open daily at 7 pm by appointment only from 1 May until 31 October. Licensed. Master Card, Visa. No smoking.

JASPER, Alberta **MAP 97**
BECKER'S
Highway 93 **$130**
(780) 852-3779 l

Becker's lost their long-time chef last year, but his young successor, Trevor Young, hasn't made many important changes. The setting here may not be as spectacular as at the Edith Cavell (see below), but the dining-room does have a fine view of Mount Kerkeslin and the Athabasca River. The menu is small and well organized. Trevor Young has added one or two new appetizers, but otherwise he's left the list pretty much as it was. The steaks are all triple-A Alberta beef. The lamb, like the beef, comes from Alberta, the chicken is all free-range. Mussels, halibut and Pacific salmon come in fresh once a week. Game—venison, ostrich, elk and bison—appears as a daily special. The wine-list is quite modest, but if you come early in the morning you'll find that they have a marvellous breakfast buffet.
Open daily 8 am to 11 am, 5.30 pm to 10 pm from early May until Thanksgiving. Licensed. Amex, Master Card, Visa. No smoking. ♿

JASPER **MAP 97**
THE EDITH CAVELL ☆☆
Jasper Park Lodge **$225**
(780) 852-3301

The spectacular views of Mount Edith Cavell, the highest peak in Jasper National Park, hardly prepare you for the Edith Cavell, which has an extraordinary (and very expensive) kitchen. The mountain, which rises more than 11,000 feet from the surrounding plain, was a landmark in the days of the fur trade. It was renamed in 1916 to honour the English nurse who was shot by a German firing-squad the year before. The floor-to-ceiling windows make the mountain an integral part of any dining experience. The kitchen is highly professional and one hardly notices the arrival of one chef or the departure of another. They have a tasting menu for 75.00 (120.00 with wine), as well as an à la carte that begins with salt-cured foie gras and a twice-baked goat-cheese soufflé, goes on to rack of fallow venison, excellent maple-glazed tenderloin of wild boar and rack of curried Alberta lamb and ends with rum baba soaked in citrus juice and a warm sticky-toffee pudding. The wine-list is large and very expensive, concentrating on wines from the Pacific Northwest and the Pacific Rim. *Open Thursday to Saturday 6 pm to 10 pm from 1 January until 31 March, daily 6 pm to 10 pm from 1 April until 31 December. Closed Sunday to Wednesday in winter. Licensed. All cards. Book ahead.* ♿

KAMLOOPS, B.C. **MAP 98**

ACCOLADES ☆

Food Training Building **$95**

U.C.C. Campus

900 McGill Road

(250) 828-5354

Accolades has long been known as the best place to eat in Kamloops, though it's open only in term-time, when students in the training program are in residence. When the school is in session, there are white table-cloths and good silver on every table in the big, bright dining-room, as well as excellent service. This year they've added lunch on Thursday and Friday for between 14.00 and 15.00. There are two table d'hôte menus that change every two weeks. One costs 32.50 for four courses, the other 29.95 for three. There's also a daily fresh sheet. The young chefs know exactly how long to cook fish, how to make a pie crust, how to season with salt and spices. The appetizers run from vegetable terrines to foie gras de canard and on to stilton pâté and blackened linguine with seafood. Every menu has six entrées, from breast of chicken rubbed with Indian spices to grilled Arctic char and pan-seared scallops. There's a different hot soup every day and several salads. Sweets come on a trolley, but look again. The ice creams are all made in

the kitchen, the chocolate ganache is a masterpiece. The wine-list is small and inexpensive.
Open Tuesday to Friday 6 pm to 7.15 pm by appointment only from mid-September until mid-December and from late January until late May. Closed Saturday to Monday. Licensed. Master Card, Visa. No smoking.

KAMLOOPS **MAP 98**
BROWNSTONE ☆
118 Victoria Street **$90**
(250) 851-9939

Connie and Dale Decaire have taken over the old Imperial Bank building in downtown Kamloops. It was built in 1904 and makes a splendid setting for their upscale restaurant. Dale trained under Bruno Marti of the Belle Auberge in Ladner (see VANCOUVER below), and like Marti he uses nothing but the finest and freshest of local ingredients. Like Marti, he prepares them with superb skill. His vocabulary is basically continental (try his frogs' legs, for instance), but there are a number of dishes that show the influence of modern Thai cooking. Try the goat-cheese soufflé and the Yom Tom soup, which is subtle and rich rather than fiery. There are other good things too: the shrimp-and-scallop brochettes, served with gnocchi and wild mushrooms, the rack of lamb with thyme and the trio of duck. The splendid chocolate cake makes a fine ending to any meal.
Open Tuesday to Sunday 5 pm to 10 pm. Closed on Monday. Licensed. Master Card, Visa. No smoking. ♿

KAMLOOPS **MAP 98**
RIC'S MEDITERRANEAN GRILL
227 Victoria Street **$100**
(250) 372-7771

Ric's is part of a chain that began six years ago in Prince George and soon will have twelve locations. Its flagship restaurant is in Kelowna, but we prefer the Ric's in Kamloops. The success of the chain has been based on

a strong food culture, combined with low prices. The menus seldom change and always feature fish as well as meat. They cook in the West Coast style and there's really nothing Mediterranean about either the menu or the cooking. They have perfectly-prepared steaks and a rack of lamb, which is tender and full of flavour They also have Ahi tuna with a wasabi-and-lime glaze and barbecued ribs with lime and tequila. The Ric's in the Sheraton Hotel at 1175 Rogers Way (telephone (250) 377-3113) has a wonderful view of the Thompson River from its deck, high on the hillside. The menu is much the same as the menu downtown, but there's also a selection of tapas-style dishes, all sold at bargain prices. Our favourites are the coconut-crested prawns with mango chutney, the Ahi tuna carpaccio and the lamb sirloin with grilled vegetables. The wine-list is carefully chosen and the holdings of Okanagan vintages are steadily expanding.
Open Monday to Friday 11 am to 10 pm, Saturday and Sunday 4.30 pm to 10 pm. Licensed. Amex, Master Card, Visa. No smoking. ♿

KELOWNA, B.C. **MAP 99**
LA BOULANGERIE ☞
3140 Lakeshore Road **$40**
(250) 762-3466

The Boulangerie makes a dozen different kinds of French bread and they're all good. It also has a café that serves breakfast and lunch. Tired of tinned pâté? The Boulangerie makes its own, in fact it makes four different kinds. Breakfasts are in the French style, which means croissants and coffee. Lunch is served cafeteria-style and that means a clear soup, a cream soup, sandwiches made with homemade bread, a quiche and sometimes a velouté of chicken. The sweets are all wonderful—millefeuille, tarte tatin, opera cake and lemon-meringue tart on sugar dough. There are about 40 seats in the café, but don't come in for dinner. It's not open in the evening.

Open Monday to Saturday 8 am to 5.30 pm. Closed on Sunday. No liquor. Master Card, Visa. No smoking.

KELOWNA **MAP 99**
FRESCO ☆☆
1560 Water Street **$150**
(250) 868-8805

Fresco occupies an old brick building that was completely restored a couple of years ago. This means that at last Rodney Butters has a setting worthy of his talent. His menu is full of pleasures: heirloom-tomato salad with the most delicate of goat-cheese, the sweetest of crab soup, oat-crusted Arctic char, baked Queen Charlotte halibut with sundried olives, oak-smoked pork tenderloin, rack of range-fed lamb with coriander and grilled beef tenderloin with peppercorn mayonnaise. The kitchen has all the important virtues: a lively imagination, restraint and the habit of understatement. This year it's probably at its best with its Arctic char and its lamb, but you can pick almost anything you like. As for the list of Okanagan wines, it has few equals anywhere. There's a Nota Bene cabernet sauvignon from Black Hills, a merlot from Burrowing Owl and a delightful chardonnay (for only 30.00) from the See Ya Later vineyard at Hawthorne Mountain. And as for the service, it's perfect.
Open Tuesday to Sunday 5.30 pm to 9.30 pm from mid-May until mid-October, Tuesday to Saturday 5.30 pm to 9.30 pm from mid-October until mid-May. Closed on Monday in summer, on Sunday and Monday in winter. Licensed. Amex, Master Card, Visa. No smoking. ♿

KENORA, Ontario **MAP 100**
THE PLAZA
125 Main Street S **$95**
(807) 468-8173

There's now a third generation at the Plaza in Kenora. Last year, Dimitri Adamopoulos and his sister, Tina, bought out their parents and acquired a third partner, Bonnie McCardle. Bonnie is a trained chef, but Dimitri and Tina have spent years in the kitchen, learning their grandmother's recipes. In recent years, they've become increasingly committed to a healthy diet—more grilling, less pan-frying, more olive-oil and less butter. Their Greek-style ribs are now dry-roasted over charcoal; chicken and beef souvlaki come with a Mediterranean salad, which is even more popular than the traditional Greek salad. People usually start with either saganaki, made with goat-cheese, or with squid cooked till crisp—they serve a half-portion as a lunch-time special. Between May and October they offer fresh-caught wall-eye pickerel from the Lake of the Woods, lightly breaded and sautéed in butter. Dimitri and Tina have ideas of their own, of course. They stay open until well past midnight on weekends, serving tapas after 10 to live music, and if you like you can tie up your boat at the dock and stroll up to the Plaza for some excitement. Bonnie has added cheesecake to such old favourites as crème caramel and ekmek. (In case you didn't know, ekmek is a Greek pastry made of biscuits soaked in honey and cointreau and served with custard and whipped cream. The restaurant has a licence, but if you're willing to pay a corkage fee of 18.00 you can bring your own bottle.

Open Monday to Wednesday 11 am to 9 pm, Thursday to Saturday 11 am to 1 am (tapas only after 10 pm). Closed on Sunday. Licensed. All cards. No smoking. ♿

KINCARDINE, Ontario **MAP 101**

HARBOUR STREET BRASSERIE

217 Harbour Street **$125**

(519) 396-6000

Four years ago we were talking about the Harbour Villa, which occupied the same site and had the same telephone number as the Harbour Street Brasserie. Its owners had spent a fortune renovating their Regency-style cottage and they'd hired a first-class chef. Sadly, they failed. Diane and Derek Griffiths, formerly of the Red Pump in Bayfield, bought the place a year or so ago. Harbour Street has been named an historic area, which helps, and they have a large terrace overlooking the lake, which also helps. The menu changes every night and features as much fresh produce as they can find. Everything is well cooked and beautifully presented. This summer you can expect fine poached halibut, fresh scallops and mussels, wild sockeye salmon and wonderful smoked wild sablefish. Their salad of spring greens is tossed with dried cranberries, toasted pecans and fresh blossoms. Their grain-fed chicken comes with local strawberries, lavender and wildflower-honey vinaigrette. Their lamb comes from Ontario, their beef from Bruce County. There are two samplers, one of homemade ice creams, the other of chocolate confections, and they're the most successful of the sweets.

Open Tuesday to Saturday 5 pm to 10 pm from Easter until 31 October, Wednesday to Saturday 5 pm to 10 pm from 1 November until Easter. Closed on Sunday and Monday in summer, Sunday to Tuesday in winter. Licensed. All cards. ♿

KINGSTON, Ontario — *MAP 102*

Like most university towns, Kingston has a number of pubs and cafés that'll give you a good, square meal for a fair price. Luke's at 264 Princess Street (telephone (613) 531-7745) is a popular place for brunch. They make good breads (which they also use at lunchtime for their sandwiches), homemade soups and salads and are known for their smoked cheese, smoked ribs and smoked meat, which they smoke for 21 days. The staff sandwich, so called because it was invented by the staff themselves, has the moist, dark meat from a roasted chicken leg between two thick slices of garlic bread. Wooden Heads at 192 Ontario Street (telephone (613) 549-1812) offers gourmet pizzas in an old stone building with a brick pizza oven. You can choose one of the ten or twelve classic combinations or build your own. If you don't want pizza, you can have a crostini or one of several tapas. Tango at 331 King Street E (telephone (613) 531-0800) is an elegant bar with great cocktails, a selection of draught beers and what they call tapas. Actually, many of the tapas are big enough for two. Try the grilled scallops with mustard and mesclun greens; if you want sweet-potato fries as well it'll cost you all of 11.00. Luke's is open Tuesday to Friday for lunch and dinner, Saturday for brunch and dinner and Sunday for brunch; Wooden Heads is open every day from noon to midnight; Tango is open every day until midnight. Wooden Heads, Luke's and Tango are licensed. Wooden Heads and Tango take all cards, Luke's takes Amex and Visa. No smoking.

KINGSTON **MAP 102**
ACQUATERRA BY CLARK
Radisson Hotel **$90**
1 Johnson Street
(613) 549-8100

You can't count Clark Day out. He keeps coming back with new ideas. This time he's formed a partnership with the local Radisson, who call him their consultant, though in fact he plans the menus, supervises the kitchen and puts on wine-tastings once a week. If you choose to go along with his three-course *prix-fixe*, you'll start with a tarte flambé and go on to lamb shanks with garlic mash and red wine, finishing off with poached pears and homemade ice cream. If you want to make a night of it, there's an excellent four-course dinner for 45.00 that might begin with tomato consommé with pea-shoots, followed by a salad of Belgian endive in apple-truffle vinaigrette. The main course might be a trio of venison, beef and lamb in a basil-and-lychee sauce, a holdover from the old Clark's on King. The sweet may be a crème brûlée. For 20.00, you can have four wines by the glass with your meal, and coffee is included. There's also an ample à la carte with at least one memorable dish, Wolfe Island bison with pecan bread pudding. There's an extensive wine-list that emphasizes New World wines (a number from the Okanagan) and offers plenty of good drinking for less than 25.00. Unless you're having the bison, you'll do

very well with the gewurztraminer from Hawthorne Mountain.
Open Monday to Saturday 11 am to 11 pm, Sunday 11 am to 10 pm. Licensed. All cards. ♿

KINGSTON **MAP 102**
CHEZ PIGGY ☆
68 (rear) Princess Street **$125**
(613) 549-7673

Zal Yanovsky's daughter returned to Kingston last year to take over the management of Chez Piggy from her late father. Chez Piggy has been a Kingston institution since 1978, when it opened in a nineteenth-century livery stable in the heart of the city. To be sure, the cooking has always been less seductive than the setting, though it has taken a great step forward in recent years. They now have excellent suppliers and a stable team of chefs. They make all their own breads and sweets and import their cheeses from France. The menu changes frequently, but old standbys remain. At lunchtime they still have the shrimp fried with garlic on fresh greens, the Thai chicken salad, the grilled teriyaki salmon with wasabi mayonnaise and the fisherman's soup of mussels, monkfish and shrimp. In the evening they add deep-fried quail, salt-cod fritters with mango chutney and goat-cheese salad, as well as Muscovy duck with braised red cabbage and white-bean purée and Mayan chicken with pumpkinseeds, black beans and rice. If you're looking for a Sunday brunch, Chez Piggy has Spanish eggs (poached in olive-oil) and Newfie fishcakes. There are 200 wines in the cellar (French, Italian and Canadian), sixteen of which are available by the glass, as well as grappas, vintage ports and single malts.
Open Monday to Saturday 11.30 am to midnight, Sunday 11 am to midnight. Licensed. All cards. No smoking. ♿

The map number assigned to each city, town and village gives the location of the centre on one or more of the maps at the start of the book.

KINGSTON **MAP 102**
CHIEN NOIR
69 Brock Street **$115**
(613) 549-5635

The Chien Noir is situated in an old stone block in the heart of downtown Kingston, not far from Cooke's celebrated grocery store. Its pressed-tin ceiling, bare stone walls, zinc bar and brown-paper table-cloths are meant to make the place look like a bistro in Paris. The menu makes much of steak and fries, mussels, poutine, duck confit and lamb. Some of the more imaginative dishes of the early days have disappeared, but free-range breast of chicken is still on the menu, served with sundried tomato, spinach and gorgonzola. And they still have a good terrine of foie gras. Their top price is for a nine-ounce beef tenderloin with green peppercorns. For the same price you can have a three-course *prix-fixe* with soup or a green salad, roast chicken or steak and your choice of sweet (chocolate mascarpone, fresh-berry galette). The sweets are fairly priced but they're not exciting. They do have draught beer and 22 wines by the glass, however, all sold at remarkable prices. The Georges Duboeuf beaujolais costs just 6.00 a glass.
Open Monday to Saturday 11 am to 2.30 pm, 5 pm to 11 pm, Sunday 11 am to 2 pm, 5 pm to 11 pm (shorter hours in winter). Licensed. All cards. No smoking. Book ahead if you can.

KINGSTON **MAP 102**
THE CURRY ORIGINAL ☞
253A Ontario Street **$55**
(613) 531-9376

The Curry Original has an attractive location overlooking the lake. They serve all the Indian classics—kormas, vindaloos, dhansaks, bhoonas, saags and tandooris, as well as a few special dishes like butter chicken, made with coconut, yogurt and raisins, shrimp phatia, a spicy, sweet-and-sour curry with coconut,

green peppers, tomato and lemon and lamb dopiaza, made with tomatoes, green peppers, fenugreek and fried onions. Vegetarian alternatives are available for every course—onion bhajis, say, or a vegetable biryani perfumed with saffron. There aren't many wines, but there are five or six private-stock vintages, as well as Indian beer on tap. The Curry Original is very cheap. At noon you can get soup, a salad, a simple curry and a bowl of rice for only 7.00 or 8.00.
Open Tuesday to Saturday 11.30 am to 2 pm, 5 pm to 9.30 pm, Sunday 5.30 pm to 9.30 pm. Closed on Monday. Licensed. All cards. ♿

KINGSTON **MAP 102**
PAN CHANCHO
44 Princess Street **$110**
(613) 544-7790

The estate of Zal Yanovsky appears now to have sold Pan Chancho, which he opened just before his death. The bakery and delicatessen, however, both still enjoy the support of all sorts of Kingston people. Pan Chancho opens early for breakfast and prepares meals all day, though dinner is now offered only in summer. Lunch brings excellent homemade soups that change every day—still served with homemade bread for just 4.00 a bowl. Then there are salads, among them an innovative Caesar made with sourdough croûtons, pancetta and shaved parmesan, and sandwiches (cumin-spiced lamb on a grilled pita with watercress, onion and chickpeas and wild salmon on rye with pickled red onions. Steak and fries and grilled fresh sardines with lemon-thyme roast potatoes come for much the same price. Dinner is, of course, more expensive, featuring entrées of wild mushroom on seared polente and wilted baby spinach or loin of lamb with a coriander chutney served with coconut-lime jasmine rice and a Thai cucumber salad. There are wonderful sweets, all made in the bakery, as well as a number of superb cheeses. Many wines are available by the glass as well as the bottle and

there's great espresso.
Open Monday 7 am to 11 am (breakfast), 11 am to 5 pm (lunch), Tuesday to Saturday 7 am to 11 am, 11 am to 5 pm, 5 pm to 9 pm (dinner), Sunday 7 am to 11 am, 11 am to 5 pm from early June until late September, daily 7 am to 11 am, 11 am to 5 pm from late September until early June. Amex, Master Card, Visa. No smoking. ♿

KITCHENER, Ontario **MAP 103**
TWENTY KING ☆
41 King Street W **$140**
(519) 745-8939

Peter Martin first opened in downtown Kitchener in 1988, almost twenty years ago. A few years later he moved across the street to much larger quarters in an old bank building. Diners still come from Toronto and Stratford to fill the front of the house and Peter is still to be seen in his open kitchen at the back. We've always praised his way with vegetables and greens and we've always been grateful for the care he takes with the appearance of every dish. Most of the entrées we find too rich, but others disagree. Typical is the seafood laksa, which is an Asian version of bouillabaisse in a lightly-curried coconut broth. The appetizers, on the other hand, are light, clean and delicate. The beet salad with roquefort is one of the best. Others are the steamed mussels with mustard and tarragon and the crabcakes with salmon and yellow peppers. The sweets make a welcome break from crème brûlée. There's a warm butterscotch-pecan tart and there's bread pudding with pumpkin and bourbon. Lunch is a simpler and cheaper affair. There's a selection of pizzas and sandwiches, served with soup or a salad and fries for no more than 10.00. The wine-list is large and there are several draught beers. The service is attentive.
Open Monday to Friday 11.30 am to 2 pm, 5 pm to 10 pm, Saturday 5 pm to 10 pm. Closed on Sunday. Licensed. Amex, Master Card, Visa. No smoking. ♿

KITCHENER
See also WATERLOO.

KLEINBURG, Ontario **(MAP 223)**
CHARTREUSE
10512 Islington Avenue **$125**
(905) 893-0475

Chartreuse occupies a rather plain little house, not far from the McMichael Gallery. The dining-room, however, has always been surprisingly ambitious. We miss Fay Millet in the kitchen, but there are still fresh flowers on every table and classical music on the soundtrack, no doubt because Tony Bonos, the *patron*, keeps an eye on every detail. There may be more steaks on the menu these days, but the fish is all fresh, the liver the best that money can buy. The lamb comes in fresh from Australia. It's a pity, however, that the cooks are so preoccupied with chartreuse. They prepare their shrimps with yellow chartreuse, their sea-bass with green chartreuse, regardless of whether shrimps or sea-bass go with chartreuse of either colour. If the sea-bass runs out you can fall back on Atlantic salmon, though you'll be disconcerted to find that it's also served with green chartreuse. Next door at Longchamp, a pub that's open all day every day, the same kitchen offers a hot-pot of chicken or lamb for just 12.50. Double Diamond is no longer on tap at Longchamp, but they have Krombacher instead.
Open daily 11.30 am to 3 pm, 5 pm to 10 pm. Licensed. Amex, Master Card, Visa. No smoking.

LADYSMITH, B.C. **MAP 105**
PRINTINGDUN BEANERY ☞
341 1 Avenue **$40**
(250) 245-7671

If you ask anybody around here where to go for something to eat, they'll be sure to suggest the Beanery in Ladysmith. The surroundings are comfortable and

relaxed and the coffee is the best in town. They have a variety of pastas, quiches, paninis, enchiladas and chillis —just about anything, in fact, that hungry people will eat for lunch. They do all their own baking and everyone likes the carrot cake and the cherry-and-raspberry vanilla cake. The service is fast and friendly, no matter how busy they are.
Open Monday to Friday 9 am to 5 pm, Saturday 10 am to 5 pm. Closed on Sunday. No liquor. Master Card, Visa. No smoking. ♿

LAHAVE, N.S. **(MAP 115)**
LAHAVE BAKERY ☞
(902) 688-2908 **$25**

People on the South Shore have been involved in a love-affair with the LaHave Bakery for at least twenty years. Small wonder. Where else would you find a piece of the maritime past, of a time when people worked for something more than money? Gael Watson and her employees—there are 22 of them now—get up before dawn every day of the week, summer and winter, to begin baking. Every day they bake fifteen varieties of bread. Our favourites are the cheese-and-herb bread and the potato bread, but one visitor from America considered the black-pepper-and-parsley bread inspired, to use her word. All the breads are made with honey and olive-oil, not fat or sugar. They also make fabulous Queen Elizabeth cakes, cookies, scones, bagels, tarts and real, old-fashioned oatcakes. Everything is sold to take out, but if you like you can sit at one of the rickety tables inside and eat your pizza there. The place is steeped in atmosphere, with high ceilings, old display counters and artifacts of all sorts—check out the skeleton of a huge fish in the dining-room. Lunch means made-to-order sandwiches as well as pizza. There are always people coming and going—the ferry terminal is just along the street. A cable ferry has been operating here since 1832.
Open Monday to Saturday 9 am to 4 pm, Sunday 10 am to 5 pm. No liquor. Master Card, Visa. No smoking.

LAKE LOUISE, Alberta **MAP 107**
BAKER CREEK BISTRO
Bow Valley Parkway **$120**
(403) 522-3761

Baker Creek is about six miles from Lake Louise on the old route from Banff to Lake Louise. The Bistro, which dates back to 1949, has been owned by the same family since 1986. Chefs have come and gone, but the kitchen has always had a good reputation. John Udell, who opened the Bonterra in Calgary, is as good as any of his predecessors, if not better. He does everything himself and that means the bread, the soups and the sweets. There are no cans in the kitchen and no boxed puddings. Dinners are distinctly ambitious and feature organic greens, wild mushrooms, foie gras, confit of duck and Alberta lamb. Travellers have written to us about the lamb shanks with ricotta gnocchi, the venison chops with savoury corn, the loin of pork marinated in beer and the gorgonzola poutine. They get in both fresh Pacific salmon and Alaska black cod on a regular basis and use nothing but Callebaut chocolate for their chocolate cake. On Saturday morning they serve brunch with vanilla-bean yogurt, wild-mushroom frittata and buttermilk pancakes with maple syrup from Quebec. The service is every bit as good as the cooking.
Open daily 8 am to 11 am, noon to 2 pm, 5 pm to 10 pm from 1 June until Thanksgiving, Tuesday to Sunday 5 pm to 9 pm from Thanksgiving to 31 May. Closed on Monday in winter. Licensed. Master Card, Visa.

LAKE LOUISE **MAP 107**
POST HOTEL ☆☆☆
200 Pipestone Road **$275 ($600)**
(403) 522-3989

The Post Hotel is the best place to stay between Golden and Banff. It's also one of the best places to eat anywhere in the country. They have an extensive à la carte,

but this is probably a good time to ask for the tasting menu, which costs 90.00 for six courses. As we've said before, the menu is extraordinary, the presentation spectacular, the cooking beyond compare. Meals begin with a cold appetizer, something like green-and-white-asparagus salad with cress and mustard-and-chive dressing, red and yellow tomatoes, Ahi tuna crusted with mustard seed and bison carpaccio. Next comes a hot appetizer, perhaps foie gras de canard with acorn squash and quince. Then a fish course (Atlantic salmon, say, with vermouth, Pacific sea-bass with star-anise carrots or Alaska black of with fresh tomatoes. Bison and caribou are available for those with expensive tastes; otherwise, there's braised osso buco with a mushroom risotto and rack of Alberta lamb with fig-and-date couscous. There's a lovely caramelized-lemon tart with sour-cream ice cream and an astonishing wine-list, with several amazing half-bottles. If you're looking for something you can afford, ask for the Latour premier-cru, the Caymus conundrum or the Cakebread sauvignon blanc. Only the Latour is really expensive.
Open daily 11.30 am to 2 pm, 5 pm to 9.30 pm from mid-December until mid-October. Licensed. Amex, Master Card, Visa. No smoking. Book ahead. ♿

LAKE LOUISE
See also CASTLE JUNCTION, FIELD.

LANGENBURG, Saskatchewan **MAP 108**
CONVERSATIONS CAFE ☆
212 Carl Avenue E **$80**
(306) 743-5111

Langenburg is just west of the Manitoba border on Highway 16, which runs from Portage la Prairie to Yorkton and Saskatoon. It's a small town and it's a long way from almost anywhere. The Café occupies an old school building right on the highway and it's run with a lot of pride—when we pointed out that they didn't make their own pasta they started making it right away.

(They sell a lot of pasta because the durum wheat from which it's made is important to neighbouring farmers.) They do everything they can to promote local products. Pickerel, for instance, is brought in from northern Saskatchewan. Lamb, which is raised nearby, is known all over the country. You can expect local pork and local organic beef as well, and everyone asks for their beetniki, which is a kind of bread wrapped in young beet greens seasoned with dill. They have a big vegetable garden at the door and they raise all their own herbs and vegetables. In season they fill their pies with locally-picked raspberries, currants and Saskatoon berries.

Open Thursday to Saturday 11 am to 10 pm from 1 February until 31 October, Thursday to Saturday 2 pm to 10 pm from 1 November until 31 January. Closed Sunday to Wednesday. Licensed. Master Card, Visa. No smoking.

LANIGAN, Saskatchewan **MAP 109**
JAN'S STEAK HOUSE ☞
17 Hoover Street **$65**
(306) 365-4366

The Americans still aren't travelling. B.S.E. keeps them away from the West, S.A.R.S. keeps them away from the East. If you're running a steak house on the Yellowhead Highway about midway between Winnipeg and Edmonton, you notice every missing car. Jan's winters were always lonely. This year she's filling in time by selling gourmet spices, candles and hand-crafted jewelry. Jan left Broadway almost 30 years ago, because she wanted to live closer to home. She misses the stage, but she's happy in Lanigan Her family is close by and she has two great-grandchildren in Yorkton. Her father still has his driver's licence at 93—he was driving before anyone had heard of licences. Her mother is 84 and helped in the kitchen until a couple of years ago. Jan does all the baking (banana cream, coconut cream, chocolate cream and pumpkin pie). She makes 60 different highballs. Her salad bar is the equal of any on the

Prairies. She herself makes the marinated mushrooms, the water-chestnuts, the hot peppers, the cucumbers and bacon. Her daughter, Debra, makes the pickled beets and brings them all the way from Yorkton. Jan makes a good clam chowder as well as mushroom and tomato soup. Her beef is all custom cut. The best of her steaks is the twelve-ounce T-bone, but most of her customers like their steaks well done, so she recommends the top sirloin for them. She sells a lot of baked ham with black currants and, in summer, a lot of roast pork, stuffed and served with an orange-red-wine sauce. St. Patrick's Day brings Irish soda bread and corned beef and cabbage, but the highlight of Jan's year are the two Scandinavian weekends, one in April, the other in November. That's when she makes her wonderful verdens beste or two layers of cake and two of meringue, served with whipped cream and a thick custard filling. If you book ahead, you can have one of these baked to order, in January or July. And remember: her coffee is just 1.00 a cup, no matter how many refills you have.
Open daily 5 pm to 11 pm. Licensed. Master Card, Visa. No smoking. ♿

LETHBRIDGE, Alberta **MAP 110**
MIRO'S
313 5 Street S **$115**
(403) 394-1961

At the moment, this is probably the best place to eat in Lethbridge. It calls itself a bistro, but the menu goes well beyond standard bistro fare. For instance, they offer such things as a salad of roasted beets and oranges in hazelnut oil, seared scallops in a warm yam vichysoisse, caramelized-pear pizza with stilton cheese and pecans and fettucine with smoked salmon and crème fraîche. The entrées are more nearly mainstream. Their lamb all comes from Alberta, their beef dishes—châteaubriand, beef with a potato pancake and beef with field mushrooms—are all made with well-aged beef tenderloin. They prepare everything from

scratch—breads, soups, sweets—and there are at least 150 wines in the cellar.
Open Tuesday to Friday 11 am to 2 pm, 5 pm to 10 pm, Saturday 5 pm to 10 pm. Closed on Sunday and Monday. Licensed. All cards. No smoking. ♿

LIVERPOOL, N.S. **MAP 111**
LANE'S PRIVATEER INN
27 Bristol Avenue **$95**
(800) 794-3332

This place has been in the Lane family for 40 years. The restaurant, which remains open all day every day year-round, is big and bright, the menu extensive. Meals usually start with solomon gundy, seafood chowder or steamed mussels with ginger. Then there's roast turkey, lamb chops, salmon, scallops and an excellent haddock burger for only 5.95. They have an all-day breakfast as well as a lazy-weekend brunch featuring everything from strawberry pancakes to maple-smoked salmon, eggs benedict and fishcakes with beans. Adjoining the restaurant there's a well-stocked gourmet shop with a large takeout menu. It's a good place to know about if you want to have a picnic on one of the spectacular beaches in the area.
Open daily 7 am to 10 pm (earlier in winter). Licensed. All cards. No smoking. ♿

LIVERPOOL
See also SUMMERVILLE BEACH.

LONDON, Ontario **MAP 112**
J.J.'S BISTRO
1304 Commissioner's Road W **$85**
(519) 474-3868

It's a long way out to J.J.'s, long and sad. It's in a strip mall, one of many on Commissioner's Road. But J.J.'s is a comfortable place with comfortable cooking. The chef has a sure hand with both his fish and his steamed

vegetables. For starters, try either the Caesar salad or the salad of mesclun greens. The risotto is made with wild mushrooms, asparagus and prosciutto. There's no veal, but the beef liver with caramelized onions and lingonberry sauce is a delightful dish. Poached salmon has disappeared this year and been replaced by pan-seared salmon with leeks and tarragon. There's a nice rack of lamb with a sweet-potato purée and rosemary pesto and, if you have money to spare, a fine fillet of beef. The sweets are all likeable and the twenty wines on the wine-list are all offered by the glass as well as the bottle. They're all extremely cheap: the Lindemans Bin 45 cabernet sauvignon costs only 21.00 a bottle.
Open Tuesday to Friday 11.30 am to 2 pm, 5 pm to 9.30 pm, Saturday 5 pm to 9.30 pm. Closed on Sunday and Monday. Licensed. All cards. No smoking. Book ahead if you can.

LONDON **MAP 112**
ON THE FORK
Museum London **$120**
421 Ridout Street N
(519) 850-3675

We had hoped that Chris Squire of the old Petit Prince would remain in the kitchen here, but he didn't and neither did his successor. Instead, the former sous-chef, Josie Olazevson-Pontarelli, is now in charge, and she describes On the Fork as a bistro. If Moroccan-spiced lamb shanks with apricot-onion chutney, couscous and fine green beans make a place a bistro, so be it. The Museum and Art Gallery in which the restaurant is housed are on a fork of the Thames River and from the restaurant windows there's a fine view of the river, with the old brick jailhouse in the foreground. While some of the early charisma may have disappeared, lunch here is still a happy experience, if only because of the expert service. The salads are too big; so start instead with a sweet-corn soufflé or a dish of sea scallops with green-apple-and-jicama slaw. Go on to crisp-skinned organic breast of chicken with rhubarb chutney or handmade ricotta gnocchi with tomato and basil. Most of these dishes reappear, in a slightly different form, on the dinner menu, along with grilled salmon glazed with maple and served with soba noodles and braised-beef short-ribs with mashed potatoes and horseradish crème fraîche. The sweets are all made with excellent pastry and real Callebaut chocolate, and the French-roast coffee is lovely. The Sunday brunch is the best meal of the week and it has a top price of just 16.00 for beef tenderloin with rostii potatoes, a baked tomato and a fried egg. *Open Tuesday 11.30 am to 2.30 pm, Wednesday to Saturday 11.30 am to 2.30 pm, 5 pm to 10 pm, Sunday 11 am to 3 pm (brunch). Closed on Monday. Licensed. Amex, Master Card, Visa. No smoking.*

LONGVIEW, Alberta **MAP 113**
THE STEAK HOUSE
Highway 22 **$70**
(403) 558-2000

At the moment the Steak House is staying open all day every day, because after all there's nothing else to do in town. But now that one son has left for Montreal to take over a restaurant the family has opened there, the rest of the family are toying with the idea of putting a sign on the door saying they're closed on Sunday or Monday—or whatever. The father of the family is Moroccan and when he started he decorated the place with Moroccan rugs and scenes of Marrakech. But the youngsters had other ideas and the rugs have now all disappeared. You can still get a Moroccan dinner (30.00 for two) if you give them two or three days' notice. But what you come here for are the steaks, which are magnificent. The owners learned about ageing and preparing steak when they were at the Châteaubriand in Calgary. They also know how to make salads and salad-dressings (honey-mustard, Caesar without anchovies) and they're pretty good with greens and root vegetables. They make all the blueberry and apple pies in house, all the bread and bread puddings, all the

cheesecakes. You'll find Longview less than an hour from Calgary, on the road to Kanaskis via Okotoks and Black Diamond. It's a small town with long views toward the Rocky Mountains—hence the name.
Open daily 8 am to 8 pm. Licensed. Master Card, Visa. No smoking. ♿

LORNEVILLE, N.S. **MAP 114**
AMHERST SHORE COUNTRY INN ☆
Highway 366 **$115 ($200)**
(800) 661-2724

Robert and Mary Laceby may allow themselves a few compromises—their orange-juice, for instance, isn't freshly squeezed and their scallops are frozen. But they run this small country inn, which Robert inherited from his parents, with real skill and rare passion. It's the sort of place where it's tempting to spend the night and there are several comfortable bedrooms in the main house and four luxurious suites behind the barn. They have big vegetable gardens as well, where they grow most of the vegetables that appear on your plate. Dinner is served every evening at 7.30 by appointment only. The meal begins with a whole loaf of multi-grain bread, cut at the table. Soup comes next. It may be a simple consommé or it may be something like creole-onion, potato-curry or squash-and-peach. The salads are full of local greens and vegetables from the garden. There's always a choice of main course—meat or fish. Fish often means salmon, grilled, poached or steamed; meat may mean chicken or pork (usually with dijon and cassis). The best of the sweets is the fresh-fruit pavlova, made to a recipe invented by Robert's mother. The small wine-list features seven chardonnays from Nova Scotia. If you want to spend money, they have a 2002 Caymus conundrum for only 85.00.
Open daily at 7.30 pm by appointment only from 1 May until 31 October, Friday and Saturday at 7.30 pm by appointment only from 1 November until 30 April. Closed Sunday to Thursday in winter. Licensed. Master Card, Visa. No smoking. ♿

LUNENBURG, N.S. **MAP 115**
BLACK FOREST ☞
Highway 3 **$80**
Martin's Brook
(902) 634-3600

The Black Forest stands in a patch of open space halfway between Lunenburg and Mahone Bay. Thomas and Barbara Heimert call their place a café, but it's really more of a gasthaus. They do everything themselves and they do it well. They offer fish, but we usually choose one of the German specialties, like maultaschen, a German-style ravioli stuffed with veal, onions and mushrooms. The à la carte starts with Hungarian goulash, grilled sausage with fries and wonderful sauerkraut and ends with pork schnitzels and zwiebel rostbraten, which means striploin with onions and krautspaetzle. The sweets are all made on the premises and you'll really notice the difference with the Black Forest cake. Mrs. Heimert covers the front of the house all by herself, but she's always quick, always friendly. The wine-list is tiny, but it includes a few local beers as well as the usual wines. *Open Tuesday to Sunday 11.30 am to 9 pm from mid-April until mid-December. Closed on Monday. Licensed. Master Card, Visa. No smoking.* ♿

LUNENBURG **MAP 115**
FLEUR DE SEL ☆☆
53 Montague Street **$115**
(902) 640-2121

Fleur de Sel was opened two years ago by Sylvie MacDonald and Martin Ruiz Salvador. Visually, the place is stunning: all brilliant yellow outside, butter-yellow inside with Palladian arches, French porcelain and white table-linen. The menu changes every few weeks. Lunch means terrine de campagne and young squid stuffed with saffron risotto. In the evening there may be a cold garlic soup or a hot lobster bisque with crème fraîche. Bouillabaisse will come next, or butter-poached lob-

ster, or perhaps local lamb or local tuna. The vegetables are all organic and there's a small wine-list offering a dozen reds and a dozen whites. Prices aren't high except for the seven-course tasting menu, which costs 70.00, or 107.00 with matching wines.
Open daily 11.30 am to 2 pm, 5.30 pm to 9 pm from 1 May until 15 October, Thursday to Sunday 5.30 pm to 9 pm from 16 October until 31 December. Closed Monday to Wednesday in winter. Licensed. Amex, Master Card, Visa. No smoking. ♿

LUNENBURG **MAP 115**
MAGNOLIA'S ☞
128 Montague Street **$90**
(902) 634-3287

Magnolia's is as good as ever, but it's no longer particularly cheap. You eat in a booth, the menu is chalked up on a blackboard and the atmosphere is funky—but char-grilled Atlantic salmon still costs 19.25, as do butterflied Old Bay shrimp. Indian Point mussels—steamed with white wine, carrots, onions and garlic—are a much better buy at 7.50. And so is the blackened-chicken Caesar salad, which comes for 9.75. There are several excellent soups—creole peanut, tomato-and-cheddar, mushroom-and-barley—as well as solomon gundy and broiled chicken wings. They have fine lemon buttercream cake, and the key-lime pie with real whipped cream is a marvel. The best thing to drink is fresh-squeezed lemon juice, which costs just 2.95 a glass. As for the bread, it's all made in house and it's wonderful.
Open Monday to Saturday 11.30 am to 9 pm. Closed on Sunday. Shorter hours in the spring and fall. Licensed. Amex, Master Card, Visa. No smoking. ♿

LUNENBURG
See also LaHave, Mahone Bay, Martin's Brook.

Nobody can buy space in this guide and nobody can buy his way out of it.

MABERLY, Ontario **(MAP 162)**
FALL-RIVER GRILL
21980 Highway 7 **$100**
(613) 268-2882

This little grill occupies what was once a general store and gas-station in Maberly, which is ten or twelve miles west of Perth. The cooking is country-style, but everything is handled with care and a good deal of sophistication. They always stress local produce and most of the produce they use is organic—and this includes the wines. Summer menus generally feature pickerel, sole, duck, venison, pork, organic chicken, lamb and Alberta beef. In the winter they serve things like smoked duck and smoked salmon. Everybody likes the appetizer of seared scallops, garnished with mushrooms and a hint of onion. New York steaks they like to smoke and chargrill with a crust of herbs. Lamb shanks may be braised with shiraz; duck is garnished with polente and a rich stew of root vegetables. (The steak comes with no fewer than seven perfectly-grilled vegetables.) Crème brûlée, made with Guinness, is the most popular of the sweets, though you won't go far wrong with the chocolate torte in a coulis of raspberry or the apple strudel with a glaze of ginger and cranberry. This isn't a large restaurant; it wouldn't seat more than 30. But it's been tastefully renovated with hand-hewn beams, a millstone at the door, hunter-green walls and an open fireplace. They're now building an outdoor patio, where they hope to have live jazz on Sunday evenings. Note: recent reports indicate that the food and service at noon have become indifferent. Come for dinner or not at all.
Open daily 11 am to 8 pm (later on weekends) from mid-May until mid-October, Thursday to Sunday 11 am to 8 pm from mid-October until mid-May. Closed Monday to Wednesday in winter. Licensed. Amex, Master Card, Visa. No smoking. ♿

If you use an out-of-date edition and find it inaccurate, don't blame us. Buy a new edition.

MABOU, N.S. **(MAP 170)**

DUNCREIGAN COUNTRY INN

Highway 19 **$115**

(800) 840-2207

Rooms at the Duncreigan Country Inn are all big and comfortable and just a step or two away from the main building across a flowered courtyard. The dining-room, where dinner is served every evening (except Sunday in winter), is more severe. There's a printed menu offering three courses for 37.00 and four for 42.00. Dinner begins with a plain soup (cream-of-tomato, perhaps), followed by salmon, often in a coulis of mustard, honey and lemon, or scallops in a creamy dill sauce. The kitchen is better with fish than with meat, and the lamb, which is said to be local, is usually more than a match for its sauce, even when it comes with black currants. This is blueberry country, but the blueberry tart, though a marvel, is no match for the apple pie, made with gravenstein apples from the Annapolis Valley and the equal of any we have ever tasted. The wine-list is growing and now offers some first-class chardonnays and merlots from Australia and California. Prices remain very low: the Wolf Blass Red Label shiraz cabernet still costs only 30.00 a bottle.

Open daily 5.30 pm to 8.30 pm from late June until the middle of October, Monday to Saturday 6 pm to 8.30 pm from the middle of October until late June. Closed on Sunday in winter. Licensed. Master Card, Visa. No smoking. You must book ahead. ♿

MAGDALEN ISLANDS, Quebec ***MAP 118***

There are sixteen islands in the 60-mile arc of the Magdalens, but more than half the population live on Ile Cap-aux-Meules. The next largest is Ile Havre-Aubert, at the southern end of the chain. Everywhere there's fine hiking, swimming and sailboarding. The Madelon Bakery at 355 chemin Petitpas on Cap-aux-Meules (telephone (418) 986-3409) has a wealth of baked goods, cheeses and made-to-order sandwiches, and it's a good place to go if you want a packed lunch. The Islands are known for their soft raw-milk cheese, which resembles reblochon and is produced by the indigenous breed of cow, known as Canadienne. You can get it at the Fromagerie Pied-de-Vent on Havre-aux-Maisons (telephone (418) 969-9292). The restaurant at the Hôtel Vieux Couvent, also on Havre-aux-Maisons (telephone (418) 969-2233), is a gay, lively spot. Mussels are cultivated in a nearby lagoon and cooked on the kitchen stove. Try the squid or the bouillabaisse or the mussels in a blue-cheese broth. On the west side of Ile Havre-Aubert is La Grave, where old fishing huts have been converted into galleries, museums, boutiques and restaurants. Here you'll find the Chocolaterie Diane at 2026 Etang des Caps (telephone (418) 937-5757), a small shop full of the most exquisite chocolates. The Café de la Grave, located next to the theatre (telephone (418) 937-5765), has some lovely, thick sandwiches, two-salmon bagels and wonderful custard cakes with meringue icing. The Four à Pains (telephone (418) 937-5244) is right on the beach. They serve first-class cod-cakes and fries, coleslaw and tortes. Few travellers get to the Magdalens, which is a pity because there are many pleasures to be had on the Islands, including some outstanding cooking. If you don't like the idea of a five-hour ferry trip from Souris in Prince Edward Island, you can board the new cruise-ship, Le Vacancier. It leaves Montreal every Friday night in season, stops in Quebec City and Matane and spends three days in the Magdalens.

MAGDALEN ISLANDS — **MAP 118**
AUBERGE DE LA P'TITE BAIE — **ONE**
187 route 199 — **$90 ($170)**
Ile Havre-aux-Maisons
(418) 969-4073

Each of the Magdalen Islands has its own distinctive style and flavour. There's an old-fashioned, old-world air about the P'tite Baie on Ile Havre-aux-Maisons. Little changes from year to year. The century-old house has four comfortable bedrooms and the cooking is simple and traditional. The à la carte is set in stone. There's

always poached cod in lobster sauce, grilled salmon with smoked-herring butter, pork tenderloin marinated in garlic, ocean snails with mushrooms and seafood chowder made with lobster, shrimps and scallops. The kitchen makes the most of fresh local produce, from smoked herring and *prie-de-vent* cheese to Island fruit and vegetables. Seal bourguignon and seafood pie with seal, lobster and shrimp are both regular features of the five-course *prix-fixe* menu. The *prix-fixe*, which changes every day or two, begins with a homemade soup or, better still, with two soups in a bowl (one cream-of-broccoli, the other cream-of-carrot). The proprietor considers this dish a masterpiece and he's right. They buy Quebec lamb from the mainland for their lamb tenderloin, which is grilled and finished with thyme and rosemary. In summer, the kitchen likes to stuff crêpes with strawberries and *pâtisserie* cream. In the fall there might be banana-and-rum crêpes or an apple-and-maple-syrup tartlet. The cooking here is genuine and likeable and prices are modest—the table d'hôte, for instance, costs only 30.00 a head with coffee.
Open daily 5 pm to 10 pm from 1 June until 30 September. Licensed. Master Card, Visa. No smoking.

MAGDALEN ISLANDS **MAP 118**
AU BOUT DU MONDE
951 route 199 **$90**
Ile Havre Aubert
(418) 937-2000

Au Bout du Monde opened only last summer, so we don't have much to go on as yet, though we do know that the cooking is promising. The menu is Italian, local ingredients are plentiful. Crab-cakes are made with fresh crab, linguine comes with lobster fresh from the sea. The risotto, made with pancetta and a local cheese, tombes des demoiselles, so impressed one diner that he came back the next evening to have it again, this time with asparagus and pied de vent. The dining-room has a sea-view from every window. The service is friendly and very charming.

Open daily 5 pm to 10 pm from late May until the end of September. Licensed. Master Card, Visa. No smoking.

MAGDALEN ISLANDS **MAP 118**
LA MAREE HAUTE ☆☆
25 chemin des Fumoirs **$120 ($210)**
Ile Havre Aubert
(418) 937-2492

The Marée Haute stands near the edge of a bay, from which its gets its name, which means High Tide. Every room in the newly-renovated inn has a view of the dunes and the sea beyond. Ducks swim in a pond by the door, where they're fattened for the table. The dining-room is spacious and comfortable. The place is run by Patrick Maphey and his partner, Pascal St.-Jean, who came to Canada from France a dozen years ago. Most of the guests are French speaking, though Maphey and St.-Jean both speak a little English. The kitchen makes full use of the abundance of fresh local produce available at the doorstep. In summer they make the most of local fish and shellfish, serving different seafood every evening—razor clams, sea snails, sea-urchin and sea parsley. In February you get to eat seal, in July fresh crab. The smoked fish, with which dinner generally begins, is drier than most, because it's all hot-smoked, but everyone likes the cured fish, which is marinated in olive-oil with crushed peppercorns and coarse sea-salt. We like to start with bouillabaisse, which is crammed with big pieces of fish and shellfish. The scallops that follow are a joy. Sometimes they have local lamb, sometimes rabbit cooked three ways. The duck is correctly prepared and served in a fan, each slice cooked rare, with blueberries. Dinner ends with île flottante with plenty of caramelized sugar, or perhaps with a sorbet or a wedge of fruit pie.
Open daily 6 pm to 10 pm from late February until early December. Licensed. Diners, Master Card, Visa. No smoking. ♿

MAGDALEN ISLANDS **MAP 118**

LA TABLE DES ROYS ☆☆☆

1188 route 199 **$160**

La Vernière

Ile Cap-aux-Meules

(418) 986-3004

The Table des Roys is almost invisible from the highway. There's a delightful garden in front and hanging flower-baskets on the verandah. Inside there are only twelve tables. This once used to be Joanne Vigneault's family homestead. When André and Francine Roy bought the place and turned it into a restaurant, Joanne, then fifteen, asked for a job in the kitchen. She knew nothing about cooking, but Francine was a master cook and, Joanne will tell you, "I watched and I learned." The two women became firm friends and, when the Roys opened another restaurant in Beaupré near Quebec, they encouraged Joanne to take charge of the Table des Roys. Today she is one of the best and best-known chefs in the province. Her bouillabaisse is famous and never leaves the menu, but recently she's been experimenting with such Asian dishes as tataki of tuna, sashimi of scallops with sesame and ginger and Vietnamese crab soup. The table d'hôte is more familiar, featuring poached cod with barley and Cornish game hen; the à la carte offers duck with honey and five spices and a sauté of Oriental vegetables. The à la carte is expensive, but the table d'hôte is quite limited. It's probably best to settle for the bouillabaisse and one of the exquisite sweets. The wine-list reaches from France to California and back, but there aren't many wines by the glass. There is, however, an important list of ports and grappas. One traveller writes: "I really feel that this was one of the great meals of my life. It's wonderful to be so far from the mainstream and yet dine in such elegance."

Open Monday to Saturday at 6 pm by appointment only from 15 June until 30 September. Closed on Sunday. Licensed. Master Card, Visa. No smoking. ♿

MAHONE BAY, N.S. **(MAP 115)**

THE BISCUIT-EATER
16 Orchard Street **$25**
(902) 624-2665

Mahone Bay has a delightful new café. It's called the Biscuit-Eater and it's just off the Main Street, not far from the centre of town. It occupies the ground floor of a big, bright-yellow house. As you enter you face a fireplace surrounded by bookshelves. There's also a counter where orders are placed. In fine weather it's a good idea to head outside to the garden, where you can have a quiet lunch. They offer soup and sandwiches, as well as biscuits, cakes and brownies, with coffee or any one of a number of loose teas. Magnificent chocolates are handmade and packaged by a pâtisserie in Eastern Passage. The Biscuit-Eater is also a bookshop and music nights and reading nights help to promote the sale of local books.
Open Monday to Saturday 9 am to 6 pm, Sunday 11 am to 6 pm from Victoria Day until Thanksgiving, Thursday to Saturday 9 am to 5 pm, Sunday 11 am to 5 pm from Thanksgiving until Victoria Day. Closed Monday to Wednesday in winter. No liquor. Master Card, Visa. No smoking.

MAHONE BAY **(MAP 115)**

SALTSPRAY CAFE
621 S Main Street **$65**
(902) 624-0457

The Saltspray in Mahone Bay has a new owner this year. Joyce Dennison had worked at the Café for three years and presumably knew a good thing when she saw it. So far she's made no important changes, except to raise the prices. The Saltspray has an excellent seafood chowder that comes with half a lobster sandwich for only 11.35, which is as good a buy as you'll get in this part of the world. They also make a good haddock dinner, as well as a roast turkey dinner with all the trimmings. But it's important to save room for one of the homemade pies, which are all made from scratch.
Open daily 8 am to 8 pm. Licensed. All cards. No smoking.

MAITLAND, N.S. **_MAP 120_**
CRESTHAVEN BY THE SEA
19 Ferry Lane **_$95 ($260)_**
(902) 261-2001

Maitland is a forgotten village on the south shore of Cobequid Bay, 30 minutes from Truro by Highway 236, 60 minutes from Halifax by Highway 215. Cresthaven is the loveliest house in the village and each of the four bedrooms has a view of the tidal flats below. The food, however, isn't all it should be. They won't make you a boiled egg in the morning and in the evening the salmon is usually overcooked. Scallops are served very conservatively with white wine, piped potatoes and cheese—the sole stuffed with shellfish is more interesting. The lemon curd is delightful, though the lemon-meringue pie is not. The house wines are by Jost and they're not good, but there's a scattering of wines from Italy, Australia, Chile and E. & J. Gallo. Prices may be high, but there's nothing better this side of Halifax. Cresthaven is open daily 5 pm to 9 pm from mid-May until mid-October, Friday to Sunday 5 pm to 9 pm from mid-October until mid-May. They have a licence and take Master Card and Visa. No smoking. ♿

MANITOULIN ISLAND, Ontario **MAP 121**
GARDEN'S GATE ☆
Highway 542 **$75**
Tehkummah
(705) 859-2088

Every year Rosemary Diebolt and her husband search the vineyards of Niagara for new and exciting wines. They track down local craft beers with the same passion. Andy Stimpson of Neustadt Springs, for instance, makes only two beers, both in small batches. One is a Scottish-style lager, the other a Belgian country-style lager. Both are in the cellar here. If you turn west off Highway 6 in Tehkummah, you'll be at the Garden's Gate in two minutes. The gate leads into a pretty garden, beyond which you'll find the restaurant, with an old barn and a split-rail fence in the middle distance.

Here Mrs. Diebolt makes all her own salad-dressings, her own bread-rolls, even her own hamburger buns. Fresh vegetables are hard to buy on the Island, so she grows as many herbs and vegetables as she can, buying the rest—green beans, baby carrots, kale, cherry tomatoes, big beets (for bortsch), potatoes (for roasting with garlic) from local suppliers only she knows about. One brings her an eleven-quart basket of blueberries once a week all the way from Sudbury; a second, who lives half a mile down the road, brings her organic raspberries and strawberries in the spring; a third brings her the greatest prize of all, fresh local garlic scapes—300 pounds of them last summer. There are six entrées every day, from breast of chicken to char-broiled lamb, and at least ten sweets. A month in Germany last winter inspired Mrs. Diebolt to make her own quartsanne torte, which is essentially quark cheese and whipped cream on a biscuit base coated with raspberry jam. One holdover is her old-fashioned Dutch apple pie, which is known all over the Island. To end the meal they're now offering organic fair-trade coffee and any one of a number of loose teas. Before you leave, you can buy a jar of peach relish or a jar of Grandma's old-fashioned chili sauce to take home with you.
Open Tuesday to Sunday 11 am to 8 pm from 1 April until 30 June, daily 11 am to 10 pm from 1 July until 31 August, Tuesday to Sunday 11 am to 8 pm from 1 September until 31 October. Closed on Monday in the spring and fall. Licensed. Master Card, Visa. No smoking. Book ahead if you can. ♿

MANITOULIN ISLAND **MAP 121**
ROCKY RACCOON CAFE ☆
24 Water Street **$75**
Gore Bay
(705) 282-8111

Three years ago Robin Pradham and Shelley Beniz of the Rocky Raccoon in Dyers Bay (see above) came upon the Red Roof in Gore Bay and fell in love with

the place. When the previous owners decided to move away, Robin took a ten-year lease. This year his brother, Suman, a trained curry chef, has joined him and the three take turns cooking, along with a sous-chef in training. The menu is the same in both locations, which means that it changes almost daily but always makes the most of fresh local products. Gore Bay, however, is twice the size of Dyers Bay and seats 90. "Come as a customer," as Mr. Pradham likes to say, "and leave as a friend."
Open daily 10 am to 1 am from early May until late October (or when the ferry closes down). Licensed. All cards. No smoking.

MANITOULIN ISLAND **MAP 121**
THE SCHOOL HOUSE ☆
Providence Bay **$105**
(705) 377-4055

Greg and Heather Niven have just had one of their best years at the School House. That was because the Lake Huron Fish and Chips, which opened last year, did a roaring business in its first full year. Everything there is fresh, everything is made from scratch—the batter, the chips and the tartare sauce. The whitefish itself comes straight from Lake Huron. At the School House, they make the most of the fabulous Island beef and lamb. When they can't get the local product, they bring in beef from Alberta and lamb from New Zealand. Greg Niven was trained as a French chef and every year he does more and more French cooking, though he's still interested in the Thai and Indian cuisines. Chanterelles are becoming scarce on Manitoulin Island, but summer still; brings local fish and whatever the Nivens can grow in their garden. There's a good selection of Niagara wines in their cellar as well as a number of first-class Australian cabernets.
Open daily 5 pm to 9 pm from Victoria Day until Labour Day, Tuesday to Sunday 5 pm to 9 pm from Labour Day until 31 October. Closed on Monday in the fall. Licensed. Master Card, Visa. No smoking. ♿

MANSONVILLE, Quebec ***MAP 122***

L'AUBERGINE

160 chemin Cooledge ***$100 ($225)***

Knowlton Landing

(450) 292-3246

This is an old coaching inn on the Montreal-to-Boston road. It was built in 1812 in a small hamlet on the western shore of Lake Memphramagog. It opened to the public again a generation ago and quickly became a success. In 2002 it was sold to Didier Perrault from Bordeaux. Perrault was always good in the kitchen, but standards declined in the front of the house and beyond. In the last year or two, however, things have improved and we now need further reports. There are only seven bedrooms and a handful of tables in the dining-room and they don't always take non-residents, so a reservation is essential. The Aubergine is open every day in season, but closes on Monday and Tuesday in November and April. They have a licence and take Master Card and Visa. No smoking. You must book ahead

MAPLE CREEK, Saskatchewan **MAP 123**

CURRAH'S BAKERY

107 Maple Street **$35**

(306) 662-3811

It must be twenty years since we first heard of Currah's Bakery. At that time they had only four tables, but the baker's wife made excellent soups and sandwiches and, in summer, first-class saskatoon-berry pies and tarts. Saskatoons were a rarity then. Now Currah's buys more than a thousand pounds every summer and freezes half for the coming winter. The saskatoon-berry pie and the one-person carrot cake are in such demand that they keep them on the menu all year. Last year they bought a small grill, so they can add a few hot dishes to their serve-yourself breakfast with its celebrated cinnamon buns. They're always experimenting with such novelties as carrot-and-blueberry muffins and flatbread made without sugar or shortening. This year they're offering

some new varieties of bread, among them flaxbread and sourdough. Their bagels—blueberry, cheese and multi-grain—are softer and heavier than most and they're very popular with visitors. Every day at noon, they bring out two big tureens of soup, one a clear broth, the other a cream of mushroom, potato or corn. Then, while you wait, sandwiches are made on sliced bread, a kaiserbun or even a croissant. After your meal, you just go up to the cash and tell them what you've eaten and they charge you accordingly. The Trans Canada Highway passes just north of the Cypress Hills between Regina and Medicine Hat. Turn off on Highway 21 south and you'll find Maple Creek.
Open Tuesday to Saturday 6 am to 6 pm. Closed on Sunday and Monday. No liquor. Master Card, Visa.

MARGATE, P.E.I. **(MAP 43)**
SHIPWRIGHT'S CAFE ☆
11869 Highway 6 **$100**
(902) 836-3403

The Shipwright's Café occupies an old farmhouse built in the eighteen-eighties in one of the prettiest parts of the Island. Calvin Burt moved here from Tyne Valley several years ago and now has a huge organic garden as well as an extensive fruit-and-vegetable farm. Travellers can't believe that plain country cooking can be this good. The seafood chowder, made with blue mussels, shrimps, scallops and whitefish, is famous in these parts, but the cream-of-asparagus soup is almost better. Malpèque oysters, mussels, fresh Atlantic salmon and beef tenderloin are the things to look for, as well as a well-known local dish called Mrs. Montgomery's chicken, stuffed with bread-crumbs laced with summer savoury. The most expensive dish in the place, believe it or not, is the paella with aioli, the rice cooked (for once) exactly as it should be. The breads are all home-made; if you want to sample the oat-bread, have a sandwich for lunch. They also make their own bread pudding and, in September, their own pumpkin pie.

There's a children's menu too. Just don't expect quick service. Island people like to move slowly, and think you should too. Prices look high but they always give value for money, and are proud of it.
Open Monday to Friday 11.30 am to 2 pm, 5 pm to 8 pm, Saturday and Sunday 5 pm to 8 pm from 1 June until 30 September. All cards. No smoking. ♿

MARTIN'S BROOK, N.S. (MAP 115)
OLD BLACK FOREST CAFE
Highway 3 **$80**
(902) 634-3600

The Old Black Forest stands right on the road between Lunenburg and Mahone Bay. It's an unassuming place, but there are always plenty of cars parked outside. Nobody comes here for the view, and there's no atmosphere at all. But the food is excellent and there's plenty of it—Oktoberfest sausages, schnitzels and pan-fried haddock. We ourselves make a point of asking for the maultaschen or ravioli stuffed with veal, mushrooms and onions. It comes with a remarkably light and tasty gravy. There are also superb side dishes of spaetzle and sauerkraut. The best of the sweets, needless to say, is their own Black Forest cake. One thing: you won't be hungry when you leave.
Open Tuesday to Sunday 11.30 am to 9 pm from mid-April until mid-December. Closed on Monday. Licensed. Master Card, Visa. No smoking.

MARY'S HARBOUR, Newfoundland MAP 126
RIVERLODGE
Highway 510 **$60**
Labrador
(709) 921-6948

Mary's Harbour is the starting-point for the two-hour boat trip to Battle Harbour, a restored nineteenth-century Labrador fishing-station. Riverlodge looks unassuming from the highway, but inside it's warm and attractive. If you sit at the back you can watch the salmon fishermen working the Salmon River, which runs right behind the lodge. Barb loves to cook and loves making every plate look right. She makes all her own bread and bread-rolls and all her own fruit pies and bake-apple cheesecakes. She likes to talk about her salads, which she finishes with chicken, oranges and slivered carrots. There's always a daily special, but if you don't want that ask for one of the old standbys like seafood chowder and cod au gratin. In season, Barb can get crablegs straight from the fish-plant. Scallops, tiger shrimps and salmon are sautéed in the kitchen and beef and turkey soup are always on the hob. There's a big breakfast every morning and there are always plenty of take-out choices for the kids.

Open daily 6 am to 10 pm from 1 June until 30 September, daily (but call ahead to make sure) 8 am to 6 pm from 1 October until 31 May. Licensed. Amex, Master Card, Visa.

MATANE, Quebec **MAP 127**

LA TABLE DU CAPITAINE

260 rue du Barachois **$85**

(800) 463-7468

Matane is a big place with a number of restaurants, but we think the Table du Capitaine is the best. The east end of Matane is rather like a vacant building lot and the captain's nearest neighbour is a brand-new, flashy motel. They have nothing in common. The restaurant is open all day in season, which makes it convenient for motorists. For 20.00 to 25.00 you can get homemade soup, the catch of the day, a shrimp stir-fry or grilled salmon, sweet and coffee. They have an à la carte as well, offering sandwiches, pizzas, and a warm seafood salad filled with the small shrimps de Matane, salmon, cod, scallops and mussels. There are also some interesting appetizers, among them cods' tongues, seafood chowder and a *dégustation* plate with salt cod, smoked salmon and herring sautéed in maple syrup. All the fish is perfectly fresh and the fillet of cod can be had for just 13.95. Lobster, of course, is more expensive.

Open daily 10 am to 10 pm from early June until early September. Licensed. All cards. No smoking.

MATTAWA, Ontario ***MAP 128***

For years we recommended Draper's at 510 Valois Drive (telephone (705) 744-2323), a bright and very clean little café—their highway billboard used to advertise clean washrooms, with the words underlined twice. They underwent a major expansion, but pretty soon we began to get adverse reports and so the place was dropped. There are still people, however, who admire their soups and sandwiches. Around the corner at 610 McConnell Street (telephone (705) 744-2274) you'll find Myrts. It's been around forever and was recently rebuilt after a fire. It's probably as good as Draper's, but it's on a bad curve and its early closing seems to have discouraged the truckers whose rigs once filled the parking-lot. They make all their own soups, all their own pies (they sell a lot of the peanut-butter) and their own fish and chips, made with halibut. They like to say they use "real beef" in their hamburgers. If you know what that means please let us know.

MAYNE ISLAND, B.C. **(MAP 230)**
OCEANWOOD ☆
630 Dinner Bay Road **$175 ($450)**
(250) 539-5074

There's good news from Oceanwood this year. Stephen Kruse, who was away all last year, will be back in the kitchen this summer. Kruse is a graduate of the Stratford chef school who's spent some time at the Sooke Harbour House (see below). In season he serves a four- or five-course dinner every day of the week. He's always made a point of seeking out the freshest of local produce. Organic vegetables, herbs and edible flowers grow in the garden. Lamb comes from an organic farm on Mayne Island, goat-cheese from Saltspring Island. The wines come from most of the important vineyards of the Pacific Northwest, and a dozen or more can be had by the glass as well as the bottle. Dinner begins with

soup, a crab-and-mussel consommé with ginger and scallions, say. Next comes a salad of local greens and edible flowers, or perhaps something like octopus in a ragoût of sea-asparagus, sweet peppers, eggplant and day-lily buds. The main course might be trout with chick-pea fritters, caribou marinated in red wine or roasted halibut with an onion glaze. The sweets are ambitious—crème brûlée with sunflower-seed biscotti, goat-cheese cake with a walnut sabayon and roasted apples in caramel sauce. Oceanwood is a hideaway retreat for the rich and weary of Vancouver and Victoria. The contemporary building of bleached grey cedar and plate-glass overlooks Navy Channel and every room has a view. If you spend the night, which is a good idea, they give you a sumptuous breakfast next morning.
Open daily 6 pm to 9 pm from mid-March until the end of October. Licensed. Amex, Master Card, Visa. No smoking. Book ahead.

MEDICINE HAT, Alberta **MAP 130**
ZUCCHINI BLOSSOM
62 3 Street NE **$55/$100**
Riverside
(403) 526-1630

This is a small, casual café with someone in the kitchen who really knows how to cook. Regulars claim he turns out the best food in southern Alberta. If you come early you'll be given granola with yogurt, muffins, scones and a cup of capuccino. If you come at noon (and can find an empty seat), they'll give you splendid red-lentil soup, a pizza and a lemon slice so fresh it's hard to believe. On Friday and Saturday nights they put on a changing four-course menu. It might be French in style or Mexican, whatever they feel like. It's usually Italian, because that's what they do best—just try their ravioli. They have a few wines and a small delicatessen selling first-class pasta and extra-virgin olive-oil.
Open Monday to Thursday 8 am to 5 pm, Friday and Saturday 8 am to 9 pm, Sunday 8 am to 5 pm. Licensed. Master Card, Visa. No smoking. ♿

MILL BAY, B.C. **(MAP 60)**
THE AERIE ☆☆
Spectacle Lake Road **$175 ($475)**
(250) 743-7115

The cooking has improved at the Aerie this year. The tasting menu that Christopher Letard puts on every night of the week is as spectacular as ever. Meanwhile, the kitchen has regained its old form at noon. The fish is no longer overcooked. The steamed local halibut is beautifully served with ratatouille. If wild Pacific salmon is offered as a daily special, be sure to ask for it. If you're lucky, it'll be prepared with cream and pernod, in which case the sauce will be light and clean and nicely understated. If your tastes are more conservative, go for the beef tenderloin from Alberta. Lunch begins gorgeously with green-pea vichysoisse or, more demurely, with dungeness-crab terrine. The wine-list is very splendid: there are eleven Spottswoode vintages from Napa, eight Blue Mountain chardonnays from the Okanagan, thirteen Mouton Rothschilds from Bordeaux. If you're drinking by the glass, there's a millifiore from Venturi-Schulze and a lovely syrah from Burrowing Owl. It costs 14.00, but it's worth it.
Open daily noon to 5 pm (lunch), 5 pm to 10 pm (dinner). Licensed. Amex, Master Card, Visa. No smoking. ♿

MOBILE, Newfoundland **(MAP 195)**
THE CAPTAIN'S TABLE
Highway 10 **$80**
(709) 334-2278

Arthur Jackman and his wife opened the Captain's Table twenty years ago in a small cabin they bought in two sections and fitted up as a restaurant. They started out small and cozy (their words); then, as they prospered, they expanded until they both had to work all day to keep up with the business. Before long they'd retired from the kitchen, employing cooks they'd trained for the purpose. But Arthur Jackman had a real feeling for the stove, and with his departure the cooking has lost its edge. You can still get a good enough meal here and it's a lovely drive to Mobile, which is on the east coast of the Avalon Peninsula, not far from the Witless Bay ecological reserve. The two most successful dishes now are the pan-fried cod and the cods' tongues with salt-pork scrunchions. The fish and chips are as good as any in this part of the country and the seafood chowder is outstanding. So are the sweets. Most people go for the pecan tart topped with ice cream and caramel sauce, but we still like the warm apple dumpling and the bumbleberry pie.

Open daily 11.30 am to 8.30 pm from early April until late September. Licensed. Master Card. Visa. No smoking. Book ahead. Wheelchair access.

MONCTON, N.B. **MAP 133**

THE WINDJAMMER ☆☆

Hôtel Beauséjour **$185**

750 Main Street

(506) 854-4344

It's many years since we recommended the Windjammer and, frankly, we seldom change our mind. But Stefan Mueller has been praised by chefs from all over the province He's been awarded four diamonds by the C.A.A. for eight years running and the Delta management has been astute enough not to send him off to a hotel in Halifax or Vancouver. Certainly, he has a lavish setting in the Beauséjour, and superb service. The menu is expansive, the cooking both imaginative and disciplined. You can start with a five-onion soup, local oysters on the half-shell or (best of all) a smoked-salmon martini shaken up with iceberg vodka and a twist of won-ton. Local char is offered as a main course on warm lentils with a trace of truffle-oil. Ragoût of crab is infused with coconut, loin of venison wrapped in a blanket of pumpkinseeds and spiced berries. Mueller uses fresh local ingredients whenever he can, buying all

his lamb from neighbouring farmers. He goes to Bouctouche for his bison, to the North Shore for his mussels and lobster. His wine-list is dazzling.
Open Monday to Saturday 5.30 pm to 10 pm. Closed on Sunday. Licensed. All cards. No smoking. Book ahead if you can. ♿

MONTAGUE, P.E.I. **(MAP 43)**
WINDOWS ON THE WATER
106 Sackville Street **$85**
(902) 838-2080

Windows on the Water is the sort of place you can always count on. The menu, the cooking and the service are all extremely consistent. Betty Higgins and Lillian Gurnham had worked there for years before they bought the place. Now Lillian has bought her sister out, so she's running the place alone. She's going to open a month later than usual, but otherwise she plans to keep things pretty much as they've always been. The bread in the lobster sandwich is too thick for our taste and as for the tuna melt, it has no virtues at all, but everything else is very good. The seafood chowder, made with haddock and scallops, has been voted the best on the Island. She makes a lot of other soups as well, but the broccoli-and-cheddar and the carrot-and-zucchini are her favourites They do several salads, all with fresh local greens. In the evening they add steak, salmon and haddock to the menu, sometimes halibut and scallops as well. They sauté their scallops and serve them with homemade tartare sauce, and it's a popular dish. You can finish off with cheesecake if you like, but it's better to ask for the apple crisp and better still to ask for the bread-and-butter pudding, which is one of a kind. Montague was founded by British settlers in 1765 and it's still an attractive place. As for Windows on the Water, the setting is irresistible, especially if you book a table on the deck overlooking the harbour.
Open daily 11.30 am to 9.30 pm from the beginning of June until late September. Licensed. Amex, Master Card, Visa. No smoking. ♿

MONTREAL, Quebec **MAP 135**
AIX
Hôtel Place d'Armes **$135**
711 Côte de la Place d'Armes
(514) 904-1201

The Place d'Armes is one of a number of *boutique* hotels that have opened recently in Old Montreal. Its dining-room, is especially attractive at lunchtime, when there's an interesting choice of dishes at bargain prices. In season you can expect to start with a poultry mousse with grape jelly or a really delightful carrot soup with fish fumé. After that you should look for striped sea-bass, wapiti with a mushroom torte, lamb shanks with squash or an omelette with asparagus and oka. Janick Bouchard is interested in cuisine au terroir, that is, dishes based on regional produce bought from local suppliers. In this case that means home-smoked salmon (which they also sell to take out), wild boar from the Eastern Townships, bison, lamb, root vegetables and a number of local farm-house cheeses. Sad to say, however, the kitchen is given to serving its vegetables hot raw. As for the *pâtissier*, he works with a heavy hand—better the farmhouse cheeses than any of the pastries. The open wines change every day at the whim of the *sommelier.* Pouilly fumé makes a delightful companion for fish and shellfish, but it costs all of 14.00 a glass. You might do better with a bottle of the Beringer fumé blanc at 45.00. If you want to spend money, there's an Opus One for 450.00.
Open Monday to Friday 11.30 am to 2.30 pm, 5.30 pm to 10 pm, Saturday and Sunday 5.30 pm to 10 pm. Licensed. All cards. No smoking. ♿

MONTREAL **MAP 135**
ANISE ☆
104 avenue Laurier o **$200**
(514) 276-6999

Anise is a tiny place with ten or twelve tables on two levels. There's s small à la carte, but it's best to ask for the six-course set dinner, which costs 65.00 a head (nine

courses cost 90.00). Anise certainly isn't cheap, but the cooking of Racha Bassoul is impeccable, the service immaculate. You start with several kinds of home-baked bread (wholewheat, cardamom, fig) and a tiny, captivating *amuse bouche* (fresh marinated salmon, perhaps, wrapped in cucumber and topped with caviar), then go on to a mouthful of oyster-mushroom or cauliflower soup and market-fresh fish (red snapper, say, on a bed of squid-ink pasta with milk of asparagus). Sometimes they have salmon poached in olive-oil with tarragon and green peppercorns, and it's a delightful dish. Meats mean venison shawarma, sweets a beautiful chocolate fondant or cheese. The wines are mainly French, but the best buy isn't French at all. For 90.00 you can get a bottle of Edna Valley chardonnay—sadly, there are no bargains on this list.
Open Tuesday to Saturday 6 pm to 9 pm. Closed on Sunday and Monday. Licensed. Amex, Master Card, Visa. No smoking. Book ahead.

MONTREAL **MAP 135**
BOULANGERIE PREMIERE MOISSON ☞
1490 rue Sherbrooke o **$25**
(514) 931-6540

This place is a bakery first and foremost and the breads are all lovely: viennoises (garnished with chocolate and cranberries), ficelles, croissants and baguettes. There's a case filled with charcuterie and another filled with salads. There's a case filled with marvellous chocolate confections: ménuphars, piquants truffés, cakes of all sorts. There are quiches, lemon tarts and linzer tortes, orange charlottes, profiteroles and lingots of apple and caramel. Every day there's a hot soup, as well as espresso and capuccino. There's brunch on Saturday and Sunday, when for 6.95 they'll bring you either eggs or pancakes, with toast and coffee. At lunchtime a few dollars will buy you a cake or a tart and a cup of café filtre—and leave you feeling you've been on the Left Bank.
Open daily 7 am to 7 pm (later on Thursday and Friday). No liquor. Master Card, Visa. No smoking.

MONTREAL **MAP 135**

BRONTE ☆☆☆

1800 rue Sherbrooke o **$190**

(514) 934-1801

We were skeptical when Brontë first opened. Other restaurants had failed on this site, which is right next to the Hôtel Meridien. Besides, some of Joe Mercuri's combinations left us unconvinced, to say the least. Then we ordered Mercuri's seafood risotto with yellow beets and our doubts disappeared. Here is a chef given to wild but wonderful inventions, and he deserves to be heard. His risotto is certainly not about rice. It's about perfectly fresh, perfectly-cooked shellfish. Scallops, shrimps and lobster come with tiny slices of red beet and rice in a reduction of yellow beets with crème fraîche. The menu is short and features regional produce, like Boileau venison with butternut squash, Quebec foie gras de canard with a fig compote and an emulsion of parsnip and shredded guinea-fowl with pickled raspberries. Like other chefs, Mercuri is finding it harder and harder to find suppliers for much of the fish and shellfish that play such an important part in his cooking. Suzuki, a delicate white-fleshed fish, comes from Japan, lobster from Maine, lemoncello-cured organic salmon from Ireland, fresh cod from Iceland. Take whatever he offers on any given day, whether it's charred octopus, soft-shell crab, sturgeon, rabbit, venison (in the autumn) or even a ragoût of oxtail. The soups are a joy. When did you last see a parsnip-and-pea velouté garnished with roquefort tortellini and poached breast of duck? It's best to end your meal with a plate of perfectly-maintained Quebec farmhouse cheeses. Otherwise, ask for the panna cotta with a hint of honey tangerine and cardamom. There's a good selection of wines from France, Italy, California and the Pacific Rim, as well as wines from Niagara, but the open wines are all seriously overpriced. The service is very slow and one misses a fishknife. But these are small imperfections.

Open Tuesday to Saturday 5.30 pm to 11 pm. Closed on Sunday and Monday. Licensed. Amex, Master Card, Visa. No smoking. Book ahead. Valet parking. ♿

MONTREAL **MAP 135**
BU
5245 boulevard St.-Laurent **$85**
(514) 276-0249

Bu is a wine-bar with a spare, minimalist décor and a small, sophisticated menu, where everything is served tapas-style in small, delicate portions. The cooking is what you might hope to encounter in a country town in Tuscany. Meals begin with a number of *pronto* dishes, of which the best is the zuppa di canederli, which is a bowl of hot, clear chicken broth filled with dumplings stuffed with prosciutto. Next comes a choice of two hot dishes—a pasta and a piatto del giorno—and a longer list of *freddo* tastes that runs from vegetable antipasto, octopus with potatoes, bresaola with lemon and extra-virgin olive-oil to beef carpaccio with shaved parmesan and veal with cream of tuna. Aside from tiramisu and panna cotta, there's an interesting array of Tuscan black chocolate from Amedei. There are five wine flights and a long list of bottled wines from France and Italy. There aren't many wine-bars that have a 1988 solaia and a 1990 sassicaia in their cellar. Don't ask what they cost. The coffee is lovely.
Open Monday 5 pm to 2 am, Tuesday to Friday noon to 2 am, Saturday 5 pm to 2 am. Closed on Sunday. Licensed. Amex, Master Card, Visa. No smoking. ♿

MONTREAL **MAP 135**
LES CHEVRES ☆
1201 rue Van Horne **$165**
(514) 270-1119

Some of the magic has gone out of this place in the past year or so, perhaps because of the departure of Eric Dupuis, who is now at Decca 77 (see below). But

Stelio Perombelon and Patrice Demers are still in the kitchen and some things—the bread, the mignardises, the gnocchi with oyster mushrooms and pearl onions—are still very well done. The tuna, however, though aptly served in a crab broth with asparagus spears and fingerling potatoes, is habitually overcooked. Ask instead (if you don't like gnocchi with mushrooms and onions) for the local lamb, roasted with spinach and served with a 25-year-old vinegar. Dinners begin well with foie gras pan-fried with white turnips, truffles and honey or, for the daring, with smoked eel. The butternut-squash soup is spoiled by its Cortland apple—apples and squash don't mix. The wines, mainly French and Italian, are wildly expensive and the service is painfully slow. You have to plan to spend three hours over dinner—and a lot of money as well. Next door there's a new restaurant called Le Chou (1205 rue Van Horne, telephone (514) 270-2468). It's served by the same kitchen and nothing on the menu costs more than 8.00 or 9.00. We'll tell you more about it next year.
Open Monday to Saturday 5.30 pm to 10.30 pm. Closed on Sunday. Licensed. Amex, Master Card, Visa. No smoking. ♿

MONTREAL **MAP 135**
CHEZ L'EPICIER ☆
311 rue St.-Paul e **$135**
(514) 878-2232

This one-time grocery store is a visual delight All brick and stone, its shelves are stocked with such things as biological carrot oil and sel de Camargue. The menu, printed on a brown-paper bag, is expanding and new dishes often speak with an Asian accent. Salmon now comes with Thai gremolata, sweet-potato rostii with Chinese spices, gnocchi stuffed with Jerusalem artichokes with eggplant, baby turnips, molasses and lovage. Portions are small. Escalope de foie gras, for instance, is served with a scrap of butternut squash between two slivers of toast. If you come for dinner,

order the shoulder of suckling pig with maple vinegar, bulgur wheat and beets. It's a fine, substantial dish. The same is true of the salmon simmered in mustard and the venison osso buco. The wines are expensive, but there's a barbera d'Asti from Val Fieri for only 8.00 a glass. The bread is noteworthy and so is the coffee.
Open Monday to Friday 11.30 am to 2 pm, 5.30 pm to 10 pm, Saturday and Sunday 5.30 pm to 10 pm. Licensed. All cards. No smoking.

MONTREAL **MAP 135**
LE CLUB CHASSE & PECHE ☆
423 rue St.-Claude **$135**
(514) 861-1112

Late last year a new restaurant opened on the site of the Fadeau, Henry Wojcik's wonderful restaurant of the nineteen-sixties and seventies. The Chasse & Pêche—it's no club—is dark and stylish inside, the service elegant and composed. The menu is small. There's salmon tartar, grilled squid and red snapper for lunch, followed by calf's liver with mushrooms and polente, croustillant of sweetbreads with celery root, salmon with green apple and fennel and striped bass with sorrel and shitake—all this for just 19.00 a head. The kitchen is restrained in all its effects, always persuasive and usually convincing. It's at its best with croustillants; try the crispy sweetbreads and see for yourself. The dinner menu is broadly similar, though meals that start with things like suckling pig cost twice as much as at lunchtime. The wine-list is full of interesting buys. The 2002 Liberty School cabernet sauvignon costs only 35.00, which is an opportunity no-one should miss.
Open Tuesday to Friday 11,30 am to 2 pm, 6 pm to 11 pm, Saturday 6 pm to 11 pm. Closed on Sunday and Monday. Licensed. Book ahead if you can. No smoking.

We accept no advertisements. We accept no payment for listings. We depend entirely on you. Recommend the book to your friends.

MONTREAL **MAP 135**
DECCA 77 ☆☆☆
1077 Drummond Street **$150**
(514) 934-1077

Overnight, this one-time jazz-bar has become a civilized restaurant. The interior (glass, suede and stainless steel) is ultra-cool. The menu is wild, as wild as any in the city. As for the prices, they're more than reasonable: 25.00 for three courses at noon, 35.00 for three courses at night. Not long ago we began with a warm salad of lamb's lettuce and went on to sablefish with patty-pan squash, coriander and ginger, followed by chocolate financier. Others tell us about the beet salad with three kinds of beet, the oysters on the half-shell, the flank steak with a purée of turnip, the minced lamb with green onions and arugula, the pineapple ravioli with tarragon and the ginger-clementine terrine. They offer a platter of raw-milk cheese as well for just 6.00, which is no more than the chocolate financier. At Decca they care about the little things: the bread, the warm milk that comes with the coffee, the presentation and the service. In fact, they seem to care about everything.
Open Monday to Friday 11.30 am to 2.30 pm, 5.30 pm to 10.30 pm, Saturday 5.30 pm to 10.30 pm. Closed on Sunday. Licensed. All cards. No smoking.

MONTREAL **MAP 135**
DA EMMA
777 rue de la Commune o **$165**
(514) 392-1568

Da Emma is a family-run operation and it has real Italian cooking. Look for it in the basement of a converted prison near the old port. Inside, it's all steel, polished concrete and rough stone, its washrooms, with their free-standing fixtures of stainless steel, a brilliant contemporary statement. The menu, which is brought to your table on a small blackboard, offers such things as carciofi, carpaccio, bocconcini cheese, bistecca

fiorentina and fegato veneziana, all cooked *à point*. The wine-list is big and extravagant, featuring a tignanello and a solaia from Antinori, an ornellaia from Boligheri and a sassicaia from San Guido. They all cost hundreds of dollars, though no vintages are given for any of them. This year it's hard to find anything for less than 50.00 a bottle and there's still no choice of open wines. Console yourself with a glass of Jacopo Poli grappa. It costs at least 20.00 a glass, but it's worth it.
Open Monday to Friday noon to 2 pm, 5.30 pm to 10.30 pm, Saturday 5.30 pm to 10.30 pm. Closed on Sunday. Licensed. Amex, Master Card, Visa. No smoking.

MONTREAL **MAP 135**
L'ENTRECOTE ☞
2022 rue Peel **$65**
(514) 281-6492

When we started this guide 35 years ago we were looking for good cooking. We didn't care very much for atmosphere or even service. We're still looking for good cooking, though maybe other things matter more than they used to. At the Entrecôte on Peel good cooking is about all they have to offer. There's no choice. For 22.40 they give you soup and a salad (both excellent, the salad made with Boston lettuce and walnuts), a strip-loin steak with *sauce maison*, fries and a chocolate profiterole. For 17.70 you can have the same meal without the soup and the profiterole, but that would be a mistake because the profiterole, like the soup, is excellent. It's made with the lightest of pastries, vanilla ice cream and hot, bittersweet chocolate sauce. The steak and the fries are good too. As for the *sauce maison*, it tastes like a *sauce marchand de vin*, with thyme and a little cream thrown in. The long, narrow dining-room is trim and pleasing, with white-paper place-mats over white linen. The service is everything it should be.
Open Monday to Friday 11.30 am to 11 pm, Saturday and Sunday 5 pm to 11 pm. Licensed. All cards. No smoking. ♿

MONTREAL **MAP 135**
GARCON! ☆☆
1112 rue Sherbrooke o **$150**
(514) 843-4000

This is a new restaurant. It's on Sherbrooke Street W at the corner of Peel, not far from the Ritz-Carlton. Inside, it's suave and very well served. The menu is small and the wine-list smaller still. (There are only twelve or fifteen clarets and a similar number of wines from each of Burgundy, Italy and California.) For lunch they offer a soup (asparagus, say), terrine de foie gras with figs, an omelette, croque monsieur, gigot d'agneau, pork belly and a *poisson d'arrivage*. In the evening they add wild salmon, rabbit prepared in three ways and pan-seared Chilean sea-bass in a purée of salsify with oxtail ravioli. Sweets are not a feature. It's the cooking that makes Garçon! what it is. The asparagus soup really tastes of asparagus. The terrine of foie gras is made by its relish of figs and its dressing of hazelnuts. The pork belly is beautifully tender and the Arctic char, served as a *poisson d'arrivage* on a bed of gorgeous fresh vegetables, is a rare delight. Each dish (except the chocolate tart, which is much too dry) is perfect in its own way. Few restaurants venture to travel on the strength of their kitchen alone, but that's exactly what Garçon! is doing.
Open Monday to Friday 11.30 am to 2 pm, 6 pm to 10 pm, Saturday and Sunday 6 pm to 10 pm. Licensed. Amex, Master Card, Visa. No smoking. Book ahead. ♿

MONTREAL **MAP 135**
JOE BEEF ☆
2491 rue Notre-Dame o **$160**
(514) 935-6504

The kitchen at Joe Beef is run by David McMillan, who came here from a string of up-market restaurants, among them the Globe and Rosalie (see below). "I wanted," he'll tell you, "to have some *integrity* in the kitchen." There's plenty of integrity at Joe Beef, which

is emphatically down-market. The place is named for a man who assumed the sobriquet more than a century ago in Montreal. A working-class hero, his nickname came from his ability to scrounge food for the British troops serving in the Crimean War. He kept wild animals in the basement of his tavern and fed them liquor and table scraps. He was known as a generous man who would search the streets at night and bring derelicts to his tavern for food and shelter. When he died, bears, foxes and wildcats took part in his funeral procession. Today there's an oyster bar at the back of the restaurant, where they shuck oysters by the hundred from all over the Atlantic and the Pacific, and even from as far away as County Galway. (David McMillan looks with pleasure at the oyster shells that litter the sidewalk. "I like to see that," he smiles. Inside, there's no menu, only a big blackboard listing the food and drink available that day. As well as oysters, there's usually a terrine, a salad, tartar de boeuf and hot soup. Next comes spaghetti, say, with serrano ham (they carve a whole ham from a rack), gigot d'agneau, beefsteak and perhaps something like sea-bass stuffed with spinach. Everything is simple and down-to-earth. Helpings are big. The restaurant is very small and every seat is occupied until they close late at night. Don't try to get in without a reservation.
Open Tuesday to Saturday 6 pm to 10 pm. Closed on Sunday and Monday. Licensed. Master Card, Visa. No smoking. You must book ahead. ♿

MONTREAL **MAP 135**
LALOUX ☆☆
250 avenue des Pins e **$115**
(514) 287-9127

André Besson has run an impressive kitchen at Laloux for many years, but last year he turned a corner. His cooking now is delicate, imaginative and at times dazzling. The setting, with its dark colours and mirrored recesses, is delightful. The service is everything it should be. And the prices, if you stick to the table d'hôte, are

very modest. Meals begin with an *amuse bouche* of pâté maison and a beautiful purée of vegetables. The list of main courses, which governs the price of the meal, is relatively small. There's turbot, salmon (with red-wine butter), Chilean sea-bass (with mango and mint) and, best of all, pan-fried sweetbreads with truffles and port wine. The sweetbreads are made the old-fashioned way and are never too rich. Crème caramel comes with the meal, but if you're willing to pay for it there's a splendid cheese-tray featuring cheeses from the Magdalen Islands. The wine-list is strong on whites from the Loire and reds from Burgundy, and everything is priced to sell. There's a first-class vouvray, for instance, from Clos Baudoin (François Chidaine, 2002) for only 65.00.
Open Monday to Friday noon to 2.30 pm, 5.30 pm to 10.30 pm, Saturday and Sunday 5.30 pm to 10.30 pm. Licensed. All cards. No smoking. ♿

MONTREAL **MAP 135**
LEMEAC ☆
1045 avenue Laurier o **$105**
(514) 270-0999

Lemeac may be open most of the day, but you should be sure to book a table if you intend to come between noon and 3 pm, when it's always full, big though it is. The place may be noisy—the floors are of crushed marble, the walls almost all of plate-glass, but the menu is large and accessible, the prices fair. Lunch might begin with a brandade of cod or carpaccio of beef and go on to leg of lamb with cumin or sweetbreads with wild cherries. On the à la carte you can still get the lovely Icelandic cod with fennel, as well as salmon tartar, blood pudding, braised beef with barley and calf's liver. After 10 pm they'll bring you squash soup, snails and homemade pork rillettes for 20.00. There are too many chocolate sweets, but the lemon-curd tart is wonderful. Teas are a specialty of the house.
Open Monday to Wednesday 11.45 am to midnight, Thursday to Saturday 11.45 am to 1 am (brunch 11.45 am to

3.30 pm), Sunday 11.45 am to midnight (brunch 11.45 am to 3.30 pm). Licensed. Amex, Master Card, Visa. No smoking. ♿

MONTREAL **MAP 135**

MILOS

5357 avenue du Parc **$175**

(514) 272-3522

Milos was redecorated last year and it's gorgeous. In front of the open kitchen there's now a wall of frozen snow. Fish are buried in the snow, kept fresh by jets of water sprayed from the ceiling overhead. The service is superb and all the fish, much of it from the Mediterranean, is superbly fresh. For starters there are squid, shrimp and stone crab (from Florida and 85.00 a pound). Then come blue-fin tuna, wild salmon from Alaska, barbouni from Greece, pompano from Florida and lobster from Nova Scotia. There's a fillet every day at noon (Arctic char, perhaps) and it's often the best and always the cheapest thing on the menu. Otherwise, everything is sold by the pound, which may be enough for two or even three people. All this is delightful, but too often the fish is overcooked and the vegetables are invariably served hot raw. The wine-list, like the fish, is expensive but there are many lovely things to be had, among them a Beaune premier-cru, an Antinori tignanello and a Liberty School and an Opus One from California. If you're looking for an open wine, there's a beautiful chianti classico riserva ducali for 13.00 a glass. And if you're looking for a pound or so of barbouni from the Aegean, there's nowhere else in Montreal where you can get it.

Open Monday to Friday noon to 3 pm, 5.30 pm to 11 pm, Saturday and Sunday 5.30 pm to 11 pm. Licensed. All cards. No smoking. Book ahead. ♿

Every restaurant in this guide has been personally tested. Our reporters are not allowed to identify themselves or to accept free meals.

MONTREAL **MAP 135**
AU PIED DE COCHON ☆
536 rue Duluth e **$105**
(514) 281-1114

The Pied de Cochon is on rue Duluth just west of St.-Hubert. It occupies a long, narrow room with a mirror along one wall and a bar and open kitchen on the other. It's always crowded and you need to book a table before you come. The waiters wear old jeans and the prices are very low—except for the wine. They like to serve things like fish and chips, steaks with fries, boudin noir, brandade de morue and jarret d'agneau. But a meal here is full of surprises. One is the foie gras, served in a terrine, with a poutine and (believe it or not) with chocolate. Another is the venison, which is served in a variety of ways: tartar, langue with tarragon and rognons à la moutarde—the kitchen is rather too fond of mustard. The tongue of venison—a startling, marvellous dish—is another surprise. Still another is the lemon tart, topped with hot meringue. In fact, the pastry is all remarkably delicate. As for the wine-list, that too is not what you'd expect. The wines of France rise all too quickly to a Lafite and a Mouton Rothschild, the wines of Italy to several tignanellos, solaias and sassicaias. There's almost nothing for less than 50.00 a bottle and there are no good buys. Note: don't order the pied de cochon unless you're absolutely sure of what you're doing.
Open Tuesday to Sunday 5 pm to midnight. Closed on Monday. Licensed. Amex, Master Card, Visa. No smoking. ♿

MONTREAL **MAP 135**
ROSALIE
1232 rue de la Montagne **$125**
(514) 392-1970

Rosalie was designed by David McMillan and, like the Globe on St.-Laurent, it's packed every night of the week. Like the Globe, Rosalie is pure David McMillan—though in fact he no longer works there. The food is simple and inexpensive. Everything is cooked with a casual flip of the pan—and it's good. The squid with sea-salt, for instance, is tender and full of flavour. The salmon tartar with avocado is lovely and comes with fine fresh greens. The seared tuna with noodles is almost as good, though it's more expensive. After that you can go on to steak tartar with fries or braised lamb shanks, both of which might well have come straight from the Globe. The same is true of the plain, earthy hanger steak and the calf's liver with onions. There are only five or six wines by the glass and you're encouraged to order a bottle. There's an expansive list of reds, all priced to sell, even the tignanello and the brunello di Montalcino. There's just one real drawback to Rosalie and that's the thunderous soundtrack. The volume rises as the evening progresses and unless you come before 6 pm you need to bring a pair of industrial ear-muffs. This is no joke. *Open Monday to Wednesday noon to 3 pm, 5 pm to 11 pm, Thursday to Saturday noon to 3 pm, 5 pm to midnight, Sunday noon to 3 pm, 5 pm to 11 pm. Licensed. Amex, Master Card, Visa. No smoking. Valet parking.* ♿

MONTREAL **MAP 135**
TOQUE! ☆☆☆
900 place Jean-Paul-Riopelle **$195**
(514) 499-2084

Toqué was born ten or so years ago in a small *boîte* on St.-Denis, painted in brilliant colours inside, with a bright-yellow sunburst on the door outside. Two years ago, they moved to a new location on the place Jean-Paul-Riopelle, where they occupy the ground floor of a brand-new glass-and-steel high-rise. But if the atmosphere of the new restaurant is cold, the cooking is as hot, passionate and provocative as ever. Everything starts, as it should, with the people from whom they buy their foie gras, their glasswort, their young lamb, their herbs and their vegetables—Fumoir Charlevoix, Fromentier, Pec Nord and Champignons Abitibi,

among others. They still offer their menu *surprise*, six courses for 80.00 (with wine, 125.00). They also offer a *soigné* lunch every day from Tuesday to Friday, something they never ventured to do before they moved into the old town. For what passes these days for a song, you can have a magical salad of yellow and candy-striped beets with goat-cheese or sweetbreads with red peppers, cipollini onions and shitake mushrooms. (The shoulder of lamb that comes next shows how to make a silk purse out of a sow's ear.) But the name of the game is still dinner. Dinner begins with the same sweetbreads as at lunch (at the same price) and goes on to Bas du Fleuve lamb with a purée of beets and cauliflower or roasted red snapper with raspberry vinegar, day-lily buds and maitake mushrooms. For 12.00 you can end the meal with a warm molten-chocolate cake with spices and berries in a reduction of red wine. The wine-list is still at its best with white burgundies and cabernet sauvignons from California. A stronger list of clarets would restore the balance.
Open Tuesday to Friday 11.30 am to 2 pm, 5.30 pm to 10.30 pm, Saturday 5.30 pm to 10.30 pm. Closed on Sunday and Monday. Licensed. Amex, Master Card, Visa. No smoking. Book ahead. ♿

MONTREAL **MAP 135**
AU TOURNANT DE LA RIVIERE ☆☆
5070 rue Salaberry **$180**
Carignan
(450) 658-7372

People like to say that Jacques Robert is no longer *au courant*. His meals are certainly expensive and his restaurant is certainly out of the way. In fact, it's almost impossible to find unless you have a copy of *Where to Eat in Canada* in your glove-compartment. But there's no doubt that the man can cook and, in fact, was making perfect pastries and delicate sauces long before many of today's super-chefs were born. His creations may sometimes be understated, but every ingredient he uses is the best that money can buy. When you arrive, you have the choice of the *menu de dégustation* at 75.00 and a menu *du jour* that costs between 48.00 and 60.00. The first offers a cheese course as well as the sweet of the day. The second offers a wide choice of the sweets that show the kitchen at its best: tarte fine with apples and honey, chocolate soufflé and a terrine glacé with almonds and pecans. There are six appetizers on the table d'hôte, including fish soup (notice the character and quality of the stock), endive salad with apples, nuts and smoked salmon, pot-au-feu of sweetbreads, brochette of scallops with prosciutto and ravioli stuffed with shitake mushrooms, truffles and white cheese. The main dish may be a straightforward maigret de canard with a charlotte of eggplant, a fillet of pork with a fruit chutney or a leg, rack and shoulder of lamb in a purée of olives with basil. The lamb is always remarkable. As for the wine-list, it's as impressive as ever. The service is impeccable, the seating luxurious. To get here, take Exit 22 from Highway 10 and turn almost immediately right (as if for Sherbrooke), then left on boulevard Brunelle. Jacques Robert's farmhouse stands at the corner of rue Salaberry two miles farther on.

Open Wednesday to Saturday 6.30 pm to 9 pm, Sunday 11 am to 2 pm (brunch). Closed on Monday and Tuesday. Licensed. Master Card, Visa. Book ahead. ♿

MONTREAL **MAP 135**

VERSES

Hôtel Nelligan **$120**

100 rue St.-Paul o

(514) 788-4000

The Hôtel Nelligan is one of the new generation of small, intimate hotels that have sprung up in recent years in Old Montreal. It has a comfortable bar and dining-room and it's only a step or two away from the Place d'Armes. Yann Turcotte's menu is small and conservative. He begins with such things as raw salmon with tobiko and olive-oil, asparagus wrapped in prosciutto

and foie gras with tomato jam and goes on to confit de canard with navy beans, wild salmon with a purée of leeks and vegetable couscous, fillet of beef with mashed potatoes and, most interesting of all, tuna rubbed with togarashi and served in yuzu vinaigrette. All of these, except perhaps the tuna, you've seen before, often before, but they're all perfectly prepared. The presentation is restrained, the service dignified. There's at least one beautiful sweet—the molten-chocolate cake is worth the price of the meal. The wine-list is mainly French and Italian and offers a number of premier-cru and grand-cru bottlings for less than 75.00.
Open daily 11.30 am to 3 pm, 5.30 pm to 10.30 pm. Licensed. Amex, Master Card, Visa. No smoking.

MONTREAL
See also ST.-ANDRE D'ARGENTEUIL.

MORRISTON, Ontario **(MAP 85)**
ENVER'S
Highway 6 **$125**
(519) 821-2852

Morriston is a straggle of houses at the junction of Highways 6 and 7, an hour west of Toronto by the 401. Enver's occupies an old brick building with gothic windows facing Highway 6. For years Enver Bismallah ran a charming restaurant on this site. His menu wasn't large, but it was notable for the quality of its ingredients and for dishes like the six-cheese soufflé and the soda bread. Enver sold out a few years ago. The new owners have expanded the wine-list to include 98 V.Q.A. vintages, many of them from little-known vineyards. Their menu is eclectic and features such things as duck-liver pâté, Italian sausage with penne and roasted leg of caribou, as well as a growing number of Thai dishes. There's Thai-style crab tian with avocado and dried pineapple, tea-smoked Muscovy duck with ginger, pepper-crusted ribeye of bison and curried game hen. They make all their own sweets, some of which (roasted

banana, praline crème brûlée and white-chocolate tart) have been on the list for years. There's now an impressive selection of dessert wines and ports, including a late-harvest gewurztraminer from Malivoire. The service could be improved.
Open Tuesday 5 pm to 9 pm, Wednesday to Friday 11.30 am to 2.30 pm, 5 pm to 9 pm, Saturday 5 pm to 9 pm. Closed on Sunday and Monday. Licensed. Amex, Master Card, Visa.

NANAIMO, B.C. **MAP 137**
GLOW ☆☆
7 Victoria Road **$110**
(250) 741-8858

This old firehall looks pretty unsightly from the street. Once inside, however, everything falls into place: the high ceiling, panelled in dark wood, the glitzy artwork, the dramatic lighting, even the service, which is friendly and attractive. The menu, which lists about 25 tapas dishes, is full of good things: Navajo fried bread, fried goat-cheese with organic greens, crab-cakes with chipotle mayonnaise, tamarind-glazed pork ribs, soft-shell crab, foie gras with grilled peaches, pan-seared Ahi tuna, halibut with miso and sake vinaigrette, poached lobster tail with a lemon-anise flan, seared scallops and prawns with tempura leeks. Luke Griffin's cooking is magical—light and exciting. Bottled wines, mostly from the Pacific Northwest, are listed according to price—from 30.00 to 60.00—and there are several interesting open wines, among them a lovely pinot noir from Saturna Island. Glow is probably our most important find of this year or last.
Open Monday to Friday 11 am to 2 pm, 5 pm to 10 pm, Saturday 5 pm to 11 pm, Sunday 10.30 am to 2.30 pm (brunch), 5 pm to 10 pm. Licensed. Amex, Master Card, Visa. No smoking. ♿

Our web site is at www.oberonpress.ca Readers wishing to use e-mail should address us at oberon@sympatico.ca

NANAIMO **MAP 137**

THE WESLEY STREET

321 Wesley Street **$115**

(250) 753-8057

We've been talking up the Wesley Street for at least twelve years. In that time owners have come and gone, and chefs too, but the quality of the cooking never seems to suffer. Daniel Caron, the present chef, is as good as any. He makes the most of fresh local ingredients, using them in creative ways and presenting them on plates selected to highlight the colour and texture of each dish. He likes slow cooking, which he uses not only for stews and ragoûts but also for rich, zesty soups, bisques and chowders. He gets in organic chicken and pork from the Sloping Hill Farm outside Nanaimo and his pork chops, pocketed and stuffed with apples, figs and pine-nuts, are a popular fixture on the menu. There's also Cowichan Valley duck, wild salmon and venison with a variety of lemon chutneys, wild-berry glazes and piquant vinaigrettes. The sweet list is small but serviceable. There's an impeccable crème brûlée, a delectable flourless-chocolate cake and the tartest of lemon pies. The wine-list offers a good selection of Italian reds, as well as a useful selection of reds and from Vancouver Island and the Okanagan. The setting is relaxed, the service informal. *Open Monday to Friday 11 am to 2.30 pm, 5.30 pm to 9 pm, Saturday noon to 2.30 pm, 5.30 pm to 9 pm, Sunday noon to 2.30 pm from 15 May until 15 October, Monday to Friday 11 am to 2.30 pm, 5.30 pm to 9 pm, Saturday noon to 2.30 pm, 5.30 pm to 9 pm from 16 October until 14 May. Closed on Sunday in winter. Licensed. Amex, Master Card, Visa. No smoking.*

NANAIMO

See also CEDAR.

This is a guide to Canadian restaurants from coast to coast—the first ever published and the only one of its kind on the market today

NAUFRAGE, P.E.I. **(MAP 43)**
SHIPWRECK POINT ☞
Highway 16 **$50**
(902) 687-1293

Naufrage is a small fishing-village eight or nine miles east of St. Peters. Five years ago a group of local women opened this charming café. It's small and bright, with white-lace curtains and a long view across the green meadows toward the harbour, the sandy beach and the Gulf of St. Lawrence. It's frequented by ferry passengers on their way to and from the Magdalens, travellers from as far away as Texas, cyclists with expensive touring bikes and local people out for a meal after church or before the Sunday ceilidh in Monticello down the road. They offer sandwiches and burgers, but most people come for the seafood. The seafood chowder is brimming with fish and shellfish and comes with a scone, which on the Island is called a biscuit. There are excellent scallops and clams and all the fish comes in a featherlight batter. The vegetables aren't up to the fish, so you should order a tossed salad instead. Everything is very cheap: the seafood platter at 12.95 is the most expensive thing on the menu. There's a lovely apple pie to end with and it costs just 2.95. In summer, you can take your dinner outside and enjoy the view.
Open daily 11 am to 9 pm from Victoria Day until late September. Licensed for beer and wine only. Visa. No smoking.

NELSON, B.C. **MAP 139**
ALL SEASONS CAFE ☆☆
620 Herridge Lane **$120**
(250) 352-0101

Here in Nelson the All Seasons Café has been making waves for several years. Nelson itself, which has been lovingly restored to the glory of its gold-rush years, makes an ideal base from which to explore the Kootenays. It also has some of the best powder skiing in the country at nearby Whitewater. At the All Seasons, Tracy

Scanlon and Jonathan Langille have a wine-list that has won an Award of Excellence from the *Wine Spectator* for the last three years. Their menu is strongly seasonal and largely organic. They bring in free-range chicken and turkey, fresh lamb and top-quality beef from all over the province and beyond. There are organic greens from Salmo, organic root vegetables from Dalton Farm, Pacific halibut and wild B.C. salmon. The cannelloni, with wine-braised wild game, is made on the premises and so is the bread. One of the most interesting dishes is five-spice confit of duck, another is lamb shanks with cumin, honey and puy lentils, still another pan-seared Pacific halibut on black lentils with Malay coconut curry. There's a particularly good flourless-chocolate torte. The wine-list has now moved far beyond British Columbia, but some of the loveliest things still come from the Okanagan, many of them sold by the glass.
Open daily 5 pm to 10 pm (shorter hours in winter). Licensed. Master Card, Visa. No smoking. ♿

NEW GLASGOW, N.S. **MAP 140**
THE BISTRO ☆
216 Archimedes Street **$100**
(902) 752-4988

Robert Vinton has now outlasted his predecessor at this bright orange-and-blue European-style bistro on Archimedes Street. He offers his customers good food, served in a comfortable, casual setting. His menu is small but attractive, changing every spring and fall. There are always three daily specials—perhaps grilled prawns with pancetta and sage or roast pork glazed with dijon mustard and honey bought from a nearby honey farm. The à la carte begins with clam chowder or chick-pea soup and goes on to pork tenderloin with black mission-fig butter, double-stuffed baked potatoes, szechuan-style green beans and carrots glazed with honey. The most popular entrée is duck lasagne, layered with eggplant, zucchini and goat-cheese., though the seafood pasta (scallops and mussels on penne) is also likely to disap-

pear early in the evening. The sweets seldom change. Most people seem to ask either for the chocolate-chip pecan cheesecake or the lemon crème brûlée. There's an ample wine-cellar that features a reserve list of eight or nine premium wines. For pub food the place to go is the Dock Irish Pub at 130 George Street (telephone (902) 752-0884). It occupies an old stone house by the bridge, built in 1845. It's owned by the same people and everybody goes there for draught beer and live local entertainment.
Open Tuesday to Saturday 5 pm to 10 pm. Closed on Sunday and Monday. Licensed. Amex, Master Card, Visa. No smoking. Book ahead if you can.

NEW GLASGOW **MAP 140**
CAFE ITALIA ☞
62 Provost Street **$35**
(902) 928-2233

Everyone seems to love this small, casual, inexpensive café. It's bright, it's friendly and a big slice of the pizza of the day costs all of 2.74. (If you add a soup or a salad, it'll come to 5.99.) They make all their own thin-crust pizzas, all their own pasta and all their own soups. The sweets run mainly to cheesecakes, but they have an unusual variety of teas and coffees. There aren't many wines, but what do you expect for 35.00 for two? They don't take reservations, so don't come between noon and one o'clock, when half of New Glasgow is looking for a table.
Open Monday to Saturday 7.30 am to 10 pm (later on weekends). Closed on Sunday. Licensed. Master Card, Visa. No smoking. ♿

NEW GLASGOW
See also PICTOU.

The map number assigned to each city, town and village gives the location of the centre on one or more of the maps at the start of the book.

NIAGARA-ON-THE-LAKE, Ontario **MAP 141**
EPICUREAN
84 Queen Street **$40**
(905) 468-3408

The Epicurean is no place for a Festival dinner. But at noon they still operate as an old-style cafeteria, offering salads and sandwiches to all comers. Their Caesar salad is properly made with romaine and homemade croûtons. The sandwiches, especially the seafood-and-avocado and the Cajun-chicken, are better than the quiches and the pies, which are apt to be heavy. If it's on the menu, ask for the raspberry pie with real whipped cream. In good weather you can have your lunch outside on the patio under a spreading butternut tree.
Open daily 9 am to 8 pm from 1 June until 11 November, daily 9 am to 5 pm from 12 November until 31 May. Licensed. Amex, Master Card, Visa. No smoking. ♿

NIAGARA-ON-THE-LAKE **MAP 141**
GIARDINO'S
The Gate House **$150 ($375)**
142 Queen Street
(905) 468-3263

Giardino's is as cool and suave as ever, but it's no longer a really satisfactory place for lunch. At noon the menu is short and simple (and very cheap), and there are only two or three important dishes, among them carpaccio of beef and salmon. In the evening the menu is much more ambitious, starting with things like tartar of tuna with cucumber and apple and pan-seared sea-bass with a julienne of vegetables and going on to homemade gnocchi, provimi-veal liver with caramelized onions and osso buco of lamb in Guinness. They still have a strong list of Tuscan wines and the Gate House is still, we think, the best place to stay in Niagara-on-the-Lake.
Open daily noon to 2.30 pm, 5 pm to 10 pm from mid-May until early January. Licensed. Amex, Master Card, Visa. No smoking. Free parking. ♿

NIAGARA-ON-THE-LAKE **MAP 141**

HILLEBRAND'S VINEYARD ☆☆☆

Highway 55 **$160**

(905) 468-7123

This is now the best place to eat in Niagara-on-the-Lake. It has everything—a lovely setting on the edge of the vineyards, wonderful fresh local produce and magical cooking. Tony De Luca may not do much of the cooking himself these days, but he's responsible for the Cumbrae beef, the bulgur wheat, the hand-picked mushrooms, the pea seedlings and the heirloom tomatoes. Dinner begins rather sumptuously with foie gras and beet risotto or bresaola with black truffles. The Arctic char that follows is organic and served with pickled cauliflower; the scallops are served with bulgur wheat and pea seedlings, the beef with chanterelles. If you want to sample De Luca's cooking at first hand, ask for one of his game dishes. He's the only man in the kitchen who knows how to cut, marinate and lard caribou, bison or red deer, which is brought in from New Zealand, The cheeses that come next are remarkable. They come from as far away as Camrose, the Magdalens and back-country Nova Scotia. The fact is that De Luca owes his third star to the rare and precious Dragon's Teeth that he imports from Nova Scotia and serves with local fruit for 15.00. As for the wines, they're all grown right here. There are thirteen chardonnays, four Trius reds and three Trius grand reds, rising to 100.00 a bottle for the 1998 vintage. The restaurant is only a few minutes west of town and within easy reach of the Festival Theatre. You must go.

Open daily 11.30 am to 2.30 pm, 5 pm to 9 pm (shorter hours in winter). Licensed. Amex, Master Card, Visa. No smoking. Free parking. ♿

☞ This symbol means that the restaurant is rated a good buy. This ♿ means that there is wheelchair access to both the tables and the washrooms. *Smoking only* means that the restaurant has no area for non-smokers.

NIAGARA-ON-THE-LAKE **MAP 141**
PELLER ESTATES WINERY
290 John Street E **$140**
(905) 468-4678

The dining-room at Peller is spacious and very grand—too grand, in fact, for its own good. The work of the kitchen is dwarfed by the architecture, the menu and the cooking both diminished by the pretensions of the building. The menu is in fact rather small. You begin with cold pea soup, robbed of its flavour by an excess of olive oil and served insufficiently chilled, or with foie gras with sour cherries (better at twice the price). Next comes wild salmon with horseradish, shallots and grape tomatoes, striped bass and diver scallops with chanterelle ravioli and Ontario lamb shanks. Ontario lamb is a virtue, but it's demanding and these lamb shanks are far too dry. As for the granita offered between courses, it has no virtues at all. The wine-list, however, is a delight. It may be small, but almost everything is sold by the glass as well as the bottle, which means that you can drink an expensive wine—a signature series chardonnay, perhaps, or one of the icewines—at a price you can afford.
Open daily noon to 2.30 pm, 5.30 pm to 9 pm (shorter hours in winter). Licensed. Amex, Master Card, Visa. No smoking. Free parking. ♿

NIAGARA-ON-THE-LAKE **MAP 141**
QUEEN'S LANDING
155 Byron Street **$175**
(905) 468-2195

Stephen Treadwell is still in charge of the kitchen at Queen's Landing, where the cooking has always been rather inconsistent. The yellow-pepper bisque and the ravioli of crab and morels are both less than likeable. The pan-seared fillet of salmon, on the other hand, is outstanding. No farm-fresh Atlantic salmon for Treadwell; his salmon is wild Pacific sockeye and it comes

with perfect taste and texture. The pork chop is good too, though garnished with bacon, which goes better with calf's liver than with a pork chop. At Queen's Landing they spend their money on the service, which is everything it should be—fast and very friendly. This makes the pan-seared foie gras de canard with preserved rhubarb, and even the poached Arctic char with lobster mash, seem more attractive than they would in a less efficient dining-room. The wine-list majors, as it should, in wines from the Niagara Region. Better still, all the open wines are V.Q.A. and rise to a lovely chardonnay from Lailey for 11.50 a glass.
Open daily 11 am to 1.30 pm, 5 pm to 9 pm (shorter hours in winter). Licensed. Amex, Master Card, Visa. No smoking. Free parking. ♿

NIAGARA-ON-THE-LAKE
See also WELLAND.

NOBLETON, Ontario **(MAP 223)**
DANIEL'S ☆
12926 Highway 27 **$95**
(905) 859-0060

If you come to Daniel's from Susur or Thuet in downtown Toronto expecting plain country cooking, forget it. This little restaurant in a village near King is good. Now in his twenty-fifth year on this site, Daniel Gilbert just keeps on getting better and better. He opened the place as a young man fresh out of cooking-school. He's not a young man any more and he looks tired, but his cooking doesn't show it. He offers several of his old standbys because he needs to earn a living, but you can ignore the bruschetta, the Caesar salad and the French onion soup. You'll find that smoked Pacific salmon comes to the table in a charming presentation, with red onion and celery root. Daniel is tired of the traditional squash soup and prepares his own version with roasted garlic and maple syrup. He serves his curried lamb on basmati rice with delightful homemade chutney, his roast pork with applesauce made from wild apples; his haddock Cajun-style, his osso buco with saffron. The wine-list offers selections, most of them familiar, from the Old World and the New, all priced to sell. For that matter, everything at Daniel's is cheap. But he needs better coffee.

Open Monday to Friday noon to 2.30 pm, 5 pm to 9 pm, Saturday and Sunday 5 pm to 9.30 pm. Licensed. Amex, Master Card, Visa. ♿

NORANDA, Quebec
See ROUYN.

NORTH BAY, Ontario **MAP 143**
CHURCHILL'S PRIME RIB ☆☆
631 Lakeshore Drive **$160**
(705) 476-7777

Upstairs at Churchill's there's a bar where you can get a prime-rib sandwich or a Black Angus burger with a glass or two of wine at a moderate price. Downstairs prices are much higher, but you know that they cut and age their own striploin and age their own prime rib of beef. They buy fresh rack of lamb from New Zealand and roast it with green herbs. Tenderloin of veal is crowned with crab and cream cheese and served with tarragon and cream sauce. They use a lot of cream here and they cook rich. If you want something lighter, ask for some fish. All the fish is fresh as a matter of course. When they could no longer get the pickerel from Lake Nipissing that made them famous, they started importing it fresh from elsewhere. Their salmon is all wild, imported from Scotland and served on a bed of leek-and-spinach risotto in citrus brown butter. Squid has lately become a signature dish, served Cajun-style with beans and barley. Scallops are served in a trio—pan-fried with leeks, spinach and Swiss cheese, in a chipotle sauce with pink grapefruit and cold ceviche-style. The chicken is all free-range, the greens organic. The bread is all homemade—molasses-and-raisin, sundried-

tomato, focaccia and Sardinian flatbread. The wine-list is constantly expanding and now includes at least 50 single malts.
Open Monday to Friday 11 am to 11 pm, Saturday 4 pm to 11 pm, Sunday 4 pm to 10 pm. Licensed. Amex, Master Card, Visa. No smoking. ♿

NORTH HATLEY, Quebec **MAP 144**
AUBERGE HATLEY ☆☆☆
325 chemin Virgin **$200 ($400)**
(819) 842-2451

The Auberge Hatley may change hands, or it may even become a Relais & Château, but Alain Labrie is always the man behind the scenes. His belief in discipline and detail permeates everything. Fifteen years ago we called his style simple and down-to-earth; now we call it classical. At times we felt that he was repeating himself, but there's a time for experiment and a time for execution. His prices are high, but he's always had a table d'hôte, now priced at 58.00 for three courses and coffee. It's a refuge from the high prices on the à la carte, and it offers many of the specialties of the house, like the pan-seared foie gras with cèpes, braised celery-root and smoked-duck chips. On the table d'hôte you can begin quite comfortably with pan-seared scallops in a white-bean purée or with the sweetbreads in sherry vinegar. There's always fish, lamb from the Eastern Townships and local duck with foie gras and dried figs. The sweets are masterly. There's caramel, grand-marnier and chocolate crème brûlée with poire William. There's a trio of valhrona chocolate grand crus. There's a chestnut soufflé. There's a pear tarte tatin. The presentation is always spectacular. As for the wine-list, it's beyond belief: countless California chardonnays and cabernet sauvignons, white burgundies, Lafites and Mouton Rothschilds. Prices are high, of course. That goes without saying.
Open daily noon to 2 pm, 6 pm to 9 pm from 15 May until 31 October, daily 6 pm to 9 pm from 1 November until 14 May. Licensed. Amex, Master Card, Visa. No smoking. ♿

NORTH RIVER, N.S. **MAP 145**

CHANTERELLE COUNTRY INN

Cabot Trail **$110 ($225)**

(902) 929-2263

The Chanterelle Inn is a stylish, purpose-built clapboard building standing high on a hill overlooking St. Ann's Bay at North River. It has nine elegant bedrooms, all fitted up with organically-washed sheets, fragrance-free soaps and Oriental rugs made with vegetable dyes. (One room has no rug at all, which is ideal for anyone who, because of their allergies, prefers bare floors.) In the dining-room, at least 80% of the food is organic. Fish comes in from local fishermen, meats from an organic farm now in its seventh generation. The cooking is austere. Meals begin with mushroom or fiddlehead soup—the mushrooms and fiddleheads all picked on the property—and go on to a garden salad with organic steak (on Mondays), rainbow trout (on Tuesdays), sautéed scallops (on Wednesdays) and so on. There are always one or two vegetarian dishes—quiche, eggplant parmesan or linguine with mushrooms. Most of the wines come from the New World, the best of them from Banrock Station (a chardonnay priced at 29.00, a shiraz at 30.00). The house wines are from Jost and neither the chardonnay nor the cabernet sauvignon is the best that Jost has to offer.

Open daily 5.30 pm to 9.30 pm from Victoria Day until Thanksgiving. Open in winter by appointment only. Master Card, Visa. Licensed. No smoking. ♿

NORTH RUSTICO, P.E.I. ***(MAP 43)***

BLUE MUSSEL CAFE

(902) 963-2152 ***$40***

This is an attractive little café at the end of the boardwalk, with an outside deck overlooking Rustico Bay. They serve all kinds of fish and shellfish and a variety of salads. Everything is simply prepared, everything tastes good and everything is cheap. They're open all day every day in season, have a licence and take Master Card and Visa.

OAKVILLE, Ontario **(MAP 223)**
PATISSERIE D'OR ☞
301 Robinson Street **$25**
(905) 815-8999

Jean-Luc and Monica Soulabaille come from France, where they both learned their trade as *pâtissiers*. After they came to Canada they worked in the kitchens of the Four Seasons before opening their own café here in Oakville four years ago. At the Pâtisserie d'Or, a stone's throw from the intersection of Trafalgar Road and the Lakeshore, Jean-Luc is in charge of the kitchen while Monica manages the front of the house with flair and charm. If you come early you may be able to get a quiche—the quiches are famous all over the city—but if you're late you may have to settle for a turnover stuffed with ground beef and sautéed onions. It's really no hardship, because what you come for are the pastries. Jean-Luc is a master *pâtissier*, turning out lemon tarts, gâteaux St.-Honoré, millefeuilles and madeleines by the dozen. His most remarkable creation is his buttercream-chocolate cake. It's covered in frills, bows, ribbons and flowers, all made of white chocolate. We once saw a young family take a whole cake to their table (it costs 24.00) and demolish it in five minutes. He also makes an astonishing array of ice creams—black currant, green apple, caramel, lemon, chocolate, vanilla and strawberry. The coffee is good too, but there's no liquor.
Open Wednesday to Friday 8 am to 5.30 pm, Saturday 8 am to 6 pm, Sunday 8 am to 4 pm. Closed on Monday and Tuesday. No liquor. Visa. No smoking.

OLIVER, B.C. **(MAP 160)**
SONORA ROOM ☆
Burrowing Owl Estate Winery **$140**
100 Burrowing Owl Place
(877) 498-0620

Who would miss the chance of working their way through one of the most fascinating wine-lists in the

Okanagan, even if it meant eating hot-dogs in a shack? Actually, in the Sonora Room you don't have to eat a hot-dog and the place is no shack. Sonora was built in the southwestern style and it was designed by a local architect. The building opens into a grand hall and outside there's a terrace from which in fine weather you can see across the valley to Osoyoos. Dominique Couton comes from France and his menu is Mediterranean with hints of the West Coast. It is, of course, designed to match a wine-list that changes every week, offering as it does new releases and rare library wines. To start, he might have a scallop ravioli with lemon grass or a trio of Pacific salmon. After that he might offer beef tenderloin with cabernet sauvignon, rack of spring lamb with green-tea jus or a seafood cioppino of scallops, sea-bass, shrimps, mussels and salmon. He might then suggest a dessert of bittersweet Belgian-chocolate velvet or a zesty lemon mousse-cake with cocoa craquelin. Later this year they plan to add a swimming-pool, a spa and several guest bedrooms.

Open Monday and Tuesday noon to 3 pm, Wednesday to Sunday noon to 3 pm, 6 pm to 10 pm from 15 June until Labour Day. Licensed. Master Card, Visa. No smoking. ♿

ORILLIA, Ontario **MAP 149**

WEBERS ☞
Highway 11 N **$20**
(705) 325-3696

Mike McParland, the senior chef at Webers (also called the Key Man) came to work here when he was sixteen, in 1963. The job helped put him through university. After he graduated he became an elementary-school teacher in the winter, but stayed at Webers in the summer. He can flip up to 55 burgers at a time, which makes him the fastest in the business. He lives on his teacher's pension and works for Webers because he likes it. Webers' beef is all processed in two railway cars parked right on the site. The meat is pasteurized by exposing it to a steam-blanket in a pressurized chamber at a tem-

perature of 185°F; it's then stored at 30°F, ground fresh daily and cooked to a temperature of 160°F. Each week in summer, they process and sell more than three tons of ground beef—50 tons every summer. Two or three years ago, they started selling beef patties by the pail, with buns and seasoning, to people on their way to the cottage or on their way back to the city. This year they arranged to sell their burgers in all the Loblaws stores in Ontario, so now you can buy a Weber burger year round. They sell ice cream too, as well as gravy for the french fries, made from potatoes grown, cut and packed near Cavendish in Prince Edward Island. In fine weather you can eat outside at one of the brightly-painted picnic tables and watch your children playing on the Via Rail coaches. There's even a coach, newly renovated, where you can sit inside when it's raining. Teenagers take your order, make change and see that you get what you want within two minutes, no matter how long the lineup may be. On the first Tuesday in August there's free corn for all comers. There's rock music on the soundtrack and free parking for hundreds of cars on both sides of the highway, with an overhead bridge that connects the southbound lot to the restaurant.
Open daily 10.30 am to 7 pm from 11 until 20 March, Friday to Sunday 10.30 am to 7 pm from 25 March until 17 April, daily 10.30 am to 7 pm (later on weekends) from 18 April until 26 May, daily 10.30 am to 9 pm from 27 May until 23 June, daily 10.30 am to 10 pm from 24 June until 5 September, daily 10.30 am to 7 pm from 6 September until 10 October, Friday to Sunday 10.30 am to 7 pm from 14 October until 13 November. No liquor, no cards. ♿

OSHAWA, Ontario **MAP 150**
GALLERY CAFE ☆
Robert McLaughlin Art Gallery **$110**
72 Queen Street
(905) 576-2392

The Gallery Café doesn't seem to have a worry in the world, regardless of the weakness of General Motors

stock. Last year they opened another restaurant, Bistro 238 at 1413 King Street E (telephone (905) 576-4688), barely ten minutes away from the Art Gallery, where at noon they serve imaginative sandwiches on focaccia bread and some unusual pastas. In the evening the cooking at the Gallery is far more ambitious. You can start your dinner with mixed greens and caramelized pecans in peach vinaigrette or dungeness crab with artichokes and go on to a fresh seafood strudel with a fricassee of spinach and roasted peppers, pan-seared scallops in lentil-and-spinach curry or pork loin glazed with brown sugar and served with a potato-and-apple galette. The greens are all impeccable and the vegetables nicely varied. Aside from the cheese-plate (which costs only 6.35), the best of the sweets is the vanilla bread-and-butter pudding with rum and raisins. Prices are amazingly low. Where else would you expect a rack of lamb to cost just 24.95? Wines are few and far between, but there are one or two attractive reds. If you're tired of Wolf Blass, ask for a bottle of Beringer stone cellars cabernet sauvignon It costs only 34.95.
Open Monday to Wednesday 11.30 am to 3 pm, Thursday to Saturday 11.30 am to 3 pm, 5.30 pm to 10 pm. Closed on Sunday. Licensed. Master Card, Visa. No smoking.

OTTAWA, Ontario **MAP 151**
BECKTA ☆☆
226 Nepean Street **$175**
(613) 238-7063

Stephen Beckta's kitchen is still capable of brilliant cooking—the tuna tataki, for instance, the tartar of beef (which they call carpaccio), the beet salad with cheese from the Charlevoix and apple-beet paint. But they make mistakes. The pig-cheek ravioli with local goat-cheese, glazed figs and pine-nuts is tough, in spite of the many pleasures it promises, and once the cannelloni comes to the table you realize that Stephen Vardy has no idea at all of how to make pasta. Pasta, of course, is not the whole story. There's the duck consommé, which is delicate and persuasive There's the first-class sushi (a different selection every day). There's the pan-roasted steelhead trout in an emulsion of truffled foie gras. And, perhaps most interesting of all, there's the unusual treatment of sweetbreads with charred apple, cinnamon spaetzle and tarragon. Beckta's is always at its best with its wines, no doubt because the proprietor cut his teeth as a practising *sommelier.* The wine-list is strong on chardonnays from Niagara and cabernets from California, Australia and France. Malivoire dominates the Canadian selection again this year, as perhaps it should. There's a melon at 42.00, a gewurztraminer at 43.00 and a chardonnay at 75.00, and they all provide very good drinking. The coffee is good too, and the service is extremely elegant.

Open daily 5.30 pm to 9.30 pm. Licensed. Amex, Master Card, Visa. No smoking. Book ahead. ♿

OTTAWA **MAP 151**
THE BLACK CAT ☆☆
93 Murray Street **$130**
(613) 241-2999

Richard Urquhart plays the Black Cat the way Itzhak Perlman plays the violin. The restaurant is small and intimate., and with either Richard or his young son, Rémy, one feels at home. No other restaurant in the city gives you quite this feeling. This is what you come back for, week in, week out. Of course, René Rodriguez (who came here from Arc and Select) does interesting, at times brilliant, things in the kitchen. He changes his menu several times a year, but at the moment dinner begins with an aromatic carrot soup, grilled sea scallops with spiced apricots and preserved lemon or seared tuna with sweet red peppers and black-olive purée. Preserved lemon shows up again with the fillet of salmon, but the striped bass with coriander-spiced dates and apple-and-coconut purée is even better. The rack of lamb is the only expensive dish on the menu. It's marinated in olive-oil and citrus peels and garnished with quince marmalade and sea-salt. Imported cheeses now turn up alongside the dark-chocolate torte and the hand-rolled chocolate truffles. There's roquefort, triple-cream brie and five-year-old cheddar, but so far none of the local raw-milk cheeses. Last winter they began putting on four-course tasting menus about once a month. They're quite expensive at 59.00 (with wine 90.00) plus tip and taxes, but they're in great demand and you have to book a table. The wine-list changes all the time, but it's always full of excitement. The coffee is great.

Open Monday 5.30 pm to 9 pm, Tuesday to Saturday 5.30 pm to 10 pm, Sunday 5.30 pm to 9 pm. Licensed. Amex, Master Card, Visa. No smoking (even on the patio). ♿

OTTAWA **MAP 151**

DOMUS ☆

87 Murray Street **$135**

(613) 241-6007

Domus has come into its own once again. John Dawson Taylor has given up his flirtation with the Métropolitain and returned to his roots—and they show it. His menus remain much the same as before. Dinners begin with soup, which changes daily, a green salad with bocconcini cheese, candied hazelnuts and graine de moutarde or pan-roasted foie gras with apple cider and fleur de sel. A *poisson du marché* follows, along with wild Arctic char, grain-fed chicken, loin of pork with root vegetables and gorgonzola, breast of duck with cranberry chutney and Alberta beef. Lunch is equally ambitious. Organic-squash soup is followed by smoked trout with brown sugar, a tart of eggplant and serrano ham, a frittata of homemade sausage and aged Balderson cheese and a fresh local fish. Domus may be using much the same menus as it always has, but the execution is now faultless, occasionally brilliant, something it hasn't always been in recent years. Last fall, Taylor was preparing pickerel with Swiss chard and roast potatoes—Taylor has a weakness for potatoes, but this treatment was

superb. His wine-list has always been outstanding and it still is. It features V.Q.A. wines from the Niagara Region, as well as one or two from Prince Edward County. The Peninsula Ridge chardonnay and the Angel's Gate cabernet merlot are particularly good buys at less than 40.00 a bottle. Both are offered also by the glass for less than 10.00.
Open Monday to Wednesday 11.30 am to 2 pm, 6 pm to 9 pm, Thursday to Saturday 11.30 am to 2 pm, 5.30 pm to 9.30 pm, Sunday 11.30 am to 2.30 pm (brunch). Licensed. Amex, Master Card, Visa. No smoking. ♿

OTTAWA **MAP 151**
E18HTEEN ☆☆
18 York Street **$145**
(613) 244-1188

With every year that passes, E18hteen is becoming less of a nightclub and more of a restaurant. It now has an expansive à la carte and a serious table d'hôte, and Christopher Deraiche is cooking extremely well. His seared scallops with five-spice pork belly and vanilla-bean purée is a masterpiece and so is his striped bass with white-bean purée and shitaki ravioli. His braised lamb shank with garlic mash and glazed turnips is an impressive dish too. The table d'hôte is expensive at 53.00 for four courses, but everything on the menu is individually priced, so you can order something like dark-chocolate espresso cake for just a few dollars. This is a lovely dish that comes to the table with fresh aspberries and marvelous chocolate-marsala ice cream. There are a number of open wines on the wine-list as well as a handful of great clarets by the bottle, but it's usually more fun to order one of the nine flights, each of which offers four ounce-and-a-half glasses for less than 20.00. If you order the table d'hôte, there's an interesting wine service (four glasses for 32.00) that'll bring you such unusual wines as the pinot gris from Mittnacht Klack in Alsace. The coffee is as good as ever.

Open Monday to Friday 11.30 am to 2.30 pm, 5 pm to 11 pm, Saturday 5 pm to 11 pm. Closed on Sunday. Licensed. Amex, Master Card, Visa. No smoking.

OTTAWA **MAP 151**
MAMMA TERESA ☞
300 Somerset Street W **$95**
(613) 236-3023

Mamma Teresa occupies a handsome old house in downtown Ottawa. The restaurant is well served, the menu is comprehensive, the cooking is familiar. All the traditional Italian dishes are here—a dozen veal dishes, seven or eight chicken, as well as fresh salmon, trout and scampi, all served (if you ask) with spinach, potatoes and deep-fried zucchini. (Our favourite is the chicken Mamma, which is flavoured with a simple squeeze of lemon.) All the pasta is made in house, all the sauces are fresh. (Our favourite pasta is the spaghetti carbonara, rich though it may be.) Best of all, everything is sold for bottom dollar. Even the wines are cheap: a bottle of valpolicella Folonari costs only 28.00, the Fontanafredda barbera 36.00, the Stoney Ridge chardonnay 35.00. Only the Fontanafredda barolo is expensive. It costs 65.00, the chianti classico riserva ducale from Ruffino 52.00. If you really want to spend money, you have to go down to the Cantina, where Giuliano Boselli stores his premium wines. Here you'll find a dozen old barolos priced to 450.00 a bottle, half a dozen barbarescos priced to 350.00, two tignanellos (to 275.00), two ornellaias (to 450.00), a sassicaia and a solaia (to 450.00). Most of his vintage wines are Italian (Giuliano himself comes from Parma), but he has at least one great pauillac, a 1983 Mouton Rothschild at 1200.00. Unless you're looking for a super-Tuscan (and maybe even if you are), Mamma's is the best buy in town.
Open Monday to Friday 11 am to 10.30 pm, Saturday 5 pm to 11.30 pm, Sunday 5 pm to 9.30 pm. Licensed. All cards. No smoking. Free parking.

OTTAWA **MAP 151**

PERSPECTIVES ☆☆

Brook Street Hotel **$160**

525 Leggatt Drive

Kanata

(613) 271-3555

Perspectives has a spectacular location in the Brook Street Hotel, which is part of the high-tech high-rise complex just off Highway 417 in Kanata. The dining-room is spacious, serene and very well served. Every evening they offer a three-course table d'hôte—lobster ravioli, sirloin of lamb and chestnut financier—and a five-course blind tasting menu. On the à la carte for much the same money you can get cold-smoked organic salmon, soft-shell crab or Digby scallops with baby spinach and shitake mushrooms in a soya-truffle emulsion, followed by red-curry loin of tuna, rack of lamb with huckleberry toffee, tea-crusted Atlantic salmon in a purée of sunchoke or triple-A rib-eye of beef. The salmon is a beautiful dish, perfectly understated; the ravioli, however, is heavy and should be avoided. The sushi-fusion rolls—tempura of shrimp and avocado in unagi sauce, lobster with toasted pine-nuts, seared foie gras with pink peppercorns and citrus soya—are a feature of the meal and they're all delightful. With a better wine-list, Perspectives would be worth three stars. As things stand, most of the wines are Canadian, with a few cabernets from California and a solaia from Italy. There are no outstanding clarets, though there is a zinfandel from Caymus and, better still, a Milpara Park shiraz. For just 50.00 you can sample a bottle of V.Q.A. wine from the Niagara estate of Mike Weir. We haven't tried it.
Open Monday to Friday 11 am to 2 pm, 6 pm to 10 pm, Saturday 6 pm to 10 pm, Sunday 10 am to 3 pm (brunch). Licensed. Amex, Master Card, Visa. No smoking. Free parking. Book ahead if you can. ♿

Nobody can buy space in this guide and nobody can buy his way out of it.

OTTAWA **MAP 151**
SIGNATURES ☆☆☆
453 Laurier Avenue E **$190**
(613) 236-2499

Signatures is four years old and now seems less like an extravagant curiosity on the Ottawa scene and more like a permanent fixture. Inside, it feels like a gentleman's club. Each of the dining-rooms is impeccably served. Every wine is served in a wine-glass that suits the character of the chosen wine, whether it be a chardonnay, a merlot or a cabernet sauvignon. Bread is passed to each person at the table, and then a basket is brought, full of the breads each person has chosen. Dinner begins with a gorgeous *amuse-bouche*—an enchanting purée of asparagus, perhaps, served in an egg-cup. Next you have the choice of several fixed-price menus, one of them known, rather seductively, as *délices du Canada*. If you prefer to choose your own meal, turn to the à la carte. This is where they have such lovely luxuries as snow crab with parsnips, foie gras with dates and lobster with ratatouille, followed by Atlantic flounder with squash and wild rice, Chilean sea-bass with savoy cabbage and saddle of fresh Alberta lamb with spinach *en branches*. The wine-list is, of course, mainly French, but there's also a generous list of chardonnays and cabernets from Niagara. The Malivoire pinot noir is a particularly good buy at 51.00.
Open Tuesday to Saturday 6 pm to 9 pm. Closed on Sunday and Monday. Licensed. Amex, Master Card, Visa. No smoking. Free parking. Book ahead. ♿

OTTAWA **MAP 151**
THE URBAN PEAR
151 2 Avenue **$135**
(613) 569-9305

The Urban Pear is repeating itself. The setting is as chic and sophisticated as ever, but the menu and the wine-list are small and seldom change. We've seen the pan-

seared scallops with Granny Smith apples too often before and the roasted pork tenderloin with parsnip and Anjou pears is a too-familiar treatment. There are, it's true, some new ideas in the salad of red beets, fresh oranges and toasted organic pumpkinseeds and the pan-seared ocean perch with soba noodles, pickled cabbage and ginger. And there are some interesting buys on the wine-list if you look for them. A bottle of Strewn riesling costs only 29.00, the Southbrook pinot gris only 32.00. Better still, there's a Hernder cabernet sauvignon for 70.00 and a Burrowing Owl merlot for 90.00. If 90.00 seems high for a bottle of Burrowing Owl, think again.
Open Monday to Saturday 11.30 am to 2 pm, 5.30 pm to 9 pm, Sunday 11 am to 2 pm, 5.30 pm to 9 pm. Licensed. Amex, Master Card, Visa. Free parking. Book ahead. ♿

OYSTER BED BRIDGE, P.E.I. (MAP 43)
DAYBOAT
5033 Highway 6 **$175**
(902) 963-3833

This is only the second season at Dayboat for the chef, Gordon Bailey, and his wife, Traci. (Dayboat is the term used in fish-markets for fish caught that day.) Last year they took over the old Café St.-Jean, which they completely transformed. The evening view from the big windows—sea-water, herons, sunset—is the very stuff of picture postcards. Gordon Bailey used to work at the Inn at St. Peters and at the Inn at Bay Fortune. If his cooking suffered while he was at St. Peters, it's regained its old form at Oyster Bed Bridge, where meals begin with oysters from Colville Bay or panko-breaded and deep-fried clams. Sadly, the salads are made with iceberg lettuce, but they're dressed with a black-olive vinaigrette instead of the customary raspberry vinegar. The pan-roasted cod and the pan-seared sea scallops that come next are superbly fresh and nicely garnished with zucchini, pattypan squash and leeks. People come back for the lovely dark-chocolate cake and the crème

caramel. The wine-list is small but carefully chosen and the service is very accomplished.
Open daily noon to 4 pm, 5 pm to 10 pm from mid-June until mid-October. Licensed. Amex, Master Card, Visa.

PANORAMA, B.C. **MAP 153**
EARL GREY LODGE ☆☆
1 Summit Drive **$245**
(250) 341-3641

The Earl Grey Lodge earned two stars from this guide in its first year. It had been purpose-built with every imaginable luxury—oak, granite, cedar, slate and leather. When the first chef left, Phil and Clare Marshall managed to find a replacement, Yan Therien, who has proved to be even better than his predecessor. After completing his training at Laval, he cooked at Toque! in Montreal before heading west to Panorama. Here he offers a four-course *prix-fixe* menu for 75.00, which most people regard as a bargain. His menu changes every week, so on any given night you can't be sure of getting his wonderful venison, his wild-mushroom ravioli with wilted lettuce, his medallion of Canadian bison, his apple strudel with rum-and-caramel or his molten-chocolate cake. But the Marshalls have given Therien his head and he runs the kitchen in his own way and cooks on his own terms. His wine-list, however, is still very small and badly needs to be improved.
Open daily at 7 pm by appointment only from early June until mid-October and from mid-December until mid-April. Licensed. All cards. No smoking. ♿

PAPINEAUVILLE, Quebec **MAP 154**
LA TABLE DE PIERRE DELAHAYE ☆
247 rue Papineau **$150**
(819) 427-5027

It's hard to find anything new to say about Pierre Delahaye. He has the same house and the same wife. He has the same menu. He came to Canada from Normandy,

and apples and calvados appear on his menu as often as the snails of Burgundy. Actually, he has two menus. One features things like fish, barbary duck and rack of lamb with rosemary. It costs between 25.00 and 35.00 and it's not fattening. If you haven't come here to lose weight, but to enjoy yourself, ask for the other menu, which has all the butter and cream you could hope for. You begin with cream-of-onion soup with framboise and go on to mussels en croûte in lobster sauce or snails sauced with garlic and flamed in calvados. Next comes fillet of pork dijonnaise or sweetbreads braised with apple and finished with calvados. Pierre Delahaye makes several fine pastries too, among them a chocolate tart and a French apple tart. All his wines are cheap and you can drink your fill with an easy conscience.
Open Wednesday to Friday 11.30 am to 2 pm, 5.30 pm to 9 pm, Saturday 5.30 pm to 9 pm, Sunday 11.30 am to 2 pm, 5.30 pm to 9 pm. Closed on Monday and Tuesday. Licensed. Master Card, Visa. No smoking.

PARIS, Ontario **(MAP 27)**
ROBERTS'
119-21 Grand River Street **$110**
(519) 442-5500

One of the two Roberts left Paris in 2002, but the chef is still in the kitchen. He has a good eye and his share of imagination. He changes his menu every few weeks and uses fresh local produce whenever he can. He begins his meals with mushroom salad with shallots, fig-and-brie turnovers with onions and brandy jus or seared scallops served over wilted greens. There's always a generous selection of pastas. Recently we've been offered rack of lamb with a potato-and-rosemary cake and Cajun duck in a citrus salad. The vegetables are always rather plain, though carefully cooked. For sweet we suggest the lemon tart with a Graham-cracker crust or the bread pudding with chocolate sauce. Lunch is mainly a matter of soup, salad, an omelette or a stir-fry. Most of the wines in the cellar are from Niagara and they're all priced to sell.

Open Tuesday to Friday 11.30 am to 2 pm, 5.30 pm to 10 pm, Saturday and Sunday 5 pm to 10 pm. Closed on Monday. Licensed. Master Card, Visa. ♿

PARKSVILLE, B.C. **MAP 156**
KALVAS
180 Moilliet Street **$90**
(250) 248-6933

Kalvas is the sort of place that keeps its chef for fifteen or twenty years. He stays because he likes it there, as do most of the people in town. Seafood is the backbone of the menu—wild salmon, halibut, shrimps, scallops, oysters, dungeness crab and Atlantic lobster in season. The fish is all grilled or pan-fried, the vegetables properly cooked. The cooking isn't elaborate, but everything is arranged on the plate with an eye to appearance. For instance, the scallops and prawns are served in an iron pan on a cedar plank. There's one spectacular sweet and that's a blackberry or raspberry meringue on a reduction of berry-juice, served in a cloud of whipped cream. The wine-list offers a number of big Italian reds at reasonable prices, as well as wines by the glass from Mission Hill. The restaurant is circular with massive wooden beams and a central fireplace—a pleasant combination of grandeur and intimacy.
Open daily 5 pm to 10 pm. Licensed. All cards. No smoking. ♿

PARRY SOUND, Ontario **MAP 157**
THE INN AT MANITOU ☆☆☆
McKellar Centre Road **$225 ($600)**
(705) 389-2171

The Inn at Manitou was the creation of Ben and Sheila Wise. It has grown in magnificence over the years and has become a Relais & Château with a Tom McBroom golf-course and a three-star dining-room. Sheila Wise is now carrying on alone, with the help of Bernard Ibanez in the kitchen and a well-trained corps of wait-

ers in the front of the house. The gourmet menu, which they offer every second evening, is quite small. There are usually four appetizers, four main courses and four sweets. Meals all start with a brilliant treatment of ravioli with lobster capuccino, raw oysters with lemon jelly or foie gras with a roasted peach. Grilled tuna comes next, or roast rack of lamb, caramelized breast of duck with lime and maple syrup or fillet of beef périgordine. Nothing is overstated. The best dishes, in fact, are the simplest—foie gras from Quebec, oysters from Prince Edward Island. This is classical cooking at its best and, though there may be hints of coriander here and there, lemon grass and chipotle are kept at arm's length. As for the warm chocolate tart, it's gorgeous, as is the mille-feuille of figs. The cellar is splendid too, if you can afford it. If not, look for a half-bottle (of which there are several) and save the rest of your money for a glass or two of icewine with your chocolate tart. Coffee is brought to you in the Chinese Room, where you'll find that you've spent more than you intended. Dinner costs 69.00 plus wine and service, which is added to your bill before it's placed at your elbow. Don't tip twice.
Open daily noon to 2 pm, 7 pm to 9 pm from Victoria Day until Thanksgiving. Licensed. Amex, Master Card, Visa. No smoking. Book ahead. Jacket and tie. ♿

PEMBROKE, Ontario *MAP 158*

This year we have two places to recommend in Pembroke. Ullrich's at 214 Pembroke Street W (telephone (613) 735-6025) has a good kitchen and very good service. Ullrich started out as a butcher, then added groceries and a deli counter. Finally he opened a lunchroom. His meats are all wonderful, especially his homemade sausages, which you can buy to take away at the deli counter, along with German cheeses, smoked meat and even Japanese nori. At noon the place is always packed, so you should come either early or late. They have soup, a quiche, a quesadillas or two and a smoked-meat sandwich on rye. They're open for lunch every day but Sunday, have a licence and take all cards. No smoking. ♿ *The Saffron Bistro at 133 Pembroke Street E (telephone (613) 735-1958) is very different. It's an up-market place with table-cloths and soft lighting that opened about a year ago with Mark Grenville, whose parents were part of the old restaurant of that name in Ottawa, in the kitchen. So far the menu isn't breaking any major new ground, but at noon you can have crab-cakes, phyllo-wrapped brie or a sesame steak. The fries are hand-cut, the parmesan hand-grated. In the evening the menu is ambitious. There's rack of lamb with rosemary, pork tenderloin with a reduction of bacon and apple, osso buco in a savoury tomato demi-glaze and Black Angus striploin with a stilton-and-butter demi-glaze. They're open Tuesday to Saturday for lunch and dinner, have a licence and take all cards. No smoking.* ♿

PENETANG, Ontario **MAP 159**
OLYMPIA GARDENS
104 Main Street **$80**
(705) 549-4802

One of the reasons the Olympia Gardens is still, after all these years, the best restaurant in its area is that Louis and Mary Poulias work at it every day of their lives. This year they've discovered an importer who supplies them with Greek wines of every sort, so now they're carrying no fewer than 26 Greek labels, almost all of them winners of international awards. They've had to build a new wine-cellar for their growing stock—600 labels at last count. They take the same pains with every dish on their menu. The specialty of the house is roast lamb. They slow-roast the lamb for four hours, so that by the time they bring it to the table the meat is falling off the bone. There are a number of chicken dishes as well. Our favourite is the chicken Greco, which is stuffed with black olives and feta cheese. They no longer offer endangered species of fish, so sea-bass and tuna have both disappeared from the menu, their places taken by grouper, Florida red snapper and Alaska black cod, pan-seared and served with a warm endive salad. Sweet-breads are now pretty hard to get, but they regularly offer squid and octopus. Dinner comes with a Caesar salad or a Greek salad and all the sweets are made in house. This year, besides the usual tiramisu, baklava and grand-marnier custard, they're offering a caramel-apple wrap. The Olympia is well liked, and it deserves to be. *Open Tuesday to Saturday 5 pm to 9 pm. Closed on Sunday and Monday. Licensed. Amex, Master Card, Visa. No smoking.*

PENTICTON, B.C. **MAP 160**
THE BARREL ROOM
Hillside Estate Winery **$95**
1350 Naramata Road
(888) 923-9463

The Hillside dates back to 1984 when Vera and Bohumir Klolocka began replacing their apricot orchard with wine grapes. They were among those lobbying for the Farm Gate winery policy of the Vander Zalm government, which allowed vineyards of less than five acres to sell their wines at the farm gate. This was the beginning of a whole new approach to the wine industry, including guidelines for the Vintners' Quality Alliance or V.Q.A. The first commercial release of a Hillside wine was the 1989 auxerrois, which won the V.Q.A. Gold Seal. In 1994 the winery was purchased by a group of investors, who began an impressive expansion. A 15,000-square-foot timber-frame structure with a 72-foot tower was built. Cellars were dug deep in the side of the hill, with walls of solid river rock. More recently, they've opened the Barrel Room bistro, which is open for both lunch and dinner. In the evening they do Pacific salmon in citrus and honey, sautéed sea scallops with saffron and a well-aged New York steak with blue cheese. At noon there are a variety of sandwiches on their own baguettes: baby shrimp with dill mayonnaise, sliced Granny Smith apple with goat-cheese and grilled eggplant with artichoke hearts and prosciutto. They prepare a different home-made soup every day, several very fresh salads, a thin-crust pizza and a quiche or two. Prices are all quite modest.

Open Monday to Thursday 11.30 am to 3 pm, Friday to Sunday 11.30 am to 3 pm, 6 pm to 9 pm from mid-April until 30 June, daily 11.30 am to 3 pm, 6 pm to 9 pm from 1 July until Labour Day, Monday to Thursday 11.30 am to 3 pm, Friday to Sunday 11.30 am to 3 pm, 6 pm to 9 pm from Labour Day until Thanksgiving. Licensed. Master Card, Visa. No smoking. ♿

PENTICTON **MAP 160**
GRANNY BOGNER'S ☆
302 Eckhardt Avenue W **$140**
(250) 493-2711

This big old house on a quiet back street was built in 1915. Hans Strobel, who bought the place in 1976, named it for his grandmother, who taught him how to cook in the kitchen of her hotel in the Black Forest. Strobel retired 22 years later and sold the business to Peter Hebel. Before settling in Penticton, Hebel had worked in hotels from Egypt to Tahiti. His menu is not so much German as old-fashioned, pleasantly old-fashioned: oysters casino, filet mignon béarnaise, slow-roasted lamb with rosemary. In season the kitchen tries to make full use of the abundant local produce. Wild spring salmon is brought in from the Pacific (and served with hollandaise sauce), halibut is served with a salsa of mango and papaya. You can begin with a spinach salad with parmesan croûtons or with shellfish in phyllo with tomato and basil. and finish off with apple fritters or a chocolate pâté made with Belgian chocolate and served in a coulis of fresh fruit. They have more than a hundred wines from the Okanagan, among them the great Burrowing Owl cabernet sauvignon, priced at just 50.00.

Open Tuesday to Saturday 5 pm to 10 pm. Closed on Sunday and Monday. Licensed. Master Card, Visa. No smoking.

If you use an out-of-date edition and find it inaccurate, don't blame us. Buy a new edition.

PENTICTON **MAP 160**
ISSHIN ☞
449 Main Street **$35**
(250) 770-1141

This is a standard sushi bar, but it's one of the first in this part of the country. The sushi is perfect and so is the sashimi, and both are very cheap (unless you want tuna belly). They also have first-class tempura—shrimp, vegetable and seaweed. The Gekeikken sake isn't great, but it's served very hot and a small carafe costs only 4.75. But don't come to this tiny streetfront restaurant expecting elegant surroundings. There's a small sushi bar at the back, seating four or five people. Out front there are half a dozen bare tables and chairs. No nonsense here.
Open Monday to Friday 11.30 am to 2.30 pm, 5 pm to 9 pm, Saturday noon to 2.30 pm, 5 pm to 9 pm. Closed on Sunday. Licensed. Amex, Master Card, Visa. No smoking. ♿

PENTICTON **MAP 160**
THEO'S ☞
687 Main Street **$75**
(250) 492-4019

Everyone loves Theo's. In winter they have a fire in the grate; in summer there are fresh flowers on every table. The service is enthusiastic, the helpings huge. There's a long list of appetizers, including avgolemono soup, homous, satziki, taramasalata, Greek salad and spinach pie. For 19.95 you can have a hot platter of dolmades, spanakopita, chicken livers and deep-fried squid—the squid are wonderful. They bring in fresh Pacific oysters by the bushel and get rabbits from a local farmer. Lamb is served Greek-style, deboned with spices and green herbs. They serve a lot of Greek wine too, and a lot nowadays from the Okanagan. Theo and Nikos, his son, are both very much at home on the main street of Penticton.

Open Monday to Saturday 11 am to 11 pm, Sunday 4 pm to 10 pm. Licensed. All cards. No smoking. ♿

PENTICTON
See also OLIVER.

PERCE, Quebec **MAP 161**
AUBERGE LE COIN DU BANC
315 route 132 e **$110**
(418) 645-2907

The best places to eat in Percé are no longer in the town itself. The Auberge du Gargantua is high in the hills above the town and the Auberge le Coin du Banc is four miles to the north, right on the beach. The Coin du Banc, an old frame building littered with hurricane lanterns, ships' models, wood stoves and primitive artwork, is open all day and has a wonderful breakfast that features pain doré, foie de morue, chèvre from Anse à Brillant and the lightest of crêpes, served with real maple syrup. In the evening, Fernand Rehel puts on a handsome dinner that starts with fish soup, smoked maquereau and bigorneaux from nearby Cloridorme and goes on to scallops with tartare sauce, cod béchamel and lobster in season. There's also a table d'hôte that offers such delicacies as shrimps from Rivière au Renard, cods' tongues and local crab in its shell. This is a friendly place where nobody dresses up and where prices are still relatively low.
Open daily 8 am to 10 pm from 15 April until 15 October, by appointment only from 16 October until 14 April. Licensed. Amex, Master Card, Visa. No smoking.

PERCE **MAP 161**
AUBERGE DU GARGANTUA ☆
222 route des Failles **$100**
(418) 782-2852

Pierre Péresse and his wife, Ginette, celebrated 50 years of marriage two years ago. Pierre, now 88, still comes to your table, sits down and tells you to order the turbot en croûte. If there's snow crab in the cooler, you can have that instead, or the bouillabaisse, the boiled lobster, the scallops, the fresh cod or the fresh local lamb in season. Meals all begin with a stunning platter of cold hors d'oeuvres, followed by a huge bowl of vegetable soup. Periwinkles are brought in a side-dish with a long, straight pin stuck in a cork. Where else can you get a dish of winkles for nothing? Then Ginette will bring your fish, served with a huge array of fresh vegetables, all grown in the garden just outside the window. The meal ends with a piece of sugar pie or crème caramel or fresh fruit and a cup of coffee. Gargantua is one of a kind. Pierre and Ginette bought the land more than 40 years ago, sight unseen, from a newspaper ad. They climbed to the summit of the ridge, a thousand feet above sea-level, and there they built their restaurant. It was twelve years before the road was paved, and so Pierre planted gardens and grew his own vegetables. They kept pigs for their sausages and pâtés. They kept laying hens. Today Pierre Péresse sits at the bar and gazes out the window at the neighbouring mountains and valleys. He owns them all.

Open daily 4 pm to 10 pm from mid-June until mid-September. Licensed. Master Card, Visa. No smoking. Book ahead in season. ♿

PERCE

See also ST.-GEORGES DE MALBAIE.

PERTH, Ontario **MAP 162**

THE HUNGRY PLANET ☞

2 Wilson Street W **$45**

(613) 264-9234

The Hungry Planet has a huge open kitchen where you can see everything that's going on in the kitchen. That suits Judy Dempsey right down to the ground. She has nothing to hide. Everything is made from scratch from the soups and the sweets to the amazing focaccia. There

are two halves to the menu, one of which changes every week. This is where you look for the specials, which all reflect Judy Dempsey's current interests. Her last few trips abroad took her to Thailand, Vietnam and Japan, so you may be offered Vietnamese charcoal pork or Thai tamarind soup with shrimp. The other half concentrates on burgers. This year she's found local suppliers for both her lamb and her beef. She orders four whole lambs at a time and grinds them completely, which means freezing everything for which she has no immediate use. Lamb burgers are named Border Farm burgers after the farm the lamb comes from. (The old Planet beef burger is now called the Scotch Line burger for the same reason.) Beef burgers are all seasoned with sweet peppers, fresh herbs and Tex-Mex spices and served on fresh-baked focaccia with mushrooms, Jarlburg cheese and chipotle caper mayonnaise. There are fresh-made as well as bottled drinks—mango lassi, chai, iced Vietnamese coffee and fruit shakes of all sorts. The Hungry Planet is in a downtown mall, with sixteen-foot ceilings, bold colours and a Calder-style mobile.
Open Tuesday to Thursday 9 am to 6 pm, Friday 9 am to 7 pm, Saturday 9 am to 5 pm. Closed on Sunday and Monday. No liquor. No smoking. ♿

PERTH
See also MABERLY.

PERTH-ANDOVER, N.B. **MAP 163**
KELLEY'S PLACE ☞
536 E Riverside Drive **$55**
(506) 273-3333

When Stephanie Kelley came here from Denver with her brother, she decided that what local kitchens needed was a challenge. She wasn't about to throw out comfort food, but she did make up her mind that she would make her own fries, her own soups, her own cheesecakes in winter and shortcakes in summer and her own burgers, using locally-raised beef. People write to us

about these things. But Stephanie also wanted to try out some entirely new dishes—new, that is, to New Brunswick—and that meant southwestern-style cooking. This has gone over pretty well, especially the taco salads with homemade taco chips. The wraps are popular too and so is the red chilli. They have draught beer on tap, as well as Guinness and Double Diamond, and every Saturday they put on a big, hearty breakfast.
Open Monday to Saturday 11 am to 9 pm (shorter hours in winter). Closed on Sunday. Licensed. Amex, Master Card, Visa. No smoking.

PERTH-ANDOVER **MAP 163**
YORK'S
1333 W Riverside Drive **$100**
(506) 273-2847

York's was in *Where to Eat in Canada* for more than 30 years. It had become an institution. People from Texas would make a detour to take in Perth-Andover. But institutions come and go. While the menu at York's hadn't changed in several generations, it was no longer cheap. The service had become offhand. We came to feel that York's day had come and gone, and the place disappeared from the guide. Now, however, we feel differently. The lobster is no longer salty. The gingerbread is wonderful and so are the fruit pies. The vegetables have improved. One traveller took the trouble to write to us about the pork chops, which he loved. His waitress worried that one was not enough, so she brought him a second—as well as his free second helping of scallops. There's still a lot to be said for York's.
Open daily noon (later on Saturday) to 9.30 pm from early May until late September. Licensed. Master Card, Visa. No smoking. No reservations.

If you wish to improve this guide send us information about restaurants we have missed. Our mailing address is: Oberon Press, 145 Spruce Street, Suite 205, Ottawa, Ontario K1R 6P1.

PETERBOROUGH, Ontario **MAP 164**
AASMAABIK'S
641 George Street N **$60**
(705) 876-6051

This tiny restaurant at the corner of George Street and Edinburgh is owned by Shawn Adler, whose mother is Ojibway—Aasmaabik is Ojibway for face of the rock. Adler trained at the Stratford Chef's School and later went to work at 38 Degrees. He describes his restaurant as a bakery bistro and every day he serves two homemade breads with a variety of herb butters (smoked paprika and cranberry, maple syrup and sunflower). Everything, apart from the bread, is cooked to order. Lunch might begin with a purée of potato or carrot or with spinach and caramelized onions in phyllo and go on to a sandwich, real macaroni and cheese, poached eggs with salmon or a steak. Dinner is more elaborate and usually brings something like chicken pot-pie or fillet of tilapia in a jalapeno sauce. In winter you can finish off with bread pudding with caramel, in summer with fresh berries with bannock and whipped cream. Every entrée comes with a big tossed salad and fresh fruits and vegetables. They have a few wines but, at least in summer, you're probably better with their ginger iced tea or cranberry lemonade. There are only thirteen seats, so it's important to book ahead.
Open Tuesday and Wednesday 11 am to 3 pm, Thursday to Saturday 11 am to 3 pm, 5 pm to 8 pm. Closed on Sunday and Monday. Licensed. No cards. Book ahead. ♿

PETERBOROUGH **MAP 164**
PARKHILL ON HUNTER ☆
180 Hunter Street W **$105**
(705) 743-8111

As soon as you sit down with the menu at Parkhill you'll notice the prices. Usually cooking of this calibre costs a lot of money, but this is Peterborough, not Toronto, and you'll find that ravioli stuffed with curried sweet potato and ricotta cheese, sautéed with spinach, mushrooms and sweet peppers and simmered in an orange, sage and feta cream costs only 14.25. Fresh sea scallops sautéed in lemon-thyme butter with wild mushrooms and finished with grated parmesan and black-truffle oil costs 18.00. This is modern cooking, with plenty of sweet, savoury and bitter greens, dried cranberries, red and black mustard seed, cumin and coriander and fresh basil leaves. They always have fresh fish on the menu, as well as fresh seasonal soups. You can begin with wild mushrooms and garlic in phyllo and go on to ginger-grilled lamb chops or pork tenderloin baked with a blackberry-sumac glaze. The sweets—chocolate pecan-toffee cake, fresh-fruit pavlova—are luscious and there are a number of first-class wines to go with them. On Friday night they put on a special menu that features Tuscan cooking or African fusion food. The move to Hunter Street has gone well and the restoration of their dreary, old building is a triumph.

Open Tuesday to Thursday 11.30 am to 9 pm, Friday 11.30 am to 10 pm, Saturday 5 pm to 10 pm. Closed on Sunday and Monday. Licensed. Amex, Master Card, Visa. No smoking. ♿

PETERBOROUGH **MAP 164**

38 DEGREES
375 Water Street **$85**
(705) 750-0038

The number above the front door refers, not to degrees of latitude or a street address, but to the temperature on the Fahrenheit scale judged to be best for keeping meat, fish and vegetables. This in turn means that the restaurant features fresh market produce. You'll notice, for instance, that no fewer than six hot vegetables, as well as potatoes, come with every entrée, not to mention the penne primavera or the signature vegetable platter. The house salad comes in two sizes and is made with baby greens, bib lettuce, sundried cranberries and sunflower seeds in a blood-orange vinaigrette. The

menu seldom changes. You can always get Bombay chicken, made with free-range chicken marinated in East Indian spices, char-broiled and served with mango chutney. You can always get pan-seared pickerel with lemon zest and medallions of Otonabee pork finished with brandy butter. The mussels come from Prince Edward Island and are finished with a broth of tomato, lime and ginger. The salmon is all wild. The specials of the day might be bacon-and-barley soup or confit of duck in a demi-glaze of strawberry and port, but the sweets all now come from Dufflet in Toronto. The wine-list is larger than it used to be and now features wines from France and Italy as well as Niagara.
Open Monday to Friday 11 am to 10 pm, Saturday and Sunday 4 pm to 10 pm. Licensed. Amex, Master Card, Visa. No smoking. ♿

PICTON, Ontario
See BLOOMFIELD.

PICTOU, N.S. **(MAP 140)**
PIPER'S LANDING
Highway 376 **$90**
(902) 485-1200

Matt and Brenda Vohs have been running this little restaurant overlooking the East River for more years than we can count. They claim to provide what they call the best in country cooking, which means that nobody hurries. A bread-basket is brought to the table as soon as you sit down, overflowing with warm bread and oatcakes. The menu doesn't change much, though this year more people are talking about the crêpes, stuffed with vegetables and seafood. There's also fresh haddock and salmon, poached, pan-fried with lemon or blackened Cajun-style. We ourselves like the roasted loin of pork with applesauce; others prefer the steak au poivre. You can begin your meal with either a seafood chowder or a green salad made with romaine lettuce, pears, mandarins and sesame seeds. The sweets are

always a pleasant surprise. There's a particularly good lemon-meringue pie and a German-style apple-cake with rum.
Open Monday to Wednesday and Friday to Sunday 5 pm to 9 pm. Closed on Thursday. Licensed. Amex, Master Card, Visa. No smoking. ♿

POCOLOGAN, N.B. **MAP 166**
BAYBREEZE MOTEL
6410 Highway 1 **$45**
(506) 755-3850

The Baybreeze is on Highway 1 just west of Saint John. Behind their sign there's a small café with three adjoining motel units overlooking the sea. John and Maria Lytras, the Greek couple who own and run the place, are the kind of people who stay open for latecomers and make them feel welcome. The scallops and clams are deep-fried, and so of course are the fish and chips, but they have a fresh-lobster salad, first-class lobster stew and a good lobster roll, as well as fine grilled haddock. The peas may be frozen, but the mashed potatoes are made on the premises, and so are the pies, which have a good crust and not too much sugar. John and Maria Lytras spend the winter in Greece, where they have an olive tree that supplies the olives they use all summer in the restaurant.
Open daily 8 am to 9 pm from early May until late June, daily 7 am to 10 pm from late June until late August, daily 8 am to 9 pm from late August until late October. Licensed. All cards. No smoking.

POCOLOGAN
See also DIPPER HARBOUR.

This is a guide to Canadian restaurants from coast to coast—the first ever published and the only one of its kind on the market today. We accept no advertisements. Nobody can buy his way into this guide and nobody can buy his way out.

PORT-AU-CHOIX, Newfoundland **MAP 167**
ANCHOR CAFE
Main Street **$75**
(709) 861-3665

This is a bright, lively café built to look like a ship sailing down the main street of town. The thing to have here is the fisherman's platter. It's laden with pan-fried cod, cods' tongues, catfish, halibut, scallops, shrimps and mussels and it's a great buy at 19.95. Several of these things—the shrimp (sautéed or deep-fried), the cods' tongues and the farm-fresh mussels—can also be had in appetizer portions. The shrimps come from the fish-plant across the street and they're small and sweet and incredibly fresh. They bake all their own bread and all their own pies, the best of which are the bake-apple and the partridge-berry. If you want a taste of tradition, ask for the salt fish and brewis with a side-order of pork scrunchions and onions, followed by figgy duff (steamed raisin pudding with molasses). They have a few wines and a number of local beers.
Open daily 11 am to 10 pm (longer hours in summer) from mid-April until late September. Licensed. Amex, Master Card, Visa. No smoking. ♿

PORT CARLING, Ontario **MAP 168**
MINT
Brown's Landing **$140**
(705) 765-0009

It's probably too soon to recommend Mint, which opened on the waterfront early last summer. They have too much space, the ceilings are too high and there's too much glass. Worse, they still had no licence at the end of last season and for all we know they may not have one yet. But Mint has one or two important things going for it. The menu may be small, but it's exciting. The presentation is dramatic, the cooking dazzling. Meals begin with smoked salmon or one of three or four beautiful salads—organic greens, fresh crab and,

best of all, feta cheese, avocado and watermelon. Rack of fresh Australian lamb with spinach and fingerling potatoes comes next—lamb or trout from Milford Bay, roasted whole with lemon, garlic and thyme, or Atlantic salmon with beets, avocado and orzo in a citrus emulsion. The salmon and the trout are both gorgeous presentations, but the sweets that end the meal are of little or no interest. It remains to be seen what the wine-list, when it comes, will have to offer. Meanwhile, the coffee is first class, the service exemplary.
Open Tuesday 10 am to 4 pm, Wednesday to Sunday 10 am to 10 pm. Closed on Monday. Licence pending. Amex, Master Card, Visa. No smoking. ♿

PORT CARLING **MAP 168**
REBECCA'S
3840 Highway 118 W **$120**
(705) 765-0244

Most of the fish is frozen at Rebecca's, but they do some things very well indeed, which is no doubt why the place is always full. One of their best dishes is the free-range chicken, which is one of the cheapest. The bird is coated with pecans and comes to the table beautifully moist and full of flavour. Pork is served with gorgonzola and garlic, rack of lamb with cumberland sauce. The lamb is expensive at 33.95, but you can start your meal quite cheaply with a medley of wild mushrooms and some first-class homemade bread. The wine-list is short but full of very good things, among them a Beringer chardonnay and a Duck Pond pinot noir. Both are fully priced, but don't be tempted by the white zinfandel, however cheap it may appear to be.
Open daily 5 pm to 9 pm (shorter hours in winter). Licensed. Master Card, Visa. No smoking. Book ahead. ♿

If you wish to improve this guide send us information about restaurants we have missed. Our mailing address is: Oberon Press, 145 Spruce Street, Suite 205, Ottawa, Ontario K1R 6P1.

PORT ELGIN, N.B. **MAP 169**

LITTLE SHEMOGUE

2361 Highway 955 **$115 ($275)**

(506) 538-2320

Little Shemogue is lonely and remote: a bright-red cottage hidden in the woods overlooking a marshy inlet of Northumberland Strait. Across the inlet (access from the main house is by a wooden footbridge) there's a second cottage with a spectacular interior, and that's where you should spend the night. Ask for a room in Log Point, as it's called, when you book. There's nothing else quite like it in the province or perhaps anywhere in the Atlantic region. Forget the cost. Dinner is served every evening in one of two or three small, snug dining-rooms furnished in old pine, or, in summer, on a glass-walled verandah overlooking the garden. Petra Sudbrack does the cooking; her husband looks after the front of the house. Meals are simple. They normally begin with a cream soup or with home-smoked salmon with onions and mayonnaise. A fine smooth sorbet follows, then chicken, perhaps, or local seafood or roast pork with peaches. Sweets are a strong suit—recently we had a lovely crisp meringue with chocolate sauce and fresh cream. There's no wine-list: they simply offer you the choice of a red wine or a white. Little Shemogue is about fifteen minutes from Confederation Bridge and has twelve golf courses within an hour's drive. Golf packages cost 650.00 and include a double room in Log Point for two nights, as well as a champagne dinner, breakfast and green fees for two days.

Open daily at 7 pm by appointment only. Licensed. Master Card, Visa. You must book ahead. No smoking. ♿

PORT HOOD, N.S. **MAP 170**

HAUS TREUBURG ☆

175 Main Street **$125 ($235)**

(902) 787-2116

Georg and Elvi Kargoll redesigned the front of their big, old house on Highway 19 last year, giving them-

selves a new verandah, new garden chairs and a protected site for their remarkable set of life-size chessmen, carved in beechwood by Bill Shaw—knights are seahorses, queens are mermaids, bishops are sharks. The Kargolls never seem to tire, though they've been at the job in Port Hood for upwards of twenty years. The bedrooms are all immaculate, each with duvets, four-piece bathrooms and a sea-view. As for the cooking, it just gets better and better. Meals begin with *flammkuchen* and go on to a homemade soup—perhaps cream of asparagus in June, cream of spinach and cucumber in July and August. Next comes Atlantic salmon with rostii potatoes, perhaps tuna caught off Port Hood Island, beef bourguignon, a schnitzel or a potato casserole for vegetarians. Be sure to finish off with their marvellous apple strudel, which is made to an old family recipe. All this costs just 38.00 (43.00 for lobster in season). There are several attractive house wines from Kirchheimer Schwarzerde, and these are usually better than the wines from Jost. If you spend the night you'll come down in the morning to a real feast: cereals, grains, scrambled eggs, an omelette, hot buttered toast and homemade yogurt.
Open daily at 7 pm by appointment only from 15 June until 31 December. Licensed. Master Card, Visa. No smoking. Book ahead.

PORT HOOD
See also MABOU.

PORTUGAL COVE, Newfoundland (MAP 195)
BEACHY COVE CAFE ☆
9 Beachy Cove Road **$75**
(709) 895-2920

The Beachy Cove was so busy last summer that they had to close for five weeks during the winter to renovate. The kitchen has been entirely revamped, which should speed up the service. Doug and Brenda Cole have been here for seven years now. Over the years,

they've added four modest bedrooms, as well as a 36-seat dining-room, to their century-old house. This year they've dropped filet mignon from the menu, which is no great loss, and added a seafood platter, featuring shrimps, scallops, cod and salmon. Right now, they're doing some of the best regional cooking on the Island. That means fishcakes, cod au gratin, fish and brewis and toutons (fried bread) dipped in molasses—the best in the province. The fishcakes are made with two thirds potato and one third salt fish with caramelized onions; the fish and brewis with unleavened bread soaked overnight and mixed with scruncheons, onions and fish. They also make what one traveller called the best cod au gratin in Newfoundland, as well as salmon, lobster (in season), mussels and cods' tongues. They have a lovely pea soup to start with. It's made with salted beef, carrots and turnips. Finish the meal with figgy duff or partridge-berry pie.
Open Monday to Friday 9 am to 10 pm, Saturday and Sunday 8 am to 10 pm from 1 February until 25 December. Licensed. All cards. No smoking. Book ahead.

PRINCE ALBERT, Saskatchewan **MAP 172**
AMY'S ON SECOND ☆
2990 2 Avenue W **$110**
(306) 763-1515

Amy and her chef, Michelle MacCauley, have had Prince Albert pretty much to themselves since Tannins closed. Like James Smith of Tannins, Michelle is a talented and interesting chef. Amy's has always offered a different chicken special every night of the week—but what chicken! Chicken stuffed with boursin, chicken with tomato, gin and basil, chicken with grape tomatoes, artichoke hearts and peppers and, for Valentine's Day, chicken with strawberry-peppered prawns. This year Michelle has been developing a market for lamb as well. She buys her lamb frozen from Australia, where she thinks the lamb is superior in both taste and texture to frozen lamb from New Zealand. She's also fond

of pork, stuffed with brie, red peppers, cashews and spinach and served with a cranberry-and-apple demi-glaze. But what she really likes is fish. In season she can get pickerel and cohoe salmon and she can almost always get tilapia, served as a special with red peppers and roasted garlic cream, as well as crab, scallops and shrimps. Michelle has had the same *pâtissière* for fifteen years now and she still makes all the cheesecakes, the amaretto pies and the cointreau fudge-cakes.
Open Monday to Saturday 11.30 am to 9 pm. Closed on Sunday. Licensed. All cards. No smoking. Free parking. ♿

PRINCE RUPERT, B.C. **MAP 173**
COW BAY CAFE ☆
205 Cow Bay Road **$85**
(250) 627-1212

Adrienne Johnston cooks so well that she has reservations in January for tables in June. She has recently expanded from nine tables to eleven, but that doesn't begin to solve her problem. She's always full of new ideas and her chalkboard changes every day. Fish is the backbone of her menu—lingcod and crab, halibut and wild Pacific salmon. Halibut is best in the winter; in the summer they serve more salmon, sometimes with shitake mushrooms, green onions and sake, sometimes with maple syrup and bourbon, sometimes pan-roasted with red curry and Asian slaw. The most popular dish last year was halibut in a dill-and-potato crust with roasted garlic cream. This summer they plan to feature the local side-stripe shrimps. Adrienne Clarkson makes all her own bread as well as the soups that are a growing part of the lunch menu. The sweets are all great, provided you have room for them. In summer they do seasonal fruit crisps, in winter sticky toffee cake and wonderful bread-and-butter pudding.
Open Tuesday noon to 2.30 pm, Wednesday to Saturday noon to 2.30 pm, 6 pm to 8.30 pm. Closed on Sunday and Monday. Licensed for beer and wine only. Amex, Master Card, Visa. No smoking. You must book ahead. ♿

PRINCE RUPERT **MAP 173**

RAIN

737 2 Avenue N **$110**

(250) 627-8272

Brian Lutz is a native of Prince Rupert who left for the greener fields of Vancouver and came back with a wife, Charmaine Gibson, to open Rain in his hometown. Rain was an immediate success, partly because people liked their small-plate menu and partly because they stay open late at night. You can come in for dinner at 1.30 in the morning if you like—at 6.30 in the evening the place is empty. There's a fresh list of raw oysters every day; mussels from Prince Edward Island they sell by the pound. The soup of the day might be a clam chowder; salads they make with mesclun greens, fresh tomatoes and shaved parmesan reggiano. There are big plates for big eaters, loaded with halibut from Hecate Strait and lamb shanks from New Zealand. There are pasta plates loaded with homemade pasta and gnocchi. But the small plates are better than either. So far we've tried the brandade of halibut, the ragoût of wild mushrooms, the carpaccio of beef and the calamari dijonnaise. They are all first class and the calamari are spectacular. Next time we hope to try the swimming scallops and the dungeness crab-legs from the Queen Charlottes. The sweets all cost just 6.00 and they're worth every cent. There's a rich toffee mousse and a warm Callebaut-chocolate cake that they call Chocolate Bondage.

Open Monday to Saturday 5 pm to 2 am. Closed on Sunday. Licensed. Master Card, Visa. No smoking.

PRINCE RUPERT **MAP 173**

SMILE'S

113 Cow Bay Road **$70**

(250) 624-3072

You don't usually expect good cooking from a restaurant with a history like Smile's. There's been a café on

this site, hidden away among railroad sidings and fish plants, for more than 70 years. People who used to come here with their children come today with their grandchildren. It's true, the cooks still use the old-fashioned deep-fry, but changes are on the way. Already, salmon, sole, red snapper and black cod can be had poached or pan-fried. Prince Rupert used to be the halibut capital of the world. Eventually the supplies ran out, but now halibut is once again on the menu at Smile's. Halibut and chips make a great dish. They have excellent chowders too, as well as club sandwiches made with crabmeat or shrimp. There are two dining-rooms here, one with booths, the other with fishnets and old photographs. Take your pick.
Open daily 10 am to 10 pm. Licensed. Master Card, Visa. No smoking. ♿

QUEBEC, Quebec **MAP 174**
AUX ANCIENS CANADIENS ☆
34 rue St.-Louis **$40/$120**
(418) 692-1627

For a long time we couldn't believe in the Anciens Canadiens. How can a restaurant, we asked ourselves, so old (the house was built in 1625), so picturesque, so conveniently sited, with waitresses wearing period costumes, be taken seriously? But the fact is, it has to be taken seriously. The interior is inviting, the waitresses charming, the *habitant*-style cooking skilful and well conceived. If you arrive between noon and 5.45 you can have three courses and a glass of house wine for just 14.75. That means a choice of tourtière, meatballs, breast of chicken in puff pastry, leg of pheasant with pork and beans and veal stew made from an old recipe and loaded with meat and vegetables. Soups start with the traditional split-pea and go on to tomato-and-barley and cream of pheasant. After 5.45 everything is much more expensive. This is when they give you caribou bourguignon with blueberry wine or a trio of filet mignon (venison, caribou and buffalo) with pink pep-

percorns and grated turnip sweetened with honey. Don't overlook the sweet course. The maple-syrup pie drizzled with fresh cream is the stuff of dreams. The homemade bread with beurre d'érable and heavy cream is almost better. The wine-list is big and expensive and if you want to you can spend hundreds of dollars on a bottle of wine.
Open daily noon to 6 pm (lunch), 6 pm to 10 pm (dinner). Licensed. All cards. No smoking. Book ahead.

QUEBEC **MAP 174**
APSARA ☆
71 rue d'Auteuil **$75 ($150)**
(418) 694-0323

A new generation has been in charge of the Apsara since the death of Beng an Khuong. Beng had fled Cambodia in 1975, leaving all his possessions behind. Within two years of his arrival in Quebec, he and his sixteen children had bought this lovely old house and opened a restaurant with rooms. The cooking gets better every year and the prices remain incredibly low. At noon you can get soup, spring rolls, a main course, sweet and tea for 10.95. The kitchen offers Vietnamese and Cambodian as well as Thai specialties. Our favourite is the nid jardinier, which is stir-fried vermicelli with chicken, shrimp and sauteéd vegetables. We also admire the sauteéd shrimp with lemon grass, the Thai filet-mignon with five-spice seasoning, the Cambodian oudong chicken with ginger and the Bangkok shrimps with sauteéd vegetables and spices. If you come as a couple, it's a good idea to order a complete dinner. Otherwise, ask for the mini lat desangker or tiny peanut rolls, followed by Thai beef. Everything is cooked as it should be and nothing is too sweet. There are a few wines, as well as Tsingtao beer. The service is subdued but very polite.
Open Monday to Friday 11.30 am to 2 pm, 5.30 pm to 11 pm, Saturday and Sunday 5.30 pm to 11 pm. Licensed. Amex, Master Card, Visa. No smoking.

QUEBEC **MAP 174**

L'INITIALE ☆☆☆

54 rue St.-Pierre **$210**

(418) 694-1818

L'Initiale closed for renovations for most of last winter. We were surprised, because we always thought the one-time bank at the corner of Côte de la Montagne and rue St.-Pierre in the Lower Town perfect as it was. The interior was at once comfortable and sumptuous, the tables generously spaced. You felt discriminating, but never lonely. But whatever they've done to the ambiance, which only time will tell, they've made one important improvement: they've added an à la carte to the old set menus (now priced at 59.00 and 79.00). Yvan Lebrun's cooking may seem a little less daring than in the days of his *menu contemporain*, but it has to be admitted that all the dishes on the à la carte are dazzling, every one. The winter *carte* started with one or two appetizers from the *menu grand*: one was scallops with a sheep's-milk-cheese parfait and a caramel of citrus fruits with dandelion greens, the other warm duck-liver with winter radish, sweet pepper, elder currants and chanterelles. Fillet of beef follows, or Fundy salmon with fried green asparagus or local lamb with its knuckle in red rice. There's also an offering of small plates—three courses and a sweet—that has such things as smoked salmon from the Charlevoix, sea-bass with a mousse of leeks and breast of pigeon with small onions and banyul's vinegar. The *menu grand* offers four courses as well as cheese and dessert of the day, adding wines by the glass for another 42.00. We, however, prefer the new à la carte, which is usually cheaper. The service is leisurely and most of the wines beyond our means—Haut-Brions, Mouton Rothschilds and the like—but the coffee is wonderful.

Open Monday to Friday 11.30 am to 2 pm, 6 pm to 9 pm, Saturday and Sunday 6 pm to 9 pm. Licensed. All cards. No smoking. Book ahead. ♿

QUEBEC **MAP 174**

LAURIE RAPHAEL ☆☆☆

117 rue Dalhousie **$215**

Vieux Port

(418) 629-4555

Don't look for Laurie Raphael on a back street in the old town, and don't expect the rough-hewn stone walls of the familiar *québécois* boîte, because it's not like that at all. It's big and plain and there's no parking except in off-street lots that close before you finish your dinner—the headwaiter will come and open the gate for you if you ask. They don't always respect bookings and one couple waited in a corner for 35 minutes after driving 250 miles in the rain to get there. In short, Laurie Raphael has every fault in the book. Except the cooking. Daniel Vézina is almost always good—one may be allowed to regret the sugar-candy balls that he calls sugar pie. But he's often brilliant, and occasionally—as with his golden-tomato carpaccio—he surpasses belief. He is, of course, very expensive. The seven-course *menu de dégustation* costs 89.00 and on the à la carte main courses cost as much as 45.00. The best way to get to know Vézina is to ask for the so-called Chef Chef, three courses for 56.00. This is a *menu surprise* that might begin with venison tartar and wild mushrooms, go on to grilled halibut with a purée of broccoli and peppers and end with a chocolate soufflé. The most ravishing dish on the à la carte is a dazzling reduction of foie gras from Goulu Farm with balsamic vinegar, perhaps, the tenderloin of beef served with its marrow and oil of truffles. The wine-list is mostly French, with a scattering of vintages from Italy and California. There's a Caymus conundrum for 105.00 and a Mouton Rothschild premier grand cru for 510.00. Both prices, believe it or not, are fair.

Open Tuesday to Friday 11.30 am to 2 pm, 6 pm to 10 pm, Saturday 6 pm to 10 pm. Closed on Sunday and Monday. Licensed. All cards. No smoking. You must book ahead. ♿

QUEBEC **MAP 174**
PANACHE ☆☆
Auberge St.-Antoine **$195 ($450)**
10 rue St.-Antoine
(418) 692-1022

Panache and the Auberge St.-Antoine are part of the lavish restoration of a nineteenth-century stone warehouse. The views of the St. Lawrence from the restaurant are fabulous and it's no surprise that the hotel has already become a member of the Relais & Châteaux group. Panache is extremely romantic and extremely expensive. Its menu lists most of the top Quebec suppliers. Goulu Farms duck, for instance, is spit-roasted or offered as foie gras prepared in two ways, with a candied orange brioche or pan-seared with cranberries. Partridge and quail are brought in from Cap St.-Ignace, Black Angus beef from Eumatimi Farm. Beets are supplied by M. Leblond, root vegetables by M. Bérube. Asparagus and Yukon Gold potatoes come from the Ile d'Orléans. François Blais' menu is intriguing. It offers minced emu with daisy buds, wild Atlantic sea-bass with fennel pollen, guinea-hen with truffles and an emulsion of honey and wine, macaroni with Ile-aux-Grues cheddar and wild mushrooms. The most remarkable sweet, as anyone who has picked them will know, is the goat-cheese ice cream with a compote of wild strawberries. If you come at noon, there's an appealing menu *du jour* for just 24.00. Most of the wines in the cellar come from France or Quebec, though there are a few from California and one or two from Australia as well.
Open Monday to Friday 11.30 am to 2 pm, 6 pm to 10 pm, Saturday and Sunday 6 pm to 10 pm. Licensed. All cards. No smoking. ♿

The price rating shown opposite the headline of each entry indicates the average cost of dinner for two with a modest wine, tax and tip. The cost of dinner, bed and breakfast (if available) is shown in parentheses.

QUEBEC **MAP 174**
LE ST.-AMOUR ☆☆
48 rue Ste.-Ursule **$175**
(418) 694-0667

People have always thought of the St.-Amour as Quebec's most romantic restaurant. The setting, of course, is extraordinary. The restaurant occupies a two-story atrium with skylights, brilliant art-déco panels, pier glasses and medallions of birds in flight. On the second floor there's a spectacular wine-vault that holds 12,000 bottles. Jean-Luc Boulay, the chef and part-owner, has been here for twenty years, and his cooking just keeps on getting better and better. He now shares the work with his son, Frédéric—they take turns at lunch and dinner. Foie gras has always been a specialty of the house, and foie gras de canard from the Goulu Farm still appears in a great many dishes. (They suggest you take it with such dishes as sweetbreads, caribou and young pigeon for a *supplément* of up to 20.00.) The à la carte is extremely expensive and for that reason we suggest you ask for the *prix fixe* at 48.00 a head. For less than half that, you can get a fine meal at noon, featuring fillet of salmon in balsamic vinegar and olive-oil, Nunavut caribou or shrimps and mussels in phyllo pastry. If money is no object, come for dinner and ask for the 59.00 menu, which shows the kitchen at its best. Start with the terrine of foie gras laced with armagnac and go on to something like filet mignon of bison roasted with pepper from Sarawak and crusted with potato. Or perhaps a tataki of red tuna with bitter orange in a bouillon of coconut curry flavoured with lime and coriander. The sweets are the work of Roland-Alain Blanchet, and they're spectacular.
Open Monday to Friday noon to 2.30 pm, 6 pm to 10 pm, Saturday and Sunday 6 pm to 10 pm. Licensed. All cards. No smoking. Valet parking. Book ahead.

Our web site is at www.oberonpress.ca Readers wishing to use e-mail should address us at oberon@sympatico.ca

QUEBEC **MAP 174**
LA TANIERE ☆☆☆
2115 rang Ste.-Ange **$160**
Ste.-Foy
(418) 872-4386

We thought Chantal Miclette and Laurier Therrien were terribly young when they opened La Tanière in 1977. They proved that it was possible to make a critical and commercial success of a restaurant devoted almost exclusively to game. Now, only a few years later (or so it seems), their niece, Karen Therrien, and her partner, Frédéric Laplante, have taken over, he in the kitchen, she in the front of the house. The cooking and service are still as good as ever, the cooking a little more imaginative, perhaps, the presentation a little more elegant. There are three set menus, one at 35.95 for four courses, another at 45.95 for six courses and a third at 55.95 for eight courses. Dinners all begin with hot homemade bread and superb *amuse-bouche*—confit of quail, perhaps, with tomato, endive and radish sprouts. They go on to tartar of red deer, smoked duck with a purée of salsify, tuna with corn and leeks, quail stuffed with foie gras and elk with barley and butternut squash. There's been a maple-syrup tart on the menu for over 25 years, but they now offer a splendid cheese-plate as well. There's a dazzling selection of clarets and super-Tuscans. All of them are, of course, very expensive. To get to La Tanière, take the Grande Allée to the Duplessis exit. Turn left on Highway 138 (here known as boulevard Hamel) and then right on the rang Ste.-Ange. The restaurant is just over two miles from the intersection.

Open Wednesday to Sunday 6 pm to 9 pm. Closed on Monday and Tuesday. Licensed. Amex, Master Card, Visa. No smoking. You must book ahead. ♿

We accept no advertisements. We accept no payment for listings. We depend entirely on you. Recommend the book to your friends.

QUEBEC **MAP 174**
TOAST ☆
17 Sault-au-Matelot **$190**
Vieux Port
(418) 692-1334

Toast opened in 2003. It has an enticing location in quarters that once housed Laurie Raphael (see above). It has a lovely walled garden for outdoor dining in summer. Inside there's not much to see but deftly-lit old stone walls. (Toast is no place for an intimate occasion.) Christian Lemelin, the chef, has worked in several Quebec restaurants. He's innovative to a fault and his style is all his own. He uses nothing but the best of local produce. He has a weakness for onions, garlic, capers and jalapeno peppers—is it any wonder his flavours are so robust? One traveller writes that Lemelin's cooking is "not for the faint of palate." Homemade ravioli, for instance, is stuffed with suckling pig, braised in mojo and sautéed in olive-oil with snails and parmesan cheese. Salmon tartar is perfumed with rice vinegar and sesame and served on avocado crisps with a salad and fries. Foie gras is pressed with apples and port and seasoned with a mixture of spices, sweetbreads are caramelized and served with asparagus. For sweet, beetroot crumble is served with a vanilla risotto and amaretto foam. If you can't rise to the beetroot crumble, have the banana tart. Sunday brunch is equally outrageous. There's an extensive (and expensive) wine-list, with more than a dozen wines sold by the glass as well as the bottle.
Open Monday to Thursday 11.30 am to 2 pm, 6 pm to 10.30 pm, Friday 11.30 am to 2 pm, 6 pm to 11.30 pm, Saturday 6 pm to 11.30 pm, Sunday 10 am to 2 pm (brunch), 6 pm to 10.30 pm. Licensed. All cards. No smoking. ♿

QUEEN CHARLOTTE ISLANDS, B.C. MAP 175

The newly-incorporated village of Queen Charlotte is about a mile east of the ferry dock on Graham Island. At 3207 Wharf Street you'll find the Purple Onion (telephone (250)

559-4119). It's a straight-up deli, where they serve things like soup, salads, sandwiches (including a raspberry-brie melt) and burgers. We particularly like the roast-beef-and-avocado sandwich, though it leaves little room for a helping of cake or apple pie. Everything is made on site except the bread, which comes from a local bakery. Across the street you'll find the Queen B, which isn't sure whether or not it has an address. It does have a telephone number, however, which is (250) 559-4463. It's a funky place with great cooking. Most of the dishes are vegetarian, though there's usually a salmon or a chicken entrée. The place is known for its pizzas, its enchiladas and its spanakopita, as well as its starving-artist's soup, which comes with a thick slice of bread for 5.00. In the evening they concentrate on local seafood. Both the Purple Onion and the Queen B are inexpensive. The Purple Onion takes no credit cards, the Queen B takes Master Card. Neither has a licence and neither permits smoking. Both are open all day every day. If you head north from Queen Charlotte to Masset, you'll come to Tlell, which is just south of the Rising Tide Bakery (telephone (250) 557-4677) The Bakery was opened a few months ago by a local woman who had dreamed for years of becoming a baker, and it became an instant success. What better breakfast than a cinnamon bun and a cup of strong, hot coffee? There's always a homemade soup at lunchtime, sometimes a quiche. Bread is made on the premises from organic flour imported from the Lower Mainland and ground on the premises. The coffee is organic and tea is brewed in a teapot. The Rising Tide Bakery is open all day every day in season (Wednesday to Sunday in winter), but has no liquor and takes no cards. Not far away, in Masset, there's another new restaurant, so new it hasn't got a telephone yet. It's right next door to the Naikoon Motel on Tow Hill Road and it's called the Trout House. A typical menu might start with razor-clam chowder and go on to fresh fish. Remember, fresh fish is rare on the Queen Charlottes, though there are fish-packing plants at both Masset and Charlotte.

Every restaurant in this guide has been personally tested. Our reporters are not allowed to identify themselves or to accept free meals.

QUEEN CHARLOTTE ISLANDS **MAP 175**
SANDSPIT AIRPORT ☞
Moresby Island **$45**
(250) 637-2455

The coffee shop at Sandspit Airport changed hands a year or so ago, but many of the same people are still involved in the business. Sandspit is a long way from almost anywhere, so it's a good place to know about. Where else would they leave muffins, sticky buns, cookies and coffee on the counter so travellers on the one daily flight to Vancouver can help themselves *free of charge* after closing time? When they're open, they sell a lot of sandwiches, all made with their own home-baked bread, and a lot of cinnamon and poppyseed buns. They make a different soup every day as well as the usual Nanaimo bars and chocolate brownies. There's always at least one hot special—on Wednesdays it's pizza. Last summer they added ice cream and yogurt parfait to the menu. The coffee is good and so is the cocoa.
Open daily 7.30 am to 4.30 pm (earlier in winter). No liquor. Master Card, Visa. No smoking. ♿

REGINA, Saskatchewan **MAP 176**
LA BODEGA
2228 Albert Street **$100**
(306) 546-3660

La Bodega, just south of Victoria on Albert Street, is both dark and garish. Book ahead and ask for the table by the window, where chances are you'll be more comfortable than anywhere else. This is a tapas bar, with a surprisingly short list of cold dishes. That doesn't really matter, because they have a lovely selection of sushi, perfectly prepared and yours for only 11.00. There's a much greater abundance of hot tapas—fried squid, mussels with tomatoes and cilantro, wild coho salmon marinated in whisky, snails sautéed with garlic and tomatoes, breast of chicken in red coconut curry and shrimp tempura with wasabi and soy. Everything but

the breast of chicken is well prepared and well served. On the à la carte there's local steelhead trout and several interesting salads—spinach in a strawberry coulis and mango with bacon and Thai chilli. Live lobster, served with either drawn butter or black beans, can be had on a day's notice. The best of the sweets is the chocolate-lava cake. There aren't many wines, but most of them are sold by the glass as well as the bottle.
Open Monday to Friday 11 am to 10 pm (or later), Saturday and Sunday 10 am to 2 pm (brunch), 2 pm to 11 pm. Licensed. All cards.

REGINA **MAP 176**
THE CREEK IN CATHEDRAL ☆
3414 13 Avenue **$115**
(306) 352-4448

The Creek, as they call it for short, may be inexpensive, but make no mistake, it's a very ambitious restaurant. They start all their meals with things like mussels with lemon grass, chilli and garlic and squid in a light butter sauce with a seductive tomato-and-fennel salsa. Or with a salad of organic greens with maple-glazed pine-nuts, persimmon and roquefort in a black-currant vinaigrette. The salad is good, the squid very good indeed. They don't use local lamb, sad to say, but the lamb they get from New Zealand is young, tender and well served with a reduction of golden figs and balsamic vinegar. The fish is all frozen, except the local farm-fresh steelhead trout, which is simply garnished with a julienne of properly-cooked vegetables. If you are scornful of New Zealand lamb, ask for the pork tenderloin stuffed with poached fruit and applesauce. To end the meal, there's a first-class molten-chocolate torte, but we always fall for the lemon-curd tart. There's good drinking from the Okanagan, California and the Pacific Rim, and markups are unusually low. The service is elegant.
Open Monday to Saturday 11 am to 4 pm, 5 pm to 9.30 pm (later on weekends). Closed on Sunday. Licensed. Amex, Master Card, Visa. No smoking. ♿

RENFREW, Ontario **MAP 177**

OLDE TOWNE HALL

128 Raglan Street S **$25**

(613) 432-7971

We first heard of Christine Bidgood's restaurant in Renfrew more than a year ago. Since then she's been working hard to maintain her meticulous standards at the restaurant while caring for three small children at home. If you're travelling Highway 60 between Ottawa and Muskoka, this is a good place to stop. On Saturday night she serves her famous prime rib to the music of a jazz group. All week she makes wonderful sandwiches with freshly-roasted turkey, cranberries and an assortment of vegetables. Travellers speak of her apple pie as one in a hundred, but she now prefers to make one of her cakes—lemon angel-food cake or chocolate cake with caramel sauce and whipped cream. Lunch is never the same two days running, though favourite dishes do reappear from time to time. She's forever picking up recipes for quiche—caramelized onion and bacon, perhaps—and recipes for casseroles, made with as much local, organic produce as she can find. Last year you could get a complete lunch for less than 10.00. The restaurant occupies a long, narrow room next to the town hall. It's furnished with old tables and chairs she's picked up at farm auctions. Right now, you can be sure of lunch five days a week. Dinner on Saturday night is by appointment only.

Open Monday to Friday 10 am to 3 pm, Saturday by appointment only. Closed on Sunday. No liquor. Amex, Master Card, Visa.

REVELSTOKE, B.C. **MAP 178**

WOOLSEY CREEK CAFE

600 2 Street **$60**

(250) 837-5500

Woolsey Creek is owned by two women from Quebec who got the idea of offering a menu that was cooked from

scratch by a real chef. They make all their own stocks, their own salad-dressings, their own fruit crumbles—everything, in fact, except the bread, which they buy from a local baker. They like to think that their cuisine is international. What that means is that they cook in the style of Southeast Asia—stir-fries from Indonesia, pad Thai from Thailand, curries from India They prepare a different soup every day and there's always a steak and one or two pastas for those who want them. Perhaps because it's so warm and comfortable, the place is always full of climbers.
Open daily 7.30 am to 10 pm. Licensed. Amex, Master Card, Visa. No smoking.

RIMOUSKI, Quebec **MAP 179**
LE 360 DEGRES
150 rue de la Cathédrale **$50/$120**
(418) 724-0360

This little place is located in an old area behind the boardwalk and the cathedral and its setting gives no hint that it is in fact a lively, stylish restaurant. The name is meant to suggest a cuisine of boundless possibilities, a place where old habits have been discarded, and that is exactly what Richard Duchesneau is trying to do. He has no table d'hôte, no principal dishes. You choose from a broad selection of appetizers and sweets, unless you decide to order the six-course *menu de dégustation*, which is a bargain at 45.00. (There's also a set lunch, priced from 6.00 to 16.00, that often features local organic pork.) On the tapas menu, keep an eye out for quail with bok choy, tamarind and pineapple and tartar of deer with a pear-and-cucumber salsa. The sweets are like tiny jewels and you can easily have two or three of them. Don't miss the cold caramel soufflé if it's available—the menu changes every month.
Open Tuesday 11.30 am to 2 pm, Wednesday to Friday 11.30 am to 2 pm, 5 pm to 10 pm, Saturday 5 pm to 10 pm. Closed on Sunday and Monday. Licensed. Master Card, Visa. No smoking.

ROCKY HARBOUR, Newfoundland MAP 180

JAVA JACK'S

88 Main Street N **$85**

(709) 458-3004

Look for Java Jack's in a big house in the heart of town, right across the street from the Bank of Montreal. At the top of a rickety stair you'll find a bright, lively dining-room where Jacqui Hunter will offer you a modern menu with hardly a nod to such traditional dishes as salt fish and brewis. Keep an eye out instead for Labrador-caribou sausage with partridge-berry honey mustard, mussels Thai-style with coconut and cilantro, pan-seared cod and scallops with fresh mango. After that there's New York cheesecake with bake-apples and fruit crisp with partridge-berries and whipped cream. There's a good, short list of bottled wines (Wolf Blass Yellow and Red Label, Masi valpolicella), Sawmill Creek by the glass and seven varieties of Quidi Vidi beer, which is brewed in St. John's. Java Jack's installed the town's first espresso machine a couple of years ago, and that's the thing to ask for. You'll like Jacqui, who spends all day running up and down the stairs.

Open daily 8 am to 9 pm from 1 June until 30 September. Licensed. All cards. No smoking.

ROCKY MOUNTAIN HOUSE, Alberta ***MAP 181***

MERLIN'S

5850 Main Street ***$35***

(403) 845-7711

The Timberline seemed sure to succeed. It was friendly, with a lively menu, an open fire in winter and an ice-cream parlour in summer. But it's gone and all we can do now is to suggest this reliable family-style restaurant as a safe alternative. At Merlin's they make their own soups, but their bread is baked from baker's dough and most of their desserts are brought in. They make their own cheesecakes and they bake a couple of their own pies. Rocky Mountain House is the largest town in west-central Alberta and a natural base for exploring the nearby wilderness or for cross-country skiing. This is big empty country and you'll be glad to know about Merlin's. It's open all day every day but Sunday. They have a licence and take all cards.

ROUYN, Quebec **MAP 182**
LA BROCHETERIE GRECQUE
152 rue Principale **$90**
(819) 797-0086

This is perhaps the most successful restaurant in the Abitibi region. It's a big place with a big menu and big helpings. What's surprising is that the kitchen is good at everything it touches. This year they've added rack of local lamb to their menu, with their usual success. But we usually go for the scaloppine of veal (romana, marsala, con funghi) or the fresh fillet of salmon, poached with sweet butter or with dill. They're particularly good too with scallops, but you won't be disappointed with the brochettes of filet mignon or the Greek-style souvlaki or even the Italian-style pizzas and pasta. We once had a lemon tart that tasted of Realemon, but they now have five kinds of real chocolate cake. Most of the wines are French, but there are some useful varietals from Italy and Niagara as well.
Open Monday to Thursday 11 am to 11 pm, Friday and Saturday 11 am to midnight, Sunday 9 am to 11 pm. Licensed. All cards. No smoking. ♿

ROUYN **MAP 182**
LA ROSE DES VENTS
19 Main Street E **$80**
Evain
(819) 768-8833

The Rose des Vents has always been too small to deal with suppliers on equal terms. So when the price of beef went through the roof two years ago, Ronnie Lysight simply took it off the menu. He finds it hard to get fresh Temiskaming sturgeon, as he once did. But people will drive eighty miles for his scallops in saffron. His first love has always been, not beef or fish, but stews: stewed rabbit, confit of duck, osso buco. Whatever he cooks, it's memorable; no-one else in this part of Quebec is cooking as well. The village of Evain is three miles east of Rouyn. La Rose des Vents occupies an old cottage with a verandah on two sides. In summer, you can eat on one of the verandahs or on the patio at the back, in the shade of a gigantic willow. There are usually about a dozen main dishes on the blackboard. In spring the chef brings in fresh asparagus from his garden. Every few weeks there'll be something new, like shrimp with a smidgen of garlic and basmati rice. The soups all look the same, but they're all delicious. As for sweets, there are three every night, fresh fruit in season, pear belle Hélène or flaming banana, or maybe something like a crêpe stuffed with chocolate and served with crème anglaise.

Open Wednesday to Sunday 5 pm to 10 pm. Closed on Monday and Tuesday. Licensed. Master Card, Visa. No smoking. ♿

STE.-ADELE, Quebec **MAP 183**
L'EAU A LA BOUCHE ☆
300 boulevard Ste.-Adèle **$230**
(450) 229-2991

Anne Desjardins is revered in Quebec. For 25 years she's been running a seasonal kitchen in Ste.-Adèle, cooking squash and cabbage in February instead of importing asparagus from Latin America. She was far ahead of her time in working closely with local farmers and she's always made the most of fresh local produce. She always takes care to achieve an exact balance of flavour and texture. For instance, she likes to serve wild salmon and honey-mushroom tempura with cucumber, celery and wild-ginger mayonnaise. She's now a chevalier de l'Ordre National du Quebec and her dining-room is packed on even the harshest of winter evenings. Before

you book a table, however, you should ask whether or not she will be in the kitchen on the appointed day, because if she isn't all bets are off. This is one of only three Relais & Châteaux in the province and prices are extraordinarily high, whether she's in the kitchen or not. Our experience is that she's at her best with her appetizers and her sweets. Look for such things as the winter-vegetable salad with truffle oil, goat's-milk cheddar, baby cress and toasted pumpkinseeds or the braised veal sweetbreads with baby carrots and a dash of curry. The sweets run to things like tapioca, bread-and-butter pudding and, for a few dollars more, a selection of local farmhouse cheeses. The wine-list is impressive, but it's hard to find a good buy anywhere.
Open daily 6 pm to 9 pm. Licensed. Amex, Master Card, Visa. Book ahead. No smoking. ♿

STE.-ADELE
See also ST.-FAUSTIN-LAC-CARRE.

ST.-ANDRE D'ARGENTEUIL, Quebec **(MAP 135)**
AUBERGE CHEZ DAVID ☆
216 route du Long Sault **$80 ($170)**
(450) 537-3734

At Chez David they serve dinner by appointment only every night of the week. They also have four attractive bedrooms and a great breakfast of fresh fruit, croissants, ham-and-cheese turnovers and crêpes with maple syrup. St.-André is on Highway 344. To get there you take Highway 327 south from Highway 148, just past Lachute. It's a great place to stop if you're heading into Montreal from the west. David himself was born in Morocco and worked as a chef in Spain before he came to Canada, which is why there are Spanish and Moroccan dishes on the menu as well as French. You have to order the couscous maison when you book because it takes all day to make, but the pastilla and the seafood paella are always on offer. David uses local lamb for his

rack and serves it with a Moroccan-style sauce. It's a specialty of the house, as are the sautéed squid, the kidneys and the duck. This year wild boar and rabbit are appearing on the menu more often. The table d'hôte offers six courses for 35.00 or so, depending on your choice of entrée. If you prefer to order à la carte you can start with marinated salmon or a salad of shrimp and avocado and end with a chestnut-cream torte. As for the fish, it's all beautifully cooked.
Open daily 5 pm to 9 pm by appointment only. Licensed. All cards. No smoking.

ST. ANDREWS, N.B. **MAP 185**
L'EUROPE
48 King Street **$100**
(506) 529-3818

The Café Europe was taken over six years ago by Markus and Simone Ritter, who completely refitted the place. The interior is no longer warm and intimate. Instead it's cool, immaculate and very chic, all snowy whites and soft, pale colours. Anita Ludwig was a fine natural cook who tried to maintain too large a menu. Markus Ritter is a professional, who began his career in St. Andrews with a very small menu. But, like his predecessor, he knows that there's still a lively demand for things like escargots de bourgogne, scallops au gratin and duck à l'orange with mashed potatoes. There are those who think highly of his lobster bisque, but we still prefer the cold-smoked salmon, which comes from Wolfhead Smokers on Jail Island, where the salmon is first dry-salted and then cold-smoked over low heat. The finished product is as good as any we know of. We also admire the local venison with homemade spaetzle and the wienerschnitzel, which is delicately cooked and served quite simply with buttered noodles. In season they make up to twelve varieties of ice cream and sorbet, as well as apple beignets and a number of cakes. The wine-list, still small, is expected to double in size this summer. As for the service, like the restaurant itself, it's cool and very, very elegant.

Open daily 5 pm to 9.30 pm from Easter until 15 January. Licensed. Amex, Master Card, Visa. No smoking

ST. ANDREWS **MAP 185**
ROSSMOUNT INN ☆☆
4599 Highway 127 **$110**
(506) 529-3351

The dining-room at the Rossmount is now furnished with bridge chairs and plain wooden tables. Where has the splendid room presided over by Sir James Dunn's butler in former times—where has it gone? The answer is that the old mahogany may have gone, but so has the dreary cooking that used to be David Brewin's stock in trade. The Rossmount now has the best kitchen in the province. They use things like black olive oil, wild mushrooms, fleur de sel, pickled fennel, toasted quinoa and highbush cranberries almost as a matter of course. They caramelize their scallops. They serve their Malpèque oysters not with lemon but with a salsa of apple, shallots and verjus, their lobster, served naked, with a purée of green pea, their lamb with a purée of eggplant and chick-pea. They make full use of fresh local produce—heirloom tomatoes, greens from Chamcook Farm, smoked salmon from Wolfhead, fresh salmon from Passamaquoddy Bay, lamb from Whitfield Farms. The cooking is graceful and nicely understated. With his avocado-and-salmon tartar with radish, chives and cilantro and his lobster in a chive beurre blanc with organic vegetables and a pea purée. Chris Aemi is at the very top of his form. Unless you want a piece of Swiss-chocolate truffle-cake you'd be wise to order a plate of local raw-milk cheeses—Sieur de Duplessis and Acadie bleu, with raisin-walnut bread, costs only 7.50. They offer some interesting wines—among them the Kim Crawford sauvignon blanc and the Wolf Blass red-label shiraz/cabernet—but the wine-list is very mall and includes only six French wines and five Italian. With a better wine-list and a more convincing ambience, this would be a three-star restaurant.

Open daily 5.30 pm to 9.30 pm from15 March until 31 December. Licensed. Amex, Master Card, Visa. No smoking. Book ahead in season. ♿

ST. ANDREWS **MAP 185**
THE WINDSOR HOUSE ☆
132 Water Street **$135**
(506) 529-3330

Peter Woodworth may have a menu with too little fish, too much meat and too many clichés—but he certainly knows how to cook. He can make the most unpromising of dishes taste as they never have before. He uses first-class ingredients (Windwood smoked salmon, Brome Lake duck, Alberta beef) and handles them with grace and restraint. Nothing is overstated. His Atlantic salmon, served in beurre blanc with slivered marrow and basmati rice, is a delight. So is his pork tenderloin, adorned with fig marmalade. His lamb shanks are tender and succulent, his beef tenderloin, in its demi-glaze of red wine, is tender and full of flavour. And his meals end well with maple-sugar crème brûlée and excellent coffee. Every wine that costs 40.00 or less is sold by the glass as well as the bottle, which means that a solitary diner can enjoy such things as Wolf Blass Red Label cabernet shiraz, Masi soave and Fetzer fumé blanc. The Windsor House is furnished in high-Victorian style and the service is attentive and dignified.
Open Monday to Saturday 5 pm to 9 pm, Sunday noon to 2 pm (brunch) from 15 March until 31 December. Shorter hours in winter. Licensed. All cards. No smoking.

STE.-ANNE-DES-MONTS, Quebec **MAP 186**
CHEZ PIERRE ☆
96 boulevard Perron o **$60/$120**
Tourelle
(418) 763-7446

Chez Pierre takes no credit cards, so don't come unless you have plenty of cash. That said, they have a prime location overlooking the St. Lawrence. They have fresh

fish that comes straight from the port of Tourelle, gorgeous homemade Belgian chocolate and fine French cooking. There's a menu *du jour,* priced at 13.50 at noon, at night at 27.95. It offers exotic things like Danish pastries stuffed with chicken, marmite du pêcheur, lobster à la nage, tournedos of bison with morels and osso buco of deer. They also offer a traditional beef bourguignon with potatoes gratin and it's a delectable dish. Pierre's wife, Monique, makes the sweets and her chocolate is magnificent.
Open daily 11.30 am to 1.30 pm, 5.30 pm to 10 pm from the middle of June until Labour Day. Licensed. No cards. No smoking.

ST.-ANNE-DES-MONTS
See also CAP-CHAT.

ST. ANTHONY, Newfoundland **MAP 187**
THE LIGHTKEEPERS ☆
Fishing Point Road **$80**
(709) 454-4900

When the lightkeeper's house at the mouth of the harbour came up for auction, Dwayne and Randy Cull bought it with the idea of turning it into a coffee shop. Five or six years later they started to put on Viking feasts in a stone-and-sod banquet hall they built next door. The restaurant in the lightkeeper's house is open all day in season until 10 o'clock or later. There aren't many tables and they don't accept reservations. You can order a drink and wait on the deck or go around the point and keep watch for whales. Inside, the place has the feel of a casual yacht club. Randy's wife's sister is in charge of the kitchen, and what she cooks is fish and shellfish. A good way to sample what's available is to order the Lightkeepers' platter. It costs just 25.50 and brings you grilled halibut, scallops and shrimps, pan-fried cod and cods' tongues and poached salmon, all perfectly cooked. They also have a wonderful chowder and fresh crab and lobster in season. All dishes come with fresh vegetables

and marvellous rice pilaf. If you still haven't had enough to eat, ask for one of the berry pies or a piece of cheesecake. In the banquet hall they have a buffet of local game and seafood, served in the style of a Viking court. Remember, St. Anthony is on the Viking Trail and there are the remains of an eleventh-century Viking settlement at nearby Anse-aux-Meadows.
Open daily 11 am to 10 pm (sometimes later) from 15 May (15 June in the banquet hall) until 30 September. Licensed. All cards. No smoking. No reservations except for the Viking Feasts. ♿

ST. ANTHONY
See also L'ANSE-AUX-MEADOWS, CAPE ONION.

ST. CATHARINES, Ontario **MAP 188**
BANSAREE ☞
342 St. Paul Street **$65**
(905) 684-3411

It's nearly fifteen years since Bhanu Choudhury came here from Montreal and named his restaurant Bansaree after the Hindi flute. Times have been hard in St. Catharines for most of those years, but Bansaree has never faltered. In fact, the cooking gets steadily better and better. Every dish comes to the table hot and everything tastes perfectly fresh. Helpings are huge. Bhanu Choudhury makes all the traditional Hindi and Moghal dishes, and everything he touches is light, clean and lively. If bangalore pal, made with green chilli, is too hot for you, try the chicken jalfarazi or the vegetarian panir jalfarazi. (The chicken atti and the new chicken filfila are made with mango and cream and they're mild enough for anyone.) Chicken tikka and tandoori shrimp are still on the menu, but you might like to try such new dishes as the sweet-and-sour beef rajella or the Maharajah shrimp with dried fruit. If you order one of the combination plates, either the kohinoor or the maharajah, you can eat very cheaply—both cost around 30.00 for two. There aren't many wines, but

beer goes better with the food and mango lassi goes even better.
Open Monday to Thursday 11.30 am to 2 pm, 5 pm to 9.30 pm, Friday 11.30 am to 2 pm, 5 pm to 10 pm, Saturday 3.30 pm to 10 pm, Sunday 11.30 am to 2 pm (brunch), 5 pm to 9 pm. Licensed. All cards. No smoking. ♿

ST. CATHARINES **MAP 188**
WELLINGTON COURT ☆
11 Wellington Street **$125**
(905) 682-5518

At noon most of the action at Wellington Court takes place on the blackboard, which stands near the front door. That's where you'll find such things as carrot soup and Asian sole. In the evening, there's an ambitious à la carte that begins with carpaccio of beef with grana padano and arugula at 10.00 and goes up to poached sea scallops with white asparagus and truffled yellow tomatoes at 15.00. There's elk tenderloin to follow on cauliflower mash, tenderloin of beef with coconut velouté and rack of fresh Australian lamb with fava beans and garlic. Sticky toffee cake is the best of the sweets. They bake all their own bread as well and serve it with sweet butter. The wine-list mixes Niagara wines with wines (like the Kim Crawford sauvignon blanc) from the Pacific Rim, all sold at remarkable prices. Inside, Wellington Court is a riot of colour, and it's only an hour away from the Festival Theatre in Niagara-on-the-Lake.
Open Tuesday to Saturday 11.30 am to 2.30 pm, 5.30 pm to 9.30 pm. Closed on Sunday and Monday. Licensed. Master Card, Visa. Free parking. Book ahead in summer.

ST.-FAUSTIN-LAC-CARRE, Quebec (MAP 183)
LA CABANE A SUCRE MILLETTE ☞
1357 rue St.-Faustin **$60**
(877) 688-2101

This place will remind you of the Boustifaille in St.-Jean-Port-Joli, though the Boustifaille has a more ver-

satile kitchen. But the Cabane à Sucre is just fifteen minutes south of Mont Tremblant and it's a good choice for hungry skiers. The restaurant has been run by the Millette family on their farm for almost 50 years now, and in all that time they've never relaxed their standards. The outside walls are fashioned of square timbers; inside the walls are hung with family memorabilia. The long tables you share with your neighbours are served by waitresses in period costume and a fiddler plays traditional reels. Legend has it that the recipes come from the family cook-book. Meals all begin with thick pea soup and crusty homemade bread. Next comes an omelette, baked beans, scrunchions and maple-cured ham or sausage, both garnished with homemade pickles. Sweets mean sugar pie, waffles and maple syrup and pancakes with hot cream and sugar. With the meal you're expected to drink maple wine—before the meal there's a caribou cocktail made with maple syrup that's a lot stronger than you think.
Open Tuesday to Sunday 11.30 am to 8 pm by appointment only from 1 March until 30 April, Tuesday to Sunday 11.30 am to 8 pm from 1 May until 28 February. Closed on Monday. Licensed. Amex, Master Card, Visa. You must book ahead. No smoking. ♿

STE. FLAVIE, Quebec **MAP 190**
LE GASPESIANA
460 rue de la Mer **$95 ($210)**
(418) 775-7233

If you're travelling in the Gaspé out of season you need to know about the Gaspésiana, which has immaculate rooms overlooking the Gulf of St. Lawrence and a good dining-room that's open every day of the week year-round. There's always a large choice of fresh fish and shellfish—fish soup, mussels, scallops, cod, sole, halibut, salmon and bouillabaisse. The *menu du jour* features a ceviche of scallops, roast cod with beer and, sometimes, cods' tongues. There's tarte au sucre to follow, as well as a lovely tartine de crème, made with homemade

bread, maple sugar and fresh cream,. The wine-list remains very small and very conventional, but the service is friendly and efficient.
Open daily 6 pm to 9.30 pm. Licensed. Amex, Master Card, Visa. No smoking. ♿

ST.-GEORGES DE MALBAIE, Quebec (MAP 161)
AUBERGE FORT-PREVEL
2053 boulevard Douglas **$105 ($180)**
(418) 368-2281

If you come in for dinner at the Auberge Fort-Prével, chances are you'll find that the meal they offer you is a lot like the meal they offered you last year and the year before that. If you spend the night, you'll be offered a menu with more daily specials, and there are several good reasons to stay here. The situation is magnificent. They have a swimming-pool as well as a tennis-court and a nine-hole golf-course. The price of a room is quite modest, but if you have to move on, ask for the bouillabaisse, which is crammed with lobster, crab, cod, shrimp, salmon and scallops. Cod and cods' tongues are also on the menu, as well as pan-fried scallops with pink peppercorns, maigret of duck with port wine and lamb with goat-cheese from the farm next door. They smoke their own salmon and offer Rivière-au-Renard shrimps with white wine and dill. In the fall they like to bring in fresh caribou from Nunavut. There are four or five sweets, among them a chocolate mousse and a fresh-fruit crêpe. The children's menu still costs only about 8.00 a head.
Open daily 6 pm to 9 pm from the middle of June until the middle of September. Licensed. All cards. No smoking. ♿

ST.-HYACINTHE, Quebec MAP 192
LE PARVIS ☞
1295 rue Girouard o **$70**
(450) 774-2200

Le Parvis claims to be inexpensive, but that doesn't stop them from charging 32.95 for their filet mignon with

soup and a sweet. The sweet might be apple, made with locally-picked apples, the sweet panna cotta with fresh-picked fruit. The menu seldom breaks new ground, though recently we were surprised to be offered rabbit kidneys with mustard. The cooking is, however, extremely consistent and at noon you can get soup, an entrée and a sweet for as little as 14.95. Specials are offered every day, often pan-fried calf's liver. Fillet of venison is a new arrival on the à la carte, which has always featured fresh cod with maître d'hôtel butter and maigret of duck in a coulis of raspberry. If you don't want to start your meal with soup, ask for the terrine of red deer or the warm salad of scallops with candied ginger. Keep an eye open for the sugar pie, which is sometimes on the sweet list. Before you leave St.-Hyacinthe, take a look at the cathedral, which dates from 1878. The organ factory of Casavant Frères is also worth a visit.
Open Tuesday to Saturday 11.30 am to 5.30 pm (lunch), 5.30 pm to 10 pm (dinner). Closed on Sunday and Monday. Licensed. Master Card, Visa. No smoking.

ST.-JEAN-PORT-JOLI, Quebec **MAP 193**
LA BOUSTIFAILLE
547 avenue de Gaspé e **$45**
(418) 598-3061

The best time to come to the Boustifaille is early in the morning, when you'll be given an excellent breakfast of fresh-squeezed orange-juice, eggs and bacon or sausages, beans, home fries, tourtière and a good cup of coffee—all this for 14.40. At noon there are apt to be long lineups at the door, and no wonder. The helpings are big, the service is cheerful and the cooking is comfortable. We like to begin with split-pea soup and go on to saucisse maison or fèves au lard (pork and beans). On Monday there's chicken vol au vent, chiard blanc on Tuesday, cigares au chou on Wednesday. Keep an eye out for the graisse de rôti, which means roast-pork pan drippings served with toast with the fat on

top. Finish up with sugar pie or rice pudding—they're both lovely. There are only a handful of wines, all of them very cheap.
Open daily 7 am to 10 pm from 1 June until 24 September (shorter hours in the spring and fall). Licensed for beer and wine only. Amex, Master Card, Visa. No smoking. ♿

SAINT JOHN, N.B. **MAP 194**
BILLY'S SEAFOOD COMPANY
49-51 Charlotte Street **$100**
(506) 672-3474

Billy's is right next door to the City Market, which was built in 1876 and is said to be the oldest structure of its kind in the country. The Market offers a remarkable variety of fresh fish, meat, fruit and vegetables. Billy sells a lot of fish to take out too, and he'll deliver fresh lobster anywhere in Canada where there's an airport. In summer they have a fully-licensed patio with fourteen tables. In winter, or in bad weather, you sit inside and order your fish steamed, poached or, most commonly, baked. Malpèque oysters are served on the half-shell, lox is hickory smoked, clams and mussels are steamed, Digby scallops sautéed. The deep-fried squid and the deep-fried seafood platter are the only two deep-fries on the menu. Fresh salmon can be had either blackened or served in a honey-lime glaze. Regulars usually ask for their salmon served on a cedar plank for 18.95 or 32.95 for two. There's a good clam chowder and an excellent bouillabaisse. They have one outstanding sweet and that's chocolate cake layered with caramel and served on a coulis of mango and raspberry. The wine-list has been greatly expanded in the last two or three years, but you still won't do better than the Sutter Home sauvignon blanc, which goes very well with most of the fish.
Open Monday to Thursday 11 am to 10 pm, Friday and Saturday 11 am to 11 pm, Sunday 4 pm to 10 pm. Licensed. All cards. No smoking.

Nobody can buy space in this guide and nobody can buy his way out of it.

SAINT JOHN **MAP 194**

LEMON GRASS

42 Princess Street **$65**

(506) 657-8424

Lemon Grass, Saint John's newest Thai restaurant, is decorated in cool, minimalist style. Its menu lists such mainstays as red and green curry and chicken, shrimp and vegetarian pad Thai. Lovers of curry should look for the milder yellow or panang curries and gaeng masaman, a delicate curry from the Muslim south of Thailand. There are also a number of unusual dishes, such as hor neung pla (haddock on a banana leaf), which comes from the east coast. Yum sa (scallops with coconut and chilli) is made with fresh Digby scallops simmered in a hot-and-sweet coconut sauce over egg noodles. Some of the appetizers, especially the tung ton (chicken sautéed with ginger and peanuts) lend themselves to sharing. There's a good chicken soup with coconut and galangal, as well as the classic shrimp soup with lemon grass. The sweets run to fresh fruit—banana fritters and watermelon sorbet. The wine-list is small and inexpensive, but it's better to order a draught beer. *Open Monday to Thursday 11.30 am to 10 pm, Friday and Saturday 11.30 am to 11 pm. Closed on Sunday. Licensed. Amex, Master Card, Visa. No smoking.*

SAINT JOHN **MAP 194**

SAMPAN

Lancaster Plaza **$60**

638 Manawagonish Road

(506) 672-9050

Sampan is a gem. Eileen runs the front of the house; her husband, Alex, came from Dynasty in Toronto to run the kitchen. Saint John has a growing Chinese community and the restaurant is crowded every Saturday and Sunday morning, when two people can fill themselves with dim sum for 30.00. Tripe and cuttlefish have been dropped from the menu, but we can still rec-

ommend the stuffed eggplant, the barbecued pork bun, the sticky rice in a lotus leaf, the pan-fried turnip cake, the stuffed black mushrooms and all the dumplings. It's disconcerting to note that the dinner menu features chop suey, chow mein and foo young, but they also offer a variety of szechuan and black-bean dishes, as well as such exotic things as crab in sweet-corn soup, kung-pao chicken, beef tenderloin with black pepper and shrimps with black beans. Finish off with taro-milk tea with tapioca or just plain lemon tea. Aside from the à la carte, there are a number of nine-course set dinners, ranging from 19.50 for two to 62.00 for six.
Open Monday to Thursday 11 am to 11 pm, Friday to Sunday 11 am to midnight. Licensed. Amex, Master Card, Visa. No smoking.

SAINT JOHN **MAP 194**
SUWANNA ☆
325 Lancaster Avenue **$75**
(506) 637-9015

Franz Gehrig and his wife, Jaruwan, first made their reputation at the Stanley Inn outside Fredericton. Franz was in the business of forest management and owned 400 acres of bush in the district. "This is for my grandchildren," he was fond of saying. Six evenings a week, his wife cooked beautiful Thai dishes for the three tables in their little house. Then, to everyone's amazement, they bought the splendid mansion on Lancaster Avenue in Saint John built by Andrew Cushing in the middle of the nineteenth century. Other people had tried to develop the site, but had failed, but Franz Gehrig doesn't recognize failure. He restored the house and filled the dining-room. Saint John has never been long on good restaurants, but the Suwanna has changed all that. Jaruwan is back in the kitchen with a menu that runs to 50 different dishes. There are red, green and yellow curries of beef, pork, chicken, scallops and shrimps. She makes green-bean curries and jack-fruit curries, bamboo-shoots with beef and pork and hot

squid with lemon grass. All her dishes are served mild, medium and hot, but they're all spicy and by the end of the meal you'll be on fire. If you want something really mild, ask for the Thai duck, which is the most expensive thing on the menu but worth every cent. The pad Thai, on the other hand, is cheap but unrewarding. They keep a few wines in the cellar, as well as the fine Thai beer.
Open daily 5 pm to 9 pm. Licensed. Master Card, Visa. No smoking. Free parking. Book ahead.

SAINT JOHN **MAP 194**
TACO PICA ☞
96 Germain Street **$50**
(506) 633-8492

This is a bright little place, with lots of colour and a lively atmosphere—a flamenco guitarist plays Spanish airs every weekend. Guatemalan food isn't nearly as spicy as Mexican food in the first place, and the four Guatemalan refugees who run Taco Pica have long since learned to temper the wind to the shorn lamb. A taco stuffed with vegetables is always going to sell better than one stuffed with sweet peppers and walnuts. Actually, the flauta stuffed with mozzarella and chicken outsells everything else, though the stewed beef runs it a close second. The taste for hot spicing has been growing in Saint John and this year they've added stuffed jalapeno peppers to the menu and all the sauces, which are made to old family recipes, can be had mild, medium, hot or very hot. There are a number of Mexican dishes on the menu now, notably fajitas, chimichangas, Spanish-style paellas and quesadillas. The sweet-potato tart is a good way to end a meal and there are some great fruit and vegetable drinks for about 2.00 each.
Open Monday to Saturday 10 am to 10 pm. Closed on Sunday. Licensed. All cards. No smoking. ♿

If you use an out-of-date edition and find it inaccurate, don't blame us. Buy a new edition.

ST. JOHN'S, Newfoundland **MAP 195**
AQUA ☆
310 Water Street **$120**
(709) 576-2782

Aqua changed hands a year or two ago, just when we thought the cooking had begun to match the elegance of the décor. The former sous-chef, Mark McCrowe, is now back from chef's school in British Columbia, full of renewed vigour and new ideas. His new menu is seasonal and reveals a bias toward fusion cooking and bold flavours. As soon as you sit down, your arrival is greeted with a basket of focaccia and three fine bean spreads, followed by a complimentary ceviche. You might then begin the meal with mulligatawny soup, redolent of apple, parsnip and other root vegetables, or with a dip of crab and artichoke on pita bread. The paella is a mixture of mussels, prawns, squid and scallops on Israeli couscous, accompanied by sundried-tomato sausage. Then there's a beef-and-parsnip stew and lamb shanks marinated in stout and served on mashed potatoes. There are one or two outstanding sweets, one of them bananas and cream wrapped in phyllo and baked with nuts. Last winter the chef was offering a three-course early-bird special for 30.00 between 5.30 and 6.30 pm.
Open Monday to Friday noon to 2 pm, 5.30 pm to 10 pm, Saturday and Sunday 5.30 pm to 10 pm. Licensed. All cards. No smoking.

ST. JOHN'S **MAP 195**
BIANCA'S ☆
171 Water Street **$160**
(709) 726-9016

Nick and Bianca Tzanov, who both came to Canada as refugees from Bulgaria fifteen years ago, now work the nine-to-five shift and let their sous-chefs do most of the cooking. But they haven't forgotten where they came from. A traveller who dropped in on Sunday evening before other customers arrived had a dinner he's still talking about. He ordered one of the day's specials, which happened to be grilled halibut with crab-legs, tomatoes and mango. The halibut was perfectly cooked and came with a small green salad and vegetables baked in phyllo pastry. For sweet there was apple strudel with the most delicate of delicate pastries. Bianca's now has a lot of competitors, many of them staffed with chefs trained by Nick and Bianca themselves. But Nick and Bianca were the first to deliver consistently good cooking, especially in winter, when fresh produce is scarce and hard to find. We've always admired their tomato-and-gin soup, but last year a new soup, chestnut and quail, appeared on the menu. There's also a handsome fricassee of caribou with sour cherries and shallots and first-class halibut blackened Cajun-style and served in a bitter-lemon sauce. The list of sweets tends to repeat itself, but apart from the apple strudel there's now a bread pudding with the texture of a soufflé. Nick and Bianca claim that there's is the biggest and best wine-list east of Montreal. If you want to find out whether or not this is true, book a table in the wine-cellar. There are plenty of good open wines.

Open Monday to Friday 11.30 am to 2.30 pm, 5.30 pm to 10 pm, Saturday 5.30 pm to 10 pm, Sunday 6 pm to 10 pm. Licensed. All cards. Book ahead. ♿

ST. JOHN'S **MAP 195**

THE CASBAH

290 Duckworth Street **$60**

(709) 738-5293

The Casbah was designed as an upscale bar, built on the site of the old Restaurant 290. Neighbours, irritated by the noise, challenged their licence and the owner got around the problem by switching to meals with wine. Very quickly, they became the in place for brunch, thanks to an inviting menu, big helpings and low prices. Brunch entrées start at 8.95 and rise to 13.95. They all come with a baguette, homemade beans, stir-fried vegetables and home-fries. There are at least a dozen choices and we can vouch for the steak and eggs, the smoked salmon, the pancakes and all the Mexican dishes. If you don't want that much to eat, ask for the excellent green salad with a raspberry vinaigrette. Every week there are at least two new specials. But don't come for dinner—at the Casbah they can do brunch, but dinner is another matter. Even the service, charming in the morning, becomes ragged and disorganized in the evening.

Open Saturday and Sunday 11 am to 3 pm (brunch). Licensed. Master Card, Visa. No smoking. ♿

ST. JOHN'S **MAP 195**
INTERNATIONAL FLAVOURS
4 Quidi Vidi Road **$25**
(709) 738-4636

International Flavours began as a modest spice-and-lentil shop on Duckworth Street, offering Mrs. Jahlat Mann's daily curry, cooked on a hot-plate in the kitchen at the back. At her new location on Quidi Vidi Road she offers what she describes as Pakistani cuisine, Halal Authentication. You can have the daily special, as the saying goes, or you can have the daily special. But what a daily special! It could be curried chicken, curried vegetables and curried lentils or chick-peas on basmati rice with hot chutney. At 6.95, this has to be one of the best lunch deals in town. If you know your way around, you don't wait to be served; you go up to the cooler and help yourself. If you're alone, you pick up a magazine from the magazine rack. It's like eating at home with a mother who happens to cook Pakistani with Halal Authentication.

Open Tuesday to Saturday 11 am to 7 pm. Closed on Sunday and Monday. No liquor, no cards. No smoking.

This is a guide to Canadian restaurants from coast to coast—the first ever published and the only one of its kind on the market today.

ST. JOHN'S **MAP 195**

OLIVER'S

160 Water Street' **$110**

(709) 754-6444

Oliver's occupies the building that once housed Premier Joey Smallwood's offices. (Before that, it was used by the first suffragettes in St. John's.) Their menu is eclectic, mixing European and Asian cuisines with a number of local dishes, like scrunchions and cods' tongues. The crab-cakes, seasoned with dill and onion and served with garlic mayonnaise, are as good as any, and so are the Grand Banks scallops, basted with lime-butter and served on spinach. Blue mussels are prepared with white wine and basil, cod au gratin baked with a rich, creamy sauce and topped with cheddar cheese. Cod is a great fish, much too good to be baked in a cream sauce and served with cheese. But if you ask you can get your cod pan-fried, and they have salmon in a citrus-herb crust as well. The sweets are forgettable, but there's an enterprising wine-list.

Open Monday to Wednesday 10 am to 10 pm, Thursday and Friday 10 am to 11 pm, Saturday 9.30 am to 11 pm, Sunday 11 am to 4 pm (brunch), 4 pm to 10 pm (dinner). Licensed. Amex, Master Card, Visa. No smoking. Book ahead if you can.

ST. JOHN'S

See also MOBILE, PORTUGAL COVE.

ST. MARYS, Ontario **(MAP 211)**

SMITH & LATHAM

139 Queen Street E **$95**

(519) 284-4469

It's now three years since Robert Smith and Frances Latham reinvented their little restaurant on the main street of St. Marys. Occupying brand-new premises down the street from the original location, Smith & Latham is now a full-blown licensed restaurant offering lunch six days a week and dinner five all year round. At noon they serve things like liver and onions with sweet-potato fries, fish and chips (for 7.00) and cold poached salmon, as well as a quiche, a pasta, a crêpe and a stir-fry. In the evening, liver and onions are back at twice the price, along with lamb cutlets with garlic mash, grilled tenderloin of beef with straw potatoes, grilled salmon with rice-wine vinegar and breast of chicken with nan. Sweets are the specialty of the house. They make their own cheesecakes, pound cakes, mousse-cakes. They make a wonderful flourless-chocolate cake. They make all their own breads—rye, wholewheat, French baguettes and cinnamon rolls. The wine-list has been improved and they now have a decent list of Niagara wines, all offered at prices that haven't been seen in the Stratford area for years.

Open Tuesday to Saturday 11.30 am to 2 pm, 5 pm to 8 pm. Closed on Sunday and Monday. Licensed. Master Card, Visa. No smoking.

ST, MARYS **(MAP 211)**

WESTOVER INN

300 Thomas Street **$145 ($320)**

(519) 284-2977

The Westover Inn is still the best place to stay in Stratford, and if the dining-room is no longer the equal of the Old Prune and Rundles it's certainly a lot cheaper than either. Tony Gosselin and Ian Johnson have a lovely setting to work with, but they both cook in a very conservative style. They begin their dinners with such things as gazpacho and foie gras de canard with black-currant mustard (a real bargain at 11.00) and go on to grilled Atlantic salmon with green asparagus, rack of lamb with gorgonzola, Cornish game hen with honey and tenderloin of beef. These are all impressive dishes, and they're all served with dignity and grace, but there's nothing new or unusual about any of them. The best of the wines are from the Niagara Region. There's a V.Q.A. chardonnay from Malivoire and V.Q.A. caber-

nets from Creekside and Strewn. Wines from California and the Pacific Rim are, however, pretty thin on the ground.
Open daily 11.30 am to 2 pm, 5 pm to 8.30 pm. Licensed. All cards. Book ahead.

ST. PETER'S, N.S. **MAP 197**
BRAS D'OR LAKES INN
Highway 104 **$110**
(800) 818-5885

The chef here is a native Cape Bretoner, who came to St. Peter's last year from the Brittany in New Hamburg. The Inn is a new, nineteen—room motel on the shore of the Bras d'Or near St. Peter's Canal. It's a splendid site in any weather and they plan to stay open all year. The menu is simple and familiar, but keep an eye open for the little things: the fish knives that come with your fish, the hock glasses that come with your Dopff & Irion, the fresh vegetables, the excellent bread. There are four or five choices in each of three courses. The soup seems always to be cream-of-broccoli, so for a change ask for the baked mussels on the half-shell. After that there's beef tenderloin, rack of lamb, poached salmon and pan-fried haddock amandine. For sweet there are chocolate truffles and raspberry crumble. This is a handy place to know about if you want to break your journey between Sydney and the Canso Causeway on Highway 104.
Open daily 7.30 am to 9 pm from 1 July until 31 August (shorter hours in the spring and fall). Licensed. All cards. No smoking. Free parking.

ST. PETERS BAY, P.E.I. **(MAP 43)**
THE INN AT ST. PETERS
Greenwich Road **$135**
(902) 961-2135

The Inn at St. Peters has a fine setting overlooking the Greenwich dunes in the Prince Edward Island National

Park. The Inn is brand new and looks it, but already it has its own big vegetable garden. The dining-room is purpose-built, but the design doesn't work. The ceilings are two storeys high, the tables too large. Everyone shouts, which may be all right in downtown Toronto but not in St. Peters. The cooking was inconsistent at first, but this year the executive chef, Brad Richard, and his *chef de cuisine*, Greg Aitken, seem to have settled down together. The appetizers—foie gras with caramelized cantaloupe and red wine—are all over the top. The main courses—grilled halibut with cilantro and lime, grilled pork medallions with caramelized parsnips and small red potatoes—are less far-fetched. There's fruit and cheese to follow, as well as warm molten-chocolate cake and warm blueberry crumble.

Open daily 11 am to 2 pm, 5 pm to 9 pm from mid-May until mid-October. Licensed. All cards. No smoking. ♿

SALTSPRING ISLAND, B.C. *(MAP 230)*

Saltspring Island has become synonymous with lamb, black cod, smoked salmon and cheese. New wineries are developing an international reputation. If you want to sample some of this produce, go to the weekly public market in Ganges. It's open all day every Saturday from Easter until Thanksgiving. As for restaurants, the Hastings House (telephone (250) 537-2362) has a huge reputation, but we think the food is just as good at the House Piccolo (telephone (250) 537-1844), which is cheaper and more popular with local people than the Hastings House. We ourselves think of Saltspring Island as a place to explore and eat informally. At the moment, Calvin's (telephone (250) 538-5551) has a good kitchen and a booming business The owners are Swiss, but they like to cook in the Thai style and they have great marinated shrimps with deep-fried coconut. The Treehouse (telephone (250) 537-5379) has wonderful breakfasts and wonderful coffee. They also have a branch in Fulford Harbour (telephone (250) 653-4833) that's handy to the ferry terminal. They both have the same menu, but the service is better in Ganges.

SARNIA, Ontario **MAP 200**
MAISON ST.-AUBIN
1202 Lakeshore Road **$120**
(519) 542-9507

The Maison St.-Aubin is a real surprise. Why would Yves St.-Aubin, who comes from Montreal, have chosen to open a restaurant in a strip mall in Sarnia, hundreds of miles away from home?. Whatever his reasons, he's created a charming place, with crisp, fresh linen and warm, soft lighting. The menu is resolutely French, so look for French onion soup, escargots de Bourgogne, filet mignon béarnaise and veal de Normandie (which differs from veal normande in that it uses applesauce instead of apple cider). The vegetables are poor, but there's an attractive *prix-fixe* that offers pickerel or salmon for 31.95, with soup, sweet and coffee, and filet mignon poivrade for 38.95. The list of sweets is shorter than it used to be, but there are a few privately-imported wines, among them a Mandolin cabernet sauvignon and a Fochon crozes hermitage.
Open daily 5 pm to 10 pm. Licensed. Master Card, Visa. No smoking. ♿

SARNIA **MAP 200**
ON THE FRONT
201 Front Street N **$145**
(519) 332-4455

On the Front has a spectacular view of the lower stretches of the St. Clair River, near the point where it's spanned by the Blue Water Bridge. The restaurant is on the top floor of a fourteen-storey office tower, well away from the traffic of downtown Sarnia. The menu is seasonal. The soups are always good, though it could be said that they serve leek-and-potato too often. If you prefer, you can begin your meal instead with mussels in tomato-and-chipotle cream or marinated salmon with tarragon pancakes and salmon roe. The entrées are often quite elaborate: trout crusted in

coconut and served with cinnamon-scented basmati rice, braised leg and saddle of rabbit with pumpkin gnocchi and pan-seared salmon with rhubarb and red-onion marmalade. They have some exciting sweets (chocolate truffle-cake and a sour-cherry tartlet) and a fine wine-list with several interesting buys, among them a Smoking Loon chardonnay for 48.00, an Amity pinot noir for 46.00 and a Trimbach pinot blanc for 38.00.
Open Monday to Friday 11.30 am to 3 pm, 5 pm and 8.30 pm (two sittings), Saturday 5 pm and 8.30 pm. Closed on Sunday. Licensed. Amex, Master Card, Visa. ♿

SASKATOON, Saskatchewan **MAP 201**
GRACIE'S OFF BROADWAY
616 10 Street **$115**
(306) 664-1953

Jody Lyons came here from Australia by way of Churchill. Last year he opened a tiny *boîte* just east of Broadway. It's a bare place with a very small wine-list and a lunch menu that runs strongly to soups, salads and melts. Dinner, however, is another story. Lyons changes his menu often, but you can usually expect something like shrimps with Jack Daniel's whisky or mushrooms with caramelized onions, followed by beef wellington or lamb chops with rosemary and a reduction of port. If panna cotta is on the menu, be sure to ask for it—it's good.
Open Tuesday to Saturday 11 am to 2 pm, 5 pm to 10 pm. Closed on Sunday and Monday. Licensed. Amex, Master Card, Visa. No smoking. ♿

SASKATOON **MAP 201**
SUSHIRO ☞
737B Broadway Avenue **$65**
(306) 665-5557

Megan Macdonald trained for two years with a sushi chef in the Cayman Islands before opening her own restaurant with her partner, Todd Gronsdahl. Last year she

moved to a stylish new location just off Broadway. Here she offers some interesting salads, together with several tempuras (try the asparagus) and a variety of nigiri and maki sushis. The best of the maki sushis, we think, are the tekka maki (tuna with tomatoes and scallions) and the California roll (tuna with cucumber); the best of the nigiri sushis are probably the hokkigai (red clam), the hamachi (yellowtail) and the maguro (tuna). There's hot Gekeikkan, of course, as well as one or two premium sakes and a couple of wines. The service has improved.
Open Monday 5.30 pm to 9.30 pm, Tuesday to Saturday 11.30 am to 2.30 pm, 5.30 pm to 9.30 pm. Closed on Sunday. Licensed. Visa. No smoking. ♿

SASKATOON **MAP 201**
TAJ MAHAL ☆
1013 Broadway Avenue **$70**
(306) 978-2227

Rano Vasani has cooked every meal she and her husband, Nitu, have served at the Taj Mahal for the past fourteen years. She's a great natural cook and she insists on using nothing but the best beef and lamb, the freshest fish and shellfish. She makes all her own yogurt and all her own lassi. Her signature dishes are indicated on the menu—nawabi badami murgha, naryal prawns and naryal lobster. Actually, you'll do better with either the masala gosht (beef, ginger and spring onions) or the masala fish (fresh cod with lemon) than the nawabi badami murgha., but the best of the lot is the naryal lobster. Rano is keen on vegetables and her vegetable dishes—aloo gobi (cauliflower and potatoes with tomatoes and onions) and mutter panir (homemade cheese with garden peas)—are all outstanding. The sweet lassi and the chutney are both lovely, the appetizers rather less so. Go straight to one of the masala dishes or the naryal prawns or lobster.
Open Tuesday to Friday 11.30 am to 1.30 pm, 5.30 pm to 10 pm, Saturday 5.30 pm to 10 pm, Sunday 5.30 pm to 9 pm. Closed on Monday. Licensed. Master Card, Visa. ♿

SAULT STE. MARIE, Ontario **MAP 202**
PANNA ☆
472 Queen Street E **$110**
(705) 949-8484

Diners at Panna, if they didn't know otherwise, might think they were in Rain or North 44° in Toronto. The cooking is excellent and the service impeccable. People drive across the bridge from Michigan for the warm valhrona-chocolate cake or (in a different mood) for the roast-beef sandwich with five-year-old cheddar and caramelized onions. Everything from the bread to the sweets is prepared on the premises. Lunch is mainly a matter of sandwiches—Black Forest ham with brie, roasted tomatoes and mustard mayonnaise, portobello mushrooms with goat-cheese and roast beef with cheddar—all served on focaccia bread. Dinner is another matter entirely. There are five thin-crust pizzas, but for anyone over 30 it's better to start with a shrimp satay, baked goat-cheese with sweet peppers, chicken ravioli or a Thai salad. The Asian rice-noodles with ginger-marinated chicken in a coconut broth and the curried pork with bok choy and basmati rice are full of the bravura of Far Eastern cooking. The basil shrimp-and-scallop skewer with a butternut-squash risotto and the hand-made chicken ravioli are both more conservative treatments of traditional dishes, as is the grilled sirloin steak with its garlic mash. Aside from the valhrona-chocolate cake, there's espresso panna cotta and raspberry crème brûlée. This is the sort of restaurant where you're expected to start with a cocktail and end with a specialty coffee. If you want to go along with this, pass on the cocktail and finish off with Chocolate Bliss, which is made with white chocolate, kahlua and espresso.
Open Tuesday to Saturday 10 am to 4 pm (lunch), 4 pm to 10 pm (dinner). Closed on Sunday and Monday. Licensed. Amex, Master Card, Visa. No smoking.

Our web site is at www.oberonpress.ca Readers wishing to use e-mail should address us at oberon@sympatico.ca

SAULT STE. MARIE **MAP 202**
A THYMELY MANNER ☆
531 Albert Street E **$130**
(705) 759-3262

Maria Sicoli opened A Thymely Manner in the nineteen-eighties. In the early years, she did all the cooking, preparing the food the way her mother had taught her to, preserving fruits and vegetables in the fall, baking bread first thing every morning. She still writes up the menu and makes the bread and most of the sauces. Her daughter, Rosetta, always made the sweets and now prepares the daily specials as well. Recently, Rosetta has been touring Tuscany and her cooking has become more purely Tuscan. Last winter, for example, she was stuffing rabbit and making quail with balsamic vinegar and lamb shanks with pomegranate. For the à la carte they still pick their own mushrooms, grow their own herbs and grate their own parmesan. They import their pasta from Italy, but use local pickerel and whitefish. Lamb they buy, whenever they can, from a farmer on St. Joseph Island. They season their rack of lamb with mustard, garlic and lemon zest and serve their mixed grill of seafood on a bed of black noodles with pernod and anise. Their chicken is stuffed with spinach and smoked mozarella and wrapped in prosciutto. Duck is pan-seared and oven-roasted with a fruit glaze. Rosetta still makes baked bananas, chocolate cake and, in season, crazy strawberries.
Open Tuesday to Saturday 5.30 pm to 11 pm. Closed on Sunday and Monday. Licensed. All cards. No smoking.

LA SCIE, Newfoundland **MAP 203**
OUTPORT TEAROOM
Highway 414 **$30**
(709) 675-2432

For four centuries La Scie, close to Cape St. John on the Baie Verte peninsula, was one of the busiest harbours on the French Shore. Today, La Scie still has a

busy crab fishery. Several years ago, Valerie and Larry Whalen transformed their old family homestead into the Outport Museum. Soon after, they opened the Outport Tearoom on the spacious glass porch that runs the length of the house. For some time Valerie limited herself to teas, offering homemade fruit tarts, tea-buns and rhubarb crumbles. Then, three years ago, she enlarged her menu to include breakfast as well as such local dishes as baked beans on Wednesday, fish and brewis on Friday, Jiggs dinner on Tuesday and Thursday and roast beef on Sunday. Any day of the week, you can have crab au gratin, homemade soup or a sandwich.
Open daily 8 am to 8 pm. No liquor, no cards.

SHEFFIELD MILLS, N.S. **(MAP 245)**
BETWEEN THE BUSHES
1225 Middle Dyke Road **$100**
(902) 582-3648

Between the Bushes opened in April of 2004, serving lunches only. This summer, they'll be doing dinner as well five nights a week. The restaurant is surrounded by 60 acres of open country planted with highbush blueberries (pick your own in August and September, telephone (902) 582-1482, but remember, these aren't wild blueberries). The restaurant itself has wide windows and a fish-pond in the middle of the floor. Todd Frank has been the chef for several years and he likes to cook fish and shellfish. His Digby scallops, served with cumin and orange beurre blanc, is particularly good and so is his cider-glazed haddock. His rostii potatoes are marvellous. Most of the entrées come with a green salad made with a house dressing and lettuces that taste of the garden. We also like the seafood chowder and the fishcakes with salt-fish and Atlantic shrimp. Most of the sweets are made with the local blueberries and they're all served with real whipped cream.
Open Wednesday and Thursday 11.30 am to 3 pm, Friday to Sunday 11.30 am to 3 pm, 5 pm to 9 pm from late April until the end of May, Tuesday 11.30 am to 3 pm, Wednes-

day to Sunday 11.30 am to 3 pm, 5 pm to 9 pm from the beginning of June until early September, Wednesday and Thursday 11.30 am to 3 pm, Friday to Sunday 11.30 am to 3 pm, 5 pm to 9 pm from early September until late December. Licensed. Amex, Master Card, Visa. No smoking. ♿

SHELBURNE, N.S. **MAP 205**

CHARLOTTE LANE CAFE
13 Charlotte Lane **$120**
(902) 875-3314

The Charlotte Lane is one of the genuine pleasures of a visit to Shelburne. The owners, Kathleen and Roland Glauser, are lively, friendly people; the dining-room is charming, the service intelligent and efficient. If you want to take a picnic lunch with you, they'll make you up a hamper that's sophisticated beyond your wildest expectations. Roland Glauser makes some glorious sweets—among them lemon panna cotta with fresh raspberries and cointreau ganache on a chocolate-crumb crust. His appetizers are good too. There's chèvre with olives and red-pepper relish, Asian-style crab-cakes with a coulis of curried mango and a spectacular salad of watermelon, canteloupe and sunflower seeds on crisp rice noodles. The problem is with the main course, which for the most part is too rich, too heavy and too large for anyone over 30. You can if you like order two appetizers and a sweet. You can take a chance on the Tuscan pasta stuffed with poached vegetables or the fillet of salmon, glazed with maple-butter. Or you can go for broke and order the lobster-and-scallop brandy gratin topped with Monterey Jack cheese, which is as rich as Croesus. If you want to spend the night in Shelburne, call in at the Shady Pines Farm at 12 Roger Lane (telephone (902) 875-3495). It's right on the Roseway River, not far from the Charlotte Lane. It has 21 acres of walking trails and a great breakfast.

Open Tuesday to Saturday 11.30 am to 2.30 pm, 5 pm to 8 pm from early May until late December. Closed on Sunday and Monday. Licensed. Master Card, Visa. No smoking. Book ahead.

SIDNEY, B.C. **(MAP 230)**
DEEP COVE CHALET ☆☆☆
11190 Chalet Road **$165**
(250) 656-3541

When you turn into the driveway at Deep Cove Chalet you find yourself in a working vineyard. Part of the garden has been turned into a vineyard and you can drink Chalet semillon, grown outside the window, with your hot avocado or your cheese soufflé. (Across the street, the Chalet vineyard has been producing a cabernet/merlot as well for a couple of years now.) Pierre Koffel is not a fashionable chef. He's not interested in fusion cuisine or vertical presentation. He sticks to his last, cooking things like Malpèque oysters and lobster bisque, beef tenderloin with black peppercorns, rack of lamb provençal, avocado with shrimps and, of course, cheese soufflé. The cheese soufflé is a remarkable dish and so is the avocado—hot, intense and perfectly ripe. The wine-cellar, with all its Lafites, its Mouton Rothschilds and its glorious drinking from the Napa Valley, has few equals on the Island or anywhere else.
Open Tuesday to Sunday noon to 2.30 pm, 5.30 pm to 10 pm. Closed on Monday. Licensed. All cards. No smoking. Book ahead. ♿

SINGHAMPTON, Ontario **MAP 207**
EIGENSINN FARM ☆☆☆
Townline 10 **$545**
(519) 922-3128

Eigensinn Farm is open only two nights a week and has seating for just sixteen guests. If you want to be sure of getting a table, you need to book three months in advance. Dinner for two (without wine) costs 500.00, and for that you get to come in through a mud-room. But the fact remains that Michael Stadtländer cooks like an angel. He was born the son of a farmer and here at Eigensinn he has in a real sense come home. He has a vegetable garden so big that he's had to hire a full-time gardener. He's dug not one but two farm ponds, where he raises speckled trout and crayfish. He raises ducks and sheep. He grows fruit trees. All these things find their way onto his table. Dinners run to ten courses, starting with freshly-baked bread and a sliver of ham from his smokehouse, together with morsels of pan-fried trout and jellied rabbit with pickled cucumber. Next comes soup, an appetizer and fish—pickerel or whitefish, perhaps. Roast suckling pig may follow, or black-bellied Bermuda lamb raised on lavender, with imaginative vegetables and a choice of sweets—farm-fresh fruit in summer, perhaps something flavoured with maple in winter. To get to Eigensinn Farm, head west from Singhampton on Townline 10.

Open Friday and Saturday at 7 pm by appointment only. Closed Sunday to Thursday. No liquor, no cards. You must book three months in advance.

SOOKE, B.C. **(MAP 230)**

POINT NO POINT ☆

(250) 646-2020 **$140**

One couple writes to tell us that Point No Point was the highlight of their trip to the Canadian West. The scenery is spectacular and after a long weekend walk you'll probably be glad of one of Stuart and Sharon Soderburgh's cream teas. They come with all the trimmings—sundried-fruit scones, homemade jam, real whipped cream, finger sandwiches and a chocolate brownie—for 13.50. But it's with dinner that the chefs show what they're really made of. Every winter they sit down with local farmers and talk about what worked last year and what they'd like to do this year. That might be a salad of arugula with shaved parmesan cheese; it might be free-range Cowichan Bay chicken with olives and garlic or the celebrated strawberry shortcake. There's always fresh Pacific salmon (spring, sockeye, coho) and usually fresh dungeness crab, perhaps with potato gnocchi and dijon. There's confit of duck, per-

haps with quince. Osso buco is a favourite, as is beef tenderloin with tarragon and anchovies. Aside from the strawberry shortcake, there's a lovely, rich chocolate mousse. The nice, short wine-list features wines from Kettle Valley and Quail's Gate, but nothing from Vancouver Island. Look for Point No Point on Highway 14, fifteen miles north of Sooke.
Open Monday and Tuesday 11.30 am to 2.30 pm (lunch), 2.30 pm to 4 pm (afternoon tea), Wednesday to Sunday 11.30 am to 2.30 pm, 2.30 pm to 4 pm, 5.30 pm to 8.30 pm. Licensed for beer and wine only. Amex, Master Card, Visa. No smoking. You must book ahead for dinner.

SOOKE **(MAP 230)**
THE SOOKE HARBOUR HOUSE ☆☆☆
1528 Whiffen Spit Road **$240 ($450)**
(800) 889-9688

The menu at Sooke has been shortened this year, the prices have been raised and the kitchen is performing as it never has before. For the first time in a generation, the fabulous wine-list has had to take second place to the menu. The menu starts with three Kusshi oysters on the half-shell and goes on to weathervane scallops served three ways or Saltspring mussels cooked with heirloom tomatoes and jalapeno peppers. Next comes wild spring salmon crusted with sunflower seeds in a pine-mushroom broth and halibut with a golden-tomato emulsion in a roasted-garlic-and-watercress purée, then a white-chocolate chiboust and unpasteurized cheeses from Saltspring Island. The cooking is imaginative and beautifully spare. As for the wine-list, it offers a marvellous collection of wines from British Columbia, including wines from Saltspring and Saturna Islands, the Saanich Peninsula, the Fraser Valley, the Naramata Bench and the Similkameen, as well as the Okanagan. There are wines from Ontario, wines from Australia (Penfold's Grange), premium sakes from Japan, super-Tuscans from Italy, sauternes from Château d'Yquem and pauillacs from Lafite, Latour and Mou-

ton Rothschild. Sooke, where nasturtiums grow wild and rosemary rises to a height of eight feet at the door, is only an hour's drive from Victoria. Don't miss it.
Open daily 5.30 pm to 9.30 pm. Licensed. Amex, Master Card, Visa. No smoking. Book ahead. ♿

SPRY POINT, P.E.I. **(MAP 43)**
THE INN AT SPRY POINT
Highway 310 **$145 ($395)**
(902) 583-2400

Island chefs are an unstable lot. No sooner was Justin Ford installed in the kitchen at Spry Point than he left for Dayboat at Oyster Bed Bridge (see above). It's too soon to say who will be cooking here at Spry Point this summer, but the menu is simple and straightforward, so there's less to go wrong than at Bay Fortune. Dinners all begin with first-class bread, baked on the premises the night before, followed by an *amuse gueule*. Appetizers run from a tomato-and-feta salad to local mussels with saffron and a seafood chowder. Halibut, roasted with a white-bean ragoût, has for years been a specialty of the house both here and at Bay Fortune. As for lobster, the risotto they were serving last year was much better than the old lobster thermidor. Afterwards there are a few sweets and milk and cookies. Frankly, we'd like to see the lemon tart back on the menu instead of the milk and cookies. The wine-list is much smaller than the one at Bay Fortune, but it's well suited to the menu.
Open daily 5 pm to 9 pm from early June until late September. Licensed. Amex, Master Card, Visa. Book ahead after 15 August. No smoking.

STEWART, B.C. **MAP 210**
BITTER CREEK CAFE
311 5 Avenue **$75**
(250) 636-2166

Stewart is right on the border a few miles from Ryder in Alaska, a place famous for its grizzly bears. There are

only 700 permanent residents in Ryder, but tourists come here by the thousand in the summer months. There are plans for helicopter skiing, which may make tourism a year-round industry. But this is hardly the sort of place where you'd expect to find a good restaurant. At Bitter Creek, Debbie Kremzar makes all her own breads (lovely little pepper rolls) and all her own sweets (wild-berry cheesecake, frozen lemon mousse, apple strudel baked with Granny Smith apples). She makes all her own soups and all her own salads. She gets her greens from Vancouver, which is 850 miles away. Wild Pacific salmon is always on the menu and so is halibut. Both are char-broiled, so she bastes the fish constantly with garlic butter to keep the flesh moist. She can't get fresh crab or shrimps, but triple-A beef and Cajun chicken are always available, as well as thin-crust pizzas and a number of Mexican specialties.
Open daily 4 pm to 10 pm from early May until the middle of October. Licensed. All cards. No smoking.

STRATFORD, Ontario **MAP 211**
BIJOU ☆
105 Erie Street **$145**
(519) 273-5000

Last year Bijou closed their bakery and enlarged the main restaurant on Erie Street. The new restaurant, which is twice the size of the old, has lost some of the spontaneity and charm of the original. Prices have risen too, though you can still eat at Bijou for a lot less than at the Old Prune or Rundles (see below). Menus are chalked up on a blackboard, where things like seared tuna hamachi, escabèche of shrimp and foie gras with roasted beets, French lentils and sherry vinegar appear alongside pan-fried rainbow trout with summer squash, wild Pacific halibut with golden beets, venison with organic shitake mushrooms and beef tenderloin with avocado. They also offer two *prix-fixe* dinners, one at 39.00 for two courses, the other at 48.00 for three. The cooking is still lively and interesting, especially the beef with avocado, and all the wines are sold by the glass as well as the bottle. You won't go wrong with either the Lailey chardonnay or the Lillypilly cabernet sauvignon. *Open Tuesday to Thursday 5 pm to 9 pm, Friday to Sunday 11.30 am to 1 pm, 5 pm to 9 pm from early May until late October, Thursday to Saturday 5 pm to 9 pm from late October until early May. Closed on Monday in summer, Sunday to Wednesday in winter. Licensed. Amex, Master Card, Visa. No smoking.* ♿

STRATFORD **MAP 211**
THE OLD PRUNE ☆☆
151 Albert Street **$210**
(519) 271-5052

The Old Prune is the loveliest of restaurants: cool, elegant and very well served. Every day but Monday, they serve a delightful *prix-fixe* lunch overlooking the garden—a plate of charcuterie, gravlax with pickled cucumber, quail with couscous and charmoula, lemon-pudding cake and the best coffee in town for 52.00. Dinner costs twice that. It begins with pan-seared sea scallops or a warm salad of sweetbreads with preserved lemon, goes on to grilled Ahi tuna or slow-baked salmon with asparagus and ends with a caramelized rhubarb compote or a lovely warm chocolate cake. There's an impressive list of wines from Niagara and the Pacific Rim—Peninsula Ridge, Malivoire, Cloudy Bay, Lailey, Kim Crawford—as well as at least one surprising claret, the 1999 Pétrus la Fleur for 165.00.
Open Tuesday 5 pm to 9 pm, Wednesday to Sunday 11.30 am to 1.15 pm, 5 pm to 9 pm from Victoria Day until Thanksgiving. Closed on Monday. Licensed. Amex, Master Card, Visa. No smoking. Free parking. Book ahead.

This is a guide to Canadian restaurants from coast to coast—the first ever published and the only one of its kind on the market today. Every restaurant in the guide has been personally tested. Our reporters are not allowed to identify themselves or to accept free meals.

STRATFORD **MAP 211**
PAZZO ☆
70 Ontario Street **$140**
(519) 273-6666

Pazzo, as everyone knows, was lavishly redecorated last year and now has dark-grey walls, white linen and seductive lighting. Six days a week they put on a three-course *prix-fixe* lunch that majors in penne and panna cotta—all things of little interest. It's best to come in the evening, when Dean Elieff offers sophisticated dinners that might start with sweet-pea soup with sorrel or foie gras seasoned with kosher salt and served with a purée of white truffles and cauliflower. There's always plenty of market-fresh fish. (The scallops are browned on the bottom and lightly seared on top and they're especially good). Then there's first-class tiramisu and a lovely pecorino of fresh figs and port, as well as the panna cotta. The wine-list is at its best with Italian reds but if you have plenty of money you can't do better than the hermitage from Guigal. There are several excellent wines by the glass (Lindemans, Leaping Horse, Joseph Phelps) and downstairs you can have a glass or two of any of these with a sweet until all hours.
Open Tuesday to Sunday 11.30 am to 2.30 pm, 5 pm to 9 pm. Closed on Monday. Licensed. All cards. ♿

STRATFORD **MAP 211**
RUNDLES ☆☆☆
9 Cobourg Street **$230**
(519) 271-6442

At Rundles they've stuck closely to their original format: three *prix-fixe* dinners six nights a week, priced at 79.00, 77.00 and 67.50. For this you get to begin your meal rather grandly with a warm red and gold beetroot salad or a ceviche of ocean trout. (For a *supplément* of 20.00 you can have foie gras de canard or cold poached lobster.) Next comes hot ocean trout with lemon grass,

skate à la nage, braised shoulder of rabbit and roasted saddle of lamb. The menu is down-to-earth (saddle of lamb, shoulder of rabbit), the cooking persuasive, the presentation spare but elegant, the service cool but graceful. The sweets are lovely. There's a glazed lemon tart, panna cotta with ginger, floating islands with mango and raspberries and (probably the best of the lot) a selection of unpasteurized cheeses. The wine-list is full of good things, among them a Malivoire chardonnay, a pinot noir reserve from Thirteenth Street and (for those with lavish tastes) a Stag's Leap cabernet from the Napa Valley. The coffee is outstanding.
Open Tuesday 5.30 pm to 7 pm, Wednesday 5.30 pm to 8 pm, Thursday and Friday 5.30 pm to 8.30 pm, Saturday 11.30 am to 1.30 pm, 5.30 pm to 8.30 pm, Sunday 11.30 am to 1.30 pm, 5.30 pm to 7 pm from late May until late October. Closed on Monday. Licensed. Amex, Master Card, Visa. No smoking. Book ahead.

STRATFORD
See also ST. MARYS.

SUDBURY, Ontario **MAP 212**
ALEXANDRIA
211 Shaughnessy Street **$160**
(705) 688-1453

This year Mohamed has shortened his menu, which once seemed to be cast in stone. At the same time, he's added several daily specials, which might be roast salmon or veal marsala or, indeed, whatever takes his fancy. The regular menu offers a little of everything, an approach he likes to call international. He's expensive, as you can see, but the old place on Shaughnessy Street is well appointed and it has a serious kitchen that pays good money for organic greens, milkfed veal and vintage port. Mohamed used to be partial to Mediterranean dishes like bruschetta, smoked salmon and wienerschnitzel. This year, however, a new dish, Thai chicken with coconut, has gone over well with the customers, who also seem to like the chicken with port

and the tiger shrimps marinated with riesling. Mohamed makes all his own pasta, as well as several versions of rack of lamb. Crêpes Suzette have disappeared and the only in-house sweet left on the menu is the so-called banana Foster. Markups on wine are still about as low as ever, and Lindemans Bin 45 and Wolf Blass riesling both cost just 33.00 a bottle. Only five wines on the list cost more than 50.00.
Open Monday to Friday 11 am to 2 pm, 4 pm to 9.30 pm, Saturday 4 pm to 9.30 pm. Closed on Sunday. Licensed. Amex, Master Card, Visa. No smoking. ♿

SUDBURY **MAP 212**
PASTA E VINO
118 Paris Street **$75**
(705) 674-3050

Year in and year out, Pasta e Vino is the restaurant that most travellers write to us about. If you like it, you like it a lot. Frank Taranto never changes his menu if he can help it. He doesn't raise his prices and he doesn't sell expensive wines. The restaurant occupies a turn-of-the-century house and has thirteen tables. The atmosphere is comfortable and so is the cooking. They buy a lot of their pasta down the street, but they do make their own lasagne, gnocchi and cannelloni, and all their sauces are prepared from scratch. The kitchen is at its best with its seafood linguine, loaded with either clams, shrimps and scallops or clams, shrimps and squid. Mussels come in fresh every Wednesday and you should have them for as long as they last. The caprese is filled with marinated tomatoes and given a touch of garlic cream and a hint of garlic. The penne with prosciutto and mushrooms comes with a light gorgonzola sauce. Afterwards there are cakes and cheesecakes and a good tiramisu, but our favourite sweet is still the espresso granita, which is made with Tia Maria and whipped cream. They have excellent house wines from Abruzzo, one a montepulciano, the other a trebbiano.
Open Monday to Saturday 5 pm to 10 pm. Closed on Sunday. Licensed. All cards. No smoking.

SUMMERSIDE, P.E.I. **(MAP 43)**
FLEX MUSSELS ☞
Spinnaker's Landing **$25**
175 Harbour Drive
(902) 954-0022

If you think you're tired of mussels, come to Flex in Summerside. Here they serve absolutely fresh Island mussels. There are 23 varieties and they're all prepared to order and sold by the pound. Our favourites are the so-called Parisienne, which is made with pernod, tarragon, white wine and basil, and the Dubliner, made with Guinness, walnuts and caramelized onions. You can't go wrong, no matter what you choose. The fries are all hand-cut and twice fried, as they are in upscale French restaurants making a specialty of what they like to call *pommes frites*. The chef, Garner Quain, learned his trade at the Pan Pacific Hotel in Vancouver and later moved to Canoe in Toronto (see below). So he's used to making the most of fresh local ingredients. He even buys his Peking duck from a nearby Chinese restaurant and pairs it with black beans and mushroom broth. If it's raining, come another day—the mussels are all served in styrofoam containers, which you take to one of the picnic tables outside.
Open daily 11 am to 9.30 pm from early June until mid-December. No liquor. All cards. ♿

SUMMERVILLE BEACH, N.S. **(MAP 111)**
QUARTERDECK GRILL
Highway 3 **$110 ($250)**
(800) 565-1119

The setting of the Quarterdeck Grill will just blow you away. They have an all-weather deck that hangs over the sand. From there you can watch the shorebirds and listen to the waves breaking on the beach. The Grill is on the edge of Kejimkujik Adjunct, eight square miles of unspoiled coastline on Port Mouton Peninsula. They have a number of luxurious beachside villas that are

open year-round, though the dining-room is open only in summer. The staff are young, friendly and very well-informed. The cooking is capable. Everybody likes the lobster rolls, the seafood Caesar, the mussels and the very delicate fried squid. We usually find the planked salmon, cooked outside on the beach, overcooked, but others feel differently. Inside, there's grilled halibut, haddock and scallops, usually served with lemon-chive butter, as well as fillet of beef, apricot chicken with pickled ginger and pork tenderloin with apple and cranberry chutney. Meals end with cheesecake or what they call a triple-chocolate fix. In summer there's often blueberry grunt or strawberry shortcake.
Open daily 10 am to 10 pm from early May until late October. Licensed. Amex, Master Card, Visa. No smoking. ♿

SUSSEX, N.B. **MAP 215**
BROADWAY CAFE ☞
73 Broad Street **$40/$80**
(506) 433-5414

We remember when Judith Williams first started offering sandwiches in Sussex, 25 years ago. Sussex may have grown since then, but it's still surrounded by gentle green countryside watered by slow-flowing rivers. The town made its name with its dairy products: then it began to attract artists and artisans. Judith and her husband brought in live entertainment on weekends, expanded their menu, bought an espresso machine and persevered. Today their café is trim, bright and decidedly stylish. It still majors in sandwiches, soups, salads and sweets—we still remember the peach crisp. Last summer, however, Judith and her husband sold the café. The new owner, Randi Griffin, had worked in the kitchen for a long time, and so far she hasn't missed a beat. The menu is designed to make the most of whatever is fresh and in season. Last summer travellers were speaking of the curried beef kebabs and the dilled salmon. They also write to us about the vegetables, especially the Greek potatoes. We find the chicken paprika

a bit too dry, but the chicken linguine is excellent. The sweets are all up to scratch, especially the so-called Chocolate Decadence. The thing to drink is Pumphouse ale, which is brewed in Moncton and sold here on draught. The espresso and capuccino are both lovely.
Open Monday and Tuesday 10 am to 3 pm, Wednesday to Saturday 10 am to 9 pm. Closed on Sunday. Licensed. All cards. No smoking.

SYDNEY MINES, N.S. **MAP 216**
THE GOWRIE HOUSE ☆☆
840 Shore Road **$115 ($300)**
(902) 544-1050

The Gowrie House isn't quite what it used to be, if only because Clifford Matthews has gone. His happy-go-lucky partner, Ken Tutty, can't be everywhere at once. If he's away, make friends instead with Carolyn, who's a pretty easy person to make friends with. If you're staying at Gowrie, as you should, you'll find that everything about the place is as it should be. Two or three of the gigantic trees on the front lawn may have disappeared, but inside and out the old house gleams with fresh paint. The Spode porcelain, the eighteenth-century drinking glass and the Staffordshire figurines—to say nothing of the wonderful contemporary teapot—are all where they belong. A splendid breakfast—muesli, pancakes, eggs, muffins, toast and hot coffee—is on the table every morning. In the evening a comfortable dinner—wild-mushroom soup, perhaps, with a Thai wrap, fresh halibut or beef tenderloin and a piece of carrot cake or chocolate mousse-cake—comes with a carafe of first-class wine. The Gowrie House is definitely the place to stay in Cape Breton.
Open daily at 7.30 pm by appointment only from early April until late December. Bring your own bottle. Amex, Master Card, Visa. No smoking. You must book ahead before 3 pm. ♿

Nobody can buy space in this guide and nobody can buy his way out of it.

TELKWA, B.C. **MAP 217**

THREE BRIDGES

1705 Riverside Street **$115**

(250) 846-5631

It's 460 very slow miles from Prince George to Prince Rupert, with nowhere to eat that we knew of between them, except in Terrace. This year, however, we've discovered a place in Telkwa, ten miles east of Smithers, called the Three Bridges. They make all their own breads, soups and sweets right here in the kitchen. In summer they buy all the fruits and vegetables they can get from local organic farmers—gorgeous ripe tomatoes, strawberries and six varieties of raspberries. They bring in fresh Pacific halibut from Vancouver. The young chef is constantly experimenting with different cuisines—Mexican, East Indian, Mediterranean. The Mediterranean menu, always popular, features spaghetti vongole made with live Pacific clams. There's a good selection of wines in the cellar from both the Old World and the New. The service, all handled by local students, is keen and enthusiastic. Look for the Three Bridges in the heart of town, not far from the meeting of the Telkwa and Bulkley Rivers.

Open Monday and Thursday to Sunday 11 am to 10 pm (shorter hours in winter). Closed on Tuesday and Wednesday. Licensed. Master Card, Visa. No smoking. ♿

TERRACE, B.C. **MAP 218**

DON DIEGO'S ☆

3212 Kalum Street **$85**

(250) 635-2307

Richard and Annalee Davis have stopped working a seven-day week and taken up golf instead. Otherwise very little has changed at Don Diego's. The Davises came to Terrace more than twenty years ago, praising the virtues of Mexican cuisine. Their restaurant was an instant success. Before long, however, they started cooking in the Thai style; later still they switched to the

Caribbean and African cuisines. They're now back right where they started, with the cooking of Mexico and the American Southwest. The menu changes every day. No cuisine is ever completely discarded, so a Thai dish may show up on Monday, a Caribbean or African dish on Wednesday. They do a lot of seafood, which is brought in fresh from Prince Rupert, a hundred miles away. Halibut appears on the menu in April and stays there until November; crab comes in October. Shrimps are scarce on the West Coast, but keep an eye out for shrimp with chipotle and lime, as well as fresh Pacific salmon. They make all their own pasta. Fresh fruit and vegetables are readily available in Terrace and stirling beef comes in from Alberta. Steaks and back ribs are all served with a hot, spicy southwestern sauce. Sweets have always been a big thing here, which means fruit cobblers, spice cakes, cheesecakes, homemade ice cream and New Orleans bread pudding with whisky. The big sellers right now are San Francisco foggies. A foggy is a chocolate-pecan brownie with chocolate sauce and vanilla ice cream. The wine-list is small and most of the wines come from the Pacific Northwest, though there are several varietals from Italy and France as well. The top price is still less than 25.00 a bottle. *Open Monday to Saturday 11.30 am to 9 pm. Closed on Sunday. Licensed. Amex, Master Card, Visa. No smoking. Book ahead if you can.* ♿

THESSALON, Ontario **MAP 219**
CAROLYN BEACH
1 Lakeside Drive **$90 ($170)**
(705) 842-3330

The Carolyn Beach is a good place to know about. Thessalon is 50 miles east of Sault Ste. Marie and the motel is just off the Trans Canada Highway. The building overlooks Lake Huron from a secluded sandy beach and every bedroom has an unobstructed view of the North Channel. The Currie family owned the place for more than 40 years. In 1997 things began to fall

apart and the Carolyn was dropped from the guide. This year the motel has been taken over by Andrew and Susan Weigel. They've updated the bedrooms and renovated the dining-room. In summer there's golf and boating, in winter there are miles of groomed cross-country ski trails. There's good fishing year-round. More to the point, the kitchen is now very good indeed. Everything on the menu is cooked from scratch. Nothing is reheated. One traveller asked for a second bread-roll and was told he'd have to wait a few minutes until a new batch had been baked. In the evening—they cook better in the evening than at noon—keep an eye out for the fresh whitefish with tartare sauce, the yellow perch in tempura batter and above all the char-broiled pickerel with lemon-butter sauce. In summer they have a number of fresh-fruit pies—strawberry, raspberry, blueberry, apple, peach. The dining-room is very well served. Indeed, everything about the place reveals the hand of a true professional.
Open daily 8 am to 11 am (breakfast), 11 am to 4 pm (lunch), 4 pm to 7.30 pm (dinner) from 15 January until 31 October. Licensed. Amex, Master Card, Visa.

THUNDER BAY, Ontario **MAP 220**
ARMANDO'S
2 N Cumberland Street **$90**
(807) 344-5833

Armando's is the kind of restaurant that everyone likes, perhaps because Armando himself is obviously so happy with his work. As he himself says, the day he stops having fun he'll shut the place down. Last year he kept himself interested by building a room for private parties. He stopped serving lunch on Fridays and that made him feel better too. Finally, he added rabbit to his menu. The rabbit is baked in the oven and served with a spicy red sauce. Armando makes all his own sauces and cuts all his own meats—Alberta beef, pork tenderloin, lamb shanks and osso buco. Veal (imported from Montreal) is popular too, whether it's served with a wedge of lemon or with black tiger shrimps. Fish comes in fresh every Friday, but Armando is disheartened by the scarcity of wild fish. He can almost always get fine fresh pickerel, which he sautées lightly with garlic and lemon—he thinks breading takes away from the flavour. Pina, his wife, makes all the soups—minestrone with black, red and white beans and the best-selling cream-of-garlic-and-mushroom. She also makes the cheesecakes and the tiramisu. Armando started out with 50 of the best Italian red wines. Now he carries wines from every corner of the New World, but he still thinks the Italians are the best.

Open Monday to Thursday 5 pm to 9 pm, Friday and Saturday 5 pm to 11 pm. Closed on Sunday. Licensed. Master Card, Visa. No smoking. ♿

THUNDER BAY **MAP 220**
BISTRO ONE ☆
555 Dunlop Street **$130**
(807) 622-2478

Jean Robillard is a serious and important chef, and at Bistro One that's what you're paying for. He has an extensive menu, which changes almost every day. Some dishes, of course, are too good to be allowed to disappear, among them the rosemary-crusted rack of lamb with gorgonzola butter and the scallops with maple syrup and champagne. Some of the dishes—Atlantic salmon with a warm lobster sauce and provimi veal with wild mushrooms and marsala—are merely comfortable. Others, however, have a real edge. Robillard likes to experiment with things like salads of chilled roasted pear, crumbled stilton, candied pecans and port vinaigrette or tenderloin of Alberta beef with chipotle and feta cheese. We for our part have always been fond of his stuffed breasts of chicken, but they'll probably be gone tomorrow. Maria Costanzas makes the sweets and her best dishes are the warm molten-chocolate cake and the maple torte with a prickly-pear coulis. The wine-list used to concentrate on the wines of California and

Australia, but in the last year or so Robillard has added a couple of dozen of the better wines from Niagara and the Okanagan, which helps.
Open Tuesday to Saturday 5 pm to 10 pm. Closed on Sunday and Monday. Licensed. All cards. No smoking. ♿

THUNDER BAY **MAP 220**
CARIBOU ☆
727 Hewitson Street **$150**
(807) 628-8588

Caribou is staffed by students and chefs-in-training from the university's culinary-arts program. They have a lot of self-confidence, and with Craig Viera in the kitchen a high degree of self-confidence is fully justified. His menu is what he calls contemporary North American, and that's accurate enough so long as you realize that everything is prepared Thai-style in a wood-fired oven. Lunch features wood-oven pizzas, along with a beef strip-loin with shoestring fries and mushroom risotto with asiago cheese and Italian sausage. At night the most popular dish is the wood-oven-roasted cedar-planked salmon with tartare sauce or (you have the choice) Asian spices and Asian garnishes. The rack of lamb, which is imported from New Zealand but tastes as if it wasn't, comes with tomatoes, spinach and egg-plant with Greek seasoning. Fresh sea-bass is marinated in Moroccan spices and served with a salsa of lime and mango. The best of the sweets is the crème caramel with fresh raspberries. It's brought to the table warm and it's delightful.
Open Monday to Wednesday 5 pm to 10 pm, Thursday 11.30 am to 2 pm, 5 pm to 11 pm, Friday 11.30 am to 2 pm, 4.30 pm to midnight, Saturday 4.30 pm to midnight, Sunday 5 pm to 9 pm. Licensed. All cards. No smoking. ♿

Where an entry is printed in italics this indicates that the restaurant has been listed only because it serves the best food in its area or because it hasn't yet been adequately tested.

THUNDER BAY **MAP 220**

GIORG

114 Syndicate Avenue N **$80**

(807) 623-8052

There never really was a Giorg. There was a Bill when the place opened with a bit of a flourish. Now Bill is a bit tired of it all and there's a Freddy who does most of the work. They still make all their own linguine, fusilli and penne with durum semolina. They pick up fresh bread twice a day and pay what they have to for a good tomato. Freddy brings in a lot of fresh fish—mussels and halibut rubbed with dijon mustard and grilled. People all seem to like the penne with sundried tomato and the mixed grill, made with Alberta beef, shrimp and chicken. There are specials that change every day or so: perhaps an inch-thick veal chop in a balsamic demi-glaze, perhaps osso buco, perhaps rabbit. They have their own pastry chef who makes all the tortes and cheesecakes, as well as the old-fashioned rice pudding, made to an old English recipe, that's served for lunch on Friday.

Open Tuesday to Saturday 5.30 pm to 9 pm. Closed on Sunday and Monday. Licensed. All cards. No smoking. ♿

THUNDER BAY **MAP 220**

GOOD NEWS CAFE ☞

116 S Syndicate Avenue **$40**

(807) 623-5001

The Good News Café has had another great year, when most other restaurants suffered reverses. Small wonder. Fernande Vezeau can dream up some wicked pastries, and a lot of people stop by the Good News for a cup of espresso and a pastry. The current favourites are the lemon-lavender torte and the strudel torte—a sponge-cake with layers of custard and mixed berries wrapped in puff pastry and baked. Or you can come in for lunch. The soups run to such things as Thai coconut, roasted-

mushroom-and-thyme and ginger-carrot. They have some great sandwiches. The so-called Mediterranean Grill, for instance, combines artichokes, tomatoes and spinach with feta cheese and garlic mayonnaise on focaccia. There are one or two outstanding salads, like the grilled sirloin with roasted vegetables and a roasted-tomato vinaigrette. They have Mexican chocolate to drink, as well as espresso and a few wines.
Open Tuesday to Saturday 10 am to 4.30 pm. Closed on Sunday and Monday. Licensed for beer and wine only. Master Card, Visa. No smoking. ♿

TOBERMORY, Ontario **MAP 221**
GRANDVIEW INN
80 Earl Street **$100**
(519) 596-2220

The Grandview is more than just a convenient place to stop if you're waiting for the ferry to Manitoulin Island. The place has been owned by the same family for almost 40 years, and it's fourteen years now since Deb Crawley took over the kitchen. She cooks her Georgian Bay whitefish every which way—fried, broiled and blackened Cajun-style, topped with asparagus hollandaise, stuffed with crab and wrapped with nori or steamed and served in a red-pepper coulis. Last summer they started serving pecan-crusted chicken, baked with blue cheese and glazed with cranberry. They also have char-grilled lamb chops, lamb ribs with a black-olive-and-anchovy tapenade, fillet of beef and, an old favourite, pork tenderloin with blueberries and cassis. There's always a soupe du jour, a nine-green salad with seasonal fruits and coconut shrimp with Asian sweet chillis. Deb Crawley makes all her biscuits and all her pies—raspberry-rhubarb, wild-blueberry—to recipes she got from her grandmother. Just about everything on the wine-list is priced to sell. Mâcon villages costs 28.00, Beringer's founder's estate cabernet sauvignon 44.00. Only the Fontanafredda barolo and the Masi amarone seem overpriced.

Open daily 5 pm to 9 pm from Victoria Day until Thanksgiving. Amex, Master Card, Visa. No smoking.

TOFINO, B.C. **MAP 222**
RAINCOAST
120 4 Street: Unit 11 **$100**
(250) 725-2215

Lisa Henderson has always been a passionate environmentalist. Even her eggs are free range. She now belongs to the Endangered Fish Alliance, however, which makes it hard for her to serve many varieties of fish. So, for the first time this year, she's serving beef tenderloin, along with lamb shanks, free-range chicken and free-range Muscovy duck (with blackberry pan-juice). She's always had a number of attractive vegetarian dishes and she still has. One is agedashi tofu dusted with gomashio and pan-fried with a sweet black-bean glaze, another is channa dal or red-lentil curry with potatoes, chick-peas, cauliflower and spinach. She often has cioppino on the menu. It's made with wild salmon, halibut, mussels and clams—none of which is an endangered species. Occasionally she'll offer swimming scallops or side-striped prawns, sautéed in ginger wine and served with daikon-and-apple slaw. She likes to cook in the Asian style, so while her salad of hand-peeled shrimps with baby greens has proved extremely popular, she prefers her clams and mussels in a sambal-coconut broth. Her sweets have always been rather conventional. The fresh-fruit crumble and the frozen peanut-butter pie are the best of an indifferent lot. The small wine-list has one or two outstanding vintages. One of these is the Wild Goose riesling, priced at just 31.00. There are also some great Okanagan ciders.
Open daily 5 pm to 9 pm (later in summer). Licensed. Amex, Master Card, Visa. No smoking. ♿

The map number assigned to each city, town and village gives the location of the centre on one or more of the maps at the start of the book.

TOFINO **MAP 222**
SHELTER ☆☆
601 Campbell Street **$145**
(250) 725-3353

Jesse Blake is doing so many good things in this three-level restaurant overlooking Clayaquot Sound that it's well worth a trip from Victoria. Even such a hackneyed dish as steamed mussels acquires new life at his hands. Seventeen large mussels are served in stout with caramelized onions and wildflower honey. What makes the dish, the most popular on the menu, is the julienned zest of preserved lemon. The fish course might be halibut wrapped in prosciutto, a treatment that gains texture from its slivers of nori, sweetness from its roasted red peppers and substance from its prawn risotto. The meat course might be Alberta rib-eye, which comes with a garnish of local chanterelles and angel-wing mushrooms. In the fall he takes advantage of the last cull of chinook and coho salmon, using only the largest and fattiest fish, which he seasons with sea-salt and cracked black pepper. The sweets are at their best when paired with one of his local icewines: chocolate-espresso mousse with merlot, vanilla parfait with blackberries, orange caramel and pistachio praline with chardonnay. The ground floor is small and crowded; ask for a table upstairs when you book.
Open daily 5 pm to 10 pm. Licensed. Amex, Master Card, Visa. No smoking.

TOFINO **MAP 222**
SOBO ☞
1184 Pacific Rim Highway **$25**
(250) 725-2341

Lisa Ahier spent years building an imposing reputation at the Cibolo Creek ranch in Texas before she moved north to Long Beach Lodge in Tofino. Before long a change of ownership at the Lodge forced her to move again, this time to a purple catering truck parked close

to the beach at No. 1084, on the site of what used to be the Café Pamplona. She's still interested in fresh local produce, organic meats and organic seafood, but at Sobo this all has to be turned into high-end takeout food. Everything is served from the back of the truck. You can eat at one of the picnic tables if you like, or you can take your meal home or to the beach. There are those who say the crab-cakes are the best on the West Coast. The blue-corn taco shells piled high with wild fish (seared spring salmon or halibut) are almost equally good. Then there's a Thai noodle salad and cornmeal-crusted oysters. Sobo (short for Sophisticated Bohemian) appeared on *EnRoute*'s list of the top ten new restaurants in Canada in its first year. Meals are served from the truck until 5 o'clock, when the operation moves indoors to the old Café Pamplona, where Richard Moore is still in charge of the kitchen. There he turns out such things as local oysters, Japanese-style eggplant and killer-fish tacos, followed by cedar-planked wild Pacific salmon, free-range chicken in mole sauce, steamed dungeness crab and braised short ribs.
Open Wednesday to Sunday 11 am to 5 pm, 5 pm to 9 pm from 7 February until 30 April, Monday and Wednesday to Sunday 11 am to 5 pm, 5 pm to 9 pm from 1 May until 30 June, daily 11 am to 5 pm, 5 pm to 9 pm from 1 July until 31 August, Monday and Wednesday to Sunday 11 am to 5 pm, 5 pm to 9 pm from 1 until 30 September, Wednesday to Sunday 11 am to 5 pm, 5 pm to 9 pm from 1 October until 15 December. Closed on Tuesday in the spring and fall, on Monday and Tuesday in the winter. No liquor, no cards in the truck. Indoors they have a licence and take Amex, Master Card, Visa.

TOFINO
See also UCLUELET.

We accept no advertisements. We accept no payment for listings. We depend entirely on you. Recommend the book to your friends.

TORONTO, Ontario **MAP 223**
BATIFOLE
744 Gerrard Street E **$110**
(416) 462-9965

Jean-Jacques Texier has left the narcissistic charms of Yorkville for a dull stretch of Gerrard Street. Here he has his own place, where the cooking is good and the prices reasonable. The menu is short and to the point. There's perfectly fresh fillet of skate. There's pork tenderloin with a truffle-cream sauce. There's a spinach tart with wild mushrooms and a beautiful crab-and-rockfish soup with saffron chantilly. M. Texier comes from Brittany and like most Bretons he's good with fish and shellfish. He's also at home with pork and such hearty vegetable dishes as oven-baked potatoes and onions with reblochon au gratin. The entrées all come to the table without any garnish, but one order of vegetables is enough for two. The wine-list is mainly French and there are a number of unusual dessert wines and digestifs. Everybody feels comfortable at Batifole.
Open Monday and Wednesday to Saturday 6 pm to 10 pm, Sunday 11.30 am to 3 pm, 6 pm to 10 pm. Closed on Tuesday. Licensed. No smoking. All cards.

TORONTO **MAP 223**
BOBA ☆
90 Avenue Road **$150**
(416) 961-2622

The green salad may have lost some of its old magic in recent years, but there are lots of other good things at Boba. There's Barbara Gordon's vegetable sushi with seared tuna for one. The tuna is perfect and the vegetable sushi is full of small surprises. There's Bob Bermann's lovely sautéed shrimp with its spicy peanut sauce and crunchy noodles. There's the fillet of tuna, offered as a main course with coconut noodles, avocado, mango and black beans. There's the ostrich, which comes from a farm near Stratford and is served

without a trace of fat—lean, intense and wonderful. The rack of lamb is served in cinzano, which may raise a few doubts, but the breast of chicken is entirely equal to its spicy rub and hot spiced eggplant. The meal ends with Barbara Gordon's marvellous trio of lemon—lemon custard, lemon buttermilk pudding and lemon ice cream. The wine-list is long on châteauneuf du pape and on cabernets from Australia and California, but weak on wines from the Okanagan and the Niagara Region.
Open Monday to Saturday 6 pm to 10 pm. Closed on Sunday. Licensed. Amex, Master Card, Visa. No smoking. Book ahead.

TORONTO **MAP 223**
BYMARK ☆
66 Wellington Street W **$250**
(416) 777-1144

Bymark is in the shopping-concourse of the Toronto-Dominion Centre, next to a toy shop. There's nowhere to park except in the basement, which like a lobster trap is easy to enter and hard to leave. The restaurant, as everyone knows, was designed by Yabu Pushelberg, which means that it's melodramatic and self-conscious. The menu could be criticized on similar grounds. Seared tuna is served with spiced mango, seared foie gras still more outrageously with calvados, rhubarb jam and a praline-apple brioche. But there are better things to be found—the terrine of foie gras, for instance, with gewurztraminer jelly, sea-salt and a roasted pear. Gravlax comes with warm potato pancakes, chives and crème fraîche, asparagus with a reduction of shrimp and a simple hollandaise sauce, a green salad with hazelnuts and sheep's-milk cheese. The kitchen is particularly good with fish: Arctic char with asparagus and corn, sea-bass in its skin with roasted tomatoes and a herb tapenade, black cod with lemon grass and ginger soy. Prices are extremely high. At noon some of the prices are lower, but the presentation is different. Striped bass, for

instance, is served at noon with fingerling potatoes, cherry tomatoes and basil for 23.95. Rufina Chombo, the *pâtissière*, makes a lovely warm chocolate torte with a warm ganache and crisp banana tuile that goes well with any of the dessert wines or a cup of loose tea. The wine-list has almost every virtue except that of economy. This could be the time to order a bottle of cabernet sauvignon from Spottswoode. Don't ask the price.
Open Monday to Friday noon to 2 pm, 5 pm to 10 pm, Saturday 5 pm to 10 pm. Closed on Sunday. Licensed. Amex, Master Card, Visa. No smoking. Book ahead. ♿

TORONTO **MAP 223**
CANOE ☆
Toronto-Dominion Bank Tower **$195**
66 Wellington Street W
(416) 364-0054

Come here, to the top floor of the Toronto-Dominion Bank Tower, for the view of the Toronto Islands, which is superb in almost any weather. Come here for the service, which is perfect. Come for the menu and the cooking, which is imaginative and, on the whole, reliable. The wild-mushroom soup is delightful and so is the organic-beet salad. The kitchen is fond of scallops, which they bring in from Yarmouth and serve with split peas. The ravioli, stuffed with ricotta cheese and black truffles and served in a coulis of wild mushrooms, is impeccable. The Atlantic salmon is lightly cooked and beautifully garnished with radishes. The lemon-soufflé pudding with tapioca and mint, an unusual treatment, is lovely, and so are the raw-milk cheeses, four of them from farmhouses in Quebec. There's a fine list of wines from Napa and the Niagara Region, as well as a scattering of super-Tuscans. Big clarets are thinner on the ground, but there are plenty of wines by the glass and the half-bottle.
Open Monday to Friday noon to 2.30 pm, 6 pm to 9 pm. Closed on Saturday and Sunday. Licensed. All cards. No smoking. Book ahead. ♿

TORONTO **MAP 223**
CELESTIN ☆
623 Mount Pleasant Road **$170**
(416) 544-9035

Everybody knows the story of Pascal Ribreau. While he was still the chef at Provence in Cabbagetown, he was involved in a car accident that left him paralyzed from the waist down. Before long he had left Provence and opened his own restaurant, where he has taught himself to stand for hours at a time. At Célestin you're meant to begin with Ribreau's celebrated dungeness-crab soup with sweet potatoes, but we prefer either the ginger-crusted tuna with shitake mushrooms and horseradish mousseline or the terrine of foie gras with apricots, szechuan pepper and fried sage. He's equally inventive with his main dishes. There's slow-cooked lamb shanks, braised with sundried tomatoes, eggplant and mascarpone cheese. There's pan-seared sea-bream with sweet onions, banana peppers and ripe olives. And there's pan-fried sea scallops on a purée of butternut squash with dried fruit and cherrystone clams. The menu is small and choice and everything is exactly as it should be, even the bread. The best wines in the cellar are not from California or Australia, still less from Niagara. They're from France (mainly the Rhône) and Italy (mainly Tuscany). The prices are outrageously high and the only good buys are to be found among the wines of the month. Don't miss the lime tart or the wonderful chocolate torte with its sorbet of passion fruit. They're both a far better buy than the solaia at ten or fifteen times the price.
Open Tuesday to Saturday 5 pm to 9.30 pm. Closed on Sunday and Monday. Licensed. Amex, Master Card, Visa. No smoking. Book ahead. ♿

☞ This symbol means that the restaurant is rated a good buy. This ♿ means that there is wheelchair access to both the tables and the washrooms. *Smoking only* means that the restaurant has no area for non-smokers.

TORONTO **MAP 223**
CHIADO ☆
864 College Street **$175/$110**
(416) 538-1910

In the old Chiado they still offer the raw sardines and salt-cod with garlic and extra-virgin olive-oil familiar in Spain and Portugal. There's also steamed clams, grilled fillet of grouper and grilled fillet of salmon. There's marinated gravlax and sometimes carpaccio of tuna as well. The new *pâtissière*, Dawn Blair, has improved the list of sweets this year, starting with a wonderful fig-and-mascarpone tart. Meanwhile, in the trendy new tapas bar next door, there's a splendid variety of hot and cold dishes at surprisingly favourable prices. For 7.00 or 8.00 you can have cold marinated sardines, salt-cod, smoked salmon, grilled octopus and carpaccio of grouper. Hot dishes start with shrimp bisque and end with blood sausage, squid and octopus. Best of all is the toasted goat-cheese on grilled eggplant. The list of Portuguese wines—douros, daos, bairradas and estremaduras—surpasses belief. Many of these are pretty expensive, but there are some excellent wines by the glass. And if you're tired of flans, they have a lovely toucinho do ceu, a traditional torte of squash, eggs and toasted almonds. The coffee is unbelievably strong; as for the service, it's wonderful.
Open daily 5.30 pm to 9.30 pm. Licensed. Amex, Master Card, Visa. No smoking.

TORONTO **MAP 223**
GAMELLE
468 College Street **$130**
(416) 923-6254

Gamelle is small, intimate and very French. They offer things like French snails, served with frogs' legs in a fricassee with wild mushrooms and a sherry reduction. Their signature dish is pan-seared foie gras with muscat de Rivesaltes and spicy bread, sliced thin and roasted in the oven. If the chef isn't satisfied he'll do the dish over again and bring both to the table for the astonishing price of 14.00. The serrano ham is dry-cured in the Spanish style and served with a small arugula salad. Main dishes start with wild-mushroom risotto with dried apples and basil and rise to Mediterranean sea-bass, maigret of Muscovy duck with local plums and roasted *pré-salé* lamb from Ile Verte, served with rosemary and mashed potatoes. The kitchen is at its best with the sweet course. The warm tarte tatin is a lovely dish and so is the flourless-chocolate cake. The wine-list majors in Niagara wines and wines from Napa and Sonoma. Several of the best of these come from Malivoire—the Old Vines Foch at 46.00, the cabernet/merlot at 55.00, the pinot gris at 38.00 and the gewurztraminer at 62.00. The Hillebrand Trius is also an excellent buy at 37.00.

Open Monday 6 pm to 10 pm, Tuesday to Friday noon to 2.30 pm, 6 pm to 10 pm (later on Thursday and Friday), Saturday 6 pm to 11 pm. Closed on Sunday. Licensed. Amex, Master Card, Visa. No smoking. Book ahead.

TORONTO **MAP 223**
GEORGE ☆☆
111 Queen Street E **$150**
(416) 863-6006

George is no part of the newly-hot strip on Queen Street East. He's farther west, between Church and Jarvis, in a faceless but elegantly-restored building, with sophisticated service and a big open kitchen. The chef, Lorenzo Loseto, came here from Rain and Hemispheres, which is an impressive pedigree. At George he's deigned a tapas-style menu in several courses. You can either go for one of the six- and eight-course surprise menus or order from the à la carte, where there are a number of wonderful things, among them Thai curried prawns on a bed of beets, poached sea scallops in a navy-bean purée, escolar tataki with ginger and pickled vegetables, Alaska black cod with wasabi, wild bar-

ramundi with pumpkinseeds and green-olive foam, miso loin of lamb with chestnuts and, most sensational of all, tuna seared rare and served with matsutaki mushrooms. Portions are small and it's a good idea to finish off with an ounce or two of one of the unpasteurized cheeses, all of which are kept in prime condition. The wines have been chosen to match the food and, if you like, you can ask Kim Cyr, the *sommelière*, to choose a wine (there are many sold by the glass) for each course. Otherwise, ask for one of the Alsatian gewurztraminers. They go well with most of the seafood, especially the curried prawns.
Open Tuesday to Saturday 5.30 pm to 10.30 pm. Closed on Sunday and Monday. Licensed. Amex, Master Card, Visa. No smoking. Book ahead.

TORONTO **MAP 223**
JACQUES' BISTRO DU PARC
126 Cumberland Street **$125**
(416) 961-1893

Jacques is spending much of his time these days in the front of the house instead of the kitchen, but everything on the plate is exactly as it has always been. That means an impeccable entrecôte maître d'hôtel or a delicate fresh fillet of salmon with a spear of broccoli and a young carrot or two, a quiche du jour or an omelette, followed by a delightful tarte au citron. Meals begin with a fillet of smoked trout with puy lentils, terrine maison, fricassee of snails or farm-fresh mussels, and end with a cup of first-class coffee. The wine-list is small and very French, with one or two New World wines, one a Santa Carolina from Chile, the other a pinot noir from Pelee Island. Book a table, if you can, near the window, where there's lots of fresh air and an unexpected view. The service is quick and unobtrusive, the prices so low they're hard to believe.
Open Monday to Saturday noon to 3 pm, 6 pm to 11 pm. Closed on Sunday. Licensed. Amex, Master Card, Visa. No smoking. Book ahead if you can.

TORONTO **MAP 223**

JAMIE KENNEDY ☞

9 Church Street **$55**

(416) 362-5586

Now in its second year, Jamie Kennedy's wine-bar is an outstanding success. You must book, even for a place overlooking the kitchen, where you can watch Jamie and the sous-chefs at work. The menu changes daily, but meals are always small, light and unbelievably cheap. There's usually a soup (mushroom with crème fraîche, say), one or two salads (Diane Kretchmar's organic greens, wild smoked salmon), milk-braised lamb with polente, short-rib stew with marrow toast and lamb-shank poutine with Yukon Gold fries. Then there may be chocolate-espresso glacé, apple crisp with caramel and upside-down quince cake. There are about a dozen open wines, among them a Reif icewine and a Malivoire late-harvest vidal. Last year Kennedy opened a full-service restaurant just behind the wine-bar (telephone (416) 362-1957). The new restaurant is crowded at all hours and you really need to book the day before. For all that, it's not very good, not yet anyway. The chef is not Kennedy himself, but Eric Walker, and maybe that's the problem. Walker changes his menu with the seasons, and last winter he was starting his meals with sashimi and terrine of wild boar glazed with apple cider. His ravioli, which comes next, is tough and tasteless and so is his lamb. The salt-crusted fish is better and people speak highly of the grilled rib-eye with marrow-bone. The wine-list is full of novel and expensive pleasures. Two great wines are offered by the glass—a premier-cru Hudelot-Noellat and a shiraz from Branson in the Barossa Valley. The first costs 29.50 a glass, the second 28.50.
Open daily 11.30 am to 11 pm (5.30 pm to 9 pm in the restaurant). Licensed. Amex, Master Card, Visa. No smoking. Reservations in the wine-bar 11.30 am to 3 pm only. At other times, be prepared to wait for up to two hours.

TORONTO **MAP 223**

JOV

1701 Bayview Avenue **$160**

(416) 322-0530

Jov was a fixture on the Leaside scene for years. It was run by Owen Steinberg and his sister Jill, he in the kitchen, she in the front of the house. Last year it was sold to Masayuki Tamaru, who hasn't changed the appearance of the place in any way. He puts on four-course and five-course tasting menus six nights a week, as well as a regular à la carte, which is short and to the point. Dinners start with something like beet salad with goat-cheese and red currants in a red-currant vinaigrette. The red currants give the vinaigrette an added tartness that makes the dish. Seared Japanese sea scallops come with a celery remoulade and apple julienne, a combination that works much better than you'd expect. Steak tartar is served with potato gaufrettes instead of the customary fries. Seared red snapper is served with double-smoked bacon in a tarragon fumet. The bacon defines the fumet without overpowering the fish. The sorbets are more interesting than the ice creams, and there's a lovely caramelized matsu-apple tart. The wine-list consists mainly of private imports, so there aren't many bargains. The service is intelligent and very well informed.

Open Monday to Saturday 5.30 pm to 10.15 pm. Closed on Sunday. Licensed. Amex, Master Card, Visa. No smoking. Book ahead if you can.

TORONTO **MAP 223**

JOY

884 Queen Street E **$125**

(416) 465-8855

Joy, which opened on this site seven years ago, is now the cornerstone of the newly-fashionable Queen Street East strip. Inside, it's crowded and warm, with diners occupying most of the seating at the curved, red-

granite bar as well as the tables on the floor. Lunch is mainly a matter of salads, sandwiches, pizzas and pasta, but in the evening the menu expands to include breast of duck stuffed with roasted walnuts, blue cheese and cherry tomatoes, breast of chicken stuffed with smoked Austrian gruyère and sundried tomatoes and slow-roasted lamb shanks with wilted spinach and rosemary mash. Atlantic salmon with grilled vegetables may appear at any time of day, and it's a brilliant and memorable dish. The wine-list is quite small, but it's notable for a chardonnay from Beringer for 46.00 and a Green Label cabernet sauvignon from Wolf Blass for 36.00. The coffee is good, the service slow.
Open daily 11 am to 4 pm (lunch), 4 pm to 11 pm (dinner). Licensed. Amex, Master Card, Visa. No smoking. Book ahead if you can. ♿

TORONTO **MAP 223**
KAISEKI YU-ZEN HASHIMOTO ☆☆
6435 Dixie Road: Unit 10 **$210/$120**
Mississauga
(905) 670-5559

Hashimoto is hard to find. Look for it in a small suburban shopping-centre a mile or so north of Highway 401, hidden behind an Esso station. Inside it's so dark that you have to feel your way to the table. If you use the washroom, you'll find that the toilet-paper is folded into a neat point after every use. That's the sort of place this is. The kitchen is run by Masaki Hashimoto, the front of the house by his wife, Sachiko. Kaiseki dinners—*kaiseki* means soft-spoken—are served daily at 12.30 and 7.30 by appointment only. The evening meal costs about 210.00 for two; at noon prices are about half that. There's no menu. Each course is brought to your table and explained in a dialect few diners (unless they're Japanese, as most are) can understand. Dinners are never repeated, but you can expect things like small pumpkins stuffed with tiny pieces of butternut squash or gingko nuts secured by a pair of red-pine needles.

Or perhaps a wafer of ocean perch or Spanish mackerel stuffed with parsnip or a pair of Japanese-style noodles (as thick as your middle finger) in clear broth, which you drink from the bowl after you've eaten the noodles. The meal may end with two tiny scoops (everything here is tiny) of green-tea ice cream decorated with shreds of pear marinated in sake. There are four premium sakes to choose from, all made in Japan and all served on ice. A small cup of green tea comes with your meal.
Open daily at 12.30 pm and 7.30 pm by appointment only. Licensed. Diners, Master Card, Visa. No smoking. You must book at least 24 hours in advance.

TORONTO **MAP 223**
KAJI ☆
860 Queensway **$245**
(416) 252-2166

Mitsuhiro Kaji no longer offers an à la carte. In fact, there are now only two set dinners, one priced at 85.00, the other at 120.00. Kaji is good, but both dinners are difficult and demanding. Neither is designed for comfort. At the moment, both dinners begin with amberjack carpaccio. If (like us) you object to eating amberjack, ask instead for the chicken cake with butternut squash or the crab, which is stuffed into a crab claw and surrounded by deep-fried potato noodles. Sushi comes next, in a brilliant variety—tuna, shrimp, eel and salmon roe. Then miso soup with egg noodles, which, unlike most others of its kind, is a masterpiece of subtle flavours and textures. The sweets are better than we remember, especially the yam with chestnuts and fresh berries. You can drink Perrier or green tea if you like, but there are several imported sakes, all made from polished rice and served hot or cold.
Open Wednesday to Sunday 5.30 pm to 10.30 pm. Closed on Monday and Tuesday. Licensed. All cards. No smoking. Free parking. Book ahead.

TORONTO **MAP 223**

LAI WAH HEEN ☆

108 Chestnut Street **$100**

(416) 977-9899

The Lai Wah Heen is a luxurious, well-served dining-room on the second floor of the old Metropolitan Hotel. You can treat yourself, if you like, to an extravagant meal of abalone or shark's-fin soup at 80.00 (or more) a head. Most people, however, ask for a table at noon and settle down to a lunch of dim sum. The first seven dishes on the list are all specialties of the chef, Terrance Chan. There's a steamed crystal purse of crab, shrimps and bamboo-shoots, steamed bean curd wrapped in minced pork and crabmeat, won-tons stuffed with scallops and water-chestnuts, pan-seared Shanghai buns stuffed with pork and shrimp and Peking beef dumplings glazed with oyster sauce. The cooking is superb and so is the service. Tea is the thing to drink, if only because the tea service is the best in the city. There's Pu Er and Dragon Well, which are both green teas, and Monkey Picked, an oolong tea. Once you've chosen, you get to watch the elaborate tea ceremony: the waiter first pours hot water over the loose leaves, then washes the tea before decanting it into your cup. There's nothing else to drink except imported Gekkeikan sake and Montai rice wine.
Open daily 11.30 am to 3 pm, 5.30 pm to 10.30 pm. Licensed. All cards. No smoking. Free parking. ♿

TORONTO **MAP 223**

LEE ☞

603 King Street W **$90**

(416) 504-7867

What Feenie is to Lumière (see VANCOUVER below), Lee is to Susur: the real thing, only cheaper. Certainly, Lee is cheap. None of the fish costs more than 15.00, none of the meats more than 14.00. Vegetables are even cheaper; none costs more than 10.00. The wine-list

may be small—twelve reds, twelve whites—but it's unbelievably cheap: bottled wines cost 20.00 and up, open wines 5.00 a glass and up. But don't think you're getting everything at these prices that Susur Lee has to offer, because you're not. The satays, for instance, are brilliantly sauced, but the meats are indifferent. The braised beef with sour cream is merely ordinary and so is the spicy lamb chop with chilli mint. On the whole, the kitchen is at its best with fish. The caramelized black cod would be a lovely dish at twice its price of 14.00. The jerk calamari and tuna ceviche are both delightful, and the matchstick potatoes with spicy mango has serious admirers all over town. At these prices you can't expect ostrich-skin seats, but the slabs of clear plastic that serve as table-tops are equally striking—and they're real. The service, like the restaurant itself, is poised and stylish, but it has one major fault: dishes are brought in no particular order and often two (or even three) at once. If you want to eat your food while it's hot, you have to hurry.
Open Monday to Friday noon to 2.30 pm, 6 pm and 8 pm (two sittings), Saturday 6 pm, 8 pm and 10 pm (three sittings). Closed on Sunday. Licensed. Amex, Master Card, Visa. No smoking. Book ahead.

TORONTO **MAP 223**
IL MULINO
1060 Eglinton Avenue W **$160**
(416) 780-1173

Il Mulino has one of the best wine-lists in the city. They have all the super-Tuscans you could hope for. They have a dozen barbarescos rising to 1200.00 a bottle, twenty barolos priced at up to 5000.00 and fifteen barolos priced at up to 1800.00. For ordinary drinkers there's a string of fine chiantis, many of them priced at less than 100.00 a bottle. This is a comfortable little place with good service and a sensible, straightforward menu offering things like grilled squid with tomato and olives, arugula with gorgonzola, pears and walnuts and pan-

seared foie gras with pears and grappa. They're better with fish than veal, unlike most Italian restaurants. Alaska black cod and European sea-bass are both often offered as daily specials and they're both wonderful. Mushroom risotto with white truffles is always available too, if you can afford it. If you can't, ask for the ravioli stuffed with ricotta and butternut squash. As a matter of fact, all the pasta is good.
Open daily 5 pm to 11 pm. Licensed. All cards. No smoking. Book ahead if you can.

TORONTO **MAP 223**
MUSA ☞
847 Dundas Street W **$70**
(416) 368-8484

Musa has a shabby address on Dundas Street W. Never mind. With your copy of *Where to Eat in Canada* in hand, take heart and open the door. Once inside, you'll find that the waiter hasn't shaved for a while, but you'll soon discover that he knows a lot about food and about his old family recipes. Start your meal with a small salad of dandelion greens or with a side order of home-cut fries, which they sell for all of 2.95. Then you have a choice of a salad of weeds, rapini and chick-peas, mussels with ginger and lemon grass, sautéed shrimp with soy sauce and sesame vinaigrette and grilled squid Cajun-style. It's a good idea to have two or three appetizers, because they're on the whole more interesting than the main courses, which run to moussaka, chicken and seafood platters. The wine-list is very small but, like everything else, extremely cheap. Musa is one of the few real bargains in the city.
Open Monday 5 pm to 11 pm, Tuesday to Friday 11 am to 11 pm, Saturday and Sunday 11 am to 3 pm (brunch), 5 pm to 11 pm. Licensed. Amex, Master Card, Visa. No smoking. ♿

If you use an out-of-date edition and find it inaccurate, don't blame us. Buy a new edition.

TORONTO **MAP 223**

NORTH 44° ☆

2537 Yonge Street **$225**

(416) 487-4897

North 44° is a comfortable, urbane restaurant with, provided you have 1000.00 to spend, a remarkable wine-list. ("If," as one waiter remarked, "you haven't got 1000.00 to spend, you shouldn't be here.") The menu, however, is disappointing. The appetizers run mainly to salads. There's a whole page of salads, as well as a handful of more inviting dishes, such as yellowfin tuna, marinated salmon (served on tiny pancakes with a morsel of caviar) and seared foie gras with apple and white wine. The salmon is spoiled, as you might guess, by its pancakes, so it's better to ask for the foie gras, which doesn't cost much more than anything else. The glory of the menu is still to come: whole Dover sole is sold, when available, at market prices. Otherwise there's roast breast of squab, roast chicken, loin of lamb, roast bison and halibut on a banana leaf. The cooking is competent rather than surprising. There are no mistakes, but not much excitement. That comes, however, with the sweets, which are as brilliant as ever. Try the sticky toffee cake and see for yourself. There are only a few wines from Bordeaux and Burgundy or, for that matter, from Australia and New Zealand, but the list of wines from California is breathtaking. Take time to explore it and buy what you can afford. Don't overlook the special-select wines from Caymus. There are seven in all, among them a 1994 cabernet sauvignon priced at almost 750.00.

Open Monday to Saturday 5 pm to 10 pm. Closed on Sunday. Licensed. Amex, Master Card, Visa. Valet parking. No smoking. Book ahead. ♿

If you wish to improve this guide send us information about restaurants we have missed. Our mailing address is: Oberon Press, 145 Spruce Street, Suite 205, Ottawa, Ontario K1R 6P1.

TORONTO **MAP 223**
ORO ☆☆
45 Elm Street **$150**
(416) 597-0155

Dario Tomaselli is one of those immaculate chefs who cook gracefully and well whatever the occasion. At lunchtime, he'll prepare sea scallops with morels and celeriac froth, followed by breast of capon with gnocchi in a blood-orange emulsion, steamed salmon with beets and tea-smoked sea-bass with sake and carrot-juice. This may be careful cooking, but it's also highly creative. When did you last see sake and carrot-juice on the same plate? In the evening they offers things like rack of lamb, tenderloin of bison, veal shanks and rare-seared tuna, as well as the salmon and the sea-bass The wine-list is rich in the big wines of Tuscany, but there are other good things as well For instance, there are eleven cabernet sauvignons from Caymus (priced to 585.00), eight clarets from Mouton Rothschild and four from Lafite, priced to 3835.00. At the other end of the list, there's a riesling from Trimbach for 32.00 a bottle and a late-harvest vidal from Malivoire for 9.00 a glass. If you're looking for a boisterous evening, don't go to Oro. Oro is elegant and understated and very well served.
Open Monday to Friday noon to 2.30 pm, 5 pm to 10 pm, Saturday 5 pm to 10 pm. Closed on Sunday. Licensed. Amex, Master Card, Visa. No smoking.

TORONTO **MAP 223**
PANGAEA
1221 Bay Street **$135**
(416) 920-2323

Pangaea has an exciting interior and exemplary service. They also have a superb *pâtissière* and a first-class wine-list. But in the last year or so the kitchen itself has lost much of its old glamour. Meals begin well with avocado soup, lamb sausages with onions and fig jam or, more grandly, with foie gras with burnt honey and orange. But the scallops that follow are disappointing—they come with beans and lobster cream in saffron. The organic salmon is served with water-chestnuts, bok choy and shitake mushrooms, the skate with lemon butter. The liver, garnished with barley, lingonberries and sage, is a livelier presentation and the veal kidneys, served with purée of apple and fried ginger, are even better. Pangaea is at its best, however, with its sweets—look for the brown-butter pear tart and hope you get lucky. The cellar is full of chardonnays from Niagara and Napa and cabernet sauvignons from Napa and the Pacific Rim. Many of these are sold by the glass as well as the bottle. This is one of the few restaurants to offer the Malivoire melon (at 44.80), to say nothing of the Old Vines Foch, which sells for 46.00. Prices aren't high by Toronto standards.

Open Monday to Saturday 11.30 am to 5 pm (lunch), 5 pm to 11 pm (dinner). Closed on Sunday. Licensed. All cards. No smoking.

TORONTO **MAP 223**
RAIN ☆☆
19 Mercer Street **$165**
(416) 599-7246

Rain is all about presentation and style. The visual impact alone is staggering. Sheets of black water pour down the walls. The bar is translucent and decorated with tulips in slender vases. The tables gleam like black lacquer and beautiful youths, dressed in black, bring the food to your place. The menu, which is neo-Asian, is the work of Guy Rubino. It's a good idea to begin with one of the side-plates and go on to a main dish. That means potato dumplings, mushroom tempura with sake and ginger foam, Japanese eggplant with sweet corn, black Thai coconut rice with mango curry and a somen-noodle roll with papaya slaw. If you order more than one of these dishes, you'll find that they all come at once. Continuity is no part of Guy Rubino's style. The main dishes are more imposing and much more expensive. There's sashimi, of course, scallops glazed with apricot-mustard, hamachi with orange, black cod with miso, squab with tea-smoked cherry glaze and red snapper with lemon grass, coconut and wasabi. The kitchen is inexhaustible and everything it touches is dramatic and exciting. The wine-list is full of unusual wines, all offered at extravagant prices. Rain is a restaurant that could easily become all show, all see-and-be-seen. So far it hasn't.

Open Monday to Saturday 5.30 pm to 10 pm (later on weekends). Closed on Sunday. Licensed. All cards. No smoking.

TORONTO **MAP 223**

ROL SAN ☞

323 Spadina Avenue **$30**

(416) 977-1128

You would never look twice at this place, on Spadina Avenue near Baldwin, if you hadn't been told to go there. It's all bright lights and plastic table-cloths. But the service is swift and everything is very cheap. Furthermore, they know how to cook and they stay open till all hours. They cook in the Cantonese style and the dishes to look for are the chicken with red chilli and deep-fried greens, the mussels with black beans, the sizzling beef with onions and black pepper. All the ingredients are amazingly fresh, the sauces delicate. The China tea is the best in the city and that's the thing to drink.

Open daily 9.30 am to 4 am. Licensed. Visa. No smoking. ♿

TORONTO **MAP 223**

SEN5ES ☆☆☆

Soho Metropolitan Hotel **$235**

328 Wellington Street W

(416) 935-0400

Claudio Aprile is almost as good as ever in the new Sen5es on Wellington Street. Almost but not quite. His cooking is still imaginative and well conceived, but it's no longer breathtaking. The menu is now quite small. He likes to begin with something like a salad of Asian pears (which is wonderful) or yu-zu-marinated tuna, served rare with basil, sesame and extra-virgin olive-oil, and go on to halibut with ravioli stuffed with peas or triple-seared squab with tonka beans and sweet potatoes in black Chinese vinegar. Have the squab and pass on the halibut. The squab is a memorable dish—at once assertive and restrained—which it has to be at 44.00 a portion. The panna cotta is an agreeable dish, but the banana parfait in its coulis of raspberries is incomparable. There's good drinking at every price on the wine-list, which really means that the wines have been chosen without regard to price. If the Liberty School cabernet is still in the cellar, ask for a bottle and damn the cost. *Open Tuesday to Saturday 6 pm to 10 pm. Closed on Sunday and Monday. Licensed. All cards. Book ahead. No smoking. Free parking.* ♿

TORONTO **MAP 223**

THE SILVER SPOON

390 Roncesvalles Avenue **$120**

(416) 516-8112

When it first opened the Silver Spoon seemed almost too good to be true. It's still doing a good job and it's still extremely popular, but the prices are no longer low. The cooking isn't as consistent as it used to be either. We've had overcooked fish and we've had lamb from New Zealand that couldn't be cut with a steak-knife. But we've also been given first-class Arctic char and fine snapper with ginger and lime. There are still a few bargains. Seared foie gras is one. It's served with pepper-squash jam and flatbread and costs only 14.00. It's a good idea to start with a soup—the wild-mushroom is lovely, the butternut-squash is brilliant. The ravioli that follows is apt to be bland. The free-range chicken with braised onions, apricots, chestnuts and a compote of ginger and cranberries is a better choice. It's very moist

and full of flavour. The vegetables are always excellent and there's at least one great sweet, a flourless chocolate ganache with crème anglaise. The service is calm and competent, no matter what the noise level.
Open Tuesday to Thursday 5 pm to 10 pm, Friday and Saturday 5 pm to 11 pm. Closed on Sunday and Monday. Licensed. Amex, Master Card, Visa. No smoking.

TORONTO **MAP 223**
SPLENDIDO ☆☆☆
88 Harbord Street **$235**
(416) 929-7788

David Lee took over the kitchen here from Arpi Magyar three or four years ago. It didn't take him long to make himself felt on the restaurant scene. He started out at Splendido, as we said at the time, with big plates and big flavours. This year he's a new man and worth every one of his three stars. His cooking is more restrained than it used to be, and more delicate. His organic Pacific salmon with horseradish and beets, for instance, is perhaps the best salmon, Atlantic or Pacific, that we have ever eaten, and that's saying something. He serves his Cumbrae beef tenderloin and his Haldimand County rack of lamb quite simply—the beef with roasted parsnips and thyme, the lamb with merguez sausage—and both are splendid dishes. Cured pork belly comes to the table in a purée of lily bulbs, yellowfin tuna with ginger and lemon grass, wild sea-bass with foie gras and chanterelle broth. Prices, however, are high: 88.00 for the three-course *prix-fixe* (without a sweet), 95.00 for the five-course tasting menu. The wine-list is absurdly expensive: a glass of Inox chardonnay from Peninsula Ridge costs 22.00. Still, it has to be admitted that you get what you're paying for. There are four Lafites on the list (priced to 1500.00), seven sassicaias (to 1200.00) and six solaias (to 925.00). There are also three gewurztraminers, two chardonnays and three Old Vines Foch (among others) from Malivoire, and they're all a bit cheaper.

Open Tuesday to Sunday 5 pm to 11 pm. Closed on Monday. Licensed. Amex, Master Card, Visa. No smoking. Valet parking.

TORONTO **MAP 223**
SUSUR ☆☆☆
601 King Street W **$225**
(416) 603-2205

Susur now serves tasting menus—seven courses for 110.00, five courses for 90.00—that show the kitchen at the top of its form. If you come with a table of four, each person will be offered a different menu, which means that you can sample up to 28 different dishes on any given occasion. The meal begins (after a different *amuse bouche* for each person at the table) with a meat course—venison, say, with a confit of garlic and squab with peanut chutney. Foie gras will follow—sliced thin and served on air-dried beef with slivers of radish. Then a fish course of cold-smoked salmon and red mullet crusted with nori, followed by shellfish—scallops, perhaps, in squid ink with truffles. Finally, a sweet course of coconut sorbet, banana cake, passion-fruit jelly or a medley of chocolate. If you order the five-course vegetarian menu, which is cheaper, you'll begin with wonderful ravioli stuffed with chanterelles and go on to crisp-fried noodles in a spicy soy sauce, a mission-fig salad or lemon tart with crème caramel. The wine-list too is remarkable in its way. The list of whites begins with ten Niagara vineyards, offering a wide range of wines from each. The list of reds begins with five Niagara vineyards (notably Malivoire and Southbrook) and a long list of wines from Antinori (notably a tignanello). There are premium sakes from both California and Japan. Susur is a brilliant restaurant. *Open Monday to Saturday 6.30 pm to 9 pm. Closed on Sunday. Licensed. Amex, Master Card, Visa. No smoking. You must book ahead.* ♿

Our web site is at www.oberonpress.ca Readers wishing to use e-mail should address us at oberon@sympatico.ca

TORONTO **MAP 223**
TEMPO ☆
596 College Street **$120**
(416) 531-2822

The way to enjoy Tempo is to make up a party of four or more and ask for a table before 8, when the place becomes crowded and noisy—too noisy for ordinary conversation. The surroundings are thoroughly down-scale, but pay no attention to that. Tom Thai is in the kitchen and that's all that matters. The meal begins with ceviche of sea-bream or lemon-grass soup, presented Thai-style with enoki mushrooms, and goes on to something like roasted mackerel with green mango or roasted whole snapper with ginger ponzu and sautéed Asian greens. If you want something less substantial, ask for a sushi plate or, better still, a sashimi plate, heaped with raw fish of all kinds—marvellous butterfish, for one, blue marlin for another. There are also vegetable sushis and a fine tuna tataki with ginger, garlic and kaffir limes. There are about a dozen wines in the house, but it's usually better to ask for a premium sake or a glass of Hakutsuru on draught. The sakes are all served cold.
Open Monday to Wednesday 5.30 pm to 10.30 pm, Thursday to Saturday 7 pm and 9 pm (two sittings). Closed on Sunday. Licensed. Amex, Master Card, Visa. No smoking. Book ahead.

TORONTO **MAP 223**
TERRA ☆☆
8199 Yonge Street **$190**
Thornhill
(905) 731-6161

Terra is now serving oysters from Aspy Bay in Cape Breton, from Hillsborough and Raspberry Point in Prince Edward Island and from Lemeque Verte in New Brunswick. This will be an eye-opener for anyone brought up to think that the sun rises and sets on Malpèque Bay. If you don't feel comfortable with oys-

ters, or don't want to pay for them, you can always start your meal with steamed local asparagus in lemon vinaigrette or Ahi tuna with soya, mirin and chilli. Stephen Perrin rather likes to prepare things like roasted rack of lamb, provimi-veal T-bone and ostrich with fava beans and wild mushrooms. But you don't need to have a steak or rack of lamb or ostrich. There are also fine treatments of steamed pickerel with romaine and Arctic char with Cookstown greens. It's best to finish off with the warm flourless chocolate torte, because the cheese plate ignores the lovely unpasteurized raw-milk cheeses of rural Ontario and Quebec in favour of such old chestnuts as roquefort and gorgonzola. There are a great many half-bottles in the cellar and a remarkable collection of Niagara chardonnays, as well as a choice list of clarets (Haut-Brion, Latour), a number of cabernets from New Zealand and Southeastern Australia and an ambitious list of Amarones from Tuscany.
Open Monday to Friday 11.30 am to 2.30 pm, 6 pm to 10 pm, Saturday 6 pm to 10 pm, Sunday 11.30 am to 2.30 pm, 6 pm to 10 pm. Licensed. Amex, Master Card, Visa. No smoking. Free parking. Book ahead. ♿

TORONTO **MAP 223**
THUET CUISINE ☆☆
609 King Street W **$225**
(416) 603-2777

A year ago Marc Thuet, fresh from the Fifth, opened his own restaurant in a second-floor walkup a few doors west of Susur (see above). The dining-room is too big, but it's mellow and warm and very well served. It's also outrageously expensive. Is it worth it? That depends on your income and your appetite. As for Marc Thuet, he cooks very well indeed. Reviewers all speak of his passion and intensity. We for our part are more impressed by his delicacy and refinement. Consommé, that most delicate of soups, Thuet makes with seafood and poached marrow. His terrine of foie gras with tuna akami is visually gorgeous and rather more venturesome

than the consommé. He makes much of truffles, offering both wild partridge and Ontario lamb with white truffles and wild-mushroom risotto with black truffles. His wild duck is glazed with honey and cumin and served with Alsatian sauerkraut. With game, Thuet is harsh and provocative, but with fish, whether a crépinette of European sea-bass or a wing of skate poached in orange court bouillon with mint, he always has a gentle hand. The wine-list is noteworthy for its holdings of Alsatian wine—in all there are 27 Alsatian whites, priced from 45.00 to 185.00. (Try the old-vines gewurztraminer from François Bléger, offered for just 60.00 a bottle.) You can end with a chocolate-and-chestnut terrine in a coulis of egg-nog if you like, but it's probably better to ask for a plate of raw-milk cheese. It costs only a dollar or two more. Note: while this edition was on press Marc Thuet decided to convert part of his large floor-space into a bakery and to add a few high-end bistro dishes to his menu at modest prices.
Open Tuesday to Friday 11.30 am to 2.30 pm, 5.30 pm to 10.30 pm, Saturday 5.30 pm to 10.30 pm. Closed on Sunday and Monday. Licensed. Amex, Master Card, Visa. No smoking. Book ahead. Valet parking.

TORONTO **MAP 223**
TOMI-KRO
1214 Queen Street E **$125**
(416) 463-6677

Tomi-Kro opened a year or two ago and since then it's helped to define Queen Street East as the place to eat—and be seen—in Toronto. It was opened by John Coronios, who came here from Lolita's Lust. There's nothing Greek, however, about Tomi-Kro. Indeed, the chef, Jefferson Alvarez, comes from Venezuela and cooks big-eye tuna, beef carpaccio and octopus ceviche in up-to-the-minute Canadian style. His menu is ambitious, his cooking adventurous. Five nights a week he offers Arctic char with fennel and orange miso, Conestoga pork with baked apples and haloumi cheese and

slow-braised lamb shanks with red wine and mint. For cooking like this, 125.00 for dinner for two with wine, taxes and tip is a steal.
Open Tuesday to Saturday 6 pm to 11 pm. Closed on Sunday and Monday. Licensed. Amex, Master Card, Visa. No smoking. Book ahead if you can.

TORONTO **MAP 223**
VIA ALLEGRO ☆
1750 Queensway **$225**
(416) 622-6677

The most amazing thing about this amazing restaurant is its wine-list. Ignoring for the moment the wonderful array of clarets, the list of Italian reds is itself beyond compare. There are pages of valpolicellas from Veneto, pages of barolos from Piemonte, pages of chiantis from Tuscany, pages of brunellos, solaias, sassicaias, tignanellos and ornellaias. There can't be another such list anywhere in the city, not even at Il Mulino (see above). If you're looking for a good buy, ask for a bottle of the 1985 barolo riserva classico from Giacomo Borgogno. It costs 290.00, but, at Via Allegro, what doesn't? The menu is surprisingly small: tuna seared rare with golden beets and (marvellous) foie gras from Quebec, lamb with mustard, garlic and horseradish, venison à la façon du chef and the signature specialty, Platinum beef. Aside from the foie gras, none of this is particularly exciting, though the presentation is always impressive, the service appropriately deferential. Everything here is on a grand scale. Few of the appetizers cost less than 20.00, few of the main courses less than 45.00. If you want to enjoy all this, order a bottle of good wine, drink it with your Platinum beef and forget the cost.. If you can't do that, go somewhere else.
Open daily 11.30 am to 10 pm (later on weekends). Licensed. Amex, Master Card, Visa. No smoking. Free parking. ♿

Nobody can buy space in this guide and nobody can buy his way out of it.

TORONTO **MAP 223**
XACUTTI ☆☆
503 College Street **$140**
(416) 323-3957

Xacutti is Yabu Pushelberg at their best, and in the kitchen Brad Moore makes the most of an extraordinary menu. This, as we've said before, is the *nouvelle cuisine* of India and the whole place hums with excitement. At last count, there were fourteen small dishes and twelve large, and it's a good idea to try as many different things as possible. Why have rack of lamb with masala potatoes when you can have tandoori-style wild salmon with pancakes, sweet-potato cakes with ginger and tamarind and sweet yam fries with soy-chilli sambal—all for the same money (or less) and half the calories? Why have spice-crusted beef tenderloin with three-jewel onion rings when you can have chicken legs with mustard and green spices, steamed mussels in tomato-coconut curry and tikka rabbit with spiced onion yogurt—or even Punjabi fish and chips. Not that the large dishes—Goan-spiced trout, Alaskan halibut with Indian pesto and striped bass with pomegranate extract and yogurt rice—are any less exciting. There's a choice of bottled waters as well as wines, and as for the waters most people agree that Voss (from Norway) is the best of the lot. As for the wine-list, it's a good idea to order one of the eight flights, each of which offers three two-ounce glasses. Most of these come from the New World and they're all good drinking. Xacutti has all the virtues—except a decent selection of Indian ales.

Open Tuesday to Friday 6 pm to 10 pm, Saturday noon to 3 pm (brunch), 6 pm to 10 pm, Sunday 10.30 am to 3 pm (brunch). Closed on Monday. Licensed. Amex, Master Card, Visa. No smoking. Book ahead.

TORONTO
See also AJAX, CREEMORE, KLEINBURG, NOBLETON, OAKVILLE, WHITBY.

TRINITY, Newfoundland **MAP 224**
FISHER'S LOFT INN ☆
Port Rexton **$135**
(877) 464-3240

Trinity, on the northwest shore of Trinity Bay, is one of the oldest settlements in the province. In 1615, only ten years after Champlain founded Port Royal, Sir Richard Whitbourne held the first Admiralty Court here. The parish church of St. Paul dates from 1734 and the rest of the town looks much as it did a century ago. Fisher's Loft is in Port Rexton, which is about ten minutes away, overlooking the old harbour of Ship Cove. The bedrooms, each with a private entrance and an ocean view, are bright and carefully furnished. Non-residents are welcome in the dining-room, which many people think as good as any outside St. John's. The kitchen gets its supplies from the sea, from fresh-water ponds, from seaside meadows (where local farmers raise *pré-salé* lamb and from their own vegetable garden. The menu changes several times a week, but a typical meal will begin with carrot-and-ginger soup or a green salad with partridge-berry vinaigrette and go on to baked cod with seasonal vegetables, ending with a chocolate torte in a blueberry coulis. Nothing is overstated and everything tastes exactly as it should. They have a useful wine-list and every night they put on a pre-theatre dinner so you can take in a show at the Rising Tide Theatre, which is a few miles from Ship Cove.
Open Monday at 7.30 pm, Tuesday to Sunday at 5.30 pm and 7.30 pm by appointment only. Licensed. Master Card, Visa. No smoking. You must book ahead. ♿

TROUT RIVER, Newfoundland **MAP 225**
THE SEASIDE
(709) 451-3461 **$70**

It's hard to believe that we've been writing about the Seaside for almost twenty years. When we first talked to May Hann, she had a small cabin by the sea, where

people could get fresh fish and fresh vegetables all summer long. Breakfast began when the first people appeared at the door; dinners ended early because the Hanns went to bed with the sun. The present Seaside, with its grey clapboard, wide windows, new deck and second-storey dining-room, is a far cry from the early days. But, though May Hann is no longer in the kitchen, her family are still doing the same job in much the same way. They offer an amazing variety of fish and shellfish. Shrimps come from Port-au-Choix, but the biggest seller by far is the snow crab, which is still fished along this coast. The salmon is farmed these days, but the cod, catfish, grey sole, caplin, flounder and ocean perch all come straight from the sea. The scallops sautéed with garlic and white wine are as good as ever, and so are the vegetarian stir-fries. The lobster season opens in late April and sometimes there are lobsters for sale by the pound at the fish-plant until late August. Stan Parsons shares his mother-in-law's scorn for the deep-fry and bakes all his potatoes to order. One of his sisters-in-law makes the seafood chowder and the splendid dinner rolls. Another does most of the sweets: blueberry and raspberry pies in late spring, partridge-berry and bake-apple pies in summer. The Parsons and the Hanns must be doing something right to keep a restaurant of this size in business so long. If you miss the personal touch, ask for a table by the window and watch the dolphins playing in the surf.
Open daily noon to 10 pm from Victoria Day until Thanksgiving. Licensed. Master Card, Visa. No smoking. ♿

TYNE VALLEY, P.E.I. **(MAP 43)**
DOCTOR'S INN
Highway 167 **$150 ($215)**
(902) 831-3057

Apparently, the reports of Paul Offer's death were exaggerated, though it's true that his heart stopped beating for a short time. However that may be, he's back in business this year. He doesn't cover the table with vegetables from his garden as he once did, but whatever he serves will be exemplary. There's a three-acre vegetable garden behind the house and it's Paul's passion. He grows at least eight varieties of carrot and 28 varieties of lettuce, not to mention tomatoes, cucumbers, cauliflower, zucchini, beets and onions, which he sells on the Farmer's Market in Charlottetown. Dinners are cooked on the old wood stove that came with the house. Jean Offer does all the baking, including the bread and the fresh-fruit pies. You book the day before and the table is set for two or four as the case may be. Four-course dinners begin with oatmeal biscuits, stuffed mushroom caps, cheese and a glass of hock. (You can bring your own bottle if you like; otherwise the Offers will choose a wine that suits the meal and serve it on the house.) We used to consider the meat and the fish a distant second to the vegetables, but this year both the lamb chops and the scallops have been excellent. The Doctor's Inn is a rambling old house in a sleepy little hamlet near the western shore of Malpèque Bay and it's surrounded by some of the loveliest country in Prince Edward Island.

Open Monday to Thursday, Saturday and Sunday at 7 pm by appointment only. Closed on Friday. Bring your own bottle. Master Card, Visa. No smoking.

UCLUELET, B.C. **(MAP 222)**
THE MATTERSON HOUSE
1682 Peninsula Road **$70**
(250) 726-2200

Ucluelet is still a backwater. But it's as close to Long Beach and the Wild Pacific Trail as Tofino. The Matterson House is a heritage building on the main street of town, with a shady porch where you can have lunch. The menu seldom changes and at least three of the five cooks have been here from the beginning. But the place has many virtues. They believe in letting food speak for itself, so their fresh clams are simply steamed, their Pacific halibut grilled with fresh herbs, their Pacific salmon poached with lemon and pepper. They make their own wholewheat bread and a number of interesting soups—cheddar-jalapeno, bacon-and-white-bean, ham-and-split-pea—as well as one or two seafood chowders. There's a monster burger that comes with a first-class green salad and homemade blackberry vinaigrette. But their most popular dish is breast of chicken crusted with almonds and cornflakes and served in a coulis of raspberry and fresh cream. The cheesecakes are made to a recipe of their own, and, if you don't want to take a chance on that, ask for one of the fruit crumbles, rhubarb, say, or mixed-berry. There's a small wine-list with a number of interesting wines from Australia, California and the Okanagan, as well as a local beer from Vancouver Island.

Open daily 7.30 am to 9 pm. Licensed. Master Card, Visa. No smoking. ♿

VAL D'OR, Quebec **MAP 228**

LE BISTRO ☞

Hôtel Forestel **$90**

1001 avenue 3 e

(819) 825-5660

There are two beautiful, luxurious motels in Val d'Or. If you're heading west toward Rouyn on route 117 there's L'Escale at 1100 rue de l'Escale (telephone (800) 567-6572. If you're heading east out of town on route 117 there's the Forestel. L'Escale has a lovely setting and it used to be our first choice. The menu is small but the cooking is very reliable. Fresh trout from St. Matthieu is a specialty, served in any way you like, even fillet of trout with scrambled eggs for breakfast. The best thing on the menu, however, is usually the fillet of beef. Dinners begin with their own smoked trout and the sweets change every day, sometimes twice a day. Prices are remarkably low. Lately, however, it's seemed to us that the Forestel has the edge. From Monday to Friday they put on a spectacular noon-hour buffet, as well as brunch on Sunday for only 9.95 a head. Every few weeks there's

a *prix-fixe* menu that features regional products, from fresh lobster to Abitibi lamb. You can start with onion soup flavoured with Taiga beer and go on to fillet of pork with braised yellow chicory or grilled Arctic trout with fennel mash. Sweets change daily, but look for the frozen goat's-milk ice with dried fruit.
Open Monday to Friday 11 am to 12.30 pm, 5.30 pm to 11 pm, Saturday 7.30 am to 1 pm, 5.30 pm to 11 pm, Sunday 11 am to 12.30 pm (brunch), 5.30 pm to 10 pm. Licensed. All cards. No smoking. ♿

VANCOUVER, B.C. *MAP 229*

Most people agree that Vancouver has the best Chinese cooking in North America. The enormous variety of Chinese restaurants is beyond the scope of this guide. All we can do is to pick out five places of unusual merit. The Shiang Garden at 4540 No. 3 Road in the Empire Centre in Richmond (telephone (604) 273-8858) has a remarkable dim-sum menu, offering things like smoked salmon with papaya, fried scallops stuffed with taro and steamed canteloupe-and-shrimp dumplings. Floata Seafood at 180 Keefer Street: Unit 400 in the heart of Chinatown (telephone (604) 602-0368) is probably the largest Chinese restaurant on the continent, with a thousand seats. A longstanding favourite for banquets, it also offers splendid cooking for a young couple who simply need a table for two. They have dim sum not seen anywhere else and the set dinner menus (especially during the Chinese New Year) are one of the best deals in town. Hon's Wun Tun House at 1339 Robson Street (telephone (604) 685-0871) belongs to a small chain. They specialize in potstickers. Everything is well prepared and you get to watch the chefs in three different open kitchens, one of which is a separate vegetarian kitchen, something that's particularly attractive to orthodox Jews. Apart from the potstickers, their best dish is the chicken with mango and cashews in a potato basket. The Szechuan Chongqing at 2808 Commercial Drive (telephone (604) 254-7434) is known for its deep-fried beef with kumquat peel and its smoked duck in camphor wood with tea-leaves. The city's large Indian population eat here often, perhaps for the orange-peel chicken, the hot, dry fried green beans or the ginger beef. The Landmark Hot-Pot House at 4023 Cambie Street (telephone (604) 872-2868) encourages you to do your own cooking at your own table, using a gas-fired burner to prepare something like a Chinese fondue, filled with meat, vegetables and spot prawns, which are put in the pot while still alive. This is Vancouver's first and perhaps its best hot-pot restaurant. Don't miss their whole geoduck, served sashimi-style.

VANCOUVER **MAP 229**
BACCHUS ☆
Wedgewood Hotel **$160**
845 Hornby Street
(604) 608-5319

The Wedgewood is deliberately and consciously old-fashioned. It is in fact a gentleman's club in the heart of a modern city. Bacchus is cut from the same cloth. The menus are comforting, offering dishes that are familiar to everyone. The cooking is cautious, which is not to say that it's dull. The service is flawless. The wine-list is equal to any occasion, offering the great wines of Lafite, Mouton Rothschild, tignanello and solaia as well as some of the best drinking from the Okanagan. Where else have you been offered Burrowing Owl by the glass—in this case a beautiful merlot good enough to transform any meal into a special occasion. The salmon is home-smoked and appropriately presented with avocado and watercress. Lightly-seared Ahi tuna is crusted with fennel seeds and served with lemon vinaigrette. The hand of Lee Parsons is easier to recognize in the evening, when dinners start with foie gras and go on to striped bass or lamb with garlic and mint. You can spend all afternoon over lunch at Bacchus, or all evening over dinner. No-one will ask for your table.
Open daily 11.30 am to 2.30 pm, 6 pm to 10 pm. Licensed. All cards. No smoking. Book ahead if you can. ♿

If you use an out-of-date edition and find it inaccurate, don't blame us. Buy a new edition.

VANCOUVER **MAP 229**

LA BELLE AUBERGE ☆☆

4856 48 Avenue **$220**

Ladner

(604) 946-7717

Bruno Marti has owned this century-old house in Ladner for a quarter of a century. The rooms occupied by the restaurant are filled with antiques. When you make your reservation, see if you can get a table in the high-windowed library. Marti was a member of Canada's first gold-medal Olympic team in 1984 and he's still there. He tries always to give international dishes a distinctively Canadian point of view. The results are impressive, though extremely expensive. The regular menu features venison, bison, musk-ox and other game dishes, but if you like you can ask the chef to design a meal specifically for you and your companion. (We suggest you ask for the quail with grapes, the rabbit with wild mushrooms or the terrine of fresh fish.) Marti grows a lot of his own produce and prowls the markets in search of new ideas. Typical of his style are the Ahi tuna tartar, the lamb carpaccio and the pan-seared foie gras with local cranberries and blueberries. Marti won the Gold Medal for his roast duck with Fraser Valley blueberries. His Arctic char is immaculately cooked and served in a Vietnamese lemon-grass broth. The sweets—fresh-fruit tart, crème brûlée, a sorbet—are rather less adventurous. But there's an excellent list of the best Okanagan vintages and the service is outstanding. The Belle Auberge is close to both the airport and the ferry terminal, though you'd never know it.

Open Tuesday to Sunday 6 pm to 10 pm. Closed on Monday. Licensed. Amex, Master Card, Visa. No smoking.

This is a guide to Canadian restaurants from coast to coast—the first ever published and the only one of its kind on the market today. We accept no advertisements. Nobody can buy his way into this guide and nobody can buy his way out

VANCOUVER **MAP 229**
BIN 941/BIN 942 ☞
1521 W Broadway **$60**
(604) 734-9421

Gordon Martin considers Bin 941 and Bin 942 as tapas parlours. By parlour he means a room reserved primarily for conversation. Conversation is impossible over the blaring techno-pop music in either Bin, but nobody seems to mind. Both, of course, offer tremendous value for money. Bin 941, the original, is tiny, crowded and noisy. It has lovely things to eat (a little bigger than the typical tapas), all carefully prepared and imaginatively presented. We especially like the grilled sirloin of lamb with a demi-glaze of cinzano, the smoked sable-fish with sticky black rice and the confit of duck served three ways—spring-roll of duck, five-spice leg of duck and shredded duck salad with green-papaya glass-noodles. Bin 942 is larger and less funky. It's just as noisy as Bin 941, but it's probably the better place to eat at the moment. The menu is similar. Our favourites are the slow-roasted loin of venison in a cognac-chestnut sauce with spiced gnocchi, chanterelles, honey-glazed baby beets and hot organic relish, the tournedos of Digby scallops with leek tempura and the confit of duck with serano-chilli cornbread. There's a generous choice of wines by the glass and if you come early you can avoid the worst of the crowds.
Open daily 5 pm to 2 am. Licensed. All cards. No smoking. No reservations.

VANCOUVER **MAP 229**
BISHOP'S ☆
2183 W 4 Avenue **$160**
(604) 738-2025

Working in a small, two-tiered streetfront restaurant on W 4 Avenue, Dennis Green does a great many things he's often done before, without ever seeming to repeat himself. If you have Saltspring Island goat-cheese marinated in olive-oil and served with organic beets in October you'll be surprised to learn that you had the same dish the previous June. Green is good at making familiar dishes seem fresh and new. He does it with his spot-prawn bisque, with his Manila clams steamed in white vermouth, with his Fanny Bay oysters crusted in cornmeal. He does it again with his organic breast of chicken—almost everything served at Bishop's is organic—with his smoked sablefish with truffles, with his dungeness crab-cakes with cranberry chutney. The list of sweets, on the other hand, is full of new ideas: warm spiced ginger cake, flourless chocolate mousse with crème fraîche, sticky toffee pudding and quince tart with caramel sauce. The wine-list is at its best with wines from the Pacific Northwest. Keep an eye out for the fine chardonnays from Blue Mountain and Edna Valley and the elegant pinot noir from Burrowing Owl. *Open Monday to Saturday 5.30 pm to 10.30 pm, Sunday 5.30 pm to 9.30 pm. Licensed. All cards. No smoking, no cellphones. Book ahead.* ♿

VANCOUVER **MAP 229**
BISTRO PASTIS ☆
2153 W 4 Avenue **$125**
(604) 731-5020

In three years the kitchen at Pastis went through three chefs. Finally, in 2003, John Blakely closed the restaurant and reopened a year later as Bistro Pastis. Already he's set the standard for bistros in Vancouver, much as Robert Feenie has set the standard for restaurants at Lumière. Sweetbreads are a good test for any bistro and here the sweetbreads are pan-seared and served with Granny Smith apples and a velouté of pumpkin. Pan-seared scallops, another good test, are cooked with the same authority. Duck is always on the menu and we can recommend it in either of its two styles. In a cassoulet confit de canard is paired with osso buco of pork; the roasted breast is served with squash, apples and walnut

gnocchi. This is hearty, homespun cooking at its best. As for the sweet course, it's an afterthought. If you're hungry, try the half-baked valhrona chocolate cake; if not, go for the lemon tart with vanilla chantilly on crisp, thin pastry. They have a five-course tasting menu for 59.50, where each of the five dishes is also sold as a daily special. Recently the chefs have begun to explore the regional varieties of French cooking, starting with Algeria and ending with Acadia. Wines by the glass are plentiful and many of them are from the Okanagan.
Open Tuesday to Friday 11.30 am to 2 pm, 5.30 pm to 10.30 pm, Saturday and Sunday 11 am to 2 pm (brunch), 5.30 pm to 10.30 pm. Closed on Monday. Licensed. Amex, Master Card, Visa. No smoking. ♿

VANCOUVER **MAP 229**
BLUE WATER ☆☆
1095 Hamilton Street **$175**
(604) 688-8078

Blue Water has a raw bar, where you can sample nine or ten varieties of sushi, as well a oysters brought here from all over the Pacific—Kusshi, Royal Miyagi, Golden Mantle, Stellar Bay, Gorge Inlet, Kunamoto an d Malpèque, among others. The green-pea soup is lovely; and so are the swimming scallops with tomato and lemon, but it's hard to beat a dish of oysters—three different varieties, say, for only 8.25, or 16.50 for six. The hot dishes are all spectacular—Pacific sablefish baked in sake with miso, Sunshine Coast sturgeon with preserved lemon, Ahi tuna with coriander and halibut from the Queen Charlottes. In the cellar they have many of the great clarets and all the big Italian reds, as well as a lavish selection from the Napa Valley, for those who can afford them. For the rest of us, there are many pleasures to be found on the list of wines from the Okanagan, among them a merlot from Hester Creek, a Poplar Grove from Benchmark on the Naramata Bench and the delightful, inexpensive gewurztraminer from Dirty Laundry.
Open daily 5 pm to 11 pm. Licensed. All cards. No smoking. ♿

VANCOUVER **MAP 229**
C ☆☆☆
1600 Howe Street **$175**
(604) 681-1164

C seems a little more realistic this year, though it still has its moments of extravagance. If you have plenty of money, start your meal with seared foie gras de canard on a plate with pickled prawns, honey and thyme for 26.00, paired with a glass of 1994 Château d'Yquem for another 70.00. But you don't have to play that game. C begins, as it always did, with a strong architectural statement, all glass and steel overlooking False Creek from the foot of Howe Street. You sit down to a choice of tuna tartar, smoked salmon, striped shrimp with caramelized garlic and licorice or carrot soup with a brandade of smoked black cod. You then go on to wild Pacific salmon, Sun Valley trout, sturgeon with poached crabapples or sablefish with orange and almonds. The cooking is impeccable, the service perfect. The wine-list is long and splendid, filled as it is with the best wines from the Pacific Northwest. There are even six premium sakes from Japan, all sold by the glass.
Open daily 5.30 pm to 10.30 pm. Licensed. All cards. No smoking. Book ahead. Valet parking.

VANCOUVER **MAP 229**
CHAMBAR ☆
562 Beatty Street **$100**
(604) 879-7119

Last year Chambar was named the best new restaurant of the year and now, a year later, it's still the toast of the town. The owner has done everything right—décor, food, service and price. No main course costs more than 20.00, though they do like to price everything on the plate separately, even the fries with the mussels. Nico Schuermans, the owner and chef, was born in Africa of Belgian parents, and his menu reflects his roots on three continents. Mussels are, of course, a feature.

They're prepared in three ways—with white wine, garlic, bacon and cream, with white wine, leeks, celery and red onions and with tomatoes, smoked chilli, cilantro and coconut cream. There's a variety of fusion dishes, all beautifully prepared and presented. Schuermans' experience in France shows in several traditional dishes, such as maigret de canard glazed with honey and assiette de chasseur with loin of Canadian elk and wild-boar bacon. There's a lovely mushroom-and-capuccino soup, as well as confit of duck in phyllo with cranberry wine and panko-seared albacore tuna with coconut and saffron. The influence of North Africa shows in the sautéed prawns with lemon and the braised lamb shanks with honey, figs and cinnamon, served with couscous and zalouk. The poached pears stuffed with dark chocolate and served with lavender ice cream is the best of a strong list of sweets. The wine-list is adequate, but they need more Belgian beers.
Open daily at 6.30 pm and 8 pm (two sittings). Licensed. All cards. No smoking. ♿

VANCOUVER **MAP 229**
CIN CIN ☆☆
1154 Robson Street **$155**
(604) 688-7338

Cin Cin has always been a warm and happy place, with its open central kitchen and colourful murals. Since the arrival of Andreas Wechselberger, formerly of Teatro in Calgary, the cooking has been more conservative than it used to be. Wechselberger began his career in one of Tuscany's top kitchens, and he uses all the natural ingredients he can lay his hands on—free-range chicken, organic eggs and local field tomatoes. The alderwood grill and oven were introduced to Vancouver at Cin Cin almost twenty years ago and they're both still in use today. At noon they make risottos of dungeness crab and pizzas of asparagus and prosciutto. At night they turn to Arctic char with a minestrone of root vegetables and chicken baked under clay—a lovely dish. Thierry Busset's pastry

kitchen is unmatched in the city for its crème brûlée with chestnut gelato, its tiramisu with chocolate espresso and its warm caramelized apple tart. They now have a thousand labels in the cellar, among them a number of rare varietals from solaia and sassicaia.
Open Monday to Friday 11.30 am to 2.30 pm, 5 pm to 11 pm, Saturday and Sunday 5 pm to 11 pm. Licensed. All cards. No smoking.

VANCOUVER **MAP 229**
CIOPPINO'S ☆☆☆
1133 Hamilton Street **$175**
(604) 688-7466

Pino Posteraro doesn't have the advantage of spectacular architecture or a luxurious menu offering the several varieties of Japanese sashimi or Pacific oysters. All he has to offer, on this crowded corner of Hamilton Street, is a superlative kitchen specializing in northern-Italian cooking. Ask for his white-asparagus soup and you'll see what he can do. Or his crab-and-asparagus salad, for that matter, or his sweet lobster bisque with fresh crab. The most typical of the main courses are the calf's liver alla Veneziana (not that it's quite in the Venetian style) and the osso buco Milanese, though he also serves seared Ahi tuna, Pacific sea-bass and, most surprising of all, Dover sole meunière. The best of the sweets, we think, is the chocolate ice cream with maple syrup and sour cherries. The wine-list offers what must be one of the best collections of big Italian reds in the country. There's more than a page of brunellos di Montalcino as well as a page of old barolos. There are nine solaias, seven ornellaias, four tignanellos and three sassicaias. Who else can match this?
Open Monday to Saturday 5.30 pm to 11 pm. Closed on Sunday. Licensed. All cards. No smoking. Book ahead if you can. ♿

Our web site is at www.oberonpress.ca Readers wishing to use e-mail should address us at oberon@sympatico.ca

VANCOUVER **MAP 229**
CRU ☆
1459 W Broadway **$115**
(604) 677-4111

The name Cru comes from the wine designation premier cru or premier grand cru. Of course, there's a lot more to this lively, colourful restaurant than wine. True, there's a list of small plates, all of which go well with a glass or two of wine: carpaccio of beef, tuna tartar, steamed local mussels and pan-seared scallops. But there's also a three-course *prix-fixe* that starts with such things as seafood soup and cellar-door Caesar, and goes on to breast of Fraser Valley duck, served rare with polente and a reduction of spiced figs and roasted halibut with thyme and glazed pearl onions. Meals end well with a lemon-curd fool or a bitter-chocolate torte. There are a number of unusual wines, among them a lovely sauvignon blanc from Township 7. The presentation is colourful, the service cheerful and enthusiastic. Cru has made a very good beginning.
Open daily 5 pm to 10 pm (later for small plates). Licensed. Amex, Master Card, Visa. No smoking. ♿

VANCOUVER **MAP 229**
DIVA AT THE MET ☆☆
645 Howe Street **$165**
(604) 602-7788

Diva has three spectacular terraced levels rising from Howe Street. It has a big, busy open kitchen, elegant service and a sumptuous menu that combines big continental dishes like osso buco with an imposing list of dishes from the Pacific Northwest. There are people who come here for the Alberta kobe-beef hamburger, served with hand-cut Yukon Gold potatoes and cheddar cheese infused with Guinness stout at extravagant prices. More to the point, they have Alaska black cod (smoked and served with white asparagus in a delicate coulis of carrot broth). They have wild sockeye salmon,

of course, with eggplant and crème fraîche. They have an interesting monkfish osso buco. They have Ahi tuna with crab salad. Scott Baechler may have left, but this is a kitchen of remarkable depth and it performs well, like the N.B.C. Symphony Orchestra in the last days of Arturo Toscanini, without a conductor. As for the sweet course, the brilliant Thomas Haas is still turning out wonderful upside-down chocolate soufflés and plum tarts in phyllo. The wine-list is weak on burgundies and wines from the Niagara Peninsula, strong (very strong) on wines from the Okanagan. Burrowing Owl is there and so is Liberty School. The coffee is superb.
Open Monday to Friday noon to 2.30 pm, 5.30 pm to 9.30 pm, Saturday and Sunday 5.30 pm to 9.30 pm. Licensed. Amex, Master Card, Visa. No smoking. ♿

VANCOUVER **MAP 229**
FEENIE'S ☞
2553 W Broadway **$105**
(604) 739-7115

Unlike Lumière, Feenie's, its sister restaurant next door, is open all day seven days a week. And unlike Lumière, it's comparatively cheap, with low markups on the wine-list right across the board. It's crowded and it's noisy. At peak hours, conversation is out of the question. The menu, however, is lively and ambitious, the cooking accomplished. You start with tartar of wild spring salmon with sesame seeds, cilantro and tamarind or, perhaps, with seared yellowfin tuna in black-olive vinaigrette and go on to seared halibut with wilted spinach and clam-and-mussel nectar, braised free-range chicken with red and green peppers or pan-seared pork chops with potato purée and sesame ginger. Feenie has a number of farmhouse cheeses from Ontario and Quebec, as well as one or two wonderful chocolate confections. This is a good buy in anyone's book.
Open Monday to Friday 11.30 am to 11.30 pm, Saturday and Sunday 10 am to 2 pm (brunch), 5.30 pm to 11.30 pm. Licensed. Amex, Master Card, Visa. No smoking. Book ahead if you can. ♿

VANCOUVER **MAP 229**
IL GIARDINO ☆
1382 Hornby Street **$175**
(604) 669-2422

The years pass and things change. Umberto Menghi was once a young man with three restaurants on Hornby Street. La Cantina was the first to go, then Umberto's. Today the charming yellow villa with white trim is used only for private parties. Umberto himself, now in his grey hairs, spends much of his time at the Villa Delia, overseeing his vineyard in Tuscany west of Florence. Or he may be found pressing olives for extra-virgin olive oil. Here in Vancouver, Il Giardino, with its Italianate garden and earthy interior, is the last survivor of the three. The menu is no longer preoccupied with game. They usually have salmon and sea-bass. There's always some first-class pasta (linguine with pesto, say). With luck, you'll be offered beautiful Alaska black cod. The vegetables, it must be admitted, are all served hot raw, and the sweets are rather predictable, even the lemon tart. The list of Italian wines is impressive. Umberto himself has a couple of his own Tuscan wines, one of them priced at 59.00, the other at 100.00.
Open Monday to Friday 11.30 am to 4.30 pm (lunch), 4.30 pm to 11 pm (dinner), Saturday 6 pm to 11 pm. Closed on Sunday. Licensed. All cards. No smoking. ♿

VANCOUVER **MAP 229**
GO FISH ☞
1505 W 1 Avenue **$45**
(604) 730-5040

Go Fish is hard to find. Look for it on the False Creek Fisherman's Wharf at the end of 1 Avenue: a trailer painted bright blue, with a blue-and-white striped awning in front. The awning shelters three or four tables from the rain, but there's no heat, so don't come in winter. In summer, they buy the freshest conceivable oysters, salmon, halibut and albacore tuna from local

fishermen. This they char-grill and make up into poboys, sandwiches and fish and chips; or they grill the fish and serve it on a bed of organic greens with white balsamic vinegar. They have nine parking spaces and washrooms in the next block. Go and see for yourself what really fresh fish tastes like.
Open Wednesday to Sunday 11.30 am to 6.30 pm. Closed on Monday and Tuesday. No liquor. Master Card, Visa. No reservations. Free parking. ♿

VANCOUVER **MAP 229**
IMPERIAL CHINESE SEAFOOD ☆
355 Burrard Street **$125**
(604) 688-8191

With its magnificent views of Burrard Inlet and the mountains of the North Shore, the Imperial is the most opulent Chinese restaurant in the city. But like the Sun Sui Wah (see below), there have been some recent doubts about the cooking. While most of the food, especially the superb Beijing duck, is prepared in-house, a number of dim-sum items are now being outsourced. There was a time when the dim sum was as good as any served in the country and we can still recommend the grilled squid, the imaginative sushi rolls, the wonderful sticky rice and the flawless custard tarts. In the evening everything tastes exactly as it should. The corn-and-asparagus soup is rich and creamy, the vegetables are crisp (without being raw). We particularly like the crab claws stuffed with shrimp paste, the honey-garlic spareribs Montreal-style and the fillet of salmon in black-bean sauce. The deep-fried rock cod is well handled too. It's cooked at a high temperature, which leaves the outside crisp and the inside moist. For sweet, try the mango pudding or the banana fritters.
Open daily 11 am to 2.30 pm, 5 pm to 10 pm. Licensed. Master Card, Visa. No smoking. Book ahead. ♿

Nobody can buy space in this guide and nobody can buy his way out of it.

VANCOUVER **MAP 229**
LUMIERE ☆☆☆
2551 W Broadway **$280**
(604) 739-8185

Robert Feenie has modified the format at Lumière this year. He still has three tasting menus, priced at 120.00, 130.00 and 165.00. But you can now choose three courses from the à la carte at the more moderate price of 100.00 a head. The dominant colour of the interior is still a subdued grey. The windows are screened from the street and conversation is possible, which it really is not at Feenie's next door. The service is stunning. The cooking is graceful, delicate and beautifully understated. The ingredients are superb. The menu is imaginative and complex—probably too complex for its own good. On the new à la carte, you can begin your meal with yellowfin-tuna sashimi with green papaya and cilantro, milk-poached Alaska black cod in grainy mustard or pan-seared Quebec foie gras with enoki mushrooms and go on to naked lobster with chanterelles, halibut in a split-pea risotto or pan-seared sea-bass in cauliflower purée and twenty-year-old balsamic vinegar. The meal ends with a splendid chocolate fondant or a praline soufflé. The wine-list is eccentric and expensive. There are, of course, the usual Lafites, Latours and Mouton Rothschilds and the usual sassicaias, but it's probably more fun to ask for a bottle of Dirty Laundry gewurztraminer—or even a basket flight of dirty laundry, which means a glass of each of the three Dirty Laundry vintages on the list.
Open Tuesday to Sunday 5.30 pm to 10.30 pm. Closed on Monday. Licensed. Amex, Master Card, Visa. No smoking. Book ahead. ♿

This is a guide to Canadian restaurants from coast to coast—the first ever published and the only one of its kind on the market today. Every restaurant in the guide has been personally tested. Our reporters are not allowed to identify themselves or to accept free meals.

VANCOUVER **MAP 229**
MONSOON
2526 Main Street **$80**
(604) 879-4001

The cooking at Monsoon gets better and better, which means that the restaurant gets busier and busier. Tables are scarce and it's best to take a seat at the bar. The menu, which used to be pure East Asian (satays and curries), now has several West Coast dishes like grilled tuna with arugula, shaved fennel and roasted red peppers. They have a new chef this year, Patrick Lynch, who might offer something like chicken soup with udon noodles and bok choy in a sesame broth or pan-seared scallops with black tagliatelle. We used to suggest starting with an order of masala fries with banana ketchup, but his year we prefer the spicier paprika fries with a lime-chilli aioli. Most of these dishes come with a bowl of steamed rice with a quartered cinnamon pod in the centre. Afterwards you have the choice of a chocolate-custard pot with cardamom ice cream or a chai brûlée, which will spoil you for anyone else's crème brûlée. The service is young, bright and cheerful.
Open daily 5 pm to 11 pm. Licensed. All cards. No smoking. No reservations.

VANCOUVER **MAP 229**
MONTRI ☆
3029 W Broadway **$85**
(604) 738-1278

Montri's menu seldom changes, but the place is always packed, which isn't surprising, because Montri is a wonderful place. For six straight years it's been named the city's best Thai restaurant. Unless you know a lot about Thai cuisine, it's best to ask Montri to choose (or create) a dinner for you. Chances are he'll suggest that you start with a soup, perhaps Tom Kha Gai, or chicken-and-coconut soup. Or perhaps he'll suggest the Tod Mun fishcakes. If you asked us, we'd suggest the boneless stuffed chicken wings or the red curry of duck.

Montri has a number of favourite dishes, which he calls Aroy-D, which means delicious. We particularly like the beef and the prawn, served with peanuts, galangal, lime and coconut on a bed of flash-fried spinach. The décor here on West Broadway is minimal. If you're more interested in ambience than food, head over to Simply Thai in Yaletown. It's a bit more up-market.
Open Tuesday to Thursday 5 pm to 9.30 pm, Friday and Saturday 5 pm to 10.30 pm, Sunday 5 pm to 9.30 pm. Closed on Monday. Licensed. Master Card, Visa. No smoking. ♿

VANCOUVER **MAP 229**
THE NAAM ☞
2724 W 4 Avenue **$60**
(604) 738-7151

The thing that brings us back to the Naam over and over again is the consistency of its kitchen. Few restaurants have survived in this guide for 30 years, as the Naam has. This is down-home vegetarian cooking. The Naam is where the hippies first gathered and where they now bring their children and their grandchildren. Even people who expect three meat meals a day come here for breakfast. Here they get a perfectly-cooked omelette, great pancakes with real maple syrup and the best fried eggs with home-fries on the side you'll find anywhere. The menu hasn't changed in years, but there's always a hot special not on the list. On our last visit we came up with a wonderful combination of spinach, chick-peas and potatoes in a hot, hot curry. The list of sweets features double fudge-cake and ginger cake with butterscotch sauce. Regulars go for one of the hearty, thick-crusted pies filled with blueberries, cranberries or Dutch apples—and they're right.
Open daily 6 am to 6 am. Licensed for beer and wine only. Master Card, Visa. No smoking. No reservations.

If you use an out-of-date edition and find it inaccurate, don't blame us. Buy a new edition.

VANCOUVER **MAP 229**

THE PEAR TREE
4120 E Hastings Street **$100**
Burnaby
(604) 299-2772

The Pear Tree is the first good restaurant we've found in Burnaby. Scott Jaeger has been chosen to represent Canada at the Bocuse d'Or culinary competition in Lyons in 2007. His small, elegant restaurant in Burnaby is in a low-rent area, which allows him to spend what money he has on top-quality produce. His menu is small and carefully chosen and his three-course table d'hôte changes frequently. Wild game, especially caribou, pheasant and partridge, features prominently. So do truffles. We can recommend the roast caribou with mashed potatoes and asparagus as well as the lamb shanks braised in red wine and served with seared scallops and roasted pears. Jaeger is also good with fish and shellfish: scallops drizzled with truffle oil and served on a bed of orzo and (our favourite) pan-seared halibut in a truffle broth. Pears appear in every form in salads, savouries and sweets. The sweets are exquisite. Try the lemon tart with a lattice of caramelized sugar garnished with sliced grapes and diced papaya.
Open Tuesday to Saturday 5 pm to 10 pm. Closed on Sunday and Monday. Licensed. All cards. No smoking. ♿

VANCOUVER **MAP 229**

PROVENCE
1177 Marinaside Crescent **$110**
(604) 681-4144

The new Provence has a splendid view of False Creek. It also has a brand-new menu, offering a variety of fresh oysters—Beach, Golden Mantle, Gorge Inlet, Kusshi and Royal Miyagi—as well as a number of seafood dishes, among them grilled Ahi tuna, lobster and crab mayonnaise and seared sable-fish. As for the cellar, it's full of magnificent wines: sassicaia, Mouton Rothschild and hermitage, as well as a large selection from the Okanagan and the Pacific Northwest. Markups are modest. Wines from Benchmark on the Naramata Bench, for instance, sell here for less than 60.00, some vintages from Burrowing Owl for less than 50.00.

Open Monday to Friday 8 am to 11.30 am (breakfast), 11.30 am to 3 pm (lunch), 5 pm to 10 pm, Saturday and Sunday 10 am to 3 pm (brunch), 5 pm to 10 pm. Licensed. All cards. No smoking. ♿

VANCOUVER **MAP 229**
QUATTRO ON FOURTH ☆☆
2611 W 4 Avenue **$210**
(604) 734-4444

People have been filling Quattro's tables, and lining up in summer for the covered seats in their garden, for more than ten years now. The antipasto plate is known all over town, but you may prefer to begin, as we like to do, with the radicchio bocconcini—grilled radicchio stuffed with cheese, wrapped in prosciutto and served in cherry vinaigrette. Others prefer the crab-and-smoked-salmon cakes, the grilled squid with ground cerignola olives or the wild-mushroom pâté. If you've come for pasta, just ask for the pasta pazza a pezzi, which will bring you five perfectly-cooked pastas for 19.95 a head. Main courses now cost at least 30.00, something you used to see only in Toronto. But even at this price, we still admire the rack of lamb with figs and mustard and the sea-bass with pistachios and sweet peppers. A new favourite is the involtini stuffed with Italian sausage, apple and fennel. The service is friendly and watchful and the cellar is full of the best Italian wines. Quattro on Fourth is the flagship of the Corsi fleet, but they've recently improved the kitchen at Il Gusto di Quattro at 1 Lonsdale Avenue in North Vancouver (telephone (604) 924-4444). This was the family's first restaurant and it's still small and intimate and comparatively inexpensive, at least at lunch, which isn't served

at Quattro on Fourth. At Il Gusto they offer several of the same dishes, as well as a hearty mixed-seafood cioppino in a zesty broth of tomato and fennel.
Open Monday to Thursday 5 pm to 10 pm, Friday and Saturday 5 pm to 11 pm, Sunday 5 pm to 10 pm. Licensed. All cards. No smoking. Book ahead if you can. ♿

VANCOUVER **MAP 229**
RAINCITY GRILL
1193 Denman Street **$130**
(604) 685-7337

If it doesn't grow west of the mountains it won't be used in the kitchen at Raincity. That means no Ahi tuna, no Chilean sea-bass, no Prince Edward Island mussels, no Bay of Fundy lobster, no avocado, no olive-oil and of course no Atlantic salmon. If you aren't familiar with Albacore tuna, this is a good place to start. Albacore-tuna sashimi is rubbed with mustard-seed and served with wilted spinach. The duck foie gras doesn't come, like most, from Quebec; it's local and served on a compote of figs with small greens. Smoked wild Pacific salmon is garnished with Indian candy and horseradish crème fraîche. Lamb comes from Prince George, where the meat is more consistent than that from Saltspring Island. The bouillabaisse is crammed with Pacific fish. Moon Farm rabbit is served three ways—the shoulder braised in cider, the leg stuffed with wild boar, the loin grilled with roasted onions. In the kitchen, Sean Cousins cooks with easy authority, but the front of the house is standing-room only except at the beginning of the week, and the service suffers. The wine-list, of course, is astonishing, extending far beyond the Okanagan to Washington, Oregon and California. Ten local wines are featured, among them Sandhill cabernet franc, Jackson-Triggs merlot, Gray Monk pinot gris and Quail's Gate chardonnay. The pinot gris from Gray Monk is a surprising choice, but this is a very personal list, prepared by the *sommelier*, Brent Hayman.

Open daily 11.30 am to 2.30 pm, 5.30 pm to 10 pm. Licensed. Amex, Master Card, Visa. No smoking. Valet parking. ♿

VANCOUVER **MAP 229**
LA REGALADE
2232 Marine Drive **$115**
West Vancouver
(604) 921-2228

This stylish little bistro is located in West Vancouver, which should mean that it's expensive. Actually, it's not. An omelette costs less than 10.00, rognons de veaux less than 20.00. The cooking is bold and vigorous, bistro-style. Don't start with the quenelle of fish à la Lyonnaise. Better the vegetable tart or the rillette of pork. Next comes beef bourguignon, a dish you probably haven't tasted since the mid-fifties. There's also veal short ribs with lemon and rack of pork with polente. The rognons de veau, served with mustard, is, however, the best of the lot. Most of the wines come from the Okanagan and you can get things like Blue Mountain gamay and Burrowing Owl chardonnay at reasonable prices. The service is friendly and very prompt.
Open Tuesday to Friday 11.30 am to 2 pm, 5.30 pm to 10 pm, Saturday 5.30 pm to 10 pm. Closed on Sunday and Monday. Licensed. Master Card, Visa. No smoking. ♿

VANCOUVER **MAP 229**
SUN SUI WAH ☆
3888 Main Street **$100**
(604) 872-8822

This is one of the most spectacular restaurants in Vancouver. You enter by a circular staircase that climbs out of a water-garden under a huge kite-shaped mobile and leads to a spacious dining-room lit by a graceful skylight. Dim sum is the thing to order. It comes on a dim-sum cart, or you can have it made to order from a printed menu. The menu offers shark's-fin soup (23.50

a head), fresh Australian abalone (29.80 and up) and fresh geoduck (39.80 for four), as well as several smaller dishes, the best of which is the pan-fried clams in black-bean sauce. There's also pan-fried silver-fish with spicy sea-salt and deep-fried won-ton and bean curd. Seafood is the specialty of the house and there are tanks filled with live lobster and shrimps, crabs and geoduck. Seafood dishes are prepared in the traditional way, steamed in ginger broth with green onions and garlic. If you come with a number of friends you can make a banquet of a whole rock cod, steamed with shredded ginger. The presentation is elegant, the service quick and to the point. There have of late, however, been some doubts about the cooking.

Open Monday to Friday 10.30 am to 3 pm, 5 pm to 10.30 pm, Saturday and Sunday 10 am to 3 pm, 5 pm to 10.30 pm. Licensed. Amex, Master Card, Visa. No smoking. ♿

VANCOUVER **MAP 229**
TOJO'S ☆☆☆
777 W Broadway **$125**
(604) 872-8050

They have all the usual sushis and sashimis here, but that's not the best way to approach a meal at Tojo's. You can either ask Tojo to design a dinner for you—he charges upwards of 50.00 a head for this—or you can design your own meal from the list of Tojo's own creations. There are about a dozen of these, each described on the menu with the year in which they first appeared. There's Golden Roll (prawns, salmon and crab, 1974), Spider Roll (soft-shell crab and avocado, 1996), Great Pacific Roll (salmon and avocado, 1990), Dynamite Roll (prawn tempura) and Pacific Northwest Roll (crab and avocado). Each is a dazzling dish and one you've never tasted before. It's a good idea to order at least one sashimi as well, and in fact Tojo's tuna sashimi outsells everything else on the menu. You can drink Asahi beer if you like, or rice wine, but it's best to ask for a carafe of hot premium sake (it comes hot or cold). If money is no object, ask for Yashi no Gawa Dai Ginjo, a super-premium sake that sells for 200.00 a bottle. If you want to be sensible, go for Mazukagami, a premium sake that sells for just 35.00 a carafe. They both make Gekkeikan taste like yesterday.

Open Monday to Saturday 5 pm to 10 pm. Closed on Sunday. Licensed. All cards. No smoking. Book ahead. ♿

VANCOUVER **MAP 229**

VIJ'S ☆☆

1480 W 11 Avenue **$125**

(604) 736-6664

Vikram Vij and his wife, Meeru, take fragments of ideas from other cultures and other cuisines, and reshape them in their own image. In the early days of their marriage, they travelled all over India, sampling meals they were offered in private homes. They brought the recipes with them when they came to Canada. So theirs is a real vernacular kitchen, where dishes are prepared according to the traditional ways of the people. Vikram and Meeru work out their ideas together, Meeru taking charge of the vegetarian dishes, Vikram the meats, the marinades and the sauces. Everything is made fresh daily, so at the end of the day there's nothing left in the kitchen but a few potatoes. The so-called lamb popsicles are their most successful dish, and it's ordered by every second customer. Lamb chops are marinated in mustard and wine and served with spinach and potatoes seasoned with turmeric. Vegetarians are in their element at Vij's, where every imaginable kind of vegetable is prepared in every imaginable way. We suggest you start with jackfruit with black cardamom and cumin and go on to an eggplant-and-papaya curry with black chick-peas and a lentil chapatti. They have a few wines, but it's better to drink beer or a ginger-lemon squash. Just remember: there are no reservations and people have been known to wait two hours in the rain for a table.

Open daily 5.30 pm to 9.30 pm. Licensed for beer and wine only. All cards. No smoking. No reservations. ♿

VANCOUVER **MAP 229**
VIJ'S RANGOLI
1488 W 11 Avenue **$50**
(604) 736-5711

Rangoli is a market café offering a wide range of South-east Asian spices, vacuum-packed, refrigerated and frozen Indian meals and a small but choice menu of Vij's Indo-Canadian lunch dishes. The interior is industrial in style—stainless steel, light wood, an open kitchen and rows of coolers and freezers—but the atmosphere is pure Vij, the service impeccable. So far there are only five dishes on the menu, all priced at less than 12.00. There's usually lamb saag (tender, perfectly-seasoned meat in a rich spinach curry) and grilled tamarind-chilli breast of chicken served with dal and rice. Sometimes there's wild salmon blended with chick-peas, cilantro and curried coconut milk. There's a good selection of local and imported beers.
Open daily 11 am to 4 pm. Licensed for beer and wine only. Master Card, Visa. No smoking. ♿

VANCOUVER **MAP 229**
WABI SABI ☆
4422 W 10 Avenue **$125**
(604) 222-8188

Wabi sabi is the name of a Japanese tradition, the tradition of celebrating the beauty in something old or worn, like a chipped teabowl, reglazed and used in a zen tea ceremony. The use of the phrase to identify a fashionable sushi bar has to be regarded as a gesture of self-deprecation. Here East meets West in the partnership of Chantelle Chouinard and Tak Katayama. Together they've made Wabi Sabi into a restaurant that promises to challenge Tojo's as the best in the city. There's the usual broad range of sushis and sashimis, but they're at

their best with their innovative sashimis. Start with the hamachi chinois, which features thinly-sliced yellowtail garnished with a julienne of bell peppers, kaiware, beets and crispy leeks. Then try the panko-crusted salmon wrapped in nori and basil, breaded and deep-fried in soy and wasabi butter. Travellers have also recommended the aigamo duck with its distinctive balsamic miso dressing (expensive but worth every dollar), the salad of albacore tuna encrusted with rock salt and black pepper, the tataki of beef tenderloin, the Asian honey-garlic salmon tartar and the tuna carpaccio with organic greens, chilli mayonnaise and a spicy mango dressing. They have an excellent assortment of sakis, as well as a number of first-class chardonnays from the Okanagan. Wabi Sabi was the first of what is now a growing number of izakaya-style eating-places in Vancouver. The most promising of these new arrivals is the Shiru Bay Chopstick Café at 1193 Hamilton Street in Yaletown (telephone (604) 408-9315).
Open daily 5 pm to 11 pm. Licensed. Amex, Master Card, Visa. No smoking. ♿

VANCOUVER **MAP 229**
WEST
2881 Granville Street **$200**
(604) 738-8938

West is unbelievably expensive. Appetizers cost 15.00 to 20.00, main courses 35.00 to 40.00. For all that, the menu offers few temptations. This the restaurant of the year? Hardly. Needless to say, David Hawksworth still has a few surprises up his sleeve. His beetroot salad shows what can be done with beets. He knows how to prepare weathervane scallops and Queen Charlotte Islands halibut. His braised and roasted veal tongue and his risottos have all the virtues. His potato-and-leek ravioli, on the other hand, is as heavy as lead. Markups on the wine-list are higher than they need to be—a bottle of Burrowing Owl costs more than 60.00. Of course, there's plenty of good drinking on the list if you can afford it. But the kitchen has never regained its footing

since the restaurant changed its name from Ouest to West, which was supposed to signify a renewed commitment to West Coast cuisine.
Open Monday to Friday 11.30 am to 2.30 pm, 5.30 pm to 11 pm, Saturday and Sunday 5.30 pm to 11 pm. Licensed. Amex, Master Card, Visa. No smoking. Book ahead.

VICTORIA, B.C. **MAP 230**
THE BLACK OLIVE
739 Pandora Avenue **$90**
(250) 384-6060

Most Greek restaurants in this country are glorified souvlaki diners. The Black Olive isn't like that at all. Paul Psyllakis works outside the box. He's interested in the cooking of Crete and Cyprus rather than that of mainland Greece. His dining-room is warm and inviting, and instead of putting up Greek travel posters he's had local artists decorate his walls. If you come in at noon, try the grilled-salmon sandwich with goat-cheese and red-pepper mayonnaise or the lamb burger with bell peppers, feta cheese and pesto mayonnaise. Though the Black Olive is not an Italian restaurant, they're good with pasta—try the linguine or the seafood cannelloni. We like to start the evening meal with the sautéed squid with a glaze of honey and lime or the phyllo purse stuffed with wild mushrooms. Their signature dish is the six-bone pan-seared rack of lamb, crusted with dijon mustard, coated with a rich demi-glaze and priced lower than anywhere else in town. They also have a lovely fisherman's pot, filled with prawns, scallops, clams, mussels and halibut in a zesty black-olive broth. Paul Psyllakis has a nose for good wines at bargain prices, so ask for his advice and take it.
Open Monday to Friday 11 am to 2 pm, 5 pm to 10 pm, Saturday and Sunday 5 pm to 10 pm. Licensed. All cards. No smoking. ♿

Our web site is at www.oberonpress.ca Readers wishing to use e-mail should address us at oberon@sympatico.ca

VICTORIA **MAP 230**
BRASSERIE L'ECOLE
1715 Government Street **$110**
(250) 475-6260

This is a true bistro, serving things like onion soup and mussels and fries (for 18.00). Better still, you can have a glass of any still wine in the cellar for one-fifth the price of the bottle, provided you order at least two glasses. The cellar is full of French wines at all prices, which means that you can order a glass of the 1999 Lafite for yourself and your companion for just two-fifths of 450.00. That may sound like a lot of money and it is, but is it a lot of money for a Lafite? Apart from the onion soup, they have organic greens in honey-and-thyme vinaigrette, mussels from Quadra Island with white wine, parsley and garlic and Pacific oysters on the half-shell. There are only four or five main dishes—rockfish with white beans and watercress, trout from Sooke on a bed of Swiss chard with butternut squash and fried chick-peas. If tarte tatin is on the menu, be sure to ask for it. The apples are sliced thin, properly cooked and drenched with caramel. It's lovely.
Open Tuesday to Saturday 5.30 pm to 10.30 pm. Closed on Sunday and Monday. Licensed. Master Card, Visa. No smoking. Book ahead. ♿

VICTORIA **MAP 230**
CAFE BRIO ☆
944 Fort Street **$135**
(250) 383-0009

Ask almost anyone about their favourite restaurant in Victoria and they'll name the Café Brio. We used to feel the same way, but last year another new chef, Chris Dignan, was installed in the kitchen and we were disappointed. This year things have improved. When Dignan is good he's very good indeed—which he'd have to be at these prices. Brio is expensive by Victoria: standards. An appetizer of veal sweetbreads costs 17.00;

entrées sell for upwards of 30.00. But Greg Hays has a legendary reputation for insisting on the best ingredients that money can buy. No kitchen has ever worked such miracles with vegetables. The organic vegetables grown on Vancouver Island are in a class by themselves. All the poultry is free-range, all the seafood is perfectly fresh. One traveller considered his sirloin steak the best he had had in his life. Last year we weren't impressed with the halibut poached in olive-oil, but this year we've been more fortunate with the smoked sablefish, the pan-seared scallops and the albacore tuna. The sweets are fabulous. There's a quince tarte tatin, pumpkin gingerbread and a lovely crème brûlée They still have a big list of Okanagan wines, but they're a lot more expensive this year. Australians are a better buy—the Wolf Blass Yellow Label still costs just 37.00, which makes it a great bargain.

Open daily 5.30 pm to 10 pm. Licensed. Master Card, Visa. No smoking. ♿

VICTORIA **MAP 230**
MATISSE ☆☆
512 Yates Street **$135**
(250)480-0883

We were always impressed by Ludovic Renaud's cooking at Matisse, though we were daunted by the prices. In the last year or two these have been cut and you now pay no more here than in any other restaurant of its class in Victoria. Nor has the cooking faltered. Every evening Renaud offers a four-course set menu for 47.00, which is such a good buy that one may almost be tempted by the seven-course menu for 85.00. His cooking still smacks of the bistro style. Take, for example, the rillettes of pork, the winter pâté made with pork belly, ham and wine, the steak au poivre and the tarte tatin. But Renaud comes from LaRochelle, the seafood capital of France, and he certainly has a way with fish. His celebrated bouillabaisse is crammed with clams, mussels and prawns in a broth of tomato, lobster and

anise. His wild Pacific salmon is poached in pineau des charentes and finished with whipped butter. His lobster bisque is finished with brandy and cream, his fresh sea scallops served in a lobster sauce. His salmon is roasted for five hours in a slow oven until the skin is crisp while the flesh is still moist; the whole fish being then served in its own drippings. The service is intelligent and very well informed.
Open Wednesday to Sunday 5.30 pm to 10 pm. Closed on Monday and Tuesday. Licensed. Amex, Master Card, Visa. No smoking. ♿

VICTORIA **MAP 230**
PAPRIKA ☆
2524 Estevan Avenue **$150**
(250) 592-7424

Paprika is first and foremost a bistro and George Szasz cooks as if he knew it. His flavours are strong, his textures earthy. He likes such things as grilled wild-boar sausages with grainy mustard, pork belly and veal cheeks. He's not at his best with his crab bisque. You'll do better with the seared scallops, the Cowichan Bay breast of duck, the Metchosin spring lamb or the braised lamb shanks with polente. Everybody's favourite sweet is the crème brûlée, but we actually prefer the crêpes stuffed with lemon cream—a beautiful creation. The wine-list has been chosen with great care and features such things as Hester Creek barrel-select merlot, Wolf Blass brown-label shiraz, Burrowing Owl chardonnay and Smoking Loon viognier. Apart from these, there's serious drinking at all prices.
Open Monday to Saturday 5 pm to 10 pm. Closed on Sunday. Licensed. Amex, Master Card, Visa. No smoking. Book ahead. ♿

The price rating shown opposite the headline of each entry indicates the average cost of dinner for two with a modest wine, tax and tip. The cost of dinner, bed and breakfast (if available) is shown in parentheses.

VICTORIA **MAP 230**

RE-BAR ☞

50 Bastion Square **$65**

(250) 361-9223

Re-Bar begins every day with a big, earthy breakfast. On weekends they put on a fabulous brunch that starts with cranberry granola and goes on to an omelette (stuffed with butternut squash, say, fresh sage and old cheddar), buttermilk corn-cakes (with toasted coconut butter), huevos rancheros (a tortilla with scrambled eggs and Monterey Jack cheese), a burrito with roasted corn, brown rice and pumpkinseed cilantro and a tofu scramble. Lunch starts at noon with miso soup, filled with brown rice, barley, soba noodles, organic tofu, Asian greens and sesame seeds. Then there are baked portobellini mushrooms stuffed with goat-cheese, sundried tomatoes and balsamic greens, szechuan-noodle salads (buckwheat noodles with seaweed, avocado, cucumber and cashews) and corn tortillas filled with green chilli, black beans and Mexican greens. There are several wheatgrass drinks, of which our favourite is still Pharaoh's Sneakers. Capital Iron Basement, made of carrot, spinach and parsley, is the best of the vegetable juices. There's a whole page of fruit drinks—orange, apple, ginger, strawberry, lemon, lime and mint among others. There are also eight or nine bottled wines, all from the Pacific Northwest, as well as beers from microbreweries in Victoria, Cobble Hill and Kelowna. Re-Bar is bright, attractive and crowded. No wonder: it's one of the best vegetarian restaurants we know of.
Open Monday to Thursday 8.30 am to 9 pm, Friday 8.30 am to 10 pm, Saturday 8.30 am to 3.30 pm (brunch), 3.30 pm to 10 pm, Sunday 8.30 am to 3.30 pm (brunch). Licensed. All cards. No smoking. No reservations.

Where an entry is printed in italics this indicates that the restaurant has been listed only because it serves the best food in its area or because it hasn't yet been adequately tested.

VICTORIA **MAP 230**
ROSEMEADE ☆☆
English Inn **$110**
429 Lampson Street
(250) 412-7673

It's almost a century since the noted B.C. architect, Samuel McClure, drew up the plans for Rosemeade Manor, a Tudor-style mansion with five acres of gardens in Saxe Point, now a seedy district of downtown Victoria. The interior is a bizarre mixture of Edwardian and contemporary design. The million-dollar kitchen is run by Richard Luttman and has a chef's table that can be reserved for special occasions. The menu features appetizers like mushroom-bean-and-bacon soup with a gratin of bone marrow, mussels in crème fraîche and sautéed sweetbreads in a brown-butter hollandaise with capers. Organic Cowichan Valley chicken is paired with mustard and foie gras, lamb cheeks are braised in olive-oil, wild Alaskan scallops are seared and served with a terrine of celeriac and a sabayon of pears in cognac. There's a magnificent breakfast, featuring granola crêpes, eggs benedict West Coast style and pancakes made with barley flour, topped with figs and sauced with maple syrup. Breakfast will cost you about 40.00 for two.
Open Monday to Friday 8 am to 10.30 am, 5 pm to 10 pm, Saturday 8 am to 11 am, 5 pm to 10 pm. Closed on Sunday. Licensed. All cards. No smoking. ♿

VICTORIA **MAP 230**
ZAMBRI'S ☞
911 Yates Street **$90/$60**
(250) 360-1171

Zambri's is hidden behind a London Drugs store in a small shopping-centre on Yates Street. It's packed all day long and you need a reservation at night, though you'll probably have to wait for a table anyway. It's cheap, it's cheerful, the helpings are big and the food—everything

is prepared to order—is likeable. The open kitchen is tiny, but every day Peter Zambri turns out a three-course tasting menu for 38.00 plus 20.00 for wine. A recent tasting menu began with clams, went on to organic chicken-liver, pine mushrooms with marsala and lamb with stewed figs, sweet peppers, polente and mint, ending with a well-made tiramisu. The fish is all very fresh, the meats (shoulder of pork, striploin of beef) all very tender. You can get a half-portion of any of the pasta dishes. The coffee, made from Illy beans, is great. If you come in for lunch, you choose your meal from the blackboard and go up to the cash, where you choose one of four or five wines, all served in a toothbrush glass, pay your bill and take a seat at one of the bare wooden tables. Maybe they'll be offering something like rockfish with spinach, roast chicken with spicy tomatoes or liver with barlotti beans. But whatever it is, you can be sure it'll be cheap.
Open Tuesday to Saturday 11.30 am to 2.45 pm, 5 pm to 9 pm. Closed on Sunday and Monday. Licensed for beer and wine only. Amex, Master Card, Visa. No smoking. No reservations. Free parking. ♿

VICTORIA

See also BRENTWOOD BAY, MAYNE ISLAND, SALTSPRING ISLAND, SIDNEY, SOOKE.

VICTORIA, P.E.I. (MAP 43)

THE LANDMARK CAFE ☞
Main Street **$75**
(902) 658-2286

Eugene Sauvé does all the cooking at the Landmark, keeping up a steady conversation with the customers at the same time. He's a charmer, and so is his son, who waits on table. They both work just four months, from June to September, and spend the rest of the year in Australia, New Zealand, India, Europe or Latin America—wherever their fancy takes them. In the kitchen, Sauvé has a style of his own, and he cooks more or less

what he feels like cooking. Generally speaking, that means lots of garlic and plenty of hot chilli. You can start your meal with local mussels with mustard and garlic and go on to a meat pie, a quiche or (in season) a lobster roll. There's no longer any cod, sad to say, but there's Cajun-style halibut and shrimp, as well as steamed salmon. Strawberry-rhubarb pie comes with every meal and there's Folonari valpolicella for 20.00 a bottle and Houghton shiraz for 25.00. Prices on the wine-list are unbelievable and the halibut and salmon are almost as cheap. If you're looking for entertainment, the Victoria Playhouse, the oldest legitimate theatre on the Island, is just across the street. The Island Chocolate Company, a block away (telephone (902) 658-2320) has gorgeous handmade chocolates filled with local strawberries, raspberries and cranberries. If Linda Gilbert is in the kitchen this summer, you'll be able to sample her superb baking: muffins, brownies, gingerbread and either a chocolate cake or a cream pie (banana or chocolate). They have coffee, capuccino and espresso from beans roasted right here on the Island.
Open daily 11.30 am to 3 pm, 5 pm to 9 pm from 1 June until 30 September. Licensed. Master Card, Visa. No smoking. ♿ *The Island Chocolate Company is open daily 10 am to 8 pm from 1 July until 31 August, Tuesday to Sunday 10 am to 5 pm from 1 until 30 June and from 1 until 30 September. Closed on Monday in the spring and fall. No liquor. Master Card, Visa. No smoking.* ♿

VICTORIA **(MAP 43)**
VICTORIA VILLAGE INN ☆☆
(902) 658-2483 **$120**

Victoria has been discovered. People who live there complain that more visitors come every year. But the old houses built in the middle of the nineteenth century are still where they've always been, and in fact most of them have now been restored. The Village Inn itself is next door to the summer theatre, and every day they make up box dinners for theatre-goers. But this is a

kitchen that's moved far beyond its setting. In fact, it would probably earn three stars if it had a better wine-list. This is true even in the absence of Stephen Hunter, the owner and chef, who has recently bought a share in the nearby Wharf. In his absence, Paul Lucas is running the kitchen at the Village Inn. His menu is strong on organic fruits and vegetables, as well as local fish and shellfish in season. All the soups—purées, creams, consommés and broths—are wonderful. Every dish that follows is carefully thought out: the lovely roulade of roasted sweet peppers with goat-cheese, the lobster risotto with asparagus, parmesan and white truffle-oil, the pan-seared salmon with its sesame-butter crust. The caramel crème brûlée is good, of course, but it's the abundance of fresh fruit that you should be looking for: apples marinated in apple wine, blueberries sautéed in maple syrup and served in a phyllo cup with vanilla-bean crème anglaise and mango purée. The wine-list, however, leaves almost everything to be desired and there isn't much that's worth drinking except the chardonnay and cabernet sauvignon from Wolf Blass.
Open daily 6 pm to 10 pm from 1 June until 30 September. Licensed. Amex, Master Card, Visa. No smoking.

WAINWRIGHT, Alberta **MAP 232**
THE HONEY-POT
Highway 14 **$75**
(780) 842-4094

The Honey-Pot has been an institution in Wainwright ever since Helen and Bruce Middleton opened the place in 1979. It passed to their son, Steve, and his wife about ten years ago, and now is in the hands of their son-in-law, Alex Heath, and his wife, Jeanie. Nobody has ever had a bad word to say about the Honey-Pot. People all like the Alberta beef, the pasta and the vegetables, which are always fresh and change every day. There's also a first-class chicken fajita and an excellent Cajun rib-steak. They make as many of the sweets as they can, and import the rest. They do still make a

McIntosh-apple and caramel torte and a rich chocolate confection they call their Suicide Cake. There's a growing children's menu and a pub, where you can order from the regular menu. Beer is the thing to drink and six beers are on tap, among them Big Rock and Rickard's Red. If you're on your way from Edmonton to Saskatoon, the Honey-Pot is a good place to know about.
Open Monday to Saturday 11 am to 9.30 pm, Sunday 11 am to 2 pm (brunch). Licensed. Amex, Master Card, Visa. No smoking. ♿

WAKEFIELD, Quebec **(MAP 92)**
LE MOULIN ☆
60 chemin Mill **$140**
(819) 459-1838

Georges Laurier has moved here from his stylish little restaurant on boulevard Montcalm, after a brief stop at the Café Henry Burger. At the Wakefield Mill, now known to the politically correct as the Moulin, he's developed an entirely new menu that shows just what he can do in the kitchen. The Moulin, as its name implies, was once a mill and to this day the dining-room overlooks the mill-stream. Meals begin with chicken-liver pâté, served with port and honey. Needless to say, he does other things as well, among them house-smoked Atlantic salmon, Papineauville goat-cheese with McIntosh apples and foie gras from Carignan seared *à la façon du chef.* There's confit of Brome Lake duck to follow, as well as lamb from Moreau Farm braised in a minestrone of red lentils and black beans and sesame-crusted wall-eye in lemon-grass beurre blanc. (Both the wall-eye and the lamb are better than the Brome Lake duck.) There's a charming sugar pie to end the meal, as well as a short, sensible wine-list—eight red burgundies, a dozen clarets. Frankly, we usually settle for a bottle of Orpailleur, the local wine from Quebec. The service is always warm and friendly.

Open Monday to Saturday 11.30 am to 2 pm, 5.30 pm to 9 pm, Sunday 9.30 am to 2 pm (brunch), 5.30 pm to 9 pm. Licensed. Amex, Master Card, Visa. No smoking. ♿

WATERDOWN, Ontario **(MAP 89)**
DODY'S OYSTER BAR
9 Franklin Street **$115**
(905) 689-1055

Waterdown is on Highway 5 between Highway 6 and the Guelph Line. Dody's is located in a small strip mall, but it's a more ambitious (and more expensive) restaurant than it appears from the outside. You'll probably be tempted to start with oysters on the half-shell, but the oysters are served with bacon, cheddar cheese, basil and garlic, so you should resist the temptation. You'll do a lot better with either the butternut-squash soup with crème fraîche or the more exciting green salad with cranberries, candied walnuts, blue cheese and balsamic vinegar. The best of the main courses is the Alaska black cod with mango and asparagus, though the breast of pheasant with local apricots and a garnish of riesling and edible flowers runs it a close second. They use a lot of sugar in the cooking, which may discourage you from ordering a sweet. That would be a mistake, because all the sweets are made in house and they're the best part of the meal. There's a Callebaut-chocolate terrine, a tart lemon flan and a particularly good banana bread pudding. Don't try to book a table on their message machine because they seldom pick up their messages.
Open Tuesday to Friday noon to 11 pm, Saturday and Sunday 5 pm to 11 pm. Closed on Monday. Licensed. Master Card, Visa. No smoking. Book ahead if you can. ♿

Every restaurant in this guide has been personally tested. Our reporters are not allowed to identify themselves to the management or to accept free meals. We accept no advertisements. We accept no payment for listings. We depend entirely on you. Recommend the book to your friends.

WATERLOO, Ontario **(MAP 103)**
BHIMA'S WARUNG
262 King Street N **$130**
(519) 747-0722

Don't come to Bhima's Warung on either a Friday or a Saturday night. On weekdays the cooking and the service are calm and composed and you can be sure of a warm welcome. On weekends you better remember their warning that if you take too long over your meal you'll be asked to move to the bar. The prices here are about as high as they get in the area, but everything is fresh and beautifully prepared. You'll be expected to begin your meal with something like mussels steamed in lemon grass and Thai basil or shrimp and crab wrapped in rice paper and deep-fried. (The oysters with garlic, lemon grass, ginger and chilli are probably too hot for most people.) Next comes roast breast of duck on a bed of egg noodles with Thai curry or smoked and grilled tiger shrimp with a coconut-and-lychee curry, black sticky rice and red-pepper dumplings. Sweets are wild: white-chocolate baked pudding, crispy won-tons filled with pumpkin and served with basil ice cream and crème brûlée, oddly paired with black sticky rice. The helpings are all big and there's a big wine-list too, with several wines by the glass, mostly from the New World. On the other hand, you won't go wrong with the tamarind soda or any of the draught beers.
Open Tuesday to Thursday 5 pm to 10 pm, Friday and Saturday 5 pm to 11 pm, Sunday 5 pm to 10 pm. Closed on Monday. Licensed. All cards. No smoking. Free parking. ♿

WATERLOO **(MAP 103)**
JANET LYNN'S ☆
92 King Street S **$140**
(519) 725-3440

Janet Lynn died last year, soon after she came back from an earlier illness. The restaurant, which was the first in the area to offer anything but German-style country cooking, had been running for more than twenty years. Kevin Wong is still in charge of the front of the house, which explains the impeccable service. The menu is made up of French and Italian dishes, all presented in contemporary style. The kitchen has always paid close attention to detail: the vegetables in the lobster bisque are cooked *à point*, the seafood pie is thick with lobster, scallops and shrimp, all perfectly fresh and skilfully enhanced by a puff-pastry crust. The vanilla-bean ice cream is full of the taste of vanilla bean. One visitor reported last winter that they had given him the best quail he had ever had in his life. Wild salmon is on the menu almost every night, always with a different sauce. The duck two ways (confit and roasted) is well conceived too and so is the breast of chicken wrapped in prosciutto. The lamb is imported fresh from New Zealand. Risottos, a pasta and a couple of thin-crust pizzas appear as daily specials. The sweets are usually cold and very rich. As for the so-called chocolate sin cake, it's been on the menu since day one. The wine-list offers a good selection of inexpensive wines, as well as several wines by the glass.

Open Tuesday to Friday 11.30 am to 2 pm, 5.30 pm to 10 pm, Saturday 5.30 pm to 10 pm. Closed on Sunday and Monday. Licensed. Amex, Master Card, Visa. No smoking. ♿

WATERLOO **(MAP 103)**
MASALA BAY ☆
3B Regina Street N **$100**
(519) 747-2763

Ritesh Bhargava has more than twenty years' experience as a chef in Canada and, before that, in New Delhi. Here in Waterloo he has a very small restaurant, with awkward, crowded seating and a big Pepsi-Cola cooler in the background. The inspiration for the cooking comes from the north of India. The chef grinds and roasts his own spices, and his spicy dishes are all beautiful. Helpings are big and most of the dishes on the à la carte are enough for two. At noon the all-you-can-eat buffet costs just 9.99. It offers a remarkable array of authentic Indian dishes: light and highly-spiced samosas, cauliflower with coriander, saag panir, green chana salads, hot stuffed peppers, wonderful goat curry and fresh, warm nan. The evening meal might begin with a purse of potatoes and peas wrapped in flaky dough or, better still, with a pakora platter loaded with cauliflower, eggplant and onion fritters. The chana masala is made with real chick peas, soaked overnight and served crisp. Tandoori murgh, mildly spiced and cooked moist, is a specialty of the house. The lamb pasanda is almost better, layered as it is with cashews and saffron. Take note that once a month there's a belly-dancer on the floor.

Open Monday to Thursday 11.30 am to 2.30 pm, 5 pm to 10 pm, Friday 11.30 am to 2.30 pm, 5 pm to 10.30 pm, Saturday 5 pm to 10.30 pm. Closed on Sunday. Licensed. All cards. No smoking. Book ahead if you can. ♿

WATERLOO **(MAP 103)**

SOLE ☆

83 Erb Street W: Building 2 **$160**

(519) 747-5622

Solé is located in one of the original Distillery buildings, which date from around 1858. Inside, there's an expanse of exposed brick two storeys high with a ceiling of massive oak beams. The effect is impressive. When the place first opened, we felt that the kitchen wasn't equal to the challenge of its setting. That is less true today. We admire the sautéed squid with a spicy orange aioli, the shrimps and scallops in a brandy-and-tarragon sauce and the carpaccio of beef with camembert, pistachios and mango chutney. The best of the main courses, we think, are the sea-bass with sweet potato and honey-mustard and the Australian lamb with a hazelnut, mint and honey crust. The sweets are still rather predictable. The wine-list is large and well chosen and there's live jazz on Saturday night.

Open Monday to Saturday 11.30 am to midnight, Sunday 4.30 pm to 9 pm. Licensed. All cards. No smoking. Free parking. ♿

WATERLOO **(MAP 103)**
VERSES ☆☆
182 Victoria Street N **$170**
(519) 744-0144

Verses occupies an abandoned church, built in 1946. The exterior is essentially unchanged, but the interior has been completely redone. The ceiling soars high above an elegantly-appointed dining-room. Debbie McFadden and Brett Shantz have carefully retained the best of the original architectural features: stained-glass windows, hardwood floors and delicate chandeliers. Several of the old pews have been turned into harvest tables on which they've laid out wine and cheese. If you want a more intimate space, book a table in the choir loft. The menu is basically French, with small touches from Asia and Italy. The presentation is superb, the service professional. Pan-seared scallops, for instance, are served with a salad of pea tendrils, shaved fennel, avocado and lemon in a vinaigrette of anise and black sambuca. Sambuca sand (sambuca reduced to crystals, then ground with a mortar and pestle) is used to garnish the plate. The menu itself is fairly small. There are four salads, five appetizers and nine entrées. The best of the entrées is the milkfed-veal osso buco braised in pinot grigio and the Ontario lamb (in combination with a navarin of New Zealand lamb) in a reduction of lamb jus. Our favourite sweet is the cacao trio, which is a slice of white-chocolate cheesecake with a dark-chocolate bourbon brownie and malted-milk ice cream. There's a modest list of New World wines.
Open Tuesday to Friday 11.30 am to 2.30 pm, 5 pm to 9 pm, Saturday 5 pm to 9 pm. Closed on Sunday and Monday. Licensed. All cards. No smoking. Free parking.

Nobody can buy space in this guide and nobody can buy his way out of it.

WELLAND, Ontario **(MAP 141)**
VENICE
128 E Main Street **$80**
(905) 714-1221

The specialty of the house at Venice is thin-crust pizza, made with hand-rolled dough cooked in a wood-burning oven. They don't make their own pasta, but buy it handmade from a small supplier in Niagara Falls. On occasion, the kitchen will turn its hand to any one of a number of Italian dishes—pollo di veneziano, perhaps, or veal scaloppine with prosciutto and sage or ravioli stuffed with cheese and mushrooms. There's always a homemade soup on the stove, as well as tiramisu for dessert. On Sunday evenings they have live jazz.
Open Monday to Friday 11 am to 10 pm, Saturday and Sunday 4 pm to 10 pm. Licensed. Master Card, Visa. No smoking. ♿

WESTBANK, B.C. **MAP 237**
OLD VINES PATIO ☆
Quail's Gate Winery **$150**
3303 Boucherie Road
(250) 769-4451

The Old Vines Patio used to have no roof, but last year it was completely rebuilt. Now it not only has a roof; it also has doors that open in summer and close in winter. Judith Knight is still in the kitchen, with an abundant supply of organic greens, Okanagan fruit and cheese and fresh fish and shellfish from the Pacific Coast. Her cooking has always been somewhat to the right of centre, even when she was at Olive Oyl's in Rossland before she settled in Westbank. Her coconut red-curry sauce, served here with prawns and scallops, first appeared in Rossland with their crab-cakes. Rack of lamb comes with a rosemary-dijon crust, fillet of beef with roquefort-and-red-pepper butter, roast breast of duck with pink peppercorns. We'd suggest a pad-Thai salad at noon, the hazelnut-crusted goat-cheese with

beet jelly at night. All the sweets—sticky banana-and-date pudding, caramel torte and caramel ice cream—are made on the premises. There's also, if you prefer, a platter of ripe Okanagan cheese. Most of the wines on offer come from the Quail's Gate vineyards, though the celebrated icewine is now available only by the bottle, which puts it beyond the reach of most people.
Open daily 11.30 am to 3.30 pm, 5 pm to 10 pm. Licensed. All cards. No smoking. Free parking. Book ahead.

WHISTLER, B.C. ***MAP 238***

If you're looking for a casual place where you can take the children, try Caramba at the Town Plaza in Village North at 4314 Main Street (telephone (604) 938-1879), Splitz in the Alpenglow Hotel at 4639 Main Street (telephone (604) 938-9300) or Portobello in the Fairmont Château Whistler (telephone (604) 938-2040). Caramba is owned by Mario Enero of La Rua (see below). It's a lively, colourful place with big helpings and prompt, friendly service. They have super free-range chicken rubbed with rosemary, but what everyone talks about is their wonderful calamari. Splitz has the best burgers in town—five different kinds with 30-odd add-your-own toppings. They make their own fries, their own onion rings and their own old-fashioned milkshakes. Portobello is very much of a family restaurant with food stations that offer a wide choice of salads, seafood, pasta and beef. Kids love the freedom to move around. They're open all day every day, have a licence and take all cards. Caramba and Splitz are also open all day every day. Caramba has a licence, Splitz is licensed for beer and wine only. Both take most cards.

WHISTLER **MAP 238**
BEARFOOT BISTRO ☆☆☆
4121 Village Green **$280**
(604) 932-3433

The Bearfoot Bistro is now offering casual dining in its Champagne Restaurant, which is somewhat cheaper than the original bistro. Cheaper it may be, but the food is outstanding, the service second to none. The menu is deceptively simple, but the impact can be dramatic. For instance, their steak tartar is made with Kobe beef, their pork belly glazed with honey and chilli. Their wild sockeye salmon is home-smoked. Their mussels come from Saltspring Island. Diners speak also of the bison shortribs, the Alberta beef striploin and the wild Arctic caribou. In the Bistro itself dinners start with arugula with aged balsamic vinegar, blue cheese, figs and candied walnuts or a lobster salad with lemon-grass broth and wild-mushroom cabbage and soya beans. Then there's Arctic caribou with an emulsion of foie gras and a potato-chanterelle terrine. Melissa Craig, the new executive chef, is making waves with her tasting menu priced at 130.00 a head, but the three-courses table d'hôte still costs less than 100.00. The sweets aren't as impressive as they used to be, but it was always best to ask for a plate of local raw-milk cheeses, and it still is. The wine-list is extraordinary.

Open daily 6 pm to 10 pm. Licensed. All cards. ♿

WHISTLER **MAP 238**

IL CAMINETTO DI UMBERTO

4242 Village Stroll **$130**

(604) 932-4442

Il Caminetto may not aspire to equal the Bearfoot Bistro or La Rua (see below), but it's a lot cheaper than either. After a hard day's skiing, a dish of fresh pasta and a bottle of good red wine have a lot to be said for them. And there's a lot more than fresh pasta here. Ivo Marinov makes excellent venison carpaccio with truffle oil, a fine caprese salad of bocconcini cheese and roma tomatoes and a good piccata of veal parmigiana, to say nothing of his osso buco milanese, his roasted sea-bass and his grilled Pacific salmon in saffron and lemon. The wine-list offers a great choice of Italian reds. If Il Caminetto is full, as it usually is, take a look at the Trattoria di Umberto in the Mountainside Lodge (telephone (604) 932-5858. It's cheaper and, some think, just as good.

Open daily 5 pm to 9.30 pm. Licensed. All cards. No smoking. ♿

WHISTLER **MAP 238**
LA RUA ☆☆☆
Chamois Hotel **$210**
4557 Blackcomb Way
(604) 932-5011

La Rua is probably the best restaurant in Whistler. The dining-room is beautiful and full of warmth and colour. The service is polished. The wine-list is full of rare vintages. For all this you can expect to pay and pay a lot, but that's Whistler. R.D. Stewart cooks in the West Coast style, working with the best of local produce. Everyone remembers his flaky, translucent halibut and his Pacific bouillabaisse, crammed with fresh seafood of all sorts. Wild Pacific salmon roasted with preserved lemon and horseradish is still on the menu and so are the tempura prawns, lightly battered and served with a chilli-soy dip. The meats are all remarkable: Fraser Valley quail with spinach and old cheddar, red deer sautéed with oven-dried blueberries and grilled lamb chops with a relish of mint, pesto and fresh tomato. The apple croustade, made with Granny Smith and Pink Lady apples, is still the best of the sweets. The wine-list is enormous, offering handsome barolos from Bertani and Antinori and splendid clarets from Mouton Rothschild and Château Pétrus. The list of New World wines is long on California vintages and short on vintages from the Okanagan.
Open daily 6 pm to 10 pm (sometimes later). Licensed. All cards. No smoking. ♿

WHITBY, Ontario **(MAP 223)**
NICE BISTRO
117 Brock Street **$95**
(905) 668-8839

In Nice where Bernard Alberigo grew up, a bistro is a small family-owned restaurant where the neighbours

like to gather for food, wine and conversation. He and his wife, Manon, run this little place on Brock Street with this in mind. Most people think the cooking is getting better and better, but, as one traveller put it, there's a lot more to this place than food. The artwork is lively, the conversation is interesting and the atmosphere is very genuine. Where else in these parts would you be likely to get a cup of *café allongé*? The menu has everything you'd expect to find there: salade niçoise, bouillabaisse, confit of duck. On Tuesday they offer mussels and fries, on Wednesday steak frites or fillet of salmon. There's also a menu *du jour*, written up on a chalkboard, offering such things as local venison, fresh Atlantic salmon and crêpes stuffed with roasted vegetables. Bernard maintains an ambitious cheese-board and Manon prepares four winning sweets every day, among them a fine tarte tatin made with Spy apples.
Open Tuesday to Saturday noon to 3 pm, 5 pm to 10 pm. Closed on Sunday and Monday. Licensed. No smoking. ♿

WHITEHORSE, Yukon **MAP 240**
GIORGIO'S ☆
206 Jarvis Street **$110**
(867) 668-4050

Everybody likes Giorgio's. Giorgio makes a real effort to get Black Angus beef from Nebraska and he's the only place in town that has it. His lamb comes from Alberta and his salmon is all wild. But he sees no point in making his own pasta, which probably wouldn't be as good as what he can buy. He also gets his sweets (except for the baklava and the tiramisu) from a baker in Vancouver. Fresh produce is more plentiful in the Arctic than it used to be. Vegetables come from Edmonton. Local farms supply ostrich and buffalo, fresh char, salmon and halibut come in from Vancouver. But all these things are expensive—quails are priced at 4.50 each and customers expect three on their plate. But ostrich is available year-round and buffalo is on the menu by spring. In the winter Giorgio can get flash-

frozen halibut and sea-bass from a local supplier. He's big on health. He grills his fish and fowl with olive-oil, lemon and dill. He makes an excellent Caesar salad, with anchovies and aged parmesan cheese. There's no cream anywhere. His wine-list is updated regularly and he carries wines from Italy, France, California and Australia as well as a few Okanagan vintages, all at very fair prices.
Open daily 4.30 pm to 11 pm. Licensed. Master Card, Visa. No smoking. ♿

WHITEWAY, Newfoundland **MAP 241**
BROWN'S
Highway 80 **$65**
(709) 588-2347

Barbara and Cecil Brown started out with a small chip-wagon on their front lawn. Before long they had moved to their present location. Business is now so brisk that last year they enlarged their dining-room to seat 100. Their menu offers the usual chicken and steak, as well as several Canadian-Chinese platters. Their best dishes, however, are all about fish. Our favourites are the fisherman's platter (codfish, cods' tongues, squid, scallops and shrimp) and the so-called puncheon tub, for which they pile every possible kind of seafood—fishcakes, clam strips, mussels, cod and salmon—into a big wooden tub decorated with the local tartan. They have fish chowder too, of course, and a great pea soup with dumplings. At the end of the meal they have an ice-cream parfait featuring Newfoundland berries and the local Rodriguez wine. Whiteway is on the eastern side of Trinity Bay about six miles north of the junction of Highway 80 and the Trans Canada. It's about an hour's drive from St. John's.
Open Monday to Thursday 7 am to 10 pm, Friday and Saturday 7 am to 12.30 am, Sunday 7 am to 10 pm from 1 June until late September, Friday noon to 12.30 am, Saturday 4 pm to 1 am, Sunday noon to 8 pm from late September until 31 May. Closed Monday to Thursday in winter. Licensed. All cards.

WHITEWAY
See also DILDO.

WINDSOR, Ontario **_MAP 242_**

On Erie Street East there are four or five blocks filled with coffee shops and delicatessens. Nico at 851 Erie Street E (telephone (519) 255-7548) has two really good dishes, one an appetizer of grilled squid, the other osso buco with a dash of chilli. If you want a piece of fish, head for Zingara at 655 Erie Street E (telephone (519) 258-7555), where Pina, the chef, roasts fresh fish in a brick oven and serves it plain with rapini and roast potatoes. She also makes a good thin-crust pizza and spicy mussels, as well as a likeable chicken parmigiana. Lastly, down the street at No. 614 (telephone (519) 252-9099), Spago does a fine penne with mushrooms, ham and peas in a blush sauce and a lovely treatment of gnocchi with meat sauce. You can go into any of these places at almost any hour of the day, any day of the week. They're all licensed and they all take Amex, Master Card and Visa.

WINDSOR **MAP 242**
MAMO BISTRO
5880 Wyandotte Street E **$120**
(519) 948-0693

Ryan Odette was in New Orleans when he heard that a small, 28-seat bistro had come up for sale in Windsor, his hometown. His career was flourishing, but he missed his family, and he thought that Windsor lacked the kind of place he had in mind. So he paid his money, got in touch with an old friend, Duane Neveu from Porcino (see below), and asked him to come in as his *sommelier*. Then he chose the name MamO to honour his mother's family, capitalizing the last letter in honour of his father. He himself took charge of the kitchen, where he prepares slow-cooked leg of duck with braised cabbage, pork chops with bourbon sweet-potato mash and all-day braised-beef shortribs with horseradish mash. He makes his own gnocchi and serves it as an appetizer with mushrooms, pine-nuts and blue cheese. Four-ounce boneless quails he grills on the barbecue. Some of these things may sound improbable, but they work. For sweet, there's apple crisp, pound cake and a dark-chocolate mocha torte. The wine-list offers such interesting things as the Amity pinot noir and the Kim Crawford pinot gris. If you bring your own bottle there's no corkage fee on Thursday; otherwise it's 15.00. *Open Tuesday to Thursday 5 pm to 9 pm, Friday and Saturday 5 pm to 9.30 pm. Closed on Sunday and Monday. Licensed. Amex, Master Card, Visa. No smoking.*

WINDSOR **MAP 242**
PORCINO
3891 Dougall Avenue **$100**
(519) 972-5699

Gino Parco doesn't change his menu as often as one would wish, which is strange since he travels the world all the time looking for new food ideas. But he knows his customers and he knows better than to offer them anything they won't like. If he never gets tired of making his spinach salad with poached pears, glazed pecans and crumbled blue cheese or his rigatoni with mushrooms and gorgonzola that's because people keep asking for them that way. There are good restaurants in this guide that never take any successful dish off their menu and Gino is of that persuasion. But he never overcooks his fish (salmon with chilli and dill) or his pasta (ravioli with basil pesto, oven-dried tomatoes and toasted pine-nuts). He makes a point of his vegetables—leek or celery-root purée, Japanese eggplant, sautéed rapini, braised red cabbage. His sweets are all made on the premises. His menu is large and fairly priced. Braised lamb shanks with white-bean purée and tomato jam cost only 15.00, linguine with tiger shrimps 7.00. His wine-list is short, sensible and inexpensive. This is a good time to ask for something like the Greg Norman shiraz or the Wolf Blass Brown Label. Both cost less than 55.00. Look for Porcino in a strip mall just off

Highway 401, on the way to the tunnel to Detroit.
Open Tuesday to Friday 11.30 am to 2 pm, 5 pm to 9.30 pm, Saturday 5 pm to 9.30 pm., Sunday 11 am to 2.30 pm (brunch). Closed on Monday. Licensed. Amex, Master Card, Visa. No smoking. ♿

WINNIPEG, Manitoba **MAP 243**
AMICI
320 Broadway **$150**
(204) 943-4997

Time was when Amici set the standard for cooking and service in Winnipeg. That was when Heinz and Johanna Kattenfeld ran the place and Amici successfully married Prairie steak house to Northern Italian cuisine. The Kattenfelds have now retired and the restaurant has changed. There's still a lot of Italian on the menu and the service is still impeccable—informed, polite and swift. But the kitchen isn't what it used to be. For example, the roasted-pepper soup with a seared jumbo scallop tastes just like what it is—a pepper broth with too much cream and a single scallop floating in the middle You'll do better with the acqua-cotta soup, which costs 2.00 less. It's always a good idea to begin the meal proper with a plate of fettucine primavera, which is made with goat-cheese and cream. The seafood linguine is much more expensive and it's usually a disappointment. There's a good selection of veal as well as roast lamb and breast of chicken and duck. For sweet, there's a first-class chocolate cake and a poppyseed cake made to Johanna Kattenfeld's original recipe. The coffee is weak, the wine-list indifferent, the espresso superb. If you like, you can get many of the same dishes downstairs at Bombolini for about half the price.
Open Monday to Friday 11.30 am to 2 pm, 5 pm to 10 pm, Saturday 5 pm to 10 pm. Closed on Sunday. Licensed. All cards. No smoking. Book ahead. ♿

If you use an out-of-date edition and find it inaccurate, don't blame us. Buy a new edition.

WINNIPEG **MAP 243**

BISTRO DANSK ☞

63 Sherbrook Street **$50**

(204) 775-5662

The Bistro Dansk was created in its present form long years ago by Paul Vocadlo and his wife, Pam, who still run the place today. They cook in the Czech style, which appears in such central-European dishes as palacinka and chicken paprikash. (They stuff their palacinkas with chicken and serve them as a savoury that's as good as anything you can get in Prague.) The Danish tradition appears in the superb herring and again in the frikadeller (veal and pork patties with potatoes and cabbage). The sweets—the elegant cream puffs and the signature hazelnut pie—are amazing. Helpings are big and the sautéed mushrooms and the crab salad are both enough for two. There are a number of good buys on the wine-list, but if you want to drink beer, which goes well with the food, they have Tuborg from Denmark in the cooler, as well as Pilsner Urquell from Bohemia and Topvar from Slovakia. You can't beat the Bistro Dansk for good central-European cooking at prices almost anyone can afford.

Open Tuesday o Saturday 11 am to 2.30 pm, 4 pm to 9 pm. Closed on Sunday and Monday. Licensed. All cards. No smoking. ♿

WINNIPEG **MAP 243**

CAFE CARLO

243 Lilac Street **$90**

(204) 477-5544

Café Carlo offers elegant cooking in a sophisticated but informal atmosphere. It's situated around the corner from the bars and restaurants that line Corydon Avenue, where prices are a little lower than they are downtown. You can come here in jeans and a sweater and order corn-and-chorizo soup to start with, or chicken-and-mango salad with cashews, mussels with pernod and

cream, shrimps with ginger or squid with orange-and-lemon. The cooking is complex, but on the whole it usually works. The main courses start with the usual chicken, steak and seafood, but the preparation makes the most ordinary dish into something rich and strange. Chicken is served with goat-cheese and pesto, fettucine with chorizo and cashews, fusilli with prawns and scallops and linguine with baby clams. The wines are all carefully chosen, with an eye not just to price but also to character and quality. There are some good sauvignon blancs from New Zealand, some good cabernets from Wolf Blass and a fine châteauneuf du pape. The sweets—crème brûlée, chocolate torte, apple crisp—are all great. So is the coffee.
Open Monday to Thursday 11.30 am to 2 pm, 5 pm to 10 pm, Friday and Saturday 5 pm to 10.30 pm. Closed on Sunday. Licensed. All cards. No smoking. ♿

WINNIPEG **MAP 243**
EDOHEI
355 Ellice Avenue **$110**
(204) 943-0427

When Sada Ohno opened Edohei in 1988 he was the only sushi chef in town. He quickly found his way into *Where to Eat in Canada*, where he stayed for several years. Gradually, however, he lost more and more of his brio, and eventually he was replaced in the guide by Asahi, which is a very different sort of place (see above). Recently, his son, Makoto, joined his father at the sushi bar and since then everything has changed. Makoto is as good as his father ever was, if not better, and a meal at Edohei is a succession of unexpected pleasures. All the sushi is perfectly fresh, and all the varieties of nigiri and maki sushi are on offer. The presentation is elegant, the flavours exquisite. The tempura is served searingly hot, in the most delicate of batters. There's more to Makoto, of course, than sushi, sashimi and tempura. He's perhaps seen at his best in his omakase dinners, which run to six courses and cost 45.00 a head. Oma-

kase is the Japanese equivalent of the *menu surprise* and at Edohei it's cheap at the price. Gekkeikan is, however, still the only thing to drink, apart from a glass or two of white wine, and it's time they started importing premium sakes from Japan. Edohei is that good.
Open Tuesday to Thursday 11.30 am to 2 pm, 5 pm to 9.30 pm, Friday 11.30 am to 2 pm, 5 pm to 10 pm, Saturday 5 pm to 10 pm, Sunday 5 pm to 9.30 pm. Closed on Monday. Licensed. Amex, Master Card, Visa. No smoking. ♿

WINNIPEG **MAP 243**
INFERNO'S ☞
312 rue des Meurons **$80**
St.-Boniface
(204) 262-7400

Fern Kirouac opened Inferno's in an industrial district of St.-Boniface a couple of years ago. He began by serving mussels and fries, snails in garlic butter and something he calls billy-bi, which means mussels with wine and cream. It was a gamble but it paid off. The place is packed all day long. It's full of noise and a sense that something is about to happen. The menu is larger now, but everything is still dirt cheap. Roast bison, with soup and salad, costs about 20.00, the marvellous sandwiches (zucchini, eggplant, goat-cheese) less than 7.25. The service is very quick—in fact, what Inferno's is really about is a full plate brought to your table, if you can get one, quickly and cheaply.
Open Monday to Saturday 11 am to 10 pm. Closed on Sunday. Licensed. All cards. Book ahead. No smoking. ♿

WINNIPEG **MAP 243**
IVORY ☞
200 Main Street **$50**
(204) 944-1600

Every big city in Canada has at least a few curry houses serving up the clichés of Indian cuisine. Ivory is different. Created by Doug Arora, it's an elegant, upscale

restaurant with serene, deep-blue walls and matchless service that caters to businessmen from Winnipeg's financial district and Indians looking for some of the best and cheapest vindaloos, biryanis and panirs to be found east of Saskatoon. They start with an all-you-can-eat buffet (10.95 at noon, 16.95 in the evening), and it's a great buy. If you want to spend a bit more, there are at least half a dozen salads and as many as eight chutneys on the à la carte, as well as beef vindaloo, tandoori chicken, spinach panir and a variety of samosas and pappadums. The best of the sweets is a cashew fudge. Given the prices, it's not surprising that there are usually as many teenagers as stockbrokers at Ivory, as many baseball caps as three-piece suits.
Open daily 11 am to 3.30 pm, 5 pm to 11 pm. Licensed. All cards. Book ahead at noon and on weekends. No smoking, Free parking. ♿

WINNIPEG **MAP 243**
PALM ROOM ☆
Fort Garry Hotel **$90**
222 Broadway Avenue
(204) 942-8251

Built by the C.P.R. as a railway hotel, then allowed to fall into disrepair, the Fort Garry was saved from demolition and restored to its original Edwardian glory by a pair of economists turned hotel-keepers, Ric Bel and Ida Albo. The Palm Room is the centrepiece of the restoration, serving as a restaurant, meeting-place and salon for piano recitals by José Paniero. It offers some of the best (and cheapest) cooking in town. The concept is roadhouse *haute cuisine*. Roadhouse here means eggs and homemade sausages with fries, very good prime-rib beef burgers and a big Reuben sandwich. *Haute cuisine* means gravlax, goat-cheese, Belgian endive, a quesadilla stuffed with field mushrooms and a bruschetta with eggplant and provolone cheese. Sweets start with such clichés as crème brûlée and end with a chocolate bombe in a puddle of double cream. Frankly,

we prefer the cheese plate, which comes to the table loaded with brie, cheddar, gorgonzola, fruit and nuts. On Sundays there's a magnificent, but expensive brunch. It's well worth it if you have 34.00 to spare.
Open Monday to Saturday 11 am to 1 am, Sunday 9 am to 2.30 pm (brunch), 2.30 pm to midnight (dinner). Licensed. All cards. Book ahead for Sunday brunch. No smoking. ♿

WINNIPEG **MAP 243**
LA SCALA
725 Corydon Avenue **$85**
(204) 474-2750

La Scala is an Italian restaurant with a difference. Its game is *cucina nuova,* with a strong emphasis on the *nuova.* The place was opened several years ago by Perry Scaletta, who at that time was better known as a bicycle racer than as a cook. He has a massive fish tank in his dining-room and serious art on his walls. His cooking is experimental and up to the minute. Meals begin with such things as mussels in sambuca and cream, mushrooms baked with cambozola cheese, dumplings with chilli and chicken with spice—none of which would be recognized in Florence or Milan. No matter. There are also a number of traditional Tuscan dishes, such as veal scaloppine, osso buco and a variety of pasta. Not that Scaletta's pasta is pasta as you know it. His penne arabiatta, for instance, is served with Spanish chorizo, tomato and capers instead of the customary Italian sausage. His linguine is done with shrimps and smoked salmon in thyme and pernod. All the sweets are made in house, including the fine chocolate tart with pecans. The wine-list features some of the better Australian shirazes for those who can afford them and two or three chardonnays from Chile for those who can't. There's an outdoor terrace in summer; in winter the dining-room is warm and inviting.
Open Monday to Friday 11.30 am to 2 pm, 5 pm to 9 pm, Saturday and Sunday 5 pm to 10 pm from mid-May until late October, Monday to Friday 11.30 am to 2 pm, 5 pm to

9 pm, Saturday 5 pm to 10 pm from late October until mid-May. Closed on Sunday in winter. Licensed. All cards. No smoking.

WINNIPEG **MAP 243**
SOUP PIERRE ☞
651 Corydon Avenue **$20**
(204) 453-7687

Soup Pierre is a no-drinks diner based (or so it would appear) on Seinfeld's Soup Nazi. Exquisite broths, dulcet bisques and memorable chowders are served up by waiters who waste no time in small talk—or in any kind of talk. The soups, all fabulous, are intended to be meals in themselves. The lobster bisque, often on the menu, is full of lobster, the mushroom bisque is intense and full of flavour. The Thai satay soup is a lovely blend of peanuts and Asian spices. The soups all come with a big chunk of one of several first-class breads, and every day there's a sturdy, not to say inflammatory, chicken chowder with chorizo. The Soup Pierre on Corydon Avenue is decorated in cheap student chic, as is the downtown location at 24 Portage Avenue (telephone (204) 888-7687). Both are one-star kitchens in no-star settings.
Open Monday to Saturday 11 am to 9 pm, Sunday noon to 10 pm. Portage Avenue is open Monday to Friday 11 am to 9 pm. Closed on Saturday and Sunday. No liquor. Amex, Master Card, Visa. No smoking.

WINNIPEG **MAP 243**
SYDNEY'S AT THE FORKS ☆
1 Forks Market Road **$145**
(204) 942-6075

Michael and Kate Schafer have opened a striking new restaurant on the site of the old Prairie Oyster on the second floor of the Forks Market building. They offer a five-course table d'hôte for 45.00 that puts a premium on new and unexpected flavours, dramatic presentation and formal service. Portions are small and nobody leaves the table feeling they've eaten more than they wanted to eat. Meals begin comfortably with egg-drop soup with sweet-spinach orzo and mortadella or dramatically with a salad of roma tomatoes, cucumber and couscous in a mousseline sauce. Next come chilled mussels with piccadilli and raw tuna, then a tiny lemon-basil sorbet, followed by pan-seared Ahi tuna crusted with cashews, loin of lamb with mint or maple-cured pork tenderloin with raita. The molten-chocolate cake that ends the meal is a perfect example of its kind. Michael Schafer is sparing in all his effects and sophisticated in his choice of ingredients. One might question his use of New Zealand lamb and feel uncertain about his choice of wines—why the Quail's Gate gewurztraminer when we could be drinking Dopff & Irion? But there's no doubt that Sydney's is making an important new statement in Winnipeg.

Open Monday to Friday 11.30 am to 2 pm, 5 pm to 9 pm, Saturday 5 pm to 9 pm. Closed on Sunday. Licensed. All cards. No smoking. ♿

WINNIPEG **MAP 243**

TRE VISI

173 McDermot Avenue **$115**

(204) 949-9032

At Tre Visi they cook in the Italian style, and traditional Italian at that. There's nothing of contemporary Italian, or *cucina nuova*, about saltimbocca alla Romana or pollo Lombardo. Why should there be? The room is warm, even intimate, in feeling; the prices are low, the service all it should be. And there's more to Giacomo Appice's menu than saltimbocca. In fact, they have all the usual appetizers—straciatella, squid, carpaccio and antipasto del Borgo—and all the usual main courses—salmon poached with fresh asparagus, scaloppine di manzo with fresh tomatoes and olives and, best of all, six tiny lamb chops grilled and served with Mediterranean herbs and sea-salt. Profiteroles are the pick of the sweets. They're really small cream puffs with chocolate and caramel, and

they're wonderful. As for wine, this is a good time for one of the big Italians, and they have them all.
Open Monday to Friday 11.30 am to 2.30 pm, 5 pm to 10 pm, Saturday 5 pm to 11 pm. Closed on Sunday. Licensed. All cards. No smoking. Book ahead. ♿

WINNIPEG **MAP 243**
THE VELVET GLOVE ☆
Fairmont Hotel **$150**
2 Lombard Place
(204) 957-1350

Luxury is what the Velvet Glove is all about. It has a sumptuous menu, accomplished cooking, impeccable service and a harpist on Friday and Saturday nights. Not that luxury is all the Velvet Glove has to offer. The cooking is original and inventive. When were you last given ravioli stuffed with butternut squash and scented with sambuca? Of course, there are steaks and chops on the menu, with clarets costing 500.00 a bottle (and up) to go with them. But there's also sweetbreads, Ahi tuna, shrimp-and-scallop tempura, wild Pacific salmon with cashew butter and breast of free-range chicken glazed with calvados. The sweets, which used to be rather predictable, are now more interesting. If they're still serving cherries jubilee, they also serve tarte tatin. And if you can't afford a bottle of old claret, you'll find that there are plenty of good wines from Niagara to choose from, to say nothing of the icewines and the Louis XII cognac at 90.00 an ounce. The espresso is excellent.
Open Monday to Friday 11.30 am to 2 pm, 5.30 pm to 10 pm, Saturday and Sunday 6 pm to 10 pm. Licensed. All cards. No smoking. Book ahead. ♿

Every restaurant in this guide has been personally tested. Our reporters are not allowed to identify themselves to the management or to accept free meals. We accept no advertisements. We accept no payment for listings. We depend entirely on you. Recommend the book to your friends.

WINNIPEG **MAP 243**
VIVERE
433 River Avenue **$85**
(204) 949-2485

Here on River Avenue, Ignazio Scaletta runs a warm and charming little restaurant, a step or two from the hurly-burley of Osborne Street. His menu is Italian. He may not have an antipasto platter, but he has just about everything else: roasted chicken livers on a caramelized onion crostini, first-class pasta made on the premises, a variety of salads (tomatoes with basil) and such main dishes as gnocchi with gorgonzola, cioppino stew with shrimps, scallops and mussels, veal stuffed with prosciutto, ricotta and rosemary and grilled lamb with spinach and eggplant. Vivere started out as a pastry shop and they still offer a remarkable variety of cakes and tortes. Aside from the familiar chiantis and valpolicellas, they have an unusual selection of grappas. The service is superb.
Open Tuesday to Friday 10.30 am to 2 pm, 4 pm to 10 pm, Saturday 10 am to 2 pm (brunch), 4 pm to midnight, Sunday 10 am to 2 pm (brunch), 4 pm to 10 pm. Closed on Monday. Licensed. All cards. No smoking. Book ahead. ♿

WINNIPEG
See also WINNIPEG BEACH.

WINNIPEG BEACH, Manitoba **(MAP 243)**
CASA BIANCA ☆
22 Murray Avenue **$85**
(204) 389-5007

It takes courage to open a serious restaurant in a resort town that has an open season of only a few months. But that's exactly what Alex Vaziri has done. Vaziri was born in Iran and trained in Italy, and Casa Bianca, where the cooking is mainly Italian with occasional excursions to the Middle East, is the result. Meals start with a bruschetta or a crostini, moves on to a Greek salad, then

on to fish soup and back again to pasta and variations on chicken and veal. There's osso buco, saltimbocca and a risotto or two. Vaziri changes his menu often enough to keep the customers coming and he makes all his own sweets: crème brûlée, chocolate torte, zabaglione—whatever he feels like making. As for the service, it's exquisite. But, though Casa Bianca isn't on Lombard Place or even on Broadway or Corydon Avenue, it has a dress code. No shoes, no shirt, no service.
Open Thursday 5 pm to 11 pm, Friday and Saturday 11 am to 2 pm, 5 pm to 11 pm, Sunday 5 pm to 11 pm from 1 until 31 May, Wednesday to Sunday 11 am to 2 pm, 5 pm to 11 pm from 1 until 30 June, daily 11 am to 2 pm, 6 pm to 11 pm (later on Friday and Saturday) from 1 July until 31 August, daily 11 am to 2 pm, 5 pm to 11 pm from 1 September until 15 October. Closed Monday to Wednesday in May, Monday and Tuesday in June. Licensed. Visa. No smoking. Book ahead, especially on weekends in summer.

WOLFVILLE, N.S. **MAP 245**
BLOMIDON INN
195 Main Street **$105 ($265)**
(800) 565-2291

The splendid old houses built by nineteenth-century sea-captains keep being sold to hopeful innkeepers who think they can earn a living while restoring their houses to their former glory. One by one they give up and close down. The Blomidon Inn is one of the few exceptions. Donna and Jim Laceby, that indefatigable pair, took on an empty building, put it in shape and then passed it on to their children. The big old house has five acres of Victorian gardens, a good kitchen and a glorious wine-list. The *sommelier*, Michael Laceby, has a 37-page selection of chardonnays and cabernet sauvignons from France, Italy, California, Australia and Chile, offering good wines at all prices. Sean Laceby's menu offers good, sensible food, all carefully prepared. The fish is never overcooked. Laceby uses fresh local ingredients whenever he can. Most of the vegetables

come from the kitchen garden. The service is friendly and prompt. The prices are fair. Last year an overnight stay with dinner started at just 149.00 a couple.
Open Monday to Friday 11.30 am to 2 pm, 5 pm to 9.30 pm, Saturday and Sunday 10 am to 3 pm (brunch), 5 pm to 9.30 pm. Licensed. Master Card, Visa. No smoking.

.

WOLFVILLE **MAP 245**
TEMPEST
117 Front Street **$125**
(866) 542-0588

Tempest is a newcomer to Wolfville and it occupies the old premises of Chez la Vigne a block from Main Street. The chef has been around and he knows how to cook. He also has some interesting new ideas. One of these is lobster chowder with sweet corn; another is prawns flamed in sambuca and served in a nest filled with a bed of polente. The grilled salmon with tomato, artichokes and red peppers is less successful and so are the hake braised in extra-virgin olive-oil and the butternut-squash soup. There is, however, a likeable chicken satay with coconut and daikon and a good, straightforward tenderloin of beef with brandy and pink peppercorns. The wine-list is at once ambitious and inexpensive and it offers a number of unusual wines, like the Dopff & Irion sylvaner, the Moondah Brook chenin blanc and the Tintarra cabernet sauvignon. The two last are from Australia, the Tintarra big, intense and very impressive. See if you can get a table on the old verandah. The service, wherever you sit, is very accomplished.
Open daily 11.30 am to 2.30 pm, 5 pm to 9 pm from mid-May until mid-October, Tuesday to Sunday 11.30 am to 2.30 pm, 5 pm to 9 pm from mid-October until mid-May. Closed on Monday in winter. Licensed. All cards. No smoking. ♿

Every restaurant in this guide has been personally tested. Our reporters are not allowed to identify themselves or to accept free meals.

WOLFVILLE
See also GRAND PRE, SHEFFIELD MILLS.

WOODSTOCK, N.B. **MAP 246**
JOHN GYLES MOTOR INN ☞
Highway 165 **$50**
(866) 381-8800

The John Gyles is no longer right on the Trans Canada, which here is called Highway 165. To get there, you take Exit 200 from the new highway a few miles south of Woodstock. Turn right at the stop sign and look for the John Gyles a few hundred yards to the north on the west side of the road. Use your cellphone if you get lost. Heino Toedler cooks first-class wienerschnitzel (pork and veal), jaeger schnitzel, zigeuner schnitzel and all kinds of German sausages: bratwurst, debresziner, knackwurst and weisswurst. For 10.95 you can have three big, beautiful potato pancakes with the sausage of your choice (try the weisswurst), real mustard and fresh applesauce. There are a few imported beers and a dozen wines, three of them from Jost. The wines, like everything else on the menu, are astonishingly cheap. If you settle for a half-portion of one of the schnitzels, a bowl of chunky vegetable soup and a cup of coffee, you can have a meal here for less than 25.00 a head.
Open Monday to Saturday 5 pm to 9 pm, Sunday 5 pm to 8.30 pm. Licensed. Amex, Master Card, Visa. No smoking. ♿

YARMOUTH, N.S. **MAP 247**
THE ACADEMY
113 Main Street **$40**
(902) 749-0193

This bright-yellow house, which dates from 1835, has recently been restored as a Victorian-style tearoom, complete with loose teas, silver tea-strainers and white linen. Five days a week you can get what they call a Queen Victoria tea from 2 o'clock to 3.30 in the afternoon. That means finger sandwiches, savouries, scones, a sweet and a pot of tea. At noon they serve lunch: homemade curried-carrot soup, perhaps, a quiche, ploughman's lunch with pastrami or smoked meat and a vegetarian dish such as homous and avocado. The sweets are charming—there's a tart, crème caramel and chocolate truffles. The atmosphere is calm and serene, the prices low. Don't miss the lovely hooked rug on the wall, which depicts the tearoom in all its brilliant yellow.

Open Tuesday to Saturday 10.30 am to 4.30 pm from mid-April until mid-December. Closed on Sunday and Monday. No liquor. Visa. No smoking.

YARMOUTH **MAP 247**

CHEZ BRUNO
278 Main Street **$95**
(902) 742-0031

Bruno started out last year by moving into space vacated by Ceilidh Desserts at five o'clock every day. He called his place Bruno's After Five and he did some stunning things. He had an imaginative menu and his cooking was always up to the mark. Before long he had taken over Ceilidh Desserts lock, stock and barrel and was operating all day under the name of Chez Bruno, with a simplified menu and moderate prices. That didn't mean, however, that he'd forgotten how to cook. All his fish is fresh, his vegetables are all organic. He uses nothing but the best basmati rice. Everything—the pan-fried haddock, the scallops in garlic butter, the shrimps provençal, the salmon with lemon and pecans, the breast of free-range chicken—is served in half-size as well as full-size portions and everything is surprisingly light. Sweets aren't as important as you'd expect, but there's dame blanche as well as profiteroles and crème brûlée.

Open Monday and Tuesday 10 am to 4 pm, Wednesday to Saturday 10 am to 8 pm, Sunday noon to 7 pm. Licensed. All cards. No smoking. ♿

YELLOWKNIFE, N.W.T. **MAP 248**
BULLOCK'S BISTRO ☆
3534 Weaver Drive **$85**
(867) 873-3474

Fish doesn't get any fresher than at Bullock's—only today's catch appears on the menu. Once Renata Bullock moved down the road to the old Weaver & Devore general store, her fish-and-chips takeout overnight became a 35-seat restaurant. This isn't exactly fine dining. Customers sit on rickety chairs, surrounded by old photographs and bumper stickers, which makes it feel like eating a meal in the middle of a scrapbook. If you come alone, take a seat next to the galley counter, where you can talk to the cook while you wait. Most of the fish—whitefish, cod, pike, pickerel, trout, Arctic char, halibut and shrimp—comes from Great Slave Lake. What they serve in the restaurant depends on the catch that day. You can order your fish grilled, blackened, pan-fried, poached or deep-fried. Whether or not you get it that way is another matter. Be that as it may, the cooking is always good, very good. Every meal begins with warm homemade buns and a slab of butter. Salads in a feta-dill dressing as well as fries come on the side. At noon you can usually get a cup of fish chowder or a bowl of caribou stew. In the evening you're more likely to get sashimi of Arctic char, followed by buffalo or caribou steak and occasionally a deep-dish apple pie. Don't bother asking for beer or wine; just go to the refrigerator and take a bottle out. (It's a good idea to bring your own corkscrew.) The choice of wine is very limited (one red, one white), but there are several imported beers. Half the charm of Bullock's is that you serve yourself and pay for what you've eaten, or say you've eaten. You can book a table if you want to, but it won't make much difference.

Open daily noon to 9 pm in winter, shorter hours in summer, when Renata likes to enjoy the outdoors. Licensed. Master Card, Visa. No smoking.

YELLOWKNIFE **MAP 248**

L'HERITAGE ☆☆☆

5019 49 Street **$200**

(867) 873-9561

Running a restaurant of this calibre anywhere in Canada would be a challenge. But to do so in Yellowknife takes a leap of faith.. Pierre LePage and Julia Tate took that leap of faith six years ago. Pierre had spent several years with the Team Canada that became the first Canadian group to win a gold medal in international culinary competition. He has visited no fewer than 32 countries to study their food and wine. He chose to settle in Yellowknife, where he took over a run-down building and turned it into the epitome of *haute cuisine*. He flies in supplies from every corner of Canada and beyond. Game is a special interest, whether it's pheasant or Muscovy duck, Arctic char or free-range bison or caribou. Grilled striploin of bison is served with apple, figs and Saskatoons in bourbon and the presentation is spectacular. The menu is more continental than Canadian: onion tart à l'alsacienne, shrimp roulade, smoked oysters in a froth of pernod and egg-white, chocolate fondant and tarte tatin. The wine-list, which has won three Awards of Excellence from the *Wine Spectator*, has lavish holdings of wines from burgundy and bordeaux as well as wines from Italy, Australia, New Zealand and California. The upstairs dining-room is the sort of place you dress up for; downstairs there's a bistro with a large menu that includes four fondues. Every Saturday they have a sumptuous brunch here where you can get at least six versions of eggs benedict.

Open Monday to Saturday 5 pm to 11 pm (earlier in the bistro). Closed on Sunday. Licensed. All cards. Book ahead if you can. No smoking.

☞ This symbol means that the restaurant is rated a good buy. This ♿ means that there is wheelchair access to both the tables and the washrooms. *Smoking only* means that the restaurant has no area for non-smokers.

YELLOWKNIFE **MAP 248**
THE WILDCAT CAFE
(867) 873-8850 **$75**

Nobody comes to Yellowknife without stopping at the Wildcat. This is the way things are supposed to be: a log shanty near the Pilot Monument in the old part of town. Actually, the building dates from the nineteen-thirties and it's had extensive restoration since, but it looks like a leftover from pioneer days. Breakfast has always been an outstanding meal and it still is. This year the kitchen has been trying out some new ideas for lunch and dinner, things like fish chowder made with fresh local char, musk-ox and blueberry pancakes piled high with fresh fruit and whipped cream. Whitefish and lake trout come in regularly from Great Slave Lake. Caribou, which is more expensive than musk-ox, is back in spades, served crusted with pecans in salads and in grilled medallions with cracked peppercorns. On Saturday nights they invite a local celebrity to come in and cook his favourite dish, an idea that's proved to be wildly popular. It's a good idea to start with something like warm goat-cheese salad with caramelized onions and finish with a fruit crisp made with rhubarb and cranberries. On fine evenings they set up tables outside, so you can enjoy the midnight sun from the patio. *Open Monday to Saturday 7.30 am to 9 pm, Sunday 10 am to 5 pm (brunch), 5 pm to 9 pm (dinner) from late May until early September. Licensed for beer and wine only. Master Card, Visa.* ♿

We acknowledge the support of the Government of Canada through the Book Publishing Industry Development Program for our publishing activities.